3/29/15 to 4/4.

W9-DCM-691

WHISTLE STOP

WHISTLE STOP

How 31,000 Miles of
Train Travel, 352 Speeches,
and a Little Midwest Gumption
Saved the Presidency of
Harry Truman   **Philip White**

ForeEdge

ForeEdge

An imprint of University Press of New England

www.upne.com

© 2014 Philip White

All rights reserved

Manufactured in the United States of America

Designed by Richard Hendel

Typeset in Quadraat, TheSans, and Champion types

by Tseng Information Systems, Inc.

For permission to reproduce any of the material in this book,
contact Permissions, University Press of New England, One Court Street,
Suite 250, Lebanon NH 03766; or visit www.upne.com

Cloth ISBN: 978-1-61168-453-7

Ebook ISBN: 978-1-61168-763-7

Library of Congress Control Number: 2014937613

5 4 3 2 1

FOR NICOLE.

It's always for you.

Contents

WHISTLE STOP

Introduction THE ELECTION OF 1948

Harry Truman was never supposed to be president of the United States. Born in humble circumstances to farmers in Lamar, Missouri—pronounced "Missour-uh" by its residents—he didn't go to college, but instead tilled the land like his father and worked as a speculator, a bank clerk, and the coproprietor of a men's clothing store. These jobs came on either side of a formative stint serving as a captain of artillery in the fields of France during World War I, where Truman impressed his fellow soldiers with his calm demeanor and refusal to join their flight from heavy enemy fire.

Truman survived his military service with nary a scratch, but, like his father, he was not so lucky in business. His Kansas City haberdashery fell victim to the economic tremor of 1920–21 that preceded the 1929 fiscal earthquake, and his mine investment and attempts to save the family farm fared little better.

As he struggled to make headway in his professional life, Truman turned to a vocation that had fascinated him since he saw the great populist William Jennings Bryan deliver an impassioned speech at the 1900 Democratic National Convention in Kansas City: politics. With close friends staffing his campaigns, Truman was elected as Jackson County judge (in this case, more of an administrative position than a judicial one) in 1933 and, with the backing of influential Kansas City boss Tom Pendergast, as a US senator in 1935. After a moderately successful though not outstanding first term, Truman won re-election to the Senate by just over eight thousand votes in a bitterly contested 1940 election. He then made his mark by chairing what soon became known as the "Truman Committee," which saved the government billions by eliminating inefficient wartime contracts and minimizing profiteering.

It was Truman's performance in this role that led to the unlikeliest political event of 1944: this short, fiery, Midwest farm boy who loved to play the piano almost as much as he loved to read, which was almost as much

1

as he liked to talk, found himself as the replacement for Henry Wallace on the Democratic presidential ticket. When Franklin D. Roosevelt defeated his Republican challenger, Thomas E. Dewey, to secure a record fourth term, Truman became vice president.

Just five months after this election, FDR, who had been president for twelve years, had ushered in the New Deal to try to pull the country out of the Great Depression and had brought the United States into World War II after Japan and Germany had given him little choice in the matter, was gone, the victim of a cerebral hemorrhage. There was a cadre of Ivy League–educated, Capitol Hill–tested veterans who wanted to succeed him, including Dean Acheson, Burton Wheeler, and Speaker of the House Sam Rayburn, who had all wanted to be FDR's vice president.[1]

Yet, despite the ambitions of these capable suitors, it was Harry Truman, invented middle "S" initial and all, who took Roosevelt's place at 1600 Pennsylvania Avenue in April 1945. The Missourian's learning curve promised to be especially steep, as he had been vice president for just eighty-two days before taking on this monumental challenge and the mantle of the titan of the age whom he succeeded. When Truman asked Eleanor Roosevelt if there was anything he could do for her on the day FDR passed away, she replied, "Is there anything we can do for *you?* For you are the one in trouble now."[2]

Truman not only inherited Mrs. Roosevelt's doubts, but he also faced the scorn of elite Democratic circles on Capitol Hill. Many feared he would be another Andrew Johnson, who was wholly unfit to succeed Abraham Lincoln and whose failure as his successor was punctuated by impeachment in 1868. Liberals criticized him for not being liberal enough despite his continuation of Roosevelt's policies, some of which he carried further. New Dealers and FDR loyalists thought him uneducated and unprepared, ignoring his keen intellect and stellar work as a two-term senator. Conservatives dismissed him as a Kansas City machine pol and a less capable FDR replacement who would merely extend the New Deal reforms they so detested.[3] And the press derided his erratic, unsophisticated speaking style and occasional prickly manner in media conferences, overlooking his ability for concision and usually friendly manner. He could please no one, it seemed, no matter what competence he had proved during his two terms in the Senate.[4]

Unrealistically low expectations aside, Truman also faced a host of domestic problems and international crises, which arguably amounted to a more daunting task than that of any president save his predecessor, Washington, Wilson, and Lincoln, men who, many believed, Harry Truman was not fit to shine the shoes of, let alone follow into power.

Yet despite his perceived shortcomings and because of fate, Truman sat down with Churchill and Stalin at the Potsdam Conference in July 1945, just weeks after he became president. There he attempted to broker peace and check the advance of Russian communism across Europe and Asia. It was he who made the fateful decision to drop atomic bombs on Hiroshima and Nagasaki the following month in which more than one hundred thousand Japanese died instantly. And it was he who, with the war won, confronted the housing shortage, widespread industrial strikes, and myriad other problems that plagued America in the early postwar period with a decisiveness and determination that should have endeared him to his critics.

In the ensuing two years, he presided over the Truman Doctrine for containing communism and implemented the Marshall Plan for creating a buffer against it by rebuilding Western Europe, and then, in 1948, he stared down Stalin over the Berlin Blockade while presidential rival Henry Wallace and other detractors urged him to tuck tail and run. And, in his most controversial policy move to date, Truman announced a courageous new civil rights program that delighted progressives but horrified segregationists in the South.[5] By then, early 1948, it was an election year in the United States and the battle lines had been drawn. Yet even these were not as simple to deal with as they had been for FDR.

The desertion by the southern Democrats was just one of the splits in his party. Henry Wallace, the man who had resigned from his post as secretary of commerce at Truman's request over his relentless criticism of George Marshall's foreign policy, and particularly America's stance on the Soviet Union, now led the breakaway Progressive Party. Wallace, an able politician who for a time had been one of FDR's favorites and who was by any measure an extraordinary speaker, was not a candidate to be underestimated, and now he threatened to divert left-wing votes away from the president at a time when Truman needed every one he could get.[6] As if these two issues were not perilous enough, the whispers grew louder in the spring of 1948 that the Democrats would try to persuade the talismanic General Dwight Eisenhower to run in Truman's stead.

FDR's son, James Roosevelt, and northern power brokers such as New York mayor William O'Dwyer and Frank Hague of Jersey City preferred just about any potential candidate to the man they saw as a wholly unfit successor to FDR, and the influential, liberal Americans for Democratic Action (ADA) joined them in courting the celebrated war leader.[7] This even though Eisenhower, like Truman, was a plainspoken midwesterner without Ivy League credentials, a ritzy upbringing, or an achievement-studded career in politics.

But whatever problems and annoyances they created for him, all his critics and detractors underestimated the grit of Harry Truman. He refused to let the southern states' intimidation neuter his civil rights legislation nor allow Wallace and his crowd to steer the United States away from a position of strength abroad or moderate liberalism at home. And he would certainly not allow "Ike" Eisenhower, or anyone else for that matter, to usurp him as the presumptive nominee of the Democratic Party.[8]

Truman's other great challenge was his testy relationship with the Eightieth Congress, which was controlled by a Republican majority led by the traditionalist "old guard." The Eightieth Congress would eventually pass more than nine hundred bills and hardly lived up to the "do nothing" label placed upon it. Yet much of this legislation was designed to roll back elements of the New Deal, and the Congress failed to make significant progress on some of the main issues facing the nation, including inflation, a severe housing shortage that had been an issue since the end of World War II, and a shortfall in education funding.

When Republican congressmen took their seats after their victory in the 1946 midterms, each found a broom placed in every seat by an anonymous colleague, who had labeled each sweeping stick, "Here's yours. Let's do the job."[9] This set the tone for what was to come. Though they continued bipartisan support of Truman's foreign policy, backing the Marshall Plan, the coming together of US armed forces, and aid to bolster anticommunists in Greece and Turkey, the Republicans planted their feet firmly on domestic issues. Yes, they helped their Democratic colleagues to balance the budget and achieve a surplus (as was later highlighted in the Republican platform for the 1948 election), but they also stymied countless Truman bills, forcing the president to use executive orders to get any meaningful action through. Even the most moderate of Democratic bills were shot down once they made it to the floor. And while the Republicans delighted in halting the progressive momentum their colleagues across the aisle had built up since FDR entered the White House in 1933, they saved the full heat of their ire for his successor. When Truman spoke, they mocked. When he proposed, they stifled. And when he vetoed, they overrode. As the GOP had won control of both houses in the 1946 white-wash—giving the would-be deserters within the Democratic Party even more ammunition—Truman was effectively at their mercy.

Of course, one of the checks and balances of American democracy is for the two main parties to battle it out over issues in both houses and for each to prevent the other from having carte blanche. And Republican representatives can hardly be blamed for seeking to bring stability to the economy during postwar reconversion and demobilization by proposing legislation that supported the private sector.[10] Yet what the Republicans in the Eightieth Congress seemed to want was not the healthy back-and-forth of interparty debate or the expression of a worldview that differed with the benevolent government outlook of liberal progressives. Rather, as the historian Cabell Phillips writes, the intent of many conservative congressmen was to dine on "a joyous feast of retribution" during the Eightieth Congress.[11] So they became the bane of the president's existence, preventing him from passing substantial domestic measures he had outlined as essential.[12] Seeking redress for a generation's worth of liberal victories, the Republicans enacted in both houses a plan of obstruction that embodied and in many cases even exceeded one of Robert Taft's favorite sayings: "The duty of the opposition party is to oppose."[13]

Though Taft saw himself as the face and voice of the Republican Party and undoubtedly led the way for the GOP on Capitol Hill, he failed to capitalize on this position when it mattered most. In June 1948, the Republican National Convention selected New York governor Thomas Dewey (who had lost by just three million votes to FDR four years previously) and Earl Warren, the governor of California, to run against Truman. Taft despaired as he again lost the nomination to his bitter rival, whom he viewed as little more than a trumped-up liberal who no more believed in true conservative ideals than did Harry Truman.[14] In contrast, the media responded emphatically, hailing Dewey and Warren, widely seen as two popular moderates, as an unbeatable ticket. Certainly Dewey knew how to make a case to a crowd, as a former prosecutor and district attorney who had taken on organized crime before moving on to the governor's mansion in 1938. Though he had lost to FDR—by a margin far narrower than his Republican predecessors—Dewey had won re-election in the 1942 governor's race by the largest in state history. With his pretty wife, reasonable policies, and highly organized campaign staff, he was predicted by more than two-thirds of newspapers and most major polls to best Truman in a similar manner come November 1948. Dewey's face beamed out from the cover of *Life* magazine with the caption, "The Next President of the United States," a *New York Times* headline predicted, "Thomas E. Dewey's Election as President Is a Foregone Conclusion," and pollster Elmo Roper declared that his organization would no longer survey public opinion of the election because "Dewey is almost as good as elected."[15]

Dewey's nomination proved more straightforward than the president's. Though Eisenhower dashed the hopes of his Democratic and ADA backers by declining to be nominated, Truman ran into yet more difficulties at the Democratic National Convention in mid-July. As if Truman's seat wasn't hot enough, the gathering took place during one of the most stifling summers on record.

Minneapolis mayor Hubert Humphrey, backed by the ADA, proposed a civil rights plank that far exceeded the timid language of the official party position, a noncommittal line that the platform committee hoped would stave off a full-scale southern Democratic rebellion. When Humphrey's bold, unflinching minority plank passed despite spirited protests by southern Dixiecrats who wanted to prop up segregation, Truman was committed to pushing it in the upcoming election. The southern rebels in the party knew that the president would not back down, and so the entire Mississippi delegation and half of their brethren from Alabama walked out when Missouri governor Phil Donnelly nominated Truman.[16]

Truman, rather than attempting to pacify the mutineers, responded by attacking. Ignoring for now the ill omen of the walkout, which heralded the end of what his advisers had hoped was still the Solid South of FDR's reign, the president delivered his finest speech to date in accepting the convention's nomination. Moreover, he shocked allies and opponents alike by calling Congress back into special session to tackle the issues they had failed to address before the summer adjournment. The Republicans could either live up to the surprisingly liberal promises of their election platform or confirm once and for all that they had resolved to "do nothing" for the country's needs, as Truman had charged.[17]

They chose the latter, but Truman had little cause to gloat. In late July he still trailed in the polls—by almost twenty points in some surveys—and the press continued to fawn over his opponents. Meanwhile, the southerners who had deserted him in Philadelphia made their flight official, forming the new States' Rights Party. Their leader, the fiery orator and governor of South Carolina, J. Strom Thurmond, stared down Truman over civil rights and declared, "All the laws of Washington and all the bayonets of the Army cannot force the nigger into our homes, our schools, our churches."[18] Even as he spoke, Henry Wallace and the Progressive Party were orchestrating their campaign on the left flank of the party to capture the liberal imagination and, they hoped, the White House.

To further complicate matters, as if they needed complicating, Truman was hamstrung by not one but two scandals involving communists. In late July 1948, alleged communist spy Elizabeth Bentley told the House Un-American Activities Committee (HUAC) that another communist agent, Harry Dexter White, a US representative to the nascent International Monetary Fund, was one of more than twenty government officials who had supplied her with classified documents.[19] A few days later, as the special session of Congress (known as the Turnip Day Congress because of the Missouri harvest schedule) closed without passing any meaningful legislation, the spy scandal got even worse for Truman. Time magazine writer and editor Whittaker Chambers identified State Department director Alger Hiss as one of several government insiders who were spying for Moscow.[20] Suddenly, the persistent accusations that Truman had turned a blind eye to communist infiltration in Washington leveled by HUAC committee members Karl Mundt, Richard Nixon, and their Republican brethren seemed to be more than just partisan hot air.

There was no respite to be found for poor old Harry Truman in foreign affairs, either. Though his decisions to keep American forces in West Berlin and to conduct a massive, unprecedented airdrop of supplies into the east of the city had thwarted the Soviet plan to bring the United States to its knees over the future of Germany, the iron-willed Joseph Stalin refused to lift the blockade.[21] He was convinced that in the end, America and Britain would be forced to cave and give him carte blanche in Germany, which was still highly vulnerable as dictatorial and democratic forces vied to fill the power vacuum left by Hitler's demise. In North Korea, the communist regime periodically shut off electricity to its southern neighbors, and China was all but lost to communist forces. Despite a massive injection of US aid as part of the Marshall Plan, Greece and Turkey were still imperiled by communist rebels. Communist parties continued to grow in membership and influence across Europe. The nascent Israeli state was a continual battleground, with Palestinian forces opposed to what they viewed as nothing more than a land grab by the same infidels they had battled during the Crusades and had hated ever since.[22]

A lesser man would have crumbled under such pressures, but they merely galvanized Harry Truman. German bombardment in World War I didn't break him, nor did arduous years on his family farm or numerous failed business ventures.[23] No matter how great the pressures were at home and abroad, Truman was determined to overcome them, even as those around him doubted his ability to prevail.

Truman's primary tactic in the contentious election of 1948 was to fall back on the endurance forged long before he entered politics and simply outwork Tom Dewey, Henry Wallace, and Strom Thurmond. During his "nonpolitical" tour in June, Truman covered more than nine thousand miles by train, and beginning with a Labor Day speech in Detroit that ensured widespread union support and funding, he set off again across the country. This time he would add more than twenty-two thousand miles — or about three thousand miles short of the earth's circumference — to his personal odometer, speaking up to sixteen times a day as part of a schedule so frenetic it gave his chief counsel Clark Clifford boils all over his body and nightmares that lasted for months after the campaign ended.[24] Contrast this with FDR, who midway through the 1944 campaign had delivered just two major speeches and traveled no more than a couple hundred miles (his war-related journeys notwithstanding). Before the September Whistle Stop Tour began in earnest, an adviser asked Truman if he, a man of sixty-four who was eighteen years older than his Republican opponent, could handle such a grueling endeavor. The tireless president replied that yes, he could endure it, it was his staff he was worried about killing with the strain.[25]

Yet for all this grit and effort on the surface, Truman's campaign was not merely that of a hard worker determined to run his opponents into the ground. The whistle stop schedule had been planned meticulously to target the states Truman needed to hold and those he must capture to have any hope of overturning Dewey's lead. And the secret weapon behind the success of the Whistle Stop Campaign was the DNC's newly formed Research Division. Truman was able to tailor the start of each of his 352 addresses to the specific audience at each stop thanks to the tireless efforts of the seven young men of that unheralded organization.

Holed up in a noisy, airless office in Washington's Dupont Circle by day and the insect-plagued American Veterans Committee boarding house by night, the Research Division provided a localized fact sheet for every single stop.[26] Director Bill Batt and his six-man team also provided Clifford, his assistant George Elsey, and undersecretary of the interior Oscar Chapman with material for the major speeches, assessed the country's reaction to these addresses, made suggestions on where Truman should speak on certain topics, and critiqued the president's speaking performances. It was also Batt whose persuasive report convinced Truman (by way of Clifford) to call the special session that had exposed the Republican copycat election agenda as fraudulent.[27]

In addition to the factual bedrock and localized information he received from the Research Division, Truman had assistance from other external sources that helped him stage the most unlikely of election victories. A reporter uncovered negligence on the part of a Republican-controlled congressional committee, which had decided that there would be no additional funding for farmers' grain storage bins in 1948. This would all be very well if crop yields stayed the same or declined, but with record output for corn and many grains, the penny-pinching policy quickly backfired. Farmers could only receive government-set prices for crops in federally funded and approved facilities, so, lacking these, they either had to borrow money to build their own, let the crops rot, or get rid of them at fire sale prices. Worse still for the Republicans, the writer tipped off Clifford to evidence linking the GOP policy to grain speculators who stood to make millions from the cut-price sell-off.[28] Truman brought all this to bear in a memorable address to eighty thousand people in Iowa in September 1948, during which he accused the GOP of having "stuck a pitchfork in the farmer's back."[29]

He used similarly strong wording across the country to indict the Republican-led Congress on pricing, housing, civil rights, education, health care, and all the other major planks of his platform. He was essentially continuing the policies of the New Deal and turning the 1948 election into a values-focused campaign, in which he painted the Democratic Party as the group that had the interests of lower and middle classes at heart, while the Republicans remained the party of, as he put it over and over again, "special interests." This had been one of FDR's central themes in his campaigns, and Truman was determined to stick with it, believing that the country still favored his party's interventionist stance over the old guard Republican's contrary calls for smaller government.[30] Whether this was reality or mere political theater would be left to the voters on Election Day.

It was immaterial to Truman that Dewey, a liberal Republican who had ushered in judicial and social reforms during his time as New York governor, was in favor of most of the president's proposed measures. Unless Dewey risked alienating traditionalist party bigwigs by separating himself from the record of the Eightieth Congress, the mud Truman slung throughout his campaign was bound to stick.[31]

Dewey was desperate to avoid the ire of his party's more conservative faction, and so he said little to distance himself from it. As Truman used bold, Research Division–fueled specifics at each whistle stop, Dewey relied on canned, repetitive platitudes. Such was Dewey's overconfidence that he would win simply by showing up that he began his own tour almost two weeks after Truman's and made less than half the campaign stops of his opponent. Indeed, the governor of New York wrote to his sister in August 1948 mulling whether it was too early to start planning the new décor of his White House.

While Dewey was thinking about decorations, Truman attacked and took risk after risk, desperately clawing and scrabbling to win the election. Dewey, following Truman's route at a languid pace, tried to put in just enough effort not to lose it. And with a double-digit lead in most surveys and pollster Elmo Roper refusing to conduct any more after September because he believed Dewey's election to be certain, the Republican challenger merely had more reason not to match Truman stop for stop, barb for barb.[32]

Though Dewey can be commended for taking the high road and while Truman, in his own words after the election, often resorted to "demagoguery," the president did not bash his opponent by name. In his 352 speeches all over the country (except the South, which, other than Texas, he wrote off and did not visit) he only mentioned Dewey twice.[33] In contrast, he slammed Dewey's fellow Republican Robert Taft on thirty-eight occasions, and the "do-nothing" Congress hundreds of times. This was partly because Dewey's record as New York governor did not align with Truman's accusations against the Congress (as he knew from the Research Division's thorough dossier on Dewey) and because the media's representation of Taft was so unfavorable—even right-leaning Time called him "dull, prosy, colorless."[34] Truman's decision to focus on targets other than Dewey is also attributable to the poor public image of the Eightieth Congress, which had even lower approval ratings than he did. Truman was better able to back up his populist distinction between his "party of the people" and the "party of privilege" by going after Congress's record than if he had tried to find fault with Dewey's achievements.[35] Because his opponent refused to respond, Truman succeeded in making him guilty by association with the "do-nothing" crew—even though this label was probably hyperbole.

Truman's team also successfully courted minority votes by proposing a massive increase in visas issued to European immigrants, and Jewish voters honored him with active fund-raising and then ballot box support on November 2 for being the first leader to recognize Israel. Though Henry Wallace was a skilled orator and a brilliant mind, he was not a factor in November, and though the Dixiecrats dissolved the Solid South, whereby every southern state voted for FDR in 1944, they were able to win only four southern states. If anything, the hateful bile spewed by Thurmond and his fellow Dixiecrats pushed more independent and black voters into Truman's column than they gained for their own prejudiced, duplicitous cause.[36]

This, combined with the Research Division's fact finding, Truman's indefatigable work ethic, and his central assumption that the values of the New Deal still rang true with the American people, enabled Truman to do what had seemed unthinkable: retain the presidency and recapture both houses. He was also able to eventually gain union support, win over the traditionally Republican Midwest on the strength of his farming policy and the GOP's grain bins debacle, and capture the majority of black votes (particularly in cities in the North) because of his bold civil rights program.

This book is the story of a president who refused to lose, the capable team that worked round the clock to help him win, and the seven men of the Research Division whose ingenuity made all the difference.

There have been many books written about the 1948 presidential election and Harry Truman's extraordinary victory, but this one, which focuses on June to November 1948, examines the period from two illuminating angles. First, I explore the microcosm of the Whistle Stop Tour against a rich background of domestic and foreign crises in the United States in 1948. At home, these included the dual split in the Democratic Party, a Republican Party in search of itself, runaway inflation, a housing shortage, and a deep divide over civil rights. Abroad, communism was on the march, as the Soviet Union shut down the trade and transport links between East and West Berlin, Mao Zedong continued his takeover in China, and Greece struggled to hold off communist rebels trying to violently overthrow the government. Second, I draw on previously unused archival material to tell the full story of the Research Division—"these bright, imaginative and energetic young men," as Truman's speechwriter George Elsey later called them—to explain how they helped Harry Truman connect with the American people.[37] Truman trusted the electorate to choose the man who understood their needs, who had walked their path, and who would fight for their future. Despite the contrary predictions of the pollsters, the press, and even Truman's family, the voters of November 1948 decided that the man who could do that was not Thomas Dewey, nor Strom Thurmond, nor Henry Wallace, but the Man from Missouri, Harry S. Truman. This is the story of how he pulled it off.

An article in the Wall Street Journal began, "A Congress stymied by partisan divides, blown deadlines and intraparty squabbling gets a late chance this week to end the year with an elusive budget deal and to make headway on other fronts."[38] This paragraph described perfectly the eightieth session that Truman labeled the "do-nothing" Congress. Yet the Journal published this story on December 9, 2013. More than half a century after Truman's campaign, many of the same problems still bedevil American politics. That Truman was able to overcome his obstructive opponents with a resounding election victory, while also surmounting a double split in his party, the lurking menace of an increasingly belligerent Soviet Union, and a largely hostile press is illustrative of a way forward in such situations. Certainly, his campaign rhetoric was not bipartisan—

quite the opposite most of the time. Yet at each of the 352 whistle stops, Truman's words showed clarity, conviction, and commitment to a clear legislative program that resonated with the millions who heard him. Bill Batt, head of the Research Division, knew that Truman was not a man who could pull off "Churchillian grand-eloquence," so Truman's talking points were simple, to the point, and connected to facts dug up by Batt and his colleagues.[39] Truman also tailored each speech to the needs and interests of each local audience—whether it was flood relief in the Pacific Northwest, labor relations in Detroit, a grain bin shortage in Iowa, or civil rights in Harlem.

Though he was no Churchill, FDR, or even an oratorical powerhouse like his opponent—the States' Rights Party's Strom Thurmond—at the microphone, Truman knew his audience and understood the issues they cared about—summed up by another Research Division staffer as "peace, prices and places to live"—and told the American people what he was going to do for them.[40] As his rival candidates failed to find the mark with white supremacist rants (Thurmond), Soviet sympathizing (Henry Wallace), and dull, tired platitudes like "unity" (Tom Dewey), Truman stuck to addressing the daily challenges facing his audiences. He conveyed the passion and fire needed to convince his listeners that he would fight for their interests if they voted for him. And he displayed a folksy, good ol' midwestern boy demeanor, dismissed as unbecoming of a president by opponents but lapped up by the crowds that cheered him at train stations across the nation. This is a story of a moment in time, but the echoes of Truman's whistle stop messages resonate just as clearly now as they did from the train platforms in 1948.

June

My Dear Mr. President,

Never in my fifty one years of life have I had the temerity to write a letter to the President. However, when I tell you that I have known you personally while I served on the Ways and Means Committee of the Grand Lodge A.F. and A.M., that we have a close mutual friend in George Marquis of Independence, that we have many other mutual friends and acquaintances, then possibly you will not feel that I am being too presumptuous in offering you in all kindness a "grass roots" political suggestion.

Our Democratic Party has a hard row to hoe. We are beset on one side by reaction and on the other by a Communist dominated Progressive Party. Wallace cannot win. But his party is attracting many liberals who fail to see the dangers of Communist domination. Present trends indicate the victory of reaction at the polls this Fall. Normally the failure of a party or a candidate is not too catastrophic. But these are perilous times in the world.

I have always looked upon our Democratic Party as the truest vehicle of real progressive liberalism in the country. I still think that is true. But in order to win, its leadership is going to have to be able to electrify the electorate. Regardless of the justice or injustice I believe both popular opinion and opinions of liberals everywhere is that new leadership of the party is essential to victory this year.

Certainly none of your liberal leadership needs to be repudiated in any way. The Democratic party must continue your civil rights fight, anti inflation fight etc. You no doubt could have very great influence in the selection of a party leader for this campaign. Naturally in voluntarily stepping out of the place of leadership you would sacrifice personal prestige and political power. Yet you will recall that the Savior of mankind when upon a mountain top was confronted with this identical problem. His road to glory was the road of personal sacrifice. That has continued to be the road to glory throughout the ages.

Assuring you of my kindest personal regards, I am,

Sincerely,

H. H. Brummall[1]

He could take it from the Republicans. He could take it from the Dixie-crats and Progressives. Heck, Harry Truman could even take it from dissenting voices inside his own cabinet. But rudeness from one of his own, a guy from Missouri he knew, and a sanctimonious one at that? No. Particularly not when Brummall was asking him to invalidate all he had worked for by "voluntarily stepping out of the place of leadership." The gall of this man!

His normally sunny disposition, conveyed with a smile that broke easily across his broad yet boyishly handsome face enhanced by mischievous hazel eyes, darkened like the sky of his native Missouri when a twister is coming. Most presidential replies are merely a boilerplate with a signature stamp or at best a hastily scrawled John Hancock at the bottom. But not this time. Truman picked up his pen and angrily scribbled a personal, and less than cordial, repost to Dr. Brummall of Salisbury, Missouri:

Dear Dr. Brummall,

I read your letter of the fifteenth with a lot of interest and for your information I was not brought up to run from a fight.

A great many of you Democrats in 1940 ran off after a certain Governor [Missouri's former Governor Lloyd C. Stark], who was trying to cut my throat and he didn't do it successfully—they are not going to succeed this time either.

I am certainly sorry that you feel the way you do. It is not a good way for a Missourian to feel at this time.

Sincerely yours,

Harry S. Truman[2]

Once his rage cooled, Truman decided he could use Brummall's note to his political advantage. He wanted to fire a warning shot about his attitude to the election campaign to his detractors across the country, so he called in the tall, wiry Charlie Ross, his eloquent former boyhood friend, Pulitzer Prize–winning journalist, and now press secretary (as one of the inner circle the Republicans disparagingly called "The Missouri Gang"). Truman knew he could count on Ross—whose small, deep-set eyes focused intently on his subject when they spoke and who addressed Truman with the confidence that only comes from a decades-old association—for a frank opinion. Ross's cautious and reserved manner often served to send the unpolished products of Truman's enthusiastic and quick decision making back to the drafting table, and the president welcomed his old pal's candor.[3] The two discussed the matter for a couple of minutes and decided on a plan of action: Ross would share the sentiments of Brummall's note and Truman's reply with the press in mid-June 1948.

If it was coverage the president wanted, he most certainly got it. *Time* ran a piece on the exchange the following week, and the *New Yorker* compared Truman's unusually frank response to the impersonal, template-based one he had sent to an attorney who had joined Brummall in calling for him to bow out of the Democratic race but which had not drawn the same ire: "The President has asked me to thank you for your letter of April 23. He has read it with interest, and wants you to know that he is always glad to receive suggestions such as yours."[4] Since the Brummall incident, counsel to the president Clark Clifford, the forty-one-year-old former naval officer who had quickly risen through the ranks to become one of Truman's key advisers, had been mulling how best to put the president's determination in the face of criticism to use in the 1948 election campaign. Clifford, whose height, dash, and sophisticated speaking manner contrasted sharply with his boss and made the society pages of Washington newspapers write "gooily" about him, according to veteran reporter A. Merriman Smith, was not just a favorite of the media.[5] He was also a master planner, had a quick turn of phrase, and was trusted by Truman to oversee strategy for the coming political dogfight.

Clifford, Oscar L. Chapman (undersecretary of the interior), and several other members of Truman's inner circle met every Monday in the Wardman Park Hotel apartment of Oscar R. Ewing, who had been vice chairman of the Democratic National Committee from 1942 to 1947 and was now an unofficial adviser to the president. Clifford called the group, which aimed to advance liberal policy in the White House and reveled in the secrecy of its gatherings, the "Monday Night Group," and as they ate their usual weekly steak and downed several rounds, they talked shop.[6] At one of these bull sessions in early spring 1948, Clifford asked Chapman to find an excuse for Truman to take a train trip out West in the coming weeks, a trial run for more sustained railroad campaigning in the fall. He had come up with this idea from the November 1947 memo penned by Washington attorney James Rowe, a confidant of FDR, for budget bureau director James Webb. The lengthy and detailed missive, which soon made it to Clifford's desk and would direct many elements of the Truman team's campaign strategy, included an exhortation that Truman should focus on "Winning the West." Rowe went on to state that "political and program planning demands concentration upon the West and its problems, including reclamation, floods, and agriculture. It is the Number One Priority for the 1948 campaign." Rowe then warned that the GOP had a foothold in many key western states. Thus, Clifford thought the president should start his battle for electoral seats in the West with a tour that would enable him to address millions of voters during the spring of 1948, long before the full fall campaign began.[7]

If Truman's staff could pull this ambitious westward journey off, he would not be the first president to take to the rails to drum up support. Woodrow Wilson had tried it in 1919 to press his case for American leadership of the League of Nations, and Andrew Johnson had "swung around the circle" from Washington to Chicago in an attempt to get popular backing for his reconstruction blueprint. Clifford, however, hoped his chief would be more successful than Johnson or Wilson: the former failed in his mission and the latter's arduous time on the tracks arguably hastened his death.[8]

After hearing Clifford out, Chapman got on the telephone to Robert Sproul, his friend who was in his eighteenth year as president of the University of California Berkeley, and who he knew was searching for a commencement speaker for the school's June 1948 event.[9] Sproul was a Republican and no fan of Truman, but he couldn't pass up the PR opportunity. Truman's advisers now had their excuse. The trip Clifford dubbed "The Shakedown Cruise" was on.[10]

In Clifford's mind, such a tour was a necessity for several reasons beyond the thinking of James Rowe's memo. First, Truman had hit rock bottom in the Gallup and Roper polls. By 1946 and 1947 the glow of wartime unity had melted away and postwar problems came to the fore, including union unrest—which led to millions of work days lost to strikes—agricultural tariffs, and a shortage of available and affordable housing. As these intensified, the nation no longer seemed to support its president. As a biographer of Truman's rival, Republican Senator Robert A. Taft, put it: "To many Americans, Truman seemed inept, uncertain, vulnerable at the polls, a sad successor to Roosevelt."[11]

Truman's numbers rallied with the boldness of the "Truman Doctrine," his ambitious plan for containing Soviet expansionism that he announced on March 12, 1947. But now, in spring 1948, with the president hobbled by his continual losses to the Republican majority in Congress, his controversial decision to recognize the nascent state of Israel, and with multiple candidates and possible candidates from both parties stealing the headlines—not least the now-iconic General Eisenhower—Truman's brief surge was well and truly over.[12]

One April 1948 poll revealed that his approval rating had plummeted to a dire 36 percent, down 19 points from the September 1947 high-water mark. Another April statistical barometer had Truman losing the election by seven percentage points to Republican preconvention favorite Thomas E. Dewey, the popular, short, and debonair governor of New York, who had won his second term two years prior by a record margin. A month later, polling data suggested the Missourian would fall even harder against the capable, studious, and ambitious former governor of Minnesota and current University of Pennsylvania president Harold Stassen—a predicted loss by twenty-three points.[13] Polling was by no means an exact science, but Gallup and its competitors had been honing their methods for a dozen years and Clifford and his fellow West Wing staff could see that Truman was in big trouble if the political winds didn't shift before November.

Furthermore, Truman was stymied at every turn by the hostile Republican-controlled Congress, the sole aim of which seemed to be to stop Truman from getting any meaningful domestic legislation through. With widespread alarm at the USSR's increasing aggression in Eastern Europe and Asia and the cooperative and bipartisan leadership of Republican Arthur Vandenberg in the Senate (a longtime supporter of Truman's tough policies toward the Soviet Union) and Vandenberg's counterparts in Congress, Truman found it easier to push through foreign policy legislation. In early spring 1948, Congress passed a bill to grant more than $5 billion in aid to Western Europe, and Truman signed the European Cooperation Act on April 3. This was the major legislation of what became known as the Marshall Plan.[14] With this, he and his secretary of state George C. Marshall, the quick-minded, detail-oriented, take-charge US Army chief of staff who masterminded American victories in Europe and the Pacific in World War II, hoped to bolster Western Europe and parts of Asia against expansionist communism.

The funding approved by Congress would also bolster Turkish and Greek government forces as they continued to oppose communist takeovers. If the communists succeeded in capturing these countries, Marshall and Truman believed, it would not only embolden what Churchill called Soviet Russia's "expansive and proselytizing tendencies," but it could also start a domino effect of more democratic European nations toppling under the weight of communism's westward march.[15] And if China succumbed to the Maoist revolution and the power void in Japan was filled by Stalin's puppets, another continent would be beholden to Moscow. By working across the aisle and reaching consensus on just about the only thing most Republicans and Democrats could agree on in 1948, Truman hoped such catastrophes would never come to pass. As Marshall put it when explaining the plan that would come to bear his name: "Our policy is directed not against any country or doctrine but against hunger, poverty, desperation, and chaos. Its purpose should be the revival of a working economy in the world so as to permit the emergence of political and social conditions in which free institutions can exist."[16]

Despite continued bipartisan support for the Marshall Plan and that it marked a personal triumph for his administration, Truman was still taking a beating in the press. The criticism was particularly sharp from conservative outlets such as the *Chicago Tribune* and southern papers that resented the far-reaching civil rights proposal Truman had sent to Congress and the Senate in February 1948. This included desegregating the armed forces, guaranteeing fair employment practices at the federal level, and introducing strict new antilynching laws.[17]

The outraged reaction from Democrats below the Mason-Dixon Line was swift in coming. "50 Southern Congressman Declare War on Truman's Civil Rights Plan" screamed a front-page headline in the February 28 edition of the *Kentucky New Era*, typifying southern segregationist ire.[18] Since June 28, 1947, when Truman became the first chief executive to speak to the NAACP and told of his intention to put to rest the inequity of Jim Crow, many Democrats in southern states had either castigated or deserted their leader, or both.[19]

Mississippi senator James Eastland, dubbed "The Voice of the White South," encapsulated his region's prevailing attitude toward Truman's plans when he lamented, "The South as we know it is being swept to its destruction."[20] Despite their despondency, however, Eastland and his fellow pro–Jim Crow, anti-Truman peers were not willing to yield without a tussle. Under the leadership of the young, ambitious governor of South Carolina, J. Strom Thurmond, who combed his dark hair backwards and had a habit of raising his bushy eyebrows when vigorously making a point, the southern rebels soon became known as the Dixiecrats. Realizing that few outside their region shared their resistance to Truman's program, and recognizing the need to pull in a wider following, they rallied around the banner of states' rights, portraying the government as meddling, invasive, and, they claimed, unconstitutional in its attempts to force civil rights legislation on local authorities. These defiant southerners swore to their backward-looking constituents that they would vehemently oppose any Democratic candidate who came to the July Democratic National Convention in support of federally mandated racial equality laws—which, Truman knew well, meant him.[21] If he didn't get laws through Congress, Truman had vowed to sign executive orders to force desegregation of the armed forces, equal pay for civil servants of all races, and other proposals, which, all told, constituted perhaps the most ambitious civil rights package in a generation.

The civil rights struggle was but one of the fissures that divided the Democrats' ranks. The articulate, well-coiffed, pointy-nosed Henry A. Wallace had been on the attack ever since Truman dismissed him from his post of secretary of commerce in the fall of 1946 for openly speaking out about the White House's foreign policy. Popular even before he served under FDR and then Truman, he had further endeared himself to the far left wing of the party by demanding a more radical domestic agenda, including nationalizing industries such as energy and extending the welfare state far beyond the boundaries of the New Deal. It should be noted that Truman had no chance of getting such an agenda through the gridlocked Eightieth Congress, which had throttled even his most moderate proposals. Wallace had also espoused a noninterventionist, conciliatory policy toward Moscow and placed the blame for escalating tensions between American and the Soviet Union on his own government and big-money Wall Street influences, which he claimed were directing the positions of the Democratic and Republican parties.[22] The same springtime 1948 polls from Roper and Gallup that put the fear into Truman's team gave Wallace only 5 to 7 percent of the popular vote, but when combined with the incumbent's likely losses in the South, this could seriously diminish Truman's hopes of beating Dewey, Stassen, or whoever else secured the Republican nomination.[23]

Truman's advisers decided what he needed to overcome all these challenges was to show the people that he was no accidental president, that he was not only the leader who had successfully ended World War II, but the right person to continue to lead them in peacetime. Once the Monday Night Group had talked Truman into the June railroad expedition to the West Coast—an idea he immediately warmed to—Clark Clifford, Charlie Ross, and Oscar Chapman planned an ambitious schedule that would test any speaker's mettle. There would be five formal speeches in large auditoriums in Chicago, Omaha, Seattle, Los Angeles, and Berkeley, as well as seventy-one brief, off-the-cuff addresses from the rear platform of the train as it traversed 9,505 miles of track, cutting through towns large and small across eighteen states.[24] All this would take place in just fifteen days.[25]

Despite the impending rigors of the trip out West and the return leg to Washington, Truman's advisers had two reasons for confidence. The first was the creation of the Democratic National Committee's Research Division in late March, which would be dedicated to providing fact-based fodder for Truman's speeches—a first for the party. Whether the president addressed one hundred thousand in a college football stadium, as was expected at Berkeley, or fifteen local residents at a tiny backwoods train station in Idaho, the Research Division would provide both the factual bedrock to help Truman persuade the people and the targeted anecdotes to charm them. Since its inception in March 1948, this project had quickly evolved from a Clark Clifford pipe dream into a small team of number crunchers, journalists, and analysts that would gather, compile, and prioritize the statistics, issues, and localized information.

In addition, the team would work with local Democratic Party leaders to take the pulse of each region and adjust Truman's talking points as needed. Each Research Division member would also compile at least one thick "Files of the Facts" on housing, prices, labor, and eight other main campaign issues, depending on their prior subject matter expertise. After Truman spoke, they would not only analyze what he said but how the media responded, and communicate constructive feedback to Clifford and his team on the train, via the White House. While Truman's train had telegraph and phone equipment on board, most of the Research Division's information would be delivered to a local airport every few days, and a runner dispatched from the train to pick up the latest reports and speech fodder. This coordinated, data-heavy, localized approach would, the Democratic brain trust hoped, enable Truman to talk his way back into contention.

In "The Politics of 1948" memo that had shaped Clifford's thinking the previous year, James Rowe had identified shortcomings in the Democratic Party's infrastructure, including the lack of a dedicated research division, which the GOP had and that Rowe felt would stack the deck even more against Truman come the fall campaign.

Rowe, Clifford, Chapman, and the other strategists behind Truman's 1948 bid were aware that the GOP had established a fact-finding group in the 1944 FDR vs. Tom Dewey election, which Dewey lost by only three million votes. Conservative writer George P. Sokolsky had observed, "Mr. Dewey set out to make serious-minded speeches on issues and problems and had a mountain of research done in preparation."[26] If Truman was going to do the same four years later, he couldn't rely on the skeleton crew in the DNC's publicity department, where Jonathan Daniels and others needed to focus on press relations, creating media buzz, and contributing to the speechwriting effort.

Clifford agreed with Rowe's assessment of the need for a research division to bolster the speechwriting efforts of the special counsel, Oscar Chapman, and others. After conferring at length with DNC chairman J. Howard McGrath about how new hires would be paid from the party's threadbare budget, Clifford received the go-ahead to hire seven full-time staff members that would make up the new DNC Research Division, plus secretarial personnel. With makeshift headquarters in the Hamilton National Bank building near Washington's Dupont Circle, this group would gather data on the major issues of the campaign, provide talking points for major and off-the-cuff speeches, and assess the reaction to Truman's oratory. Though they would be only two blocks from the DNC headquarters, the Batt group would remain a separate entity, communicating with the White House through special assistant to the president Charlie Murphy and sometimes with Clark Clifford directly.[27]

To lead this group, Clifford selected William L. Batt Jr., the chairman of the ADA's Philadelphia branch. Though only a year old, the ADA was fast becoming one of the most prominent liberal political organizations in the country, and Batt was considered one of its rising stars. Batt's father had run a wartime production board for FDR and run it well, which helped open the door when his son, whom everyone called Bill, wanted to follow him into politics. Bill Jr. had also inherited his father's work ethic, enthusiasm, and ability to make friends everywhere he went. Though he had failed to win a congressional seat in the 1946 midterms, the younger Batt was involved in organizing Philadelphia's branch of the ADA, which proved to be one of the most influential in the liberal movement's first few years.[28]

Batt was still working as a sales representative for the Motor Parts Company in Philadelphia, but after Clifford and DNC executive director Gael Sullivan had several phone conversations with him, they knew they had found their man.[29] Clifford dispatched a formal offer letter, offering him a $10,000 salary (the equivalent of almost $100,000 today) to head the Research Division, with a guarantee of at least eight months on the job. As the influential campaign strategy memo from the previous year had stated, there was no time to lose in ramping up the DNC PR and research apparatus, and so Clifford requested that Batt begin his duties on March 8.[30]

Clifford's first assignment for Batt was to review Truman's podium performances in the weeks leading up to the June train tour. When reading from a text, Truman was, frankly, boring, but when he spoke off the cuff he was relaxed and convincing. For this reason, the president's close advisers had devised a new, extemporaneous approach for him whereby he used just a few bullet points for guidance rather than the word-for-word script his advisers had once given him to read from when trying, unsuccessfully, to force him into FDR's rhetorical mold. Batt was charged with figuring out if this new strategy was going to work or whether Clifford and company would once again have to try something new to elevate Truman's rhetoric from the depths of ineffectiveness. Batt believed it would work, at least based on his assessment of the address to Congress on March 17, of which he wrote, "This was the best yet, both in the writing and the presentation. He said what he had to say, then he stopped. The presentation was forthright, unpretentious and terribly sincere. I have never heard the President do better."[31] This direct approach, then, was the model Batt proposed in crafting Truman's speeches going forward, one that favored the president's own conversational style.

While he immediately started analyzing Truman's speeches, providing talking points to Democratic leaders and somehow finding time to write an article for The Nation supporting Truman's plans for universal military training, Batt's primary concern in his first few days at Dupont Circle was filling the six remaining positions McGrath had budgeted for.[32] After all, if the Research Division was to create an armory of facts with which to bombard the Republicans and the Progressives, Batt could hardly be expected to stock it by himself. To this end, he exchanged several notes with Clifford about his developing personnel wish list, mentioning such prominent writers as Merle Miller, editor of New York–based Yank magazine, and experienced operators such as Gus Tyler, political education director of the American Federation of Labor (AFL), who Batt noted had "led the successful fight against Communist infiltration within the American Veterans Committee."[33]

As he made inquiries, it became clear that many of these men—and, in the testosterone-dominated world of American politics in the late 1940s, all his candidates were men—were either indisposed, were not big fans of Truman, or simply wished to stick with the well-charted territory of their current positions.

In the coming campaign for a president who at one time had a sign reading "The Buck Stops Here" on his desk, the success or failure of the Research Division would ultimately rest squarely on Batt's shoulders. Batt knew what he needed to get the job done: a team that combined the talents of skilled writers, researchers, and policy experts, all of whom could gather, interpret, and prioritize the information needed to provide Truman's advisers with comprehensive yet highly usable speech fodder.

Batt made his first successful overture to Kenneth Birkhead, whom he had come to know through their membership in the American Veterans

Committee.[34] Like Batt, the tall, husky Birkhead liked to work long hours, had a head for numbers, and was able to quickly gather, synthesize, and present information from a wide array of sources he peered at through black, round-rimmed glasses. Herbert Tareyton cigarette boxes, with their distinctive image of a monocled, top-hatted gentleman, carried the slogan, "There's something about them you'll like," and this was certainly true of Kenny Birkhead, who liked them so much that he smoked up to three packs a day as he beavered away. Birkhead had helped the AVC free itself from communist influence in late 1947 and early 1948, an undertaking well-known to Batt given his long-standing involvement with veterans' affairs.[35] Though only a small percentage of AVC members were communists, they tried to drive the organization's agenda to the far left. Ronald Reagan biographer Edmund Morris notes that a young Reagan, himself an AVC member and at the time a Democrat, observed that at one 1946 AVC meeting, "a tiny, well organized minority of Communists manipulated the entire proceedings."[36] Negative publicity from the powerful Hearst newspaper group spurred Birkhead and others to act, and they began expelling known communists from the group.[37]

Birkhead helped Batt refine his short list for the other Research Division vacancies, and they soon settled on another American Veterans Committee member (though one Batt didn't previously know), Frank Kelly, who was also an old friend of Birkhead's from their days together at Kansas City University.[38] Kelly's grandfather, Michael, had immigrated to that Midwest town from Ireland in the 1840s and had quickly gravitated to the Democratic Party. Following his example, Michael's sons mimicked their father's voting habits, with Frank's uncle working for the same Tom Pendergast who had launched and furthered Harry Truman's late-starting political career. Kelly family lore insists that despite connections with the notorious city chief, they had, again like Truman, resisted the corruption that swirled around "Boss Tom" like a Midwest twister.[39]

As had his father and uncle, Frank Kelly became a staunch supporter of FDR as he cut his teeth as a cub reporter at the *Kansas City Star* and then honed his craft as a freelance contributor to *The New Yorker* and *The Atlantic Monthly* in the late 1930s and early 1940s.[40] During the president's 1944 campaign, though, Kelly's mind and body were elsewhere, with the thirty-year-old fighting in France as part of the American Expeditionary Force, landing on the beaches of Normandy and participating in the liberation of war-weary Paris. He finished his wartime service as an army correspondent and upon returning home after VE Day, Kelly returned to work for the Associated Press (AP), assigned to cover the early weeks and months of the United Nations. His experiences in the UN press corps in 1946 led him to write a book, *An Edge of Light*, about reporters' attempts to find out what was going on behind the White House's official releases about the standoff between the United States and Russia over the latter's refusal to withdraw troops from oil-rich Iran the year after World War II ended.[41]

Batt needed someone who not only had the writing ability needed to craft his own white papers, speech fodder, and Files of the Facts for Truman's election bid—which Kelly, whose journalism had earned him recognition as a Nieman Fellow by Harvard in 1946, could certainly handle—but could also cast an editor's wary eyes over the work of the other Research Division members. Kelly fit the bill and was another proven quantity Batt could depend on to work at the pace that the assignment demanded.

So in early April 1948, Kelly received an unexpected phone call from the White House. Sleeping off a hangover he'd acquired at New York's boisterous McSorley's Old Ale House during an overenthusiastic celebration of finishing his first book, Kelly thought the operator was merely a prankster. But when she put Bill Batt on the phone and then he passed the receiver to Kelly's college friend Kenny Birkhead, he quickly realized that the call was anything but a joke. "We're going to gather ideas and materials for the speeches Truman's going to make on trips through the country by train. We'll work on the back platform talks and some of the big ones in the cities too," Birkhead explained.

Though Batt and Birkhead were calling from Clark Clifford's office and the project was evidently for real, Kelly was still skeptical. He wasn't sure that Truman was a true liberal, and he protested, "I've never been in politics." Refusing to let his friend's doubts end the conversation, Birkhead assured him, "We'll divide the speech assignments . . . and you can work on the ones you can honestly handle." Kelly, surprised by the proposition and still battling a foggy head, asked for a couple of days to think about it. That wasn't going to happen, Birkhead explained, adding, "We haven't got much time. Call us back by four o'clock this afternoon. We've got other names on our list of writers."[42]

As was always the case with career decisions, the first person Kelly asked for advice was his wife of seven years, Barbara. "If you pass it up, you'll always feel like you missed something big," she told him. But a close friend, with whom Kelly had shared a few too many pints the night before, was of the opposite opinion, saying, "Don't do it, man. Truman is no Roosevelt. He tried to handle the job, but now he's going down the tube." Kelly's editor at The Atlantic Monthly Press agreed, warning him that "Truman is a sore loser" and offering to recommend Kelly for a professorship at Boston University instead of going to Washington. To further muddle Kelly's decision-making process, his agent advised him to join Batt and Birkhead on the campaign.[43]

Time was now running short, with the 4 p.m. deadline looming. Kelly weighed the conflicting advice from friends and family and made his choice. By now, he was convinced that Truman was doing what was best for the country and would certainly do a better job than Tom Dewey. And so Kelly favored the advice of his agent and his wife over the caution of his friend and editor and accepted the Research Division offer.[44] After saying "yes" to Batt just before the late afternoon cutoff, Kelly again called Barbara, who had taken their two-year-old son, Terry, to stay with friends in Vermont for a few days. "I've joined the Truman team, Barbie," he told her. "I've got to be in Washington next week. If we're going to save Harry, there's no time to lose."

"Now that you're on board, I'm sure he's going to win. He'll carry 30 states," the ever-supportive Barbara replied.

Carried away by a moment of exuberance about a race in which Truman was still lagging, Kelly burst out, "Why not 35?"[45]

When Kelly arrived at the Research Division offices in late April, Batt and Birkhead were already hard at work gathering every possible useful fact, quotation, and statistic for Truman's campaign. Though used to hectic work environments in the army, at the Kansas City Star, and at the New York AP bureau, Kelly was taken aback by the cramped quarters, piles of paperwork, and anthill-like activity he encountered when he first walked into the Research Division's offices in Dupont Circle. His desk, such as it was, was jammed right next to Birkhead's. While the two were friends who shared a love of wisecracking and Kansas City jazz, the prospect of practically sitting in each other's laps in a shared cubicle fifteen hours a day until late October (when Kelly would leave to take up the professorship he would soon be awarded at Boston University) was an

unpleasant one. Kelly was also taken aback by the long list of responsibilities outlined in a memo Batt handed to him, titled "Research Division
Functions," including preparing research briefs, consulting with local
Democratic leaders on the political climate in their regions, and acquir-
ing localized information to inform talking points for the more than 350
speeches Truman would deliver on the campaign trail. How could this
skeleton crew possibly provide so much in so little time, he wondered.[46]

Kelly's first assignment for the Research Division was to produce material on one of the top issues of the campaign: housing. After leaving the
AP in late 1946, Kelly had gone to work for the National Housing Agency,
a product of the New Deal. Batt was counting on Kelly to show how the
"do-nothing" Republican-dominated Congress had sabotaged the president's bold plans to extend FDR's provision for low-income housing.
Kelly had seen the results of this obstructionist stance in his previous
job, he told Birkhead as his friend banged away at the keys of his type-
writer, "The Housing Agency was kicked around when I was there. That's
why I left."[47]

Some of the first statistics Kelly uncovered were surprising though,
even to someone with his employment history: five million living in
slums, four million living in dwellings in urgent need of repair, three
million sharing houses or apartments with other families.[48] Though star-
tling, such facts would give teeth to Truman's forthcoming speeches on
housing during the campaign, such as the one he gave at Los Angeles's
Gilmore Stadium on September 23, in which he also tied Research Division fact finding on housing and inflation together to reveal that in 1940
only 5 percent of LA homes sold for more than $10,000, while eight years
later, that figure had increased to 50 percent.[49] Far from just illustrating
negative trends, the Research Division's work also provided Truman with
positive statistics, such as when he shared with a Winona, Minnesota,
audience on October 14 that "back in the Republican depression year of
1932, Minnesota farmers made less than a quarter of a billion dollars.
Last year, the income of Minnesota's farmers was a billion and a half dollars. That is the difference between the right side of a proposition so that
everybody gets his fair share of the national income, and the approach
that gives only the special privileged few the national income."[50]

In addition to trawling files sent over from the Department of Housing,
Department of Agriculture, and other federal and state government divi-

sions, Batt and his men combed through Works Progress Administration (WPA) guides to towns and cities across America.[51] Though the GOP — and particularly the old guard led by Taft — continued to criticize the Democrats for setting up "big government" programs such as the WPA, the guides gave Batt, Birkhead, and Kelly invaluable information on each of the places Truman would visit during his June "nonpolitical" trip and the even greater number his train would stop at in the fall campaign to follow. The president would refer to these local details at the start of his brief speeches from the rear platform of his train car to endear himself to the local crowd.[52]

While the WPA booklets offered invaluable insight, they didn't supply all the comprehensive know-how the Research Division needed to send to Clark Clifford and George Elsey before the presidential train car — the stately Ferdinand Magellan, hitched to the back of sixteen other cars — pulled out of Washington's Union Station on June 3. To get the rest, they visited the Library of Congress to peruse local newspapers from all over the country and compiled a list of twelve questions they sent to local Democratic Party offices:

1. What are the particular complaints the people have about high prices in your town? Give us the details and any local incidents on price.
2. What is the principal problem facing your town and its citizens right now?
3. How did your town vote in the 1944 and 1946 elections? Is it traditionally Democratic or Republican? Who are the candidates for the Senate and the House? Do they have strong popular support? What are their chances of election?
4. What is your town proudest of?
5. Who are the half-dozen notable citizens of your town? Do you have any Olympic stars? Any war heroes? Any citizens who have won the affection of your citizens, such as ministers, priests, rabbis, or well-loved people in other fields besides religion?
6. What is the size of your town? This means population, physical characteristics (hilly, spread out, etc.), main industries, etc.?
7. Give us a brief, colorful history of your town, stressing the events likely to be remembered by most citizens.

8. Does your town have a slogan, such as "the biggest little city in America," or something along such lines?
9. What are some of the local phrases, sayings, familiar jokes about your town?
10. What are the nicknames for political leaders and others?
11. What is the housing situation in your town? Are there any slums? Any public housing projects? How many units were built in the town last year? How many units are needed?
12. How many veterans do you have?[53]

The answers sent back to the Batt group by local politicians would form the basis of Truman's main points at each train stop in the coming months. It was not enough for him to see the people and for them to see them, he wanted them to feel like he knew them, understood their concerns, and would do everything he could to meet their needs if re-elected. Some of the information that the Research Division's questionnaire asked for was trivial (Olympians, movie stars, and so forth), but other questions were firmly focused on the main issues of the campaign, as defined in the Rowe-Clifford memo "The Politics of 1948," which comprehensively identified the main challenges Truman faced in 1948 and detailed how he should address each one. Frank Kelly summarized the main issues outlined in this report, which would inform Democratic strategy for the duration of the campaign as "People, prices and places to live."[54]

Batt expanded on this slogan in a memo dispatched to "All Concerned"—likely including Kelly, Birkhead, Chapman, Clifford, and George Elsey, who held a typically ambiguous Truman-bestowed title of "special assistant" and shared his boss's affinity for perfectly tailored suits—that he typed on May 8. Batt suggested that his team follow this methodology for compiling Files of the Facts on each of the "basic issues" that Truman would cover while out West the following month, and during his even longer train journeys in the fall:

The Democratic Plan for the Future
File No. 1: The Problem—How We Plan to Meet It—What that Plan Means to the American People
File No. 2: Good Quotations Explaining This Plan, Especially from President Truman

The Democratic Record

File No. 3: What We Found—What We Did—The Bills Passed and What They Provided—Democratic and Republican Votes

File No. 4: Good Illustrative Quotations, Especially from President Truman

File No. 5: Evaluations of What This Program Has Meant to America, Using All Dramatic Measurements Available

Republican Record of Blocking

File No. 6: Recapitulation of Republican (and Democratic) Votes on Key Issues. Quotations Expressive of their "Let Them Eat Cake" Philosophy

File No. 7: Draft of the Democratic Plank Platform

File No. 8: Draft of the President's Major Campaign Speech on This Issue

File No. 9: What The President Should Do and Say About This Issue—When—Where

File No. 10: What the Democratic Committee, Executive Departments and Democratic Leaders Should Do and Say—When—Where

File No. 11: Drafts of Three Ten-Minute Speeches on Specific Phases of this Issue[55]

Once Kelly and his colleagues had compiled the Files of the Facts on each major campaign issue, which, according to Batt's hyperspecific directions were housed in 12″ x 9″ folders, they sent them on to DNC chairman J. Howard McGrath or to William B. "Bill" Boyle, the barrel-chested, deep-voiced Washington lawyer who was McGrath's heir apparent and was instrumental in planning Truman's June train journey and the longer one to follow in the fall.[56] Along with his assistants, Charles Murphy sifted through the dossiers and then presented them to Matthew J. Connelly, Truman's appointments secretary. Next, Connelly sat down with Clark Clifford, George Elsey, and Charlie Ross to further condense the figures, tie them to the campaign's main messages, and tailor them to local audience demographics. Finally, the group presented the key points to Truman in the clearest, most logical manner possible.[57] Thus, once the process reached its master, he had a cohesive, empirical, fact-based launching platform for both his formal and spontaneous speeches. What leader could ask for more?

★ ★ ★

"IF I FELT BETTER, I COULDN'T STAND IT"

In addition to the "secret weapon" of the Research Division, Truman's team had another reason for optimism heading into the 1948 campaign. This was a marked improvement in Truman's public speaking, which had never come naturally to a man who far preferred informal banter with small groups. Clifford, who crafted talking points for the president along with Charlie Ross, Jonathan Daniels, and George Elsey, had tried just about everything to make Truman more confident and fluid at the podium. Memorization, detailed note cards, giant cue cards with a few high-level messages—all had proved dismal failures. It was not just his speaking style, but the seeming lack of preparedness and clear thinking when addressing the White House press corps that troubled his advisers, encouraged his opponents, and emboldened his critics. The veteran *New York Times* reporter Felix Belair wrote in 1946 that FDR's press sessions resembled "the opening night of the Ziegfeld Follies while President Truman's are like amateur night."[58] The most glaring example that backed up Belair's assertion came on September 12, 1946, hours after Henry Wallace gave a speech in New York condemning American foreign policy and, indirectly, Truman and his secretary of state James F. Byrnes.

The text of the speech was circulated among reporters before Wallace's address and they couldn't understand why the president would allow the secretary of commerce to tear his handling of the Soviets to shreds. When a writer from the *Minneapolis Star Journal and Tribune* quizzed Truman on whether he approved of Wallace's stance, Truman at first declined to comment on a speech that Wallace had not yet delivered, but on further examination from the determined scribe, he stated that yes, he approved of the speech. Then, when Wallace's unflinching rhetoric caused a media frenzy, Truman called another press conference for the 20th. He clumsily reversed his earlier claim that he approved of Wallace's speech, saying that he instead meant to defend Wallace's right to make an independent address. This was a contradiction in its own right, as the president went on to tell the press that he had asked for his resignation. Then, as hand after hand shot skyward among the reporters who demanded more than a befuddled half-explanation, Truman announced that he had nothing to add and walked away from the microphones.[59]

Predictably, Truman's performance received a near-universal thumbs down. Harold Ickes, a longtime Roosevelt servant who had himself left the Truman cabinet earlier that year, stated that the president had "humiliated himself" and then made the situation even worse by "throwing Wallace to the lions." *Time* slammed the president for flip-flopping around a colossal "lie." Even foreign newspapers commented on Truman's poor speaking performance and even worse public relations, with the *Calgary Herald* lamenting the president's "piece of bungling."[60] These were the kind of mishaps that gave Clark Clifford and Truman's press secretary, the long-suffering Charlie Ross, fits. They eventually realized that Truman simply couldn't handle reading flowery oratory in front of an audience, or, frankly, any type of speech that didn't resemble his own straightforward speaking style. So they jettisoned the artful speechcraft for the latter and only then, in spring 1948, began to help Truman rehabilitate his speaking reputation.[61]

As a first trial of this new approach on April 17, Truman addressed the American Society of Newspaper Editors at Washington's grand Statler Hotel with no speaking aids, prompts, or notes, and he surprised himself and many who listened by coming across as, well, *himself*. Thirty minutes went by easily, without Truman feeling anxious or being aware of the ticking second hand.[62] Gone were the fumbling of words, the awkward pauses, and the rigid posture of a man being forced to speak in an unfamiliar style. Truman just spoke to the crowd as he typically did to everyone else, in an uncomplicated, folksy, direct way.

Truman proved the experiment was no fluke when he again carried himself well at a Young Democrats rally a few weeks later. One of the many reporters who praised his performance raved that it was a "fighting one in the new Truman manner."[63] By jettisoning the high rhetoric of the presidency and reverting to who he truly was as a person—straightforward Harry Truman from small-town Missouri—Truman found he could connect to a working- and middle-class audience. Because, cliché aside, he fundamentally *was* one of them. Though in the future he would sometimes ask for a few bullet points to place on the podium for guidance, this was a new Truman, one who could at last articulate his views to voters in a confident, relaxed way that rang true.[64]

The third trial run came on May 6, when Truman spoke at lunchtime to a family life conference in Washington, with no manuscript, with microphones for all four major networks on the podium, and TV cameras pointed at him. Truman confided to his diary later that day that he had enjoyed the experience and felt comfortable with his new public speaking approach: "The audience gave me a most cordial reception. I hope the radio and television audiences were half as well pleased. I may have to become an 'orator.' I heard a definition of an orator once—'He is an honest man who can communicate his views and make others believe he is right.' Wish I could do that."[65]

He also recorded how his leadership style differed from FDR's and what a challenge the unexpected transfer of power between them had been:

> I think I've been right in the approach to all questions 90% of the
> time since I took over. I was handicapped by lack of knowledge
> of both foreign and domestic affairs—due principally to Mr.
> Roosevelt's inability to pass on responsibility. He was always careful
> to see that no credit went to anyone else for accomplishment. . . .
> The objective and its accomplishment is my philosophy, and I am
> willing and want to pass the credit around. The objective is the thing,
> not personal aggrandizement. All Roosevelts want the personal
> aggrandizement. Too bad.[66]

This is merely a small indication of the void that separated Truman from his predecessor. Joseph Alsop, FDR's cousin and copublisher of the Washington paper *Matter of Fact*, was shocked at the contrast between the formality of Roosevelt's White House and the informal one Truman ran. He wrote to Eleanor Roosevelt that "In Franklin's time, it had been a great seat of world power." With the Missourian in charge, however, Alsop felt it now resembled "the lounge of the Lion's Club of Independence, Missouri, where one is conscious chiefly of the odor of ten-cent cigars and the easy laughter evoked by the new smoking room story."[67]

Such haughty disdain of Truman was common among the FDR loyalists, even those who should have been grateful when they retained their places after the handover. It was also a staple feature of press reports about the president, such as the one written by *Kansas City Star* editor Roy Roberts, whose first feature about Truman in the White House dismissed him as "the average man."[68] And while such comments were certainly overly critical, they are illustrative of how dissimilar the two presidents were.

Indeed, other than sharing the same party, commitment to the cause of defeating the Axis powers in World War II, and a coherent philosophy on domestic matters, the two men could not have been more different. Roosevelt was in many ways the definitive elite patrician. He came from the right family, went to the right schools, and mixed in the right social circles to facilitate his rise to the highest office in the land. In contrast, Harry Truman was from a lower-middle-class home, was the first president in fifty years to have not attended college, and was an outsider to the circles of power brokers that FDR and his Capitol Hill peers moved in. Few noticed that Truman was arguably just as smart and multitalented as FDR—a voracious reader, a competent piano player, and an endearing conversationalist.[69]

Despite such merits, Truman was fighting an impossible battle for credibility against the rose-colored memory of a ghost. So many things about Roosevelt had become iconic—the jaunty grin and wave, the trademark white cigarette holder, his Hyde Park mansion, even his ever-present black Scottish terrier, Fala. And no matter how far Truman had come as a speaker, he would always struggle to match FDR, who one critic begrudgingly admitted "possessed a golden voice and a seductive and challenging radio technique" that was immortalized in his "fireside chats."[70] In just over two years in the White House, Truman had not yet made a similar mark on the public consciousness.

Then there was the matter of geography. Through no fault of his own, Truman's Midwest roots neither endeared him to the Democratic in-crowd in the Northeast, to whom he was too provincial, nor the southerners, who thought Missouri decidedly too far north in locale and attitude. And yet with Roosevelt now gone, it fell to Truman to avoid all-out war with the Soviet Union, prevent the Dixiecrats and progressives from irreparably rupturing the Democratic Party, and somehow keep the Republicans from snatching away the White House in November, as they seemed fated to do. To do it, he would need all his endurance, guile, and that irrepressible Midwest charm (with more than a little help from the Research Division's Files of the Facts). On the evening of June 3, Truman's driver conveyed him; his wife of twenty-nine years, Bess; their vivacious twenty-four-year-old daughter, Margaret; and Howard McGrath to Union Station in Washington D.C. Truman, clad in newly polished Oxford wing-tips and a lightweight cream suit and fedora, bantered with reporters for a couple of minutes about his imminent "grass roots" tour, and then, as he sprang up the steps to the dark green Ferdinand Magellan car, he turned and, with a grin, told them emphatically, "If I felt better, I couldn't stand it."[71]

With him on the seventeen-car train, though in less luxurious quarters than the stately, walnut-paneled presidential cabin, were thirty-nine reporters, six radio correspondents, four television presenters, four photographers, and four newsreel cameramen—a contingent similar to the one that had gone with Truman when he accompanied Winston Churchill from Washington to Missouri for the former prime minister's delivery of his Iron Curtain speech in March 1946.[72] While this year's gang would likely enjoy the trip and their access to Truman, the White House's official instructions handout made it clear that they were on board to do their jobs: "[I]f the President appears on the rear platform, correspondents, newsreel and still photographers will leave their cars and walk back to cover the proceedings."[73] To ensure that they and, more importantly, the man they were covering, could communicate with the outside world, one of the seventeen cars was dedicated to communications equipment.

Truman had a few hours before the first address in Pittsburgh, Pennsylvania, at 6:50 a.m. the following morning, more than enough time for Ross, Clifford, and Elsey to prep him with the tour's key messages once again—the special-interest Congress is failing you, I'm better able to look after farmers and laborers like you, and, most importantly, I may be president, but I'm also just a regular guy, one of your own. Truman needed little sleep and rose daily between 5:30 and 5:45 a.m., so he was all too happy to stay up to talk shop.

Though he said little in Pittsburgh, his advisers got a better chance to assess if he was sticking to their strategy a few hours later as the train rolled into the outskirts of Crestline, Ohio, right on time, at 10:53 a.m. His speech was so brief—just seven minutes—that the engine's great iron pistons barely had time to stop pumping, but Truman was in good form, telling the one thousand people who milled around that "when you get out and see people and find out what people are thinking about, you can do a better job as President of the United States." He also reiterated the pretour line about his purpose being apolitical, calling it "this nonpartisan, bipartisan trip." Local Democratic organizers did their job and stirred the crowd into applause at exactly the right moments.[74]

At least one person in attendance was impressed by the opening remarks of Truman's fall tour. Ten-year-old Joan VanHorn had been excitedly planning her prelunchtime escape from school for weeks, ever since the local paper carried news of the president's impending arrival. VanHorn's uncle and grandfather had worked on the railroad, and her mother, Stella, met Humphrey Bogart, Lauren Bacall, and Sammy Davis Jr. while working as a cleaner at Crestline's red-brick station during World War II. On this day, despite her Grandpa Morton's assertion that Truman wasn't a true Democrat and she'd be wasting her time going to see him, Joan ran all the way from the schoolhouse to watch as Truman's train pulled into the railroad crossing just outside of town. This enthusiastic, brown-haired girl was the only child in attendance, but she was undeterred as she weaved to the front of the adult crowd just before Truman came out to speak. After he spoke, the president reached down to shake VanHorn's little hand, and then asked, "Do you want to shake Mrs. Truman's hand?" VanHorn replied that yes, she would be delighted, so Bess offered her hand to the delighted child. VanHorn later thought that the president would have had an even bigger crowd if the train had pulled into the main station rather than stopping a little way down the line.[75]

Following several other brief speeches from the back of the Ferdinand Magellan in Fort Wayne and Gary, Indiana, the train picked up Senator Scott Lucas as it rolled into Illinois. Famished from his full morning, Truman quickly devoured a large plateful of bacon and eggs (served on fine White House china) as he caught up with Lucas, an old ally.[76] The senator accompanied Truman as he went on to the cavernous Chicago Stadium to address the Swedish Pioneer Centennial Association on the centennial of their nationality's putting down roots in the Midwest.[77] In addition to praising the Scandinavians for their hard work ethic and contribution to American culture, Truman gave a broad view of the domestic policies he would focus on if returned to the White House in November, which he dubbed the "goals of abundance." These seven points included providing more housing, expanding Social Security and health care provisions, and, with a nod to his desegregation efforts, ensuring "full rights of citizenship" for all.[78] Other than the latter further incensing the Dixiecrats, Truman had played it safe, introducing a populist platform that appealed to his voting base and that he hoped would also entice left-leaning independents.

As was to become the norm on this tour, there was little time for Truman to rest his body or his vocal cords after a late night. The next morning, a couple of hours after he got up at his usual 5:30 a.m., his train pulled into Omaha, where Truman would give the second major address of the tour.

Before that was an appointment that was as personal for Truman as it was presidential: watching his former World War I comrades-in-arms from the 35th Division parade through downtown Omaha. After a few minutes of his car crawling around the cordoned-off route, Truman shocked his inner circle and the Secret Service detail when he hopped out of his motorcade car, joined the parade, and marched half a mile down the main drag with his old pals. Whatever the official party's concerns, the sight of the president of the United States, clad in a crisp blue suit and red tie and marching in double time to the rat-ta-tat-tat beat of Battery D's military drums, drew frenzied cheers from the delighted crowd lining the sidewalks. And this in a town that had always voted for Republicans.[79]

Not everything in Omaha would be quite so successful. That evening, after several meet-and-greets around the city, Truman expected to address a sellout crowd at the Ak-Sar-Ben Auditorium. But because of substandard planning, lack of advance notice in the local press, and a host of other logistical snafus, only two thousand showed up to the ten-thousand-seat arena. The momentum gained in the parade had hit a wall, and the foul-up was, predictably, covered in explicit detail by the press, particularly by conservative outlets such as *The Chicago Tribune*, which declared that "Truman in Omaha . . . was as flat as a platter of beer."[80] All was not lost though; the audio still reached a nationwide audience and particularly, as Truman told his friend and Nebraska host Eddie McKim, his Midwest target demographic. "I am making a speech on the radio to the farmers," Truman told McKim. "They won't be there—they'll be home listening to the radio." Regardless, speaking to an arena in which 80 percent of the seats were empty must have been embarrassing.

Despite the setback, Truman was quickly back into rhythm. Rising before dawn the following morning from the presidential bedroom, which boasted a queen-sized bed, unlike the cramped media train cars where reporters curled up on tiny cots, Truman was invigorated and ready for another jam-packed agenda. Stopping at mid-morning in Grand Island, he received a set of gleaming silver spurs from the Grand Island Saddle Club. Two hours later, he sat with Margaret and Bess in the back of a service at the First Baptist Church in Kearney, Nebraska, in which the young Reverend Pearson thanked the president for having "honored this city and this sanctuary." As the Trumans walked out into the bright sunshine afterwards, several ebullient representatives of the Kearney Junior Chamber of Commerce gave the president a pair of brown leather cowboy boots. Truman smiled and said, "I can really take Congress for a ride now!"[81] His day got even better when he heard that Massachusetts's thirty-six delegates vowed to back him at the Democratic National Convention in July.[82]

Leaving flat Nebraska behind, the train surged west into the high plains and more varied topography of Wyoming. In the picturesque state capital of Cheyenne, with its unimpeded views of the Rockies' front range, Truman's apparel haul increased again as he received a cowboy hat. He proudly modeled it for the people who surrounded the train at his next stop in Rawlins, speaking their language when proudly calling it his "fifty-dollar hat." Then he appealed to the grit of the rugged frontiersmen in the group, telling them that the election campaign would be nothing short of "a brawl."[83]

The train, chugging steadily on as it traversed undulating, mountainous terrain, crossed over the Wyoming-Idaho border just after lunchtime. Arriving at Pocatello, Idaho, an aide introduced Bess Truman, who came out onto the rear platform before her husband, as "the boss." Though she waved the comment away dismissively, and Truman's claim that he was "hen pecked" was an exaggeration, the curly gray-haired, full-figured Bess was a pole star for her husband, with whom she would celebrate twenty-nine years of marriage later in June 1948. Bess had agreed to come on the tour at the urging of India Edwards, the vivacious head of the DNC's Women's Division. Edwards recognized that Mrs. Truman's presence (and Margaret's) positioned the president as an ambassador of family values to his prospective voters, but, while the DNC staffer's influence was important, the truth is that they simply enjoyed each other's company.[84] Both laughed easily, were frugal (he recorded his car mileage in a notebook to keep tabs on fuel economy, and she put back grocery store items that would be cheaper elsewhere), and liked nothing better than sitting around their dinner table talking long into the night, be it in their adopted home of the White House or back in Independence. She was the First Lady in name, and yet she still approached people with the courtesy and humility of what one friend called "a good American home-maker." [85]

Once Truman joined Bess on the platform in Pocatello, with the gold presidential seal below the rail seeming out of place for these off-the-cuff addresses, he talked up his administration's big plans for spurring development in the Columbia Basin. On cue, an aide handed him a three-inch thick wad of paperwork, about which Truman said, "It is really a sample of the reports the President is supposed to read and study all the time. You know, I fool them: I get up early in the morning and I read them!" [86] His audience laughed and applauded. Later that day, Truman got both a physical and political boost, first going 1,200 feet up the side of Dollar Mountain in a ski lift as he waved his fedora to the crowd far below, and then hearing the news that Idaho's twelve delegates had pledged their support.[87]

But the good times didn't last for long. The Ferdinand Magellan halted in the desert-ringed, six-hundred-resident town of Carey, Idaho, so that Truman could dedicate the new regional airport. When he was handed a garland to lay at the ceremony, Truman assumed that he was to honor a local lad killed in World War II, as his aides informed him. So, in solemn tones, he began, "I'm honored to dedicate this airport, and present this wreath to the parents of the brave boy who died fighting for his country . . ." Aghast at what she was hearing, a distraught woman, Mrs. Coates, cut him off, saying, "It was our girl, Wilma . . ."

Gathering himself, a ruffled Truman began again: "Well, I'm even more honored to dedicate this airport to a brave young woman who bravely gave her life for our country . . ."

Now the awkwardness morphed into humiliation. "No, no," the bereaved mother sobbed. "Our Wilma was killed right here." Her sixteen-year-old daughter had died when her boyfriend's small biplane nosedived into a field.[88] The haste of the White House team's preparations was again all too evident and once more prompted a media field day at the expense of their mortified chief.

Attempting to recover his pride in an unusual way as the train barreled into Montana, Truman made an atypically revealing speech at Missoula. Blinking in the early morning sun as he surveyed the mountains and the evergreens of Lolo National Forest in the distance, the pajamas-and-robe-clad Truman told surprised onlookers, "I understand it was announced I would speak here. I am sorry I had gone to bed. But I thought I would let you see what I look like, even if I didn't have on my clothes."[89]

A couple of hours later and now dressed in more presidential attire, Truman waved to forty thousand who came out to see his motorcade through the streets of Butte, Montana, which with its breathtaking mountain views was the very definition of "Big Sky Country." As his long black coupe passed by, the onlookers chanted as if at a football game, "Yeah Truman, yeah Truman, yeah Truman, yeah," while a marching band played the Missouri Waltz, the pedestrian tune that Truman heard in almost every town that received him. Moving on to Butte High School, Truman wasted little time in picking up the tempo, criticizing Congress once more as he spoke to nine thousand people in the jam-packed gymnasium. There, he also slammed the Republican Party by name for the first time, claiming that by undermining labor it was practicing "economy in the reverse" and stating that the Republican platform "is the platform of Congress now." This was a Congress, Truman knew from Bill Batt's fact sheets, that had an even lower approval rating than he, dipping as low as 22 percent in one Roper poll.[90]

Truman then changed direction, playing to the many farmers who were in the audience; he declared that one of his opponents—Robert Taft by implication—had suggested that the best way to control grain and livestock prices was not to buy, or to just eat less. "I guess he would let you starve," Truman said, "I am not in that class." This, his audience knew, was also a dig at Dewey. Then, taking aim at Congress once more, Truman stated his goal of keeping the legislative body in session until it had achieved something. He warned, "If this Congress goes away without passing an agricultural bill, without passing a housing bill, without doing something about prices, then this Congress has not done anything for the country. They should stay there until they get those things done."[91] And so was born the enduring phrase "the do-nothing Congress."

As usual, Truman spent the evening aboard the train reviewing his key messages with Clifford and Ross, and then joining them, his physician Wallace Graham, naval aide (and yet another Missourian) Major General Harry Vaughan, and whoever else there was room for at the mahogany table for a game of poker. The group, which typically pulled up extra seats between the six gold-and-green striped dining chairs, had sometimes welcomed distinguished guests into their clique, such as the time they fleeced Winston Churchill for $250 in March of 1946. Whoever was playing, the banter was continuous and the bravado unceasing. Bess and Margaret preferred the quieter, more ladylike game of solitaire, often playing the double or triple version for more of a challenge in a side room to avoid the chatter and clinking of bourbon glasses from the men.[92]

In Washington State, though, the president would focus on more serious matters than his nightly poker games. The Columbia Basin floods had devastated the area, destroying homes and businesses and causing millions of dollars of damage that would take years to repair. The Research Division, as usual, had supplied Truman's team with all the relevant facts and figures, so he could speak accurately and on demand about the situation.

Truman's train pulled into a sunny, cornflower-skied Spokane early on June 9, at 9:20 a.m., and twenty-four-year-old Margaret Truman was the first to come out onto the rear platform. "Mother sent me out," the fair-skinned, soft-spoken, aspiring singer, who was still learning the ropes on this trip, told the crowd. "She doesn't give interviews in the east, so she can't do it here." "Why not?" a beat writer wanted to know. "She never has," Truman's daughter replied. "I think she doesn't think she has anything newsworthy to say."[93] Margaret then gave way to her father, who, his audience hoped, would make up for his wife's reticence. After greeting the assembled, Truman enthusiastically pumped the hands of old friends Senator Warren Magnuson and Governor Charles "Mon" Wallgren, with whom Truman, Bess, and Margaret would stay that night. Before Truman could say much, another reporter piped up, asking the president "How do you like being in a Republican stronghold?"

Truman, well aware of the praise Washington's papers had lavished on Thomas Dewey during his visit the previous month, and how critical most were of his administration, asked the man if he was with the *Spokane Spokesman-Review*, a copy of which Truman held at arm's length as if he had just used it to clean up after a dog's morning business. When the reporter confirmed that he was, Truman said sharply, "This paper and the *Chicago Tribune* are the worst in the United States." The scribe, who had not expected such venom, was left dumbfounded. Now on a roll, Truman carried on, stating that the Republican-majority Congress was enacting all the skewed principles the *Spokesman-Review* and the *Tribune* stood for. "This Congress is the worst we've ever had," he blasted through the three loudspeakers mounted atop the platform.[94]

Following these controversial opening remarks, the president left the rails for the brief drive into the city. Alighting at Riverside and Monroe Streets, he clambered up wide wooden steps that ran up the outside of the buff-brick Spokane Club and up onto the first-floor terrace. After Wallgren's suitably laudatory introduction, Truman took the rostrum and began by offering his sympathy to residents of the nearby Columbia Valley for the ill effects of the flooding and promising government action to help. He then took another shot at Congress, slamming the Taft-Hartley Act that had prompted seventeen thousand mine workers to strike and which the chief of the powerful CIO labor federation had condemned as "domestic fascism."[95]

Though he said it in a half-joking manner, Truman then admonished his audience for their political apathy, laying the blame for electing such a partisan group at the feet of those who stayed away in the 1946 midterm elections: "Two thirds of you didn't go out and vote. Look what the other third gave you. You deserve it!" he said. Next, turning from past to future, he warned against a repetition of such inaction, telling them that if the booths were again empty in November, they would get yet more "of what you deserve."[96] More than twelve thousand people clapped as one. Then, recognizing the irony of his stated intentions for this trip, he told them, "I hope that sometime later on I can come back and talk politics to you."[97]

Truman then took a seven-mile car ride to inspect the carnage at the town of Vanport, the public housing community located between Portland and the Columbia River that had been decimated by the raging torrent. Truman hopped out of the black coupe, now stained with mud and foul-smelling river runoff, and made his way over to a temporary dock to greet army engineers. After a few minutes of serious conversation, Truman and his military aides went back up the dock, but the dock shifted and Colonel T. D. Weaver offered his stout arm to steady the president. As they carefully picked their way across the unsteady wooden planks, the murky brown floodwater soaked Truman's shoes. Once the party made its way onto dry land, he surveyed the chaotic scene, where wood-board houses jutted out in vain defiance of the water, which in some places was at roof-level. Roof tiles, planks of wood, and other debris were scattered everywhere, as if a child had just thrown an almighty tantrum in a giant bathtub. A reporter for the *Oregon Journal* told Truman, equally fascinated and aghast, that his nearby home was halfway submerged, and he recounted how he had pulled his wife and two children free at the last possible moment.[98]

The next two days were a blur, with Truman giving a dozen impromptu speeches, inspecting the Grand Coulee Dam—where he again skewered Congress for its "do-nothing" agenda—and meeting with local and state officials on flood control and response in Portland. Truman then gave his third major speech of the tour, this time addressing the Washington State Press Club in Seattle.[99]

He opened by praising the record of Lewis Schwellenbach, his secretary of labor, who had passed away the previous evening. Truman then told of his visit to the 550-foot Grand Coulee Dam, which he extolled as a symbol of industrial progress in the Pacific Northwest. Next, he recounted his struggles to get funding proposals for land reclamation, which would benefit the region by increasing agricultural yield, through a hostile Congress. Despite these challenges, Truman pledged, "This administration is determined that it will continue to move ahead with a constructive, practical program against the delaying tactics of ignorance and selfishness. It will fight in the future with the same vigor as it has fought in the past."[100]

In addition to conveying Truman's spirit of determination, the address also showed the usefulness of the DNC Research Division. Ninety percent of Truman's words were focused on the local challenges, successes, and potential of Washington and Oregon, and Truman delivered numerous items from his researchers' Files of the Facts that he then tied to several of his central campaign themes, including supporting labor, kickstarting economic development, and, of course, riding roughshod over congressional opposition from the GOP if necessary.

★ ★ ★

"WELL, I GUESS I GOOFED"

Meanwhile, reports from Europe indicated that the latest meeting between secretary of state George Marshall and his counterparts from Britain and France had provided consensus on the immediate future of western Germany. The non-Soviet zones would have some measure of home rule, though they would not be permitted to rearm. French, British, and American troops would remain, unless all three agreed to pull their forces out—which seemed unthinkable given the threat posed by the massive Red Army presence in the east and the Allied commitment to rebuilding democracy in the western zones. The goals were preventing the rise of another totalitarian government and ensuring the freedoms that had been lacking in the country since Hitler had taken control fifteen years earlier.[101]

With such developments added to his own hectic schedule, even the hardy Truman was now tired. Thankfully, that evening provided a welcome, light-hearted diversion. The Trumans left their stateroom on the train—which was next to a galley, servants' quarters, dining room, and five bedrooms—for the even grander appointments of Governor Wallgren's expansive white stone mansion in Olympia.[102] There, Truman played a couple of hours of billiards with Mon, the jovial, silver-haired former optometrist who prided himself on his prowess with a cue and who had won the amateur national championships in 1929. Meanwhile, his wife, Mabel, entertained Margaret and Bess. The two women had hit it off while their husbands were in the Senate in 1940 and now, with both men having moved onto higher office and their families separated by more than 2,700 miles, were glad for a chance to catch up. Later that evening, Mabel served up the president's favorite dish, fried chicken, with freshly picked local strawberries for dessert.[103]

At 7:30 the next morning, Friday, June 11, Truman left the governor's mansion at a brisk clip. The unrelenting sky deposited yet more rain on the president, Bess, Margaret, and their party as they made their way to their idling car. As they drove to McChord Air Force Base just outside Tacoma, the downpour intensified, and to make conditions even more treacherous, a thick mist hung in the chilly air. Undeterred, the Trumans boarded the presidential plane for Salem, Oregon.[104] Traveling by plane would enable the president to quickly complete this leg of his journey while his train was serviced and cleaned. As they crossed the Washington-Oregon border, he gazed down on the millions of gallons of water that had poured across the lower Columbia basin, turning normally verdant green fields into unsightly marshes that would produce no crops that year. With no time to tarry in Salem, the Trumans and their companions disembarked for the hour-long northward drive to Portland, where they reboarded the Ferdinand Magellan, newly cleaned and now ready to convey the president south to California. As a parting gift to Washington and Oregon, Truman signed a $10 million flood relief bill while the train idled at the station.[105]

It didn't take long for news of Truman's comments about Congress to make it to Washington. As his train rumbled down the Pacific coast, affording breathtaking views of the rugged shore through the bulletproof glass, the president's usual critics retaliated. The editors of the *Chicago Tribune*, none too happy with seeing their newspaper labeled the worst in the country, wrote a stinging editorial: "Thanks in no small measure to the *Tribune*, the people of this nation know Mr. Truman for the nincompoop that he is, and for the vote stealing, graft protecting, gangster paroling Pendergast man that he is."[106]

House majority leader Charles Halleck called Truman the worst president in US history, and his Republican colleagues were quick to join his attack.[107] Ohio congressman Cliff Clevenger, addressing the House on June 11, blustered, "High Tax Harry, like a nasty little gamin, has dipped his hands into the mud and dirt and plastered it all over our new buggy, and danced out of reach of the whip. It might well be that there will be some Congress-tanned Missouri jackass hide on the Christmas market."[108] But it was left to Robert Taft, the presidential hopeful who, like Clevenger, represented the Buckeye State, to provide the most memorable denunciation. Taft, who always wore rimless glasses and whose rhetorical prowess had made him a formidable opponent of the New Deal, slammed Truman for mounting "an attack on the very principle of representative government itself" and dismissed him as "our gallivanting president." And then, the fiery cosponsor of the controversial labor bill that Truman had dragged through the mud while in the Northwest stated his regret that Truman "is blackguarding Congress at every whistle stop in the West."[109] It would not take long for this comment to haunt Taft and his fellow Republicans.

Rather than wilting in the face of such attacks, Truman seemed to revel in them. Indeed, the morning after reading the comments from Halleck, Clevenger, and Taft, he again courted criticism in an informal talk with reporters on board the Ferdinand Magellan about the Soviet Union. Though his strong stance toward Moscow had irked isolationists and prompted Henry Wallace's leftward breakaway from the Democratic mainstream, Truman spoke kindly about "old Joe" Stalin on this particular day: "He is a decent fellow. But Joe is a prisoner of the Politburo. He can't do what he wants to."[110] Like Churchill, Truman enjoyed the company of Stalin while in the high-spirited atmosphere of the lavish dinners held at the Potsdam Conference two years before. Yet, as did the former British prime minister, Truman knew that Stalin was immovable when it came to negotiating, and he was strongly opposed to his Soviet counterpart's political agenda. Truman's comment, then, inflated the stock he put in Stalin's joviality while obscuring his true feelings about the Soviet leader's actions.

The Republicans had long criticized Truman for not being tough enough with Moscow and had ramped up such accusations in this election year, and now Truman was foolish to give them fuel for their fire. Taft and many of his fellow Republicans were predictably incensed, and Truman's team was aghast.

The 142-ton, armor-plated presidential train car was impervious to bullets, but not to criticism.[111] Clark Clifford received panicked calls from undersecretary of state Robert A. Lovett and secretary of defense James Forrestal, both insisting that Truman officially withdraw his comments. Clifford talked it over with Elsey and Charlie Ross, and the three of them shared their concerns with Truman. Ross was unconcerned about incurring Truman's ire and said, "Mr. President, we just have to tell you, frankly, that your 'I like old Joe' comment is not going over well. We are getting hammered for it." Silence followed. Then Truman recognized that he had been too flippant about the man who had killed as many as twenty million of his own people and imprisoned many more—the leading ideological antagonist to Western democracy. As the train rolled into Berkeley, he admitted to his team, "Well, I guess I goofed."[112]

Ironically, as Truman was speaking, newspapers across the country reported that the Soviets had upped the stakes in the divided German capital of Berlin, once again blocking freight shipments from the western occupation zones,[113] in protest of West Berlin's decision to issue its own currency, known as the Berlin mark. British, French, and American officials were trying to oversee a return to democratic government in West Germany and prevent communist or fascist elements from filling the void left by the fall of the Nazis. One of the elements of the Marshall

Plan was to fuel the rise of free Western Europe through economics, and so the move to issue a new currency in the Western zones was a logical step.[114] The Soviets, however, were determined to control every aspect of life on the other side of the Brandenburg Gate, and they saw this currency decision as a direct threat to their hegemony and as a sign of American provocation.

Indeed, the chief American administrator in the conflicted, divided city, the tall, angular, no-nonsense general Lucius D. Clay, had in April 1948 read his tea leaves correctly when he foresaw that it would be the push for West German currency, rather than the creation of a government in this region, that would trigger Soviet attempts "to force us from Berlin."[115] Clay would need every ounce of his war-tested resolve to maintain the uneasy peace between the Western democracies, who wanted to grant the German people economic, social, and political liberty, and the Soviet administrators, who were equally determined to deny it.

The Berlin crisis General Clay was trying to resolve was not the only turmoil in Europe. Greece had been in political turmoil since the death of military dictator Ioannis Metaxas in 1941 left a power void. From 1943 to 1944 the right-leaning National Republican Greek League (EDES) fought for control of the country with the communist National Liberation Front. The 1946 election was supposed to bring peace, but instead, with the EDES voted into power in a corrupt process, the communists restarted their violent campaign to gain power. Now, two years later, communist rebels refused to give in despite the America-supported government gaining the upper hand. Meanwhile, the Soviet Politburo expelled Yugoslavia from the Cominform, the international organization of international communist leaders, due to strong-willed Josip Broz Tito's refusal to follow Moscow's orders chapter and verse.[116] These events influenced the content and tone of Truman's address that afternoon at the University of California, Berkeley, where he spoke to his largest crowd on the trip, more than fifty thousand, who stood in a stiff breeze in the expansive concrete stands of the school's football stadium.[117] Truman praised the United Nations Charter as being "man's best hope for world order based upon law and for lasting peace based on justice." He then commented on the sacrifice of American service personnel in World War II and described how the Allies had withdrawn their troops as agreed at the wartime summits. This contrasted with the actions of the Politburo, however: "The

Soviet government has rejected the invitation to participate, freely and on equal terms, in a great cooperative program for the reconstruction of Europe." Here the president was evidently lauding the Marshall Plan as well as chiding Moscow for opposing its sentiments.

He went on, "It has used its veto excessively and unreasonably in the Security Council of the United Nations. . . . It has used indirect aggression against a number of nations in Eastern Europe and extreme pressure against others in the Middle East. . . . The refusal of the Soviet Union to work with its wartime allies for world recovery and world peace is the most bitter disappointment of our time."[118] This was his strongest denunciation of Stalin's government since his March 1947 speech at Harvard, where he declared the "Truman Doctrine" for containing communism, and was the opposite of his ill-timed, ill-conceived comments about "Uncle Joe."

Truman continued, echoing Churchill's call in his March 1946 Iron Curtain speech for active diplomacy backed by military might: "We know that peace through weakness has proved to be a dangerous illusion. We are determined, therefore, to keep strong for the sake of peace."[119] Truman was letting it be known that while he wanted to avoid conflict with the Soviets, he planned to be even tougher with them than he was on the "do-nothing" Congress — much to Wallace's chagrin, no doubt. Back in Washington, the Research Division's Frank Kelly was impressed, later recalling how he and his colleagues listened to the address on the radio "with a growing appreciation for Truman's stature as a global statesman."[120]

After the Berkeley speech, Truman refocused his narrative on domestic matters, including the Senate Judiciary Committee passing his bill to make lynching a federal crime, despite one dissenting senator, Harry Byrd of Virginia, barking that he would "fight it to the bitter end."[121]

There was more good news for Truman as he arrived in Santa Barbara on the balmy morning of June 14: a district court judge had forbidden the CIO national maritime union to lead a one-hundred-thousand-worker strike. This was a personal victory for the president, who had seen many such walkouts proceed and last a long time during his tenure.[122] Buoyed by this verdict, Truman talked casually with local reporters who had gotten up just as early as he had to make it to the train, telling them that only his most bitter opponents believed his journey to be "a low-down political trip." His real purpose, he asserted, was to "come out and tell the people what they ought to hear. I am trying to give you the picture as I see it, and if you like it, that will be wonderful for me. If you don't like it, you will do what you feel is best for the country. And I think that is the reason our country is great."[123]

Then it was on to Los Angeles. There, a writer asked him how he felt, and Truman, clad in a well-fitting brown suit and flanked by Bess and Margaret, said, "Oh, you always feel fine in California." The ladies, who were close to exhausting the wide selection of dresses they had packed, gratefully received red carnations from the wives of the newspapermen as a navy band struck up in the background. Disembarking, the Trumans and Los Angeles mayor Fletcher Bowron led a forty-car motorcade through downtown, past the mansions, movie studios, and fancy stores of Beverly Hills and on to the Hollywood Ambassador Hotel.[124] His team later estimated that more than a million people had seen his car pass by, and the Los Angeles Times described that onlookers "clung to the roofs of buildings, jammed windows and fire escapes and crowded five deep along the sidewalk."[125]

That evening, Truman again put his researchers' Files of the Facts to good use at his speech to the Greater Los Angeles Press Club, using statistics to make his case for building more houses, extending Social Security and health care coverage, and introducing price controls to curb cost of living increases. Later, he told a group that gathered to hear him speak on the palm-tree-lined Coconut Grove that since price controls expired in 1946, the consumer price index had risen from 130 to 172 — hurting the common man's pocketbook most.[126] And all the while, he asserted, Congress was protecting the fortunes of the wealthy.

The following day, Truman met with James Roosevelt, FDR's eldest son, who with his distinctive glasses, narrow face, and upright posture was the spitting image of his father. He was also chairman of the powerful California Democrats. Despite the smiles and platitudes at their outdoor photo shoot, where the president wore a tan suit and Roosevelt wore pinstripes and sunglasses, James was no friend of Truman's. He privately criticized the president just as harshly as did Eleanor Roosevelt, who thought little of FDR's successor. Truman was well aware of their hostility and later in his diary labeled James a "double-crosser."[127] With negative comments continuing from his Republican opponents as he left

Roosevelt and the city of Los Angeles behind, Truman kept up his rhetorical pressure. Stopping for a brief speech in San Bernardino, he told a ten-
thousand-strong crowd that he would "keep pouring it on Congress."[128]
Accepting the gift of a dozen eggs, he tied his thankfulness to his calls
for stronger price controls, saying, "I appreciate these eggs—the cost of
living has gone up. At least they weren't thrown at me."

"Throw 'em at Taft!" an onlooker shouted. Though Truman had in his
speech to the LA press club poked fun at the Ohio senator by calling LA
the "biggest whistle stop," he opted for tact over candor this time. "I
wouldn't throw eggs at Senator Taft," he said, though his impish grin
suggested otherwise.[129]

With the Berkeley and LA addresses now behind him, Truman had no
other major speaking engagements, though he gave another twenty-five
informal speeches from the rear platform. One of his last in California
was in Barstow, where for the second time on the "nonpolitical tour" he
appeared late at night in blue pajamas and robe. His voice was understandably strained after speaking almost without ceasing for days upon
end. One woman in the crowd piped up, "President Truman, you sound
as if you have a cold." Truman smiled and replied, "That's because I ride
around in the wind with my mouth open."[130]

The next morning, the train journeyed east through New Mexico and
Arizona before turning north to take him back into his native Midwest.
In tiny Newton, Kansas, he explained the reason for his "nonpolitical"
tour, which was sounding more political at each stop: "I am here to get
the people aroused as to what Congress ought to do, and I think the Congress ought to be aroused!"[131]

After enjoying an expectedly jubilant hometown welcome from five
thousand people who filled the platforms at Kansas City's Union Station
on a sunny June 16, the Trumans spent the night at their modest, two-
level, whiteboard house in Independence, where more than two hundred
neighbors welcomed them home to the tree-shaded neighborhood they
had not seen in months. That night, Truman tried to put out of his mind
yet another depressing poll that put his approval rating at a dire 38 percent.[132]

The next day, Truman did everything to avoid more bad news. He got
a haircut—the usual neat side part, gray hair trimmed short all the way
round—from his longtime barber, Frank Spina, visited his ninety-nine-

year-old aunt, and spent time with his brother, J. Vivian, and sister, Mary Jane. The next morning, Vivian drove them seventeen miles back through Kansas City's red brick downtown to Union Station, where Harry and Bess (Margaret would stay a few more days) reboarded the train and set off for Washington, traversing Illinois, Indiana, Ohio, Pennsylvania, and Maryland in just three days.[133]

Arriving back at the White House on June 19, an upbeat Harry Truman estimated that more than 2.5 million Americans had seen their president in person in the previous two weeks. And they had heard him loud and clear on economic policy, civil rights, housing, and, of course, on the flaws of the "do-nothing" Congress. Indeed, the western towns dismissed as "whistle stops" by Taft had angrily rejected the Ohio senator's comment as derogatory and declared their support for Truman.[134]

Yet the American people and the press corps had also seen Truman at his most vulnerable — embarrassed in a near-empty arena in Omaha, insulting the family of a dead girl in Idaho, and giving a free pass to the ruthless leader of Soviet Russia in Oregon. Meanwhile, the Republican front-runners continued to dominate the polls. Congress had overruled Truman's veto of three bills while he was away (making six vetoes overridden in his brief presidency). The most significant of the bills Truman had vetoed was House Joint Resolution 296, which Truman claimed would exclude up to 750,000 people from Social Security coverage. In vetoing the resolution on June 14, he said, "I cannot approve legislation which would deprive many hundreds of thousands of employees, as well as their families, of social security benefits when the need for expanding our social insurance system is so great. If our social security program is to endure, it must be protected against these piece-meal attacks."[135] Despite this impassioned statement, the bill became law anyway.

To add to Truman's woes, rumors were rife that General Eisenhower would undermine the president by seeking the nomination at the Democratic convention, as if Truman didn't have enough to worry about with the challenges from Wallace and Thurmond. Abroad, the challenges were no less complex, with Stalin's interference with American and British supplies in western Germany, support of the Greek communists' insurgency, and escalation of tensions in Korea, not least by shutting off the power to the democratic south.[136] Harry Truman's "nonpolitical" train trip was over. Clearly, his real work was just beginning.[137]

During the first three weeks of June the nation had its eyes and ears turned to the president, but in the final week of the month they shifted their attention to his GOP foils as they prepared for the Republican convention. The 1944 Republican National Convention had nominated suave, smooth-voiced New York governor Thomas E. Dewey to run against Roosevelt. With John Brickman running with him, he had waged a campaign in two halves, distinct in tone and intensity. The first, from August to the end of September, had seen a languid Dewey, who perhaps underestimated FDR—as unthinkable as that may seem for the man who had run the nation for so long—due to Roosevelt's war commitments and the fact that he only gave one major speech during this period.

Once October came around, Dewey, at the behest of his advisers, changed tack and went on the offensive. He attempted to unseat him, something no Republican challenger had managed since FDR claimed the White House by trouncing incumbent Herbert Hoover by 472 electoral votes to 59 in 1932 as the Democrats successfully pinned the Great Depression on the GOP. In sixteen years no Republican candidate had even come close. The dire campaign of Kansas governor Alf Landon in 1936 had claimed an almost laughable 8 electoral votes to FDR's 523. Four years later, Wendell Willkie had put up a better showing (how could anyone not?), but still, he claimed just 82 electoral votes, a long way from Roosevelt's 449.

Despite possessing charm and charisma in abundance, Willkie had never gained the full confidence of his party during the 1940 campaign, not least because the former businessman had never run for, let alone held, elected office. The fact that he was formerly a Democrat also sat ill with many of his peers. Though his unlikely surge past Robert Taft and Dewey captured the imagination of some, he was far from a unanimous choice among the Republican delegates, needing six convention ballots to finally claim the nomination. The voters were similarly halfhearted. Willkie captured ten states and won 22.3 million votes, but he failed to generate enough momentum either to upset Roosevelt in the Electoral College or the popular vote tally; FDR got the nod from 27.3 million people.

The issues that Willkie campaigned on, including ending the Great Depression by stimulating commerce and entrepreneurship, staying out of World War II, and opposing Roosevelt's unprecedented run at a third term, had become irrelevant by the time Dewey took up Willkie's mantle in 1944 and tried to prevent FDR from extending that third term into a fourth. The economy was on an upswing even before the United States entered the war, and once the need for wartime supplies, vehicles, and munitions kicked in, American industry soon reached new heights of efficiency and output. The war was already in its latter stages and bipartisan foreign policy had become accepted as a necessity for achieving the successful conclusion of Axis surrender or obliteration.

With these factors in mind, Dewey, who with his appealing baritone and easy manner at the microphone was nearly FDR's equal as a public speaker, focused his campaign on opposing the New Deal, which he condemned as nothing more than a power grab designed to extend the reach of Roosevelt and the Democrats. Despite his furious late rally, Dewey's fate proved the same as that of Willkie, Landon, and Hoover: Election Day defeat and disappointment. He improved on Willkie's performance by two states and seventeen electoral votes, and he got closer to FDR in the popular vote—with 22 million to his opponent's 25.6 million—than any other Republican presidential candidate, but he was still unable to overtake him. Explaining Roosevelt's record fourth November win, a Dewey aide said simply, "the war."[138]

It is certainly true that a nation tends to rally around its leader in wartime, as is human nature. Yet there was more to it than that. FDR had taken on the mantle of commander-in-chief and had brought the United States close to its aim of helping Britain and the other Allies extinguish the hateful inferno of Nazism, Japanese imperialism, and Italian fascism. But he had also dragged the nation out from economic despair, had offered domestic continuity in the face of global mutability, and had governed with a seemingly unshakeable, and sometimes almost regal, air even as the world plunged into what Winston Churchill later called "the awful whirlpool" of the second global conflict in three decades. It appeared to many as if FDR would be in the White House until he chose to depart.

So when sickness cruelly claimed Roosevelt in April 1945, the Republicans had, after a period of respectful silence, rejoiced on a political level. And with the ascension of Harry Truman—whom the GOP leadership, like the many detractors in his own party, saw as green, unsophisticated, and unprepared—they had yet more reason for confidence. This newfound optimism became near delirium in the 1946 midterms, when the Republicans stormed to victory across the country, recapturing the House and Senate and ending fourteen years of Democratic legislative dominance. This was, party power brokers believed, just a preview of the triumph they would unveil two years later in November 1948: an epic tale of victory over their big government, high-tax, New Deal foes.[139]

Since his defeat in 1944 Dewey had been waiting for a chance at redemption. Like most on the public stage he was not without ego.[140] This time, though, he would face stiff competition from an even broader and deeper field of Republican challengers. They would be led by Robert Taft, the son of the twenty-seventh president and the de facto leader of the old guard on the right of the party. The voluble, keenly intelligent Taft was, like his father, larger than life in person as well as in mind (though he did not quite match the former president's bulk). Taft the younger was also nursing a bruised ego from 1944 and was determined to best Dewey this time and end the career of the Man from Missouri, whom he had accused of "blackguarding Congress at every whistle stop."

Despite denigrating Truman's June tour and frequently chastising Democrats for what he saw as the boundless and damaging expansion of central government, Taft was by no means the arch right-winger that Truman portrayed in his speeches out west. Certainly, Taft was the face of the GOP that foiled the president at every opportunity, was a firm believer in limited government, and believed that the interventionism of the New Deal should be curtailed or reversed completely. But he could be more flexible than his critics gave him credit for; during the Seventy-Ninth and Eightieth Congresses he had acted on behalf of federal funding for certain programs.[141] Looking to provide $8 billion for education, Taft cosponsored the Thomas-Hill-Taft Bill with Democrats Lister Hill and Elbert Thomas. Though this failed to make it off the floor of either chamber intact, the proposal showed Taft's willingness to back reform he believed in and to work across the aisle. Taft was also eager to collaborate with Democrats to solve the housing crisis, putting his name alongside fellow Republican Allen Ellender and New York Democrat Robert Wagner on the "T-E-W" bill, which was soon diluted by Taft's more right-leaning party delegates.[142]

Taft's attempts at reform, noble as they were, did nothing to endear him to his critics to the left, the president chief among them. Truman's main source of ire regarding Taft was the formidable Ohioan's name on perhaps the most impactful legislative dent in the New Deal—the Labor Management Act of 1947. This was more commonly known as the Taft-Hartley Act and was slammed by Truman as a return to "slave labor," even though it might actually have helped him by limiting the strikes that had battered the US economy in 1946 and early 1947.[143] These strikes were so widespread and long-lasting that they prompted Truman to threaten drafting railroad workers into the army if they didn't get back to work.

Taft's selective reform proposals also caused him problems within his own party. Those to the right bemoaned his teamwork with Democrats on federal provisions, no matter how moderate these might be or that each proposal had provisions to protect states' local powers and limit those of federal overseers. Kenneth Wherry encapsulated such frustration when he said of Taft's friendship with a liberal Senator, "I like [Taft] even if we have had a hell of a time to keep him from climbing up in Claude Pepper's lap."[144]

To the younger, more liberal wing of the party, Taft was no reformer at all, but a stick-in-the-mud whose uncharismatic demeanor would give the Republicans little chance of victory if he was their nominee in the 1948 election.[145] Thomas E. Dewey, the two-term governor of New York who remained the golden boy of the centrist Republicans despite his election defeat to FDR in 1944, favored continuation of New Deal policies with certain modifications. Taft and his loyalists, on the other hand, stuck with a statement he had made a decade earlier when he entered the Senate, insisting that the country must "break with the corrupting idea that we can legislate prosperity, legislate equality, legislate opportunity."[146] Yes, he was willing to reach bipartisan accords on some domestic issues, but for the most part the Ohio senator believed that the GOP had to present a strong alternative vision for America to the public, one that advocated a smaller federal government, free enterprise, and individualism.[147]

Also in the running was Harold Stassen, the strapping 6′3″, 220-pound former governor of Minnesota and current president of the University of Pennsylvania, whose endorsement of Dewey at the 1944 convention during the keynote address had paved the latter's way to the nomination.[148] Stassen believed that it was his turn in 1948, but his candidacy, like that of Dewey, was anathema to the conservative branch of the GOP, who thought them both too liberal.

Some of them preferred Arthur Vandenberg, the brilliant, white-haired president pro tempore of the Senate and the man who had helped keep Republicans in line in supporting first FDR's and then Truman's foreign policy, on a bipartisan track.[149] And on the fringes, there were whispers that Eisenhower or his fellow World War II leader, the human tornado General Douglas MacArthur, would join; inevitably, given their track record in combat, one of them would carry the day as the GOP's pick to trounce Truman come November. Also in the running was amiable California governor Earl Warren, who was closer to Dewey in ideology than to Taft or Vandenberg. Whoever prevailed from this crowded field, the Republicans believed, would build on the success of 1946 and thrash Truman at the polls to end the Democratic stronghold on the White House.

Despite the distractions of the other candidates, the real battle was between Taft and Dewey, with Stassen poised to close in if one of the front-runners faltered. Taft had the backing of what would later be known as the "country club Republicans" and was not short on ideas or funds, but it was Dewey who had put together the superior organizational structure and campaign team. This was led by his wily, bright, and energetic campaign manager, Herbert Brownell Jr. It was he who masterminded the strategy of playing up Dewey's reputation of reform as New York governor and trust-busting district attorney with the more liberal elements of the party faithful that might otherwise plump for Stassen. Brownell also pushed Dewey's credentials as a fiscal conservative and opponent of big government to the traditionalists who would be naturally inclined to select Taft. Because Dewey's record had elements of legitimacy on both fronts, this game plan was effective with both target groups, and as Truman returned from his "nonpolitical" trip, Dewey was leading all comers as the preconvention favorite.[150]

Beginning June 21, the Republican gathering was the first of three party conferences to be held at the cavernous Philadelphia Convention Hall that summer (with the Democrats following on July 12 and the Progressive Party coming in a week and a half later). The battle for the nomination was, as with any such gathering, the headlining act, but there were plenty of bizarre sideshows to amuse the delegates and provide fodder for the television cameras, the first to ever capture the goings on at a political convention.[151]

Pro-Dewey delegates had borrowed a gigantic truck and parked the $20,000 vehicle, with its seven beds, full kitchen, and bathroom, in front of the Hotel Walton, where Dewey was staying. Taft's backers, playing up his nickname of "Mr. Republican," decided to physically embody the party mascot in the form of three papier mâché elephants on the streets leading to the hall. In case people weren't getting the hint, the Taftites brought in Eva, a baby elephant, and paraded her around the convention hall lobby.[152]

Not to be outdone, Stassen's supporters brought in 1,200 pounds of Wisconsin cheese, which, not surprisingly, Eva the elephant ignored. With temperatures climbing in what would turn out to be one of the hottest summers on record, those who got their cheddar earlier in the proceedings were more satisfied than the ditherers who waited for the effects of the heat. To help cool the attendees off, Stassen's helpers also gave iced tea flavored with California lemons.[153]

For all the showmanship and circus-like stunts, the delegates did finally get down to business on the evening of June 23. Nominating Dewey in terms that were even more glowing than the usual political convention flattery-fest, Pennsylvania senator Ed Martin called the New York governor "America's greatest administrator," "a man who towers above all others," and "tried, tested and true." Only Dewey, Martin told the delegates, "has the warmth and human qualities so necessary to inspire the loyalty and devotion needed to rebuild a party, run a great state, and now lead the greatest nation in the world."[154]

The next morning, many of the delegates showed that they agreed with Martin's assessment, with 434 voting for Dewey on the first ballot, compared to 224 for Taft and 157 for Stassen. Knowing that his chance was slipping away, Stassen tried a last-ditch attempt to get Eisenhower to run, but he failed to reach him.[155] The second ballot almost put Dewey over the top, as he captured 515 votes, just 33 short of the total needed to garner the nomination. Though Taft had moved up to 274, with Stassen slipping back to 149, a Dewey victory was now looking inevitable unless his adversaries formed a desperate, win-at-all-costs coalition at the eleventh hour.[156]

The last-minute efforts of party bigwigs to persuade Taft to drop his divisive candidacy and support someone, anyone, other than Dewey failed, even though the Ohio senator could abide neither the thought of another Dewey-led ticket nor the man himself.[157] Recognizing that he had again lost to his archrival, a despondent Taft quit the contest, citing "simple arithmetic" for his decision. Stassen and Warren also withdrew their candidacies, and the third ballot vote became a formality, with Dewey taking all 1,094 votes.[158]

"Mr. Republican" and his fellow old guard comrades received a kick in their already bruised ribs when Earl Warren, the governor of California, was named Dewey's running mate later that evening. For the first time during Taft's tenure as a Republican bigwig, the fate of the party was in the hands of two New Deal–supporting moderates who were arguably closer to Truman on many issues than they were to those in the opposing wing of their own party. The elephant, it seemed, had ambled off in another direction.

Still, while Taft was crestfallen, many of his party mates were jubilant over the selection of two capable politicians with broad appeal and solid records in the country's two most populous states. "We have a dreamboat ticket," new national party chairman Hugh Scott declared.[159] The Republicans were not just excited about the prospects of their own party's ticket, but dismissive of their opponents' chances to beat it come November. In her speech to the exultant delegates, Clare Boothe Luce, wife of *Time* and *Life* publisher and longtime Truman-basher Henry Luce, encapsulated the mood of the Republican Convention when she declared, "Mr. Truman's time is short; his situation is hopeless. Frankly, he's a gone goose."[160]

As the Republicans were crowing over what they presumed would be Truman's inevitable defeat in November and proposing a surprisingly liberal platform that likely pleased Dewey and horrified Taft, Clark Clifford's team was planning how to keep their boss in the White House. Certainly Truman himself was unfazed by his Republican opponent. After reminding his advisers that he had helped FDR best Dewey four years before, Truman told them emphatically, "I'll take Dewey like that," snapping his right thumb and forefinger for emphasis.[161]

To help make sure he fulfilled this bold, if unlikely prediction, the Research Division continued its diligent work. The group had provided fact sheets on every place Truman visited on the June tour and valuable speech fodder, and now that the president's potential foes had been named, there was no time to waste in compiling every possible useful detail.

In addition to providing speech material, Batt, Kelly, and Birkhead were also analyzing Truman's performance in almost real time via newspaper reports and editorials, constant communication with Clifford, and conversations with local Democratic Party officials whose areas the president visited. By the time Truman's train rolled back into the capital, the Dupont Circle boys had appraised the good (the president's off-the-cuff, back-platform mini-speeches) to the not so good (the logistical foul-up that led to him speaking in a near empty stadium in Nebraska) to the outright bad (the ill-conceived positive comment about "Uncle Joe" Stalin being "alright").[162]

It was not enough to analyze, but it was also necessary to put the analysis to work in proactively preparing to do things better for the four legs of the coming autumn campaign. For Truman to win, he would need more than just his by now legendary work ethic and a few witty one-liners. It would require a meticulously planned operation, facts to support every claim about his record and every attack on the Eightieth Congress, and more than a little luck. It was no secret to Clifford, Batt, or any of the others that the media had lauded Dewey's 1944 push as being a model of efficiency and good timing. Now that he was putting the old team back together, including a research staff of his own, the pressure had been turned up yet again on the Truman contingent to work quickly, work hard, and work smart.

One of the areas that the Research Division and Jonathan Daniels' PR group focused on after the June tour was media relations. They decided that the press on the train must be given "as much constructive material as possible" to get more positive coverage and help overcome anti-Truman bias, particularly among East Coast journalists.[163] Furthermore, reporters should be allowed to get closer to the president when he spoke, "so that crowd reaction will register" with them. To enhance the effect of Truman's back-platform speeches, there needed to be a better PA system on the train and staff members must stop blocking the crowd's view of the president. There should also be a better system for getting visitors on and off the train, including familiarizing Truman with the names on the guest list before they came to see him.[164]

The Batt group also offered several pointers on advance work for the train trips that would start again in September. It was better to have Truman speak at smaller venues that he would fill than at larger ones where cameras might capture shots of empty seats, as had been the case in Nebraska. Special appearance requests should be evaluated in a timelier manner, and there must be better communication with local Democratic groups to drum up crowds.[165]

In addition to poring over the problems of the June tour and proposing how to fix each one, the Research Division continued compiling information on each of the main platform planks. After putting together one of their twelve Files of the Facts dossiers on Tom Dewey, they realized that focusing Truman's criticisms on the New York governor was futile.[166] Though the spending of his office had increased considerably over the past few years and he had vacillated on several key issues, he had the proven record of a reformer who had done more about the hot button issues of education, housing, and inflation than many Republican or Democratic governors. He was a staunch supporter of civil rights, believed in continuing price supports for farmers' yields, and, as was the way of the Republican Party at that time, was not critical of Truman's foreign policy.

At almost every whistle stop on his nine-thousand-mile June trip across the country, Truman had, as Robert Taft said, been "blackguarding Congress." Why stop now? Why not continue to make the GOP-controlled legislative body the enemy? Certainly Dewey was a governor, not a congressman, so he could hardly be held responsible for the failures of the Eightieth Congress. But because he was a Republican, the same as Taft, Halleck, and the other Republican congressman Truman liked to criticize, he was by implication the same as them. Whether this was borne out by reality—which on most issues it wasn't—was immaterial. If Truman could but convince the majority of voters that all Republicans were defenders of greedy big business, hostages of special interests, and obstructers to transformative social policy, he had a chance at the ballot box. So while the Research Division and Truman's speechwriters would include some of the material they'd dug up on Dewey, they decided to let Truman keep going with his indictment of his congressional opponents for the duration of the campaign, come what may.

One topic the Truman team wanted to continue pressing was housing. On June 29, Research Division staffer Kenny Birkhead wrote to special assistant to the president Philleo Nash emphasizing how the watered-down housing bill, which fell far short of the extensive legislation Truman had proposed, was impacting urban blacks. Birkhead attached a report that asserted "some 170,000 Negro families across the countries have lost the opportunity to live in decent housing at rents they can afford to pay because the public housing provision of the housing bill was not passed by Congress."[167] Clearly, the Democratic brain trust would keep pursuing the black vote and also make it clear that it was the Eightieth Congress, not the president, that had failed to meet even the basic needs of the American people.

While such strategy communiqués were being exchanged, Truman was focusing his attention on running the country. On June 24, he signed a new draft bill that would conscript up to quarter of a million men in its first year. He also put his pen to two new spending appropriations for the US military, totaling around $10 billion. Of this, $3.7 billion would go to the navy, funding a wide range of new initiatives and vessels, including development of the world's largest aircraft carrier, an as-yet unnamed sixty-five-thousand-ton behemoth.[168]

The next day brought some positive news on a front that, for the president at least, had typically delivered just the opposite. A Truman-appointed inquiry board brokered a deal between coal mines and the United Mine Workers union (UMW), run by Truman's nemesis, the fiery, volatile John L. Lewis. In return for ending more than two years of strikes and unrelenting threats and demands, the mine workers would receive a $1 an hour pay increase and, more significantly, a $100 million annual welfare fund. Ironically, Truman's investigatory board had wielded the power of the Taft-Hartley Act, which Truman had derided so thoroughly during his June tour, to bring the warring factions to the negotiating table.[169] Talks also progressed between CIO chief Philip Murray and the steel mines over a pension plan for more than nine hundred thousand workers.

The coal mine owners' climb down was good news for Truman—not least because he had not needed to talk directly to John Lewis about the dispute—but any satisfaction he may have derived from the settlement was doused the next day by news that the liberal wing of his party was yet again calling for General Dwight Eisenhower to replace the president on the Democratic ticket. The former commander of US forces in Europe was acting in another presidential capacity in academia, at Columbia University, and had not stated his intention to run for a higher elected office or even so much as indicated his political party of choice. And yet the Americans for Democratic Action (ADA), a group that doubted Truman's commitment to continuing the New Deal, was determined to convince Ike to march in double time to the Democratic nomination the following month. Attending an ADA rally in New York, FDR's son Elliott read parts of a letter from the general to a leading ADA official's solicitation. The communication was, in reality, a study in ambiguity. Yet Roosevelt drew cheers from the crowd when he read, "I am anxious to do my duty, but felt that it was my own problem to determine whether a sense of duty could call me into the political field."[170]

It was hardly a declarative statement, but it was one that Roosevelt and the ADA clung to as evidence that Eisenhower was at least considering a run at the White House. In his absence, ADA chairman Leon Henderson believed that Supreme Court Justice William O. Douglas, who ironically had emerged as Truman's top choice for a running mate, would also be a better bet than Truman to thwart Tom Dewey.[171]

Baby-faced yet eminently capable J. Howard McGrath, the forty-five-year-old former Democratic governor of Rhode Island and acting chairman of the Democratic National Committee (one of Truman's few supporters among the party's top brass), dismissed the "Draft Ike" movement. He asserted that Truman would be nominated on the first ballot at his party's convention and dismissed further reports on anti-Truman sentiment among southern Democrats over the president's bold civil rights proposals. Facts undermined McGrath's optimism. Fifteen southern and border state governors announced that they were planning an anti-Truman meeting for July 11, the day before the convention. "All of the 15 governors are hostile to the nomination of President Truman," said J. O. Emmerich, director of the states' rights committee. "This pre-convention caucus, to plan ways and means to protect the South, will be a serious blow to the hopes of those who support Harry Truman."[172] Another report, which made the front page of the New York Times, estimated that Truman could count on just twenty-six votes from the southern delegates now known as the "Dixiecrats" when the convention opened.[173]

Further north, in the District of Columbia, Truman won the nod in a poll of Democratic leaders but saw Eisenhower come in second despite the general's repeated insistence that he would not seek the party's nomination. The District of Columbia had just three votes in the Electoral College, but with the clamor for Eisenhower growing, Truman's advisors fretted nonetheless. As if Truman wasn't facing fire from enough directions, Henry Wallace again criticized US foreign policy, stating his belief that the president was failing labor because of the country "spending vast sums in adventures overseas."[174]

Such "adventures," Wallace believed, included the continued presence of American troops in occupied Berlin, which he and his fellow Progressive Party members demanded Truman end.[175] That was certainly what Moscow was hoping for, too. On June 29, the Soviets extended their blockade between East and West Berlin that they had begun five days before, again preventing food and medical supplies from reaching the western zones where US, British, and French forces were stationed. Though there were not enough US transport aircraft to fully meet the needs of West Berliners, Truman ordered his commanders to overcome the Soviet obstruction of road, rail, and water travel with as many flights carrying vital supplies as possible. At one point, an Allied aircraft landed every three minutes at Templehof airport in the American zone. Many more would be needed if Truman were to successfully stare down Stalin.[176] Certainly the pending West German appeal to the United Nations would not intimidate Stalin, whose resolution was every bit as intimidating as the tens of thousands of Red Army troops who greatly outnumbered their former American brothers-in-arms in Germany.

So as the final hours of June slipped away, Truman looked to the following month, hoping to avoid war with the Soviets and the dissolution of his party. His aides and the Research Division planned in earnest for the fall Whistle Stop Tour, but unless he secured the Democratic nomination at the 31st Democratic National Convention, Truman's train and his career would be left in the shed to rust.

July

In the first week of July 1948, the focus of the nation had shifted from whether Dewey could secure a second straight presidential nomination to whether the incumbent Truman could unify his squabbling party members and gain their nod for November. Observers also wondered whether the defiant rhetoric of southern Democrats would manifest into an outright split on the right of the party and how damaging Henry Wallace's leftward defection would prove.[1] And it was not just the fringes of the Democratic fold that proved troublesome to the president. Party bigwigs such as Frank Hague, Jake Arvey, and William O'Dwyer were threatening to abandon Truman and push for the nomination of Dwight Eisenhower, who the increasingly influential Americans for Democratic Action (ADA) also thought had a better chance of overhauling Dewey than the president did.[2] Despite the storm clouds threatening to deluge whatever chances of re-election he still had, Truman remained bullish. Asked at a White House press conference on July 1 if he would consider pulling out of the race, he bristled, "No, certainly not. That is foolish question number one." He then predicted not just nomination on the first ballot at the Democratic National Convention, but also victory on November 2.[3]

Across town at Dupont Circle, the Research Division had no choice but to work as if Truman's first prediction had already come to pass. If it did, there were still two months to go until the president returned to the rails, but the activity at the cramped offices continued at its frenetic pace. Whatever the enduring question marks about Truman's chances, Kelly, Batt, and Birkhead continued to churn out their reports, messaging points, and fact sheets about every place on Truman's whistle stop itinerary, adding to their longer, comprehensive Files of the Facts on housing, pricing, and the other major campaign issues and making recommendations to Clark Clifford about the tone and content of Truman's speeches. Papers were strewn about, towers of read and unread folders perched precariously on the edges of too-small desks, and the click-clack of type-writer keys only added to the cacophony of drills, picks, and hammers from the road construction that continued outside the office windows.[4] Soon, the desperately overworked trio gained welcome and much needed backup in the form of Johannes Hoeber, Batt's eloquent, bespectacled friend from Philadelphia.[5]

In the few years they had known each other, Hoeber had proven his worth to Batt, not least by providing research assistance for Batt's failed attempt to wrest a Pennsylvania House of Representatives seat in pro-Republican Montgomery County away from the GOP incumbent in 1946. The following year, Hoeber had put his full rhetorical weight behind Batt's bid for the chairmanship of the Philadelphia ADA, which was successful.[6] Batt was a man of loyalty and principle, and Hoeber's reward was a glowing recommendation to Clifford penned on May 11, 1948: "Hoeber is one of the best men in the country for the work on issues. He has a combination of practical political experience and research background, and a Ph.D. from the London School of Economics"[7] (not quite accurate, as Hoeber completed his doctoral work at the University of Heidelberg and merely studied at the London School of Economics for one year as an undergraduate). Hoeber had also honed his analytical, research, and mass communications skills during his time as director of information in Mannheim, Germany, in the 1930s. In this role, he educated the bustling city's half a million citizens about the purpose and functions of democratic government and explained the bold, progressive reforms of the mayor, job experience that would serve him well in the Research Division. One of Bill Batt's key requirements for his team was the ability to handle deadline pressure. Hoeber's turbulent experience in Germany as the Nazis rose to power left no question that he could think clearly under circumstances far more extreme than anything the Research Division's heavy workload could bring to bear. The March 5, 1933, election saw Hitler seize control of Germany's key government departments despite failing to win a majority. Nazi leaders in Mannheim, backed by the muscle and firearms of the SS, stormed the city's administrative offices, tore the black-red-gold Weimar Republic flag from the pole in the city square and set it ablaze, and hoisted in its place an imposing swastika.

They then marched Hoeber and his colleagues into "protective custody" at the county prison—ironically, located just down the hall from his old office at the Rathaus—as Hoeber wondered whether he would ever see his wife, Elfriede, and their four-year-old daughter, Susanne, again. Hoeber's father secured the terrified young man's release and the family escaped to Dusseldorf, three hours drive north of Mannheim.[8]

They would not be safe for long. Hoeber worked by day in Dusseldorf for the Rhineland bureau office of the liberal newspaper *Frankfurter Zeitung*, which before Hitler rose to the highest office in the land was Germany's intellectual and political equivalent of the *New York Times*. At night, the committed anti-Nazi was politically active in the Social Democratic Party, which was now conducting its subversive activities underground. Several of Hoeber's employees at the *Frankfurter Zeitung* were careless with their anti-Nazi pursuits and were arrested in early November 1938. It didn't take long for them to give Hoeber up, too, and the Gestapo called him into their Dusseldorf office for a preliminary grilling. Hoeber somehow talked his way out of that predicament, but he knew it wouldn't be long until the full details of his subterfuge came to light. As he stepped out of Gestapo HQ and into the bright sunlight of a crisp November morning, he decided not to wait around for the inevitable. He returned home, packed a few things, said hurried good-byes to Elfriede and Susanne, and crossed the Swiss border when night fell.[9] Hoeber made his way alone to Philadelphia, where his parents had relocated after the Nazis threw his father out of his teaching post at the University of Kiel because of Jewish ancestry. As he lobbied to get his wife and daughter American visas, Hoeber worked for Walter Phillips, a wily Democratic lawyer who was lobbying for the creation of an overhauled Philadelphia City Charter. Phillips also provided an affidavit of support for Elfriede and Susanne. They set sail during a rare lull in the U-boat attacks that would soon make the Atlantic a no-go zone and reunited with Johannes on November 5, 1945, more than a year after he fled Germany.[10]

Soon after Hoeber's family joined him in Philadelphia, the City Charter plan sunk amidst the swirling waters of partisan rankling. Hoeber went to work for the Institute of Local and State Government.[11] He then became director of public relations for the Philadelphia Housing Authority. There, Hoeber advocated for implementation of the low-income housing provisions of FDR's New Deal.[12] He later used his formidable research and writing skills to prepare a wide range of background materials for Dick Dilworth's mayoral campaign from 1947 to early 1948, penning fact sheets and position papers on public housing and health, finance, social services, and scandals in City Hall. As if he didn't have enough to do, Hoeber created a wide range of materials in his voluntary role as, fittingly, chairman of the Philadelphia ADA's Research Committee.[13]

After reviewing such a comprehensive professional record and proof of Hoeber's determination in the face of odds far longer than those facing Truman, Clifford was convinced that the ex-German should indeed join the Research Division. Prying him away from his nonprofit work, however, was anything but a foregone conclusion, and Hoeber, like many of his ADA brethren, was not convinced of Truman's commitment to the liberal cause.[14] Despite the obstacles, Clifford was able to articulate the vital significance of the Research Division to Joseph D. Gibbon, Hoeber's boss, while Batt talked Hoeber into joining him at Dupont Circle.[15] Hoeber could only stay until the end of September because the Community Chest would hold its annual pledge drive in October, but by then most of the heavy lifting for the Whistle Stop Tour would already have been done.

So in the first week of July, Hoeber—whose rimless glasses, neatly combed side-parting hair, and intense eyes accurately conveyed his personality to the world—packed a suitcase. He said good-bye to his wife, Elfriede, their eighteen-year-old daughter, Susanne, seven-year-old son, Tommy, and five-year-old son, Frank, and took the train to Washington. There he swapped his tiny, shared office in downtown Philadelphia for one in Dupont Circle that was even more confined and, due to the ongoing roadwork outside, infinitely noisier. Here he would earn $175 per week, pay $40 per month for lodging at the low-end American Veterans Committee Club, and set aside $5 a day for living expenses, including his daily pack and a half of Chesterfields—then endorsed by Hollywood stars Gregory Peck and Louis Jourdan and billed as "Always Milder, Better Smoking, Cooler Tasting."

The Research Division gang could hardly waste time grousing about their less-than-ideal working conditions or the privations of their low-end accommodations at the AVC boarding house, where, Hoeber wrote to his wife, "The heat and humidity here are getting more unbearable every day."[16] Instead, they channeled all their energy into fact finding, writing, and talking with local, state, and national campaign staff members. It was a nonstop effort for Batt, Hoeber, Birkhead, Kelly, and Batt's other two new recruits, John Barriere and Phil Dreyer. Barriere was a graduate student who was studying for his PhD at the University of Chicago and was, at age twenty-nine, the youngest of the Batt group. This precocious fellow, who wore his hair spiked up in front with plenty of pomade and who Johannes Hoeber described as "very bright," had come to Batt's attention through a recommendation by a mutual friend on the Senate Banking Committee.[17] Batt immediately recognized Barriere's versatility and resolved to employ him as a "utility outfielder at Dupont Circle."[18]

Phil Dreyer was a specialist in natural resources, which the Research Division needed given the high percentage of Truman's June tour speeches in which he mentioned developing and protecting resources in the West. Hailing from the Pacific Northwest, Dreyer had met Batt through the American Veterans Committee and had become yet another example of the Research Division head preferring to hire known entities he could count on even under the most extreme pressure.[19] Before he left to serve with the 41st Field Artillery in the Pacific in World War II, Dreyer had been a staunch Republican, but upon returning to Portland, Oregon, in 1945, he found that the party's policies and his own beliefs had diverged and now "the Republicans were against everything I cared about." Dreyer also became committed to the civil rights cause after seeing how much worse blacks were treated in peacetime. Dreyer later explained that he "got pissed off at how we treated African-Americans. They couldn't go bowling, and they couldn't eat in fancy restaurants. They fought the war for liberty, but they couldn't get it at home." He was so passionate about the issue that he postponed his wedding to speak about it before the City Council.[20]

Bill Batt could certainly do with some of that passion on his skeleton crew, and he brought Dreyer to Washington at the earliest opportunity. Frank Kelly, for one, was immediately impressed by the verve of his new colleague, whom he described as "a very energetic, bouncy fellow."[21] Once Dreyer, Batt, Hoeber, and the others had prepared their Files of the Facts, white papers, speech analyses, and other documents, someone had to get these to Clifford et al., not to mention answer phone calls, schedule appointments, and process incoming correspondence. Batt also needed help dispatching the several letters and memos he composed to

Clifford each day, plus those intended for Oscar Chapman and others on the campaign team. His writing/research team was already running on little sleep, and each day refused to yield them a spare minute. So the Research Division chief sought from McGrath, and received, a budget to hire a team of well-qualified, efficient, and, most importantly for this still clandestine organization, discreet secretaries, one for each full-time Research Division member.

Though the majority of secretaries were, in the still-chauvinistic workplace, female, many men had also served in this capacity in World War II, both in regional field command centers and posts in the United States. Once the war was over, these clerks had useful skills that they plied in the peacetime economy. This explains the inclusion of Joe Clark and Johan Wallace—whose wife, Virginia, also became an administrative assistant for the Research Division—on Batt's list of administrative staff members.[22]

★ ★ ★

Harry Truman's July started much as the previous months had, with trouble abroad and uncertainty at home. The Greek government, which had received invaluable aid from the Truman administration as part of the Marshall Plan, was still unable to eliminate communist resistance. Greek troops tried five times to storm enemy positions in Kleptis Height in the northwest of the country, only to be repelled each time.[23] The picture was little better in Korea, where the US Army seized documents detailing a plan for an armed revolt in the south of the country by communist activists in the north, a region from which the Red Army had still not withdrawn despite pledges to do so.[24] And in the nascent state of Israel, which Truman had been the first world leader to officially recognize, the main highway through Tel Aviv was blocked by fierce fighting between Israeli and Arab troops.[25]

Meanwhile, in Berlin the Red Army had again completely cut off all road, rail, and water routes between its occupation zone in the east of the city and the American and British zones in the west, having allowed a few barges to pass a few days before.[26] General Marshall let the Soviets know that this renewed embargo would not force American troops to abandon Berliners, stating on July 1, "We are in Berlin as a result of the agreements between the governments on the areas of occupation in Germany and we intend to stay."[27] The president was determined to back his secretary of state and the man trying to find a peaceful way forward in Berlin, General Lucius Clay, telling reporters at a White House press conference that he had approved Marshall's statement in advance and agreed with its entirety.[28]

Even as he spoke, plans were afoot to continue breaking the blockade without the British, American, or French forces resorting to armed retaliation, which could lead to all-out war between the antagonists that eyed each other warily from either side of the Iron Curtain. Unbeknownst to the Kremlin, Truman had ordered his commanders to intensify the air sorties between the occupation zones. This had begun as a trial operation, but it was poised to become the biggest American peacetime airlift, with hundreds of aircraft redeployed from all over the world to deliver food, medicine, and other vital supplies to West Berlin. Truman had invested much effort, political capital, and hundreds of millions of dollars in reviving Western Europe and bolstering it against expansionist communism (not least in his aid package to Greece and Turkey), and he was determined that it would not be in vain because of Soviet obstructionism and brinksmanship.[29]

The task was not one to be taken lightly. General Curtis LeMay, the hawkish commander of the United States Air Force in Europe, had told the White House and his subordinates that to survive the blockade, West Berliners required eight million pounds of food a day at the absolute minimum.[30] In the first week of July, the combined efforts of the British Royal Air Force and US Air Force could only manage 750,000 pounds, a small fraction of the subsistence figure.[31] Yet hundreds of American planes would soon be diverted from Guam, Hawaii, and across the United States to participate in a daring, high-risk campaign for which they would later be dubbed "The Candy Bombers." Truman could not speak of it publicly because an official statement would give the game away and put American pilots and the lives of West Berlin's hungry citizens at risk. But behind the scenes he was in frequent communication with Marshall, LeMay, and the Joint Chiefs of Staff over the issue.[32] Even as they sent memos back and forth and talked on the phone, Truman faced criticism in the press for his Berlin policy and previous actions in foreign affairs. Veteran *Milwaukee Sentinel* beat writer David Sentner typified this when he wrote, "The grave Berlin crisis . . . was made possible by failure of President Truman at the Potsdam Conference to seek an iron-clad agreement with the Russians."[33]

In the United States, hundreds of thousands of lives were not imperiled by Soviet troops and the actions of their puppet masters in Moscow, yet Truman still faced another new and serious challenge to his presidency: the supposedly unbeatable Republican election ticket. In a meeting at the White House with DNC chairman Howard McGrath, Clark Clifford, and his other advisers, he discussed how they might best Tom Dewey and Earl Warren at the polls come November, but also, backing the cart up, how they might overcome the new challenge of Democrats calling for General Dwight Eisenhower to run in his place as what the *Washington Daily News* called "a more acceptable candidate."[34]

The Republicans had failed to convince Ike—America's most prominent war hero (though Douglas McArthur would have contested this status)—to lead their charge, but the general's appeal seemed to transcend party lines, and since April the ADA had been pushing for Truman to step aside and let Eisenhower take his place, even passing out thousands of "I like Ike" buttons. Truman was, contended ADA executive secretary James Loeb, "the ADA's great frustration" because "we cannot compete with the Wallace crowd unless and until we have a national Presidential figure to crusade for."[35]

With Dewey and Warren now joining Wallace and the potential southern Democrat mutiny over civil rights as legitimate threats to the president in November, the liberal call for "Ike" spread beyond the ADA ranks.[36] On July 5, New Jersey Democratic Party boss Frank Hague declared that the thirty-seven delegates in his state would back the army man over the Man from Missouri.[37] Two days later, party leaders in Georgia and Virginia instructed their states' fifty-four delegates to vote for Eisenhower at the Democratic convention if the general, who had become president of Columbia University just two months previously, chose to enter the fray. Georgia Democrats decried Truman as the cause of "chaos, confusion and revolt" and asserted that Eisenhower was "the one man, the only proper man, to lead the people of this nation in their fight against Communism, tyranny and slavery."[38] They then decided that Georgia senator Richard Russell was the best man to join Eisenhower on the ticket.

Even more troubling for Truman was the report in the *New York Times* that FDR's son, James, Chicago party boss Jacob Arvey, and New York mayor William O'Dwyer were going to call a meeting of state delegation chairmen for Saturday, July 10, in Philadelphia, just two days before the convention opened.[39] That same day, Truman wrote his friend Winston Churchill—who since his humiliating election defeat in July 1945 had been leader of the opposition in England—that he was "going through a terrible political 'trial by fire.'"[40]

The part of this trial that included the Democrats' push to nominate Eisenhower instead of Truman at the 1948 convention made little sense. When Truman took over from Roosevelt, his detractors had carped that he was inexperienced, was not intellectual like his predecessor, lacked public speaking polish, and was from the supposedly out-of-touch Midwest. If Jimmie Roosevelt, Hague, and the others in the "Draft Ike" crowd really thought about it logically, all the same charges could be leveled at Eisenhower, who for all of his evident qualities was a career soldier, a modest orator, and a midwesterner to boot.[41] Despite this cognitive dissonance, the growing anti-Truman faction was determined to get its man.

As he journeyed back from Bolivar, Missouri, on July 7, where he had been with Venezuelan president Romulo Gallegos to dedicate a statue honoring the liberator of that country, Simón Bolivar, Truman did not waste emotional energy fulminating against the "draft Ike" contingent. Instead, he focused on what he *would* say when nominated by the Democratic National Convention delegates, an eventuality he still fully believed in.[42] There were several givens—calling for better provisions on housing, price controls, and immigration reform among them. But one issue that was still up in the air was whether he would allow the Eightieth Congress that he so reviled to walk away from these issues or call them back for a special session after the convention.

The call for a special session was not confined to the Oval Office. Back on June 2, the *Christian Science Monitor* had posited this tactic in an editorial Batt sent to Clifford via the daily delivery pouch two days later.[43] Titled "Why Should Congress Quit," the piece stated that there were at least a dozen important measures before Congress, all of which should be resolved before the body dissolved for the summer. If Congress dissolved on June 19, it would be the briefest session in a decade, far less vigorous than the ones during the 1944 presidential and 1942 and 1946 midterm election years.

In a conclusion that sounded like it could have been penned by Clifford himself, the anonymous editor stated, "It would be a sad commentary on this great Republic if through overemphasis on the elections or through sheer weariness great national purposes should be frustrated by a failure of Congress to do its job. Last year Congress quit early and had to be called back in special session." What then, was the solution this time around? "We respectfully suggest that it reconvene this year in the middle of July . . . and finish properly important work left over when the legislators knock off for the party shindigs in Philadelphia."[44]

There was, then, a very recent instance of Congress meeting in special session over the summer and in election years. These extended sessions, however, had been decided upon by Congress. A president had not ordered Congress back to Capitol Hill during an election year since 1856, when the Missouri-Kansas border war saw proslavery Missourians burn Lawrence, Kansas, to the ground, Kansans retaliate viciously in the Pottawatomie Massacre, and South Carolina representative Preston Brooks caning Massachusetts senator Charles Sumner on the Senate floor.[45]

Bill Batt informed Clifford that the *Monitor* editorial he had passed along was just one of several "aimed at Congress inactivity" and predicted that many publications would soon be clamoring for an extended session.

By early July, Congress had ended its session without addressing housing, price controls, or the other ten issues mentioned in the *Monitor* article, although by now the Republicans had taken the audacious step of including some of these in their own platform for the election. What could Truman do to expose the disconnect between his opponents' inertia in Congress and their grand plans for the supposedly preordained Dewey presidency?

The answer was simple, Batt believed: call Congress back into session during the campaign and see if they could live up to their stated intentions. He first delivered this thesis at a midweek meeting of the Kitchen Cabinet (the Monday Night Group) at Oscar Ewing's apartment, where the idea of the Whistle Stop Tour was originally incubated and hatched. Truman's liberal advisers discussed the idea, argued about it for a few hours, and voted it down. The next morning, a downcast but not despairing Batt talked to his fellow Research Division members, who urged him to pursue the matter. So Batt got on the phone to Clifford, telling him,

"We want to pursue this idea; we think it's too darn good." Clifford replied succinctly, "Put it in a memorandum."[46]

The decisive two-page memo is unsigned, but the rhetorical devices therein, including the use of "we" (which Batt frequently used to convey the shared opinions of himself, Birkhead, Kelly, and the others at Dupont Circle to Clifford), the harsh language about the GOP, and the logical argument–counterargument–conclusion structure are classic Batt. Indeed, he later took the credit for the memo.

The special session memo opened with a challenge: "This election can only be won by bold and daring steps . . . the boldest and most popular step the President could possibly take would be to call a special session of Congress."[47]

The author then goes on to make his case:

1. This would focus attention on the rotten record of the 80th Congress, which Dewey, Warren and the press will try to make the country forget.
2. It would force Dewey and Warren to defend the actions of Congress, and make them accept the Congress as a basic issue.
3. It would keep a steady glare of publicity on the Neanderthal men of the Republican party, the reactionary men such as Martin, Halleck, Wolcott, Allen, who will embarrass Dewey and Warren. The press is with us on the 80th Congress issue.
4. It would split the Republican Party on the major questions of how to deal with housing, inflation, foreign policy, social security, etc.
5. It would give President Truman the chance to follow through on the fighting start he made on his Western tour. It would show the President in action on Capitol Hill, fighting for the people, delivering messages to Congress in person, broadcasting his messages, leading his party in a crusade for the millions of Americans ignored by the "rich man's Congress."

Despite the validity of each of these points, the author recognized that Truman calling Congress back into session in the middle of summer was not without its risks, calling it "politically hazardous." But Batt believed that the potential boost to Truman's fortunes outweighed the dangers: "President Truman faces an uphill fight to win the upcoming election—

and the American people love a fighting leader who takes bold action to help the ordinary citizens against the lobbies and the corporations."

Batt then played devil's advocate, presenting the first major peril posed by a special session: "The Republicans may invite a Southern filibuster by introducing strong civil rights legislation." It would be difficult enough for Truman to come back against Dewey—"an almost impossible task" according to *U.S. News and World Report*—and if the Solid South James Rowe had referred to in his campaign manifesto the previous November went from disquiet over Truman's civil rights plans to full-out rebellion, the president would be in real trouble at the ballot box.[48]

Still, Batt believed that even if the GOP introduced bold civil rights action that Truman was forced to endorse, the president could threaten the southern Democrats with "losing their patronage, their positions of power in the party and their prestige in the event of a Republican victory."

If this wouldn't budge the stubborn southerners, Batt believed that Truman could unite liberal Democrats and Republicans to pass a modest civil rights bill, which he could then announce by national radio to win over the nation. Here Batt seems to be overstating his case, as Truman would likely already have proposed a bipartisan measure on the issue if he and Democratic leaders in Congress and the Senate thought they had the votes to get such a proposal through.

The second danger was that the "do-nothing" Congress might actually do *something* of merit for once, which Dewey and Warren would claim the credit for. Batt, now making a more convincing case, thought such action was unlikely, as "this Congress is so closely controlled by reactionaries and lobbyists that it cannot pass satisfactory bills to stop the disastrous inflation which is frightening the people, or to start constructing the millions of homes that are needed, or to initiate a more enlightened policy . . . or to extend social security."

Even if a special session put through one or two worthwhile pieces of domestic legislation, the DNC's PR team could see to it that the nation saw their president, not Dewey, as the architect. This, Batt believed, would leave the governor of New York "standing in the wings, saying, 'Yes, we should have some housing legislation. Yes, we should stop inflation. Yes, we should extend social security. Me too. Me too!'"

This was, in fact, *exactly* what the surprisingly liberal Dewey and Warren platform was up to, Batt, Clifford, and most of Truman's advisers believed—a copycat policy aimed to dupe the electorate into believing that the Republicans, not the Democrats, were the party of reform and the voice of the common people.[49]

The third concern Batt hypothesized was that this "me too" tactic would carry over into a summer session, which could "fool the people." Not much chance of that, the Research Division director answered with his own devil's advocate argument: "On the issue of price control, which will be the hottest issue of the campaign, the Congress cannot possibly act. . . . This Congress is run by men who cannot pass price control legislation without losing their financial backers and incurring the wrath of the [lobbying organizations] N.A.M., the US Chamber of Commerce and other such groups."

So, if he had to advise for or against Truman's calling Congress back, which course would Batt pick? The Research Division chief thought the decision was a simple and logical one for Truman to make: "On housing, education, social security, health—the answer is the same. This Congress cannot meet the critical needs of the country. It is tied up by the rich interests which expect to make a killing after the Republican victory in November—if they get that victory."[50]

There was only one choice in Batt's mind: pull Congress back into session and either enable the Republicans to live up to their surprisingly liberal platform or expose them and it as fraudulent. It had likely also occurred to Batt that while Truman's party was deeply divided, the GOP was hardly a model of unity. On one side were the Republicans who wanted to reduce the size and reach of the federal government and send Harry Truman back to small-town Missouri, where they thought he belonged. And on the other were the moderate centrists such as Warren, Stassen, and Dewey, who favored social change and could even be called reformers.[51] By pulling Republicans kicking and screaming back to Capitol Hill and putting them under the microscope of the national media as Truman baited them to act, Democratic strategists hoped to expose the conflicting stances and motivations of the two factions.

Certainly, it was whispered in Washington, Taft was none too happy with the selection of Dewey for the second campaign in a row. It was not just that the New York governor had lost to FDR in 1944—after all, every Republican challenger had suffered the same ignominy—but that the energetic, industrious, and bright forty-six-year-old represented the new wave, which undermined Taft's position of mounting spirited opposition to the New Deal. And with Warren joining Dewey on the ticket, the old guard had neither the nominee for president or vice president.[52]

Taft wanted the voice of the conservative movement to be his voice, not the smooth, sonorous tones of the debonair Dewey who, Taft believed, was barely on the right at all. If anything, Dewey's positions were more aligned with those of the president than with the strong-willed party leader who had always strived to follow his father's path to the White House and had, one reporter recalled, run the party during the preceding two years like an army general.[53]

The old guard Republicans, and Taft in particular, were also none too pleased with the selection of the tactful, polite-to-a-fault Warren, whose even-tempered, centrist approach was the exact opposite of the gruff Ohio senator's strong rhetoric. Truman had been shelling the Eightieth Congress, and therefore the Republicans, for months, not least in June when Taft called him out for "blackguarding Congress at every whistle stop." To defeat him, Taft believed, the GOP needed to return fire. Were Warren and Dewey up to manning the guns? Not in Taft's view.[54]

Despite the evident divisions in the Republican Party, Clifford's number two, George Elsey, did not concur with Batt that the president announcing a special session at the convention was, on balance, a risk worth taking. He read the memo Batt sent to Clifford and immediately penned his own to the president's special counsel, taking the opposite tack: "I feel very strongly that any announcement at this time . . . would be most unwise. The Democrats on the Hill have splintered in all directions and at the moment I see little prospect of any early or happy family reunion. The time to decide whether a special session would be advisable is one month from now, after the two conventions and the two platforms."[55]

Clifford trusted Elsey implicitly, but he was won over by Batt's airtight exposition, and he recommended to Truman that he recall Congress. Going against Elsey's suggestion, the president would do so at the most dramatic setting possible, where the decision was sure to gain maximum exposure—the Democratic National Convention.

As the Truman team made its final preparations for the convergence of the Democratic delegates, one major obstacle was removed from the president's path. For all the media hype, the overtures of the ADA and New Dealers, and the breathless quotes about his leadership, Dwight

Eisenhower becoming a Democratic Party candidate was not to be. He said "no" to Frank Hague, James Roosevelt, and the rest in the first week of July, again in the second, and then, under increasing pressure, declined the opportunity to run against Truman in no uncertain terms for a third and final time. In a memo to Claude Pepper, the general wrote, "No matter under what terms, conditions or premises a proposal might be couched, I would not accept the nomination." This decision was, the loyal soldier explained to Pepper, made with "a sincere conviction as to the best interests of the country." [56]

So despite the best efforts of his Republican foes, Wallace's defection and the looming battle with the southern Democrats, Truman would go into the convention as the favorite to secure the nomination for November. His longtime supporter Henry Dockweiler, treasurer of the California Democratic Party, sided with the president over the leader of that state's delegation, telling reporters, "I am for Harry Truman and I think the majority of the delegation is, despite the machinations of Jimmie Roosevelt." [57] Whether this prediction would prove to be true when the ballots were counted remained to be seen.

★ ★ ★

"YOU CAN'T STAY COLD ABOUT A MAN WHO STICKS HIS CHIN OUT AND FIGHTS"

It was the second presidential election year in a row that the Republicans and Democrats had held their national gatherings in the same city, with Chicago hosting the two parties' delegates in 1944. Unfortunately for those in Truman's party, Philadelphia's weather had resolved to be much harsher to them on July 12 than it had been to their GOP counterparts from June 21 to 25, when it was warm but not unseasonably so. Temperatures surged into triple digits, with high humidity making it feel even more uncomfortable in Convention Hall. Add the accumulated body heat from more than 1,200 delegates, some of their spouses, administrative and serving staff, and TV crews from ABC, CBS, and NBC, and it's not surprising that the thermometer on the floor hit an almost unbearable ninety-four degrees—hardly ideal conditions for cool heads to prevail among the already combative delegates, who were witnessing what many of them saw as the long-term demise of their party.

Whatever happened between the rival groups, each struggling for a foothold at the first convention since FDR's passing, the cameras would be rolling. NBC had broken new ground during the Republican convention by showing the first live feed from a political press conference—that of Thomas Dewey. Even in TV, it seemed, Dewey was leading Truman. NBC also had on hand an illustrious lineup of presenters who had made their names on radio, not least Douglas Edwards, Eric Sevareid, and perhaps the most famous broadcaster in the country, if not the world, Edward R. Murrow, who had become a household name during World War II. Their coverage would add a new, visual dimension to the convention and the race for the White House, despite Murrow's preference for radio and his concern that television cheapened the business of news reporting.[58] Though at the time of the convention television was only available in major cities, soon enough it would supplant radio as the dominant communication medium as network coverage grew, sets went up in quality and down in price, and broadcasters began to hook viewers on regular programming.[59]

To help ensure that Truman got the election platform he wanted, Bill Batt dispatched Frank Kelly to Philadelphia to participate in the drafting meetings at the Bellevue-Stratford Hotel, the imposing French Renaissance–style building that loomed over the corner of Walnut and Broad Streets. The committee, which also included representatives from the New Deal, conservative, and liberal elements of the Democratic Party, quickly reached consensus on several of the main planks, including Truman's push for low-income housing, an increased minimum wage, and continued price controls (especially of crops, dairy, and livestock to help win back the Republican-dominated Midwest). But there were several other issues that would not be settled so harmoniously by these ideologically opposed factions. One of the key points of contention in the platform committee's jam-packed, noisy, smoke-filled conference room was civil rights and, more specifically, how proposed legislation would affect the rights of blacks in the Jim Crow South, where they were still, at best, second-class citizens.[60]

Truman had, of course, taken significant strides in establishing the Committee on Civil Rights in December 1946 and promising to act on its recommendations to eliminate segregation and the associated prejudicial treatment of blacks in early 1948. But the president and many of his top advisers didn't want to push the so-called Solid South much further in case they deserted the president altogether, so they favored a moderate, nonspecific civil rights plank.[61] This was anathema, however, to ADA president Andrew Biemiller and chairman Leon Henderson, who, with influential backers including Illinois delegate Paul Douglas and Californian Paul Shelley, pushed the platform committee to go much further. If it didn't, they worried, many more liberals might quit the party and rally around Henry Wallace.[62] Though the DNC leadership had tried to freeze the ADA out of the convention, they had acquired a few convention passes from some top figures in the party and, oddly, four from a Philadelphia bartender who somehow came to possess them. Now that they'd come in through the back door, they were determined to make their presence felt.[63]

But in the end, despite the presence of the vocal ADA leaders at the Bellevue-Stratford strategy sessions and their vigorous pleas, the platform was ratified with civil rights messaging that they and many liberals found unacceptably weak and vague.[64] Afterwards, committee members revealed to reporters that their last-minute attempt to strengthen it was drowned out in "an overwhelming thunder of 'no's.'"[65] The ADA and likeminded Democrats saw the lack of decisive wording as pandering to the anti-civil-rights element of the party in an attempt to retain their support for the daunting task of hauling in Dewey—a prospect that Truman's cautious advisers feared would become impossible if the South bolted. Having failed to impact the civil rights plank in the committee room, Biemiller, Henderson, and their band of young bucks took the only avenue open to them: action on the convention floor. Wanting to time their stand to make maximum impact, they resolved to wait until as close to the end of the event as possible.

In fact, they had little choice but to wait, because they needed to persuade a skilled and respected orator to introduce a minority plank in a way that would carry the day. The ADA zeroed in on Hubert Humphrey, a man about whom a reporter in the black newspaper the *Minneapolis Spokesman* had written three years earlier, "(He) publicly expressed his opinions on the question of Negro rights long before he ever ran for public office. He is familiar with the problems Negroes face and he is ready to help solve them, if he can get the cooperation he wants."[66]

Humphrey, now the mayor of Minneapolis, had been an ardent supporter of the Committee on Civil Rights since its inception, and a rousing speech at the group's first Midwest meeting in Chicago the previous year and his reputation as a rising star in the Democratic Party had won him the role of ADA vice chairman.[67] Despite his belief that segregation was inherently wrong and that it was up to Truman's party to end it, Humphrey was initially cautious about his role in the fight. He was overwhelmingly popular in his home state, having garnered almost two-thirds of the vote in the 1947 Minneapolis mayoral election. Now he was running for a Senate seat that he didn't want to jeopardize by championing such a divisive cause. And, after all, a Gallup poll showed that only 6 percent of the American population favored federal civil rights legislation.[68] His close friend Orville Freeman, though urging Humphrey to follow his convictions, warned him that advocating a strong civil rights plank might get him "laughed out of the hall."[69]

And yet, through the combination of his fellow ADA members' lobbying efforts during an all-night strategy session in his fourth-floor room at the Bellevue-Stratford hotel on July 13, a pep talk from his father, Hubert Sr., and his own conscience, he relented, putting principle above pragmatism. Humphrey, sweaty of brow and worried of mind, was physically and emotionally drained, losing fifteen pounds through the stress of the previous days' back and forth, fasting, and lack of sleep for the best part of a week. And yet, in this crucial moment, the weary young politician was also decisive.[70] "I'll do it," he told his friends at around 5:00 a.m., just before dawn broke on that final, fateful day of the convention. "If there's one thing I believe in this crazy business, it's civil rights. Regardless of what happens, we are going to do it. Now get the hell out of here and let me write a speech and get some sleep."[71]

After a brief nap, Humphrey did as he said, writing and rewriting a punchy eight-minute speech. Meanwhile, Alben Barkley, the talismanic seventy-one-year-old who had made a long habit of trying to get on the Democratic ticket as vice president and had been Senate minority leader since the Democrats' drubbing at the 1946 midterms, became the unlikely spark plug for the previously subdued convention.[72] With his large, soft features, gentle authority, and easy laugh, Barkley had the air of a kindly grandfather. Yet this image veiled a determination, a talent for public speaking, and a sharp mind that, along with his unparalleled political experience, made him the perfect man to frame the coming battle with the Republican Party, contrary to outward appearance.

Looking dapper in a white suit accented with a black polka dot pocket square and gray and black striped tie, the remaining strands of his wavy gray hair slicked across his broad head, the Kentuckian took the podium with twenty-four pages of notes.[73] As the convention's keynote speaker, he enunciated deliberately and consulted his talking points regularly, but the force and conviction of his words did not need bombastic delivery to impact his audience, which, almost without exception, respected his thirty-six-year record on Capitol Hill.[74]

"The Republican nominee has announced, with characteristic finality, that he proposes to sweep from the Government of Washington the cobwebs as he swept them from Albany following tenure of Democratic administration," Barkley told his fellow Democrats. "I am not an expert in cobwebs, but if my memory does not betray me, when the Democratic Party took over the Government 16 years ago, even the spiders were too weak from starvation to weave or spin a cobweb in any department of the Government of the United States."

This gained the expected laughs, but Barkley had also hammered the GOP as Truman had done as he spoke at "whistle stops" in June. Though he did not mention civil rights by name, Barkley alluded to this most controversial of issues when he quoted Jefferson's immortal "all men are created equal" line from the Declaration of Independence, and then, again criticizing the GOP, asserted that "the Republican politicians have not been closer to Lincoln in two generations than to quote him."

Barkley saved his most emphatic passage for his conclusion: "This is no partisan call, it is no appeal for the lusts of office, it is no panoply of sophistries made to perpetuate or deny power to any political party. It is the swelling of human breasts with pride that God in his wisdom has given us the power and the opportunity to inaugurate a better world and a better society. Behold, destiny itself knocks on our door."[75]

The reaction was emphatic. Barkley received a twenty-eight-minute ovation and a rendition of "My Old Kentucky Home" for his efforts, and Democratic delegates stayed in the hall for hours after the memorable keynote address.[76] James Roosevelt, who came up to Barkley on the platform and put his arm around the man who had served his father for so long, encapsulated the feelings of the audience when he told journalists it was "one of the greatest speeches I ever heard in my life."[77]

Associated Press columnist Hal Boyle was unreserved in his praise of the veteran Kentucky senator, declaring, "In 68 stirring minutes of old-fashioned sledgehammer oratory, last night he welded the quarrelling delegates together in a tremendous outburst of party enthusiasm."[78]

"As a keynote speech, it was a masterpiece," Eleanor Roosevelt wrote in her nationally syndicated "My Day" column. She then echoed one of Truman's lines from his "nonpolitical" tour the previous month: "Senator Barkley showed us that those of us who approve of the record made by the Democratic party, under both Woodrow Wilson and Franklin D. Roosevelt, must add up that record and weigh it against the record made under the Republican Administrations. Then we must decide which party we now wish to support."[79]

Buoyed by Barkley's performance and the news that the federal judge Alan Goldsborough had reached a settlement with the president's long-time foe, John L. Lewis, to end a weeklong strike by forty thousand members of the United Mine Workers union, Truman called the Kentucky senator to congratulate him on his speech.[80] Though the details of the conversation remained private, Democratic National Committee chairman J. Howard McGrath revealed to the press the next day that the president would "be most happy" if Barkley was his running mate. And with William O. Douglas, the president's first choice for the ticket, having turned down the opportunity in favor of retaining his seat on the Supreme Court, Barkley certainly seemed like a shoo-in. It also couldn't hurt that he was from the South; perhaps his selection could help heal the rift with anti-civil-rights leaders.[81]

Secretary of the Senate Leslie Biffle was less guarded in his assessment than McGrath, saying about Barkley's probable nomination, "I think it is a cinch. I think there is no question about it." New Jersey boss Frank Hague, who many had thought to be lukewarm about Barkley (much as Truman was before the keynote address), issued the most candid assessment of his fellow delegates' intentions, telling a reporter who asked about Barkley's prospects, "What the hell? You're not stupid, are you? You *saw* that demonstration, didn't you?"[82]

With Barkley enlivening the previously dour convention, the ADA knew their opportunity to make a stand for civil rights was now upon them. Prominent black St. Louis attorney George L. Vaughan proposed a motion to unseat the delegation from Mississippi because of prejudicial policies in that state's constitution that he deemed illegal. While by no means one of the best-recognized delegates in Philadelphia that day, Vaughan had garnered nationwide news attention when representing a black family of his city that was forcibly evicted from their home by a white resident's association, for no reason other than their skin color. This was the type of injustice that continued to enrage Harry Truman, as did the continued beatings and lynching of blacks in the South. What more justification could the American electorate need to bring about lasting change and equality to the nation that was supposed to be leading the world into a lasting peace?

The Missouri state court upheld real estate segregation covenants, which Vaughan, the son of freed slaves from Kentucky, passionately indicted as "the Achilles heel" of American democracy. But his subsequent appeal made it all the way to the Supreme Court, which ruled in favor of Vaughan's client and declared that such covenants were invalid because they violated the Fourteenth Amendment.

Now, six months after his victory in the *Shelley v. Kraemer* case, Vaughan would again make his mark on the national stage. Though his motion fell 115 votes short of ratification, the delegates debated his motion passionately enough for Truman, watching on a tiny television in the Oval Office with Charlie Ross, to note it in his diary.[83]

The president was also paying attention when William Levi Dawson of Illinois, the black congressman Bill Batt had recommended to lead Truman's attempts to capture the minority vote in the 1948 campaign, followed Vaughan's effort with a lively speech of his own. "These two colored men are the only speakers to date who seem to be for me wholeheartedly," an approving Truman jotted.[84]

Certainly those southern delegates who introduced a minority plank urging the Democratic Party to drop civil rights entirely from the election platform were not for Truman and were, in fact, overtly critical of a president they believed was wielding excessive federal powers at the expense of states' rights. This was in keeping with what Strom Thurmond told the southern caucus when he claimed that Truman had "stabbed us in the back with his damnable program" and then threatened that "the guilty will not go unpunished."[85]

And yet, for all the southern bluster, the prevailing wind was blowing in the other direction, and their motion was rejected. As Humphrey ascended the steps to the speaking platform with Biemiller in tow, New

York political boss Edward Flynn assured them that their minority plank to strengthen the wording of the party's stand on civil rights was essential. "Look, you kids are right," the power broker told them after instructing his state's delegates to side with the bold young upstarts. "What you're trying to do is the only way we can wake up this country." And then, moving from moral assertion to political calculation, Flynn—who were it not for his thick eyebrows would have born a passing resemblance to FDR—said, "We've got to stir up the interest of minority groups in this election, otherwise we're dead."

As Humphrey prepared to take the podium, Flynn acted on these convictions, lobbying other bosses from the urban Northeast to ensure their backing on the vote that would follow the mayor of Minneapolis's address.[86]

Though he thought the man who had turned down the chance to be Truman's running mate, William Douglas, would have a better chance on the top of the ticket than the president, Hubert Humphrey now stepped to the platform to push for Truman and his implementation of the most ambitious civil rights measures since Lincoln. With the TV cameras rolling, it was no coincidence that Humphrey sported a large yellow button with the word "Truman" on the right lapel of his double-breasted black jacket.

He backed up this visual aid with an unqualified verbal endorsement, praising Truman for having "the courage to give to the people of America the new emancipation proclamation," but asserting that the president had unfinished business. There was a "challenging task" for the delegates to undertake, "because good conscience, decent morality demands it."

And now here was the part Biemiller, Henderson, and the rest had been eagerly waiting for: "I feel I must rise at this time to support a report—the minority report—a report that spells out our democracy, a report that the people of this country can and will understand, and a report that they will enthusiastically acclaim on the great issue of civil rights."

For just a moment, Humphrey attempted to soothe the South, to make it clear that this minority report was not targeting their part of the country alone, but the entire United States: "[T]his proposal is made for no single region. Our proposal is made for no single class, for no single racial or religious group in mind. All of the regions of this country, all of the states have shared in our precious heritage of American freedom. All the states and all the regions have seen at least some of the infringements of that freedom—all people—get this—all people, white and black, all groups, all racial groups have been the victims at time[s] in this nation of—let me say—vicious discrimination."

To reinforce his point (and reinforce the feeling that after such a rousing speech earlier that day, Alben Barkley was a shoo-in for VP), he quoted Thomas Jefferson, by way of Barkley: "He did not proclaim that all the white, or the black, or the red, or the yellow men are equal; that all Christian or Jewish men are equal; that all Protestant and Catholic men are equal; that all rich and poor men are equal; that all good and bad men are equal. What he declared was that all men are equal; and the equality which he proclaimed was the equality in the right to enjoy the blessings of free government in which they may participate and to which they have given their support."

For America to achieve the full promise of its role as a leader in democracy, Humphrey stated, Truman must obtain the rights of "full and equal employment opportunity," "equal opportunity of employment," "security of person," and "equal treatment in the service and defense of our nation." There were howls of derision from the southern delegates, but Humphrey continued, his florid face lined with sweat in reaction to the ire and the unabated heat in the convention hall. "There are those who say to you we are rushing this issue of civil rights. I say we are 172 years too late."

The thirty-seven-year-old then delivered the defining line of his speech and of the convention so far, slamming the southern delegates and challenging Truman to live up to the long unfulfilled potential of the Declaration of Independence and the Thirteenth Amendment: "The time has now arrived in America for the Democratic Party to get out of the shadow of states' rights and walk forthrightly into the bright sunshine of human rights."

In closing, Humphrey made it clear that there was only one man who could make good on this promise: "I ask this convention to say in unmistakable terms that we proudly hail, and we courageously support, our President and leader Harry Truman in his great fight for civil rights in America!"[87]

The result was equally explosive among Humphrey's supporters and opponents. Biemiller and the other liberals who had pleaded with Humphrey to overcome his fears and deliver just such a speech were elated.[88] Paul Douglas was moved to tears, and once he had composed himself he led his fellow Illinois delegates and those from California and New York in a parade into the aisles, soon accompanied by the forty-piece American Federation of Musicians band, whose members had not expected to play a note until Truman's arrival.[89] Joining in with their jubilation, Frank Kelly recalled himself clapping along, though he was concerned that the fallout from Humphrey's proclamation, which Kelly agreed with, would give Truman even more trouble come November.[90]

The convention voted down the South's motion by a resounding 925 to 309 margin, and then—despite the warning of Charles Block from Georgia, echoing William Jennings Bryan's famous 1896 speech, that "You shall not crucify the South on this cross of civil rights" and the assertion from Tennessee's Cecil Sims that passing the plank would cause "the dissolution of the Democratic Party in the South"—narrowly passed Humphrey's minority plank, 651½ to 582½ (in cases where a district can't agree on a convention plank, it casts half its vote for each side).[91] Thurmond, Fielding Wright, and the other southern rebels were apoplectic. Before the convention, they had held out little hope that Truman would climb down over civil rights, but they had still believed there was a chance to intimidate him by threatening to withdraw their support and leave him unelectable. Now, if the convention nominated the incumbent, he would have no choice but to run on the full-fledged civil rights plank that Humphrey and his ADA backers had just created.

Truman, again watching with Charlie Ross on a television in the Oval Office as he prepared for his train journey to Philadelphia that evening, was dumbfounded by how far Humphrey had gone, concerned that the ADA "crackpots" had all but severed ties between the mainstream party and its backward-looking members.[92] The "Solid South" was now treacherous quicksand beneath the president's feet. He was already fraught with worry that the Progressives' efforts would lose him votes in key battleground states such as New York and Henry Wallace's native Iowa, tipping the balance there in favor of Dewey—as if the Republican candidate needed the help. While the president didn't consider Strom Thurmond and the Dixiecrats to be any more of a nationwide threat than Wallace and what Truman's former commerce secretary called his "Gideon's Army," the loss of more than a couple of southern states plus the Progressives' detraction could equal Election Day disaster.[93]

Whatever his concerns, the next day Truman had to go to Convention Hall for what he hoped, what he *believed*, would be the nomination of his party that night at around 10:00 p.m. While he turned in relatively early for a man by now well accustomed to working late nights, the young men and women who had fought for and won the stronger civil rights plank he must adopt if he triumphed in Philadelphia were in no mood to sleep.

Frank Kelly's Research Division colleague, Johannes Hoeber, had also come to the convention and to see his daughter, Susanne, who had not joined her mother and brothers on a camping trip to Maine.[94] Hubert Humphrey and his ADA supporters were eager to toast their victory, but Philadelphia's puritanical liquor laws only allowed bars to serve alcohol until midnight, and it was now past 3:00 a.m. Hoeber, who knew Biemiller and the rest of the ADA crowd from his role as one of the founders of the local branch, invited them all back to his modest brick-and-white-clapboard row house on North Ninth Street. They clambered into a few cars and drove to the Hoeber home, eager for a few drinks and the chance to finally eat, given that it had been hours since they wolfed down a hurried dinner as the marathon final evening of the convention got underway. When they'd had their fill, Susanne Hoeber, who had joined in the revelry, was happy to wash the dishes but would be darned if she was going to dry them too. So she handed a towel to a surprised Hubert Humphrey and told the new star of the Democratic Party to get to work.[95]

As Humphrey's supporters poured themselves some strong coffee and slowly made their sleepy-eyed way back to their hotels, Truman's speechwriters were hard at work revising the notes for his speech. The *New York Times* had correctly reported that Truman would speak off-the-cuff to try and use the "fire, vigor and free flowing rhetoric" that he had honed since the spring to achieve "unity in the ranks of his party."[96] This approach to the pivotal speech had been Bill Batt's idea, based upon detailed analysis of past convention speeches and Truman's own addresses throughout the first half of 1948. Batt condensed his thinking about how the president should address the convention delegates in a memo to Clark Clifford on July 9, which focused on four main points:

1. It should be a fighting talk along the lines of the Young Democrats' speech and the Western trip. It should keynote the entire campaign.

2. The President should not just exude confidence, but confidence with reasons. He should give our side some good solid substance upon which to hinge the campaign arguments. Platitudes and truisms should be avoided like the pox.

3. The speech should be short—ten to fifteen minutes maximum. It should be read after thorough study.

4. The words and phrases should be short, homely and in character. This is no place for Churchillian grandiloquence.[97]

To act on Batt's recommendations and build on the first draft he penned, Clifford had called in Samuel Rosenman, a high-profile New York lawyer who had served as one of FDR's key speechwriters.[98] Clifford, Oscar Chapman, Charlie Murphy, Dave Bell, and several others also threw in their ideas.

As the last day of the convention dragged on and on and Truman's departure time from Washington kept getting pushed back, these men hunched over the great oval table in the Cabinet Room, shirt sleeves rolled up, red pens in hand, scribbling revisions on top of revisions.[99] Working off of an outline by Charlie Murphy and Batt's draft, Rosenman composed the long list of bullet points that would spur Truman's crucial oratory. Round and round it went, to versions six, seven, and eight. Finally, as the hot afternoon drifted languidly into evening, Truman's secretary Matt Connelly received a call from treasury secretary and Truman's longtime friend John Snyder, who indicated that the president should now take the train. Clifford presented Truman with the final set of notes, and they were off.[100]

Just after dinner, Truman emerged from the White House into the muggy July evening, equipped with a black leather folder containing eighteen pages of speech notes. He followed Margaret and Bess—who had flown back from Kansas City after spending time at the family home in Independence—into the broad leather back seat of a White House limousine. Once its passengers were safely in the car, the driver pulled carefully away and down Pennsylvania Avenue, heading for the waiting seven-car train at Union Station.[101] He need not have hurried, for at Convention Hall in Philadelphia, the convention was set to go far later into the night than even the late-arriving president and his advisers had predicted.

At 8:00 p.m., the states began the roll call for nominating the president. Not waiting to find out if Truman would make the ticket, thirty-five southern delegates—the entire Mississippi delegation and half of Alabama's—got up and marched out of the hall as tall, white-haired, bushy-eyebrowed Missouri governor Phil M. Donnelly was beginning his speech to nominate the president, with the CBS cameras and Ed Murrow and his team looking on. Not feeling charitable toward their ideological enemies, some of the southerners' more tolerant counterparts bellowed, "Good riddance!"[102] It was not the first time the Democratic Party had been torn asunder by civil rights. In 1860, the walkout of eight southern delegations weakened the party so much that Abraham Lincoln won a resounding victory for the Republicans in that year's election.[103]

As he contemplated whether this new southern revolt would prove equally calamitous for his Democratic Party, Truman was forsaking the meal that the rest of his entourage tucked into and instead was poring over his speech notes with Murphy. He scribbled some minor, handwritten changes with a black fountain pen as the group listened to the convention report on the radio.[104] Once he was satisfied with the messaging, Truman excused himself to his private quarters. There he changed from a gray suit into a double-breasted white linen one, which was suitably lightweight for the heat of the evening.[105] The former men's clothing store owner accented his crisply pressed suit with gleaming black and white oxfords.

Stopping for a few minutes in Wilmington, Delaware, Matt Connelly called DNC chairman J. Howard McGrath to get the lowdown on the behind-the-scenes news that the radio broadcast didn't carry.[106] Was Truman going to win the ballot? Were the Dixiecrat–draft Ike–liberal camps joining forces to stop his nomination? Connelly did not receive a definitive answer to either of these questions.

The train started back up and trundled northeast for another thirty-five miles. When it rolled to a stop at the Baltimore and Ohio Railroad station in Philadelphia, Secret Service men ushered DNC chairman J. Howard McGrath, Pittsburgh mayor David Lawrence, and Pennsylvania senator Francis Myers aboard for a brief chat with the president, as Missouri governor Phil Donnelly was halfway through his speech on the convention floor. Several thousand other people who had clamored to catch a glimpse of Truman could not get quite so close, as 150 police officers, fearing a security breach, had created an impenetrable human cordon around the perimeter of the station. They kept rank as the president and his group walked briskly across the hot concrete to six black limousines that were idling outside the station, the hum of the engines drowned out by the whoops and hollers from the crowd.[107]

Truman's motorcade arrived at Convention Hall at 9:51 p.m., and the much-needed, if light, rain shower that fell as he strode into the building offered a little relief from the Philadelphia heat wave that had settled in since the Republicans held their gathering the previous month. It was almost as if the weather was conspiring with Truman's many other enemies to keep him off the Democratic ticket.[108]

The scheduling of Truman's advisers and the convention organizers, who had predicted that the president would make his acceptance speech between 10:00 and 11:00 p.m., was way off, not least due to the furor over civil rights and the ensuing Mississippi and Alabama walkout. Truman could not abide idleness, so he made good use of the interlude by holding court with anyone who wanted to stop by the inhospitable, windowless, concrete-walled room that had been set aside for him near the back of the building, which was even more oppressive than the stifling convention floor. Among the visitors were former Chicago mayor Ed Kelly, who had lost none of his prestige since leaving that office, New York Mayor Bill O'Dwyer, who could be counted on to share some information about his state's governor and Truman's opponent, Tom Dewey, and the man who had until just days earlier led the movement to dethrone the president: James Roosevelt. He also talked with one of Thurmond's men, Alabama senator John Sparkman. Though this was likely a difficult conversation, as was the one with FDR's son, Truman assured a friend, perhaps somewhat tongue-in-cheek, "They may be mad at me but I'm not mad at them. I believe in Christ." [109]

Though he did not want to go to the convention floor until it was time to speak to the crowd, Truman did not (as was later reported) cut a lonely figure. Instead, he used the extended waiting time with the man who had emerged as the shoo-in to be his running mate, Alben Barkley. The seventy-one-year-old Kentuckian joined Truman in that air-deprived makeshift office, with the former leaning back on a leather chair acquired from the speaker's platform and the president perched on a rather less inviting wooden one. Truman's secretary Matt Connelly paced the room.[110]

When the heat, which typically didn't faze Truman given his years of hard summer toil on the family farm in blistering Midwest summers, got to be too much even for him, the men walked the short distance to a loading ramp that faced the train yard opposite the back of Convention Hall, and there they found a refreshing breeze.[111] If there was anyone in the Democratic Party camp that knew about elections, it was Barkley, who would become the oldest candidate for vice president in US history.

Their long conversation, which Truman later described as "very agreeable and instructive," was not all business. Barkley recalled later that the two meandered easily between topics, including "politics, trivia, how to bring up daughters."[112] Partway through their talk they were joined by FDR's attorney general, Homer L. Cummings, who pulled up a chair and sat with the soon-to-be running mates as they chatted and watched the trains pass by. After more than three years as president, Truman had gotten along just fine without a vice president, despite the domestic strife that now plagued him. And during his own brief spell as number two to Roosevelt, Truman's isolation from the president had made it clear that FDR certainly didn't *need* him in the role, either. Yet there was something comforting about Barkley's decades of experience, something reassuring in his fatherly manner that put Truman at ease with the man who would soon, if everything went according to plan, be his deputy.

As the evening wore on, their discourse was noisily interrupted by three loud bangs, which sent Secret Service agents and police scurrying outside to investigate. Truman and Barkley were relieved to discover that it was fireworks, not gunfire, that rudely disturbed the three men's conversation.[113]

Going into the convention, the balloting had all the potential for being equally explosive, and the partial southern walkout had given credence to that concern. Yet at 12:42 a.m., the votes were tallied and Truman had carried the day on the first ballot, garnering 948 votes to the 263 that the southern holdouts gave to the hastily nominated Richard Russell, who they had hoped would "see that the South is not crucified on the cross of the so-called civil rights program."[114]

Still, despite the certainty that Thurmond's crew had been bested, the "draft Eisenhower" instigators foiled, and the liberals, with Humphrey's bold civil rights plank, placated, Truman could not yet make it to the speaker's rostrum. It took another hour and a quarter before the procedurals abated and then, at long last, he walked into the hall to address the party, which was, his detractors be damned, still his party.

With Barkley in tow, Truman strode confidently to the platform, showing no signs of the stomach upset that had plagued him a few hours earlier or the tiredness that many politicians would have succumbed to by 2:00 a.m.[115] The sight of their president caused his supporters to cheer, the band that had celebrated Humphrey's earlier triumph struck up again and, for some odd reason, an official thought it fitting to release a passel of pigeons. The birds had no sense of ceremony or decorum and flitted around the dais, their fluttering wings knocking some of the microphones upward. Rather than displaying outrage, as a more pompous politician might, Truman's face creased in laughter. "I am sorry that [they] are in your way," he told the audience and, more so, the photographers assembled below the platform, flashbulbs ready to burst if only the birds would clear off, "but they have to be where they are because I've got to be able to see what I'm doing—as I always am able to see what I am doing."[116]

The comic interjection helped Truman to forget the expectations of the moment. He flicked through his notes, which he had removed from their leather folder and placed on the podium, one last time. When he got into his rhythm, it became clear that, on this night, he would have little need for them.

After accepting the nomination and confirming Barkley, whom he called "a great man and a great public servant," Truman indulged a little demagoguery, calling on the Democrats to "get together and beat the common enemy." The contrast between the two sides was simply defined, he believed: "[T]he Democratic Party is the people's party, and the Republican Party is the party of special interest."

He then went through the list of achievements under his administration and FDRs: greater agricultural income, increased wages, and a bipartisan foreign policy that "has been turned away permanently from isolation."

Next, he outlined the sins of the Republican-controlled Congress, which he said proved that the GOP was beholden to "special privilege." They had failed to back his initiatives on pricing controls, housing, the minimum wage, education, health care, and, as Truman channeled

Humphrey, civil rights. "I got nothing," Truman insisted. "Congress has still done nothing."

The only significant legislation that the legislators did pass, he contended, was the Taft-Hartley Act, which, instead of helping ensure the rights of working people, merely "disrupted labor-management relations and will cause strife and bitterness for years to come if it is not repealed." Though Congress couldn't or wouldn't address the pressing needs of the nation, the president contended, "they did find time to take social security benefits away from 750,000 people, and they passed that over my veto" and also passed "a rich man's tax bill" that "sticks a knife into the back of the poor."

Ironically, Truman told his listeners, the Republican platform promised to advocate for the very issues that the Eightieth Congress had failed to act on. Despite their stripping away of benefits, they had the audacity to propose boosting Social Security. "I wonder if they think they can fool the people of the United States with such poppycock as that!" Truman said.

Was he going to let the Republicans get away with this ruse? Truman asked. Certainly not.

"My duty as President requires that I use every means within my power to get the laws the people need on matters of such importance and urgency," he said. "I am therefore calling this Congress back into session July 26th. On the 26th day of July, which out in Missouri we call 'Turnip Day,' I am going to call Congress back and ask them to pass laws to halt rising prices, to meet the housing crisis—which they are saying they are for in their platform."

He then reiterated all the things the GOP claimed to be for in its platform but had actually either voted against or just ignored during the eightieth congressional session. With his recall, they would have one last chance to act constructively. Truman, and the nation, would hold them accountable: "They are going to try to dodge their responsibility. They are going to drag all the red herrings they can across this campaign, but I am here to say that Senator Barkley and I are not going to let them get away with it. Now, what that worst Eightieth Congress does in this special session will be the test. The American people will not decide by listening to mere words, or by reading a mere platform. They will decide on the record."

Hoping that those who had stayed up to hear him via a national radio broadcast were paying attention, Truman closed with an impassioned plea:

> Now my friends, with the help of God and the wholehearted push which you can put behind this campaign, we can save this country from a continuation of the Eightieth Congress, and from misrule from now on.
>
> I must have your help. You must get in and push, and win this election. The country can't afford another Republican Congress.[117]

It was telling that, in all his 2,709 words, Truman did not mention Tom Dewey or Earl Warren once. He did, however, say "Congress" twenty-four times, accompanied by "worst," "done nothing," "greed," "failed," "sabotage," "anti-Semitic," "anti-Catholic," and several other terms of indictment. This tactic would set the pattern for the campaign to come.

Truman's approach certainly hit its mark among the delegates, who gave him a thirty-eight-minute standing ovation that even eclipsed the ones Barkley and Humphrey enjoyed.[118] They were a far different bunch now from what Truman's assistant David Bell called "a tired, dispirited, soggy mass of beaten humanity" before the president stepped to the microphone.[119] One delegate was most impressed with Truman's defiance and willingness to go toe-to-toe with the so-called Republican "dream ticket" of Tom Dewey and Earl Warren. "You can't stay cold about a man who sticks his chin out and fights," the newly impassioned Democrat said.[120] Venerated NBC radio commentator Earl Godwin told Truman's secretary Matt Connelly, "I never heard a better political speech. This should do it."[121]

A party "insider" told the *Washington Daily News* that Truman's special session call had put the GOP in an impossible position: "It's a case of heads he wins, tails they lose."[122] Despite his preconvention backing of Eisenhower, New York mayor William O'Dwyer told reporters after the president's speech that he had a strong "feeling" Truman would prevail come November.[123]

It wasn't just veteran politicians who left the buzzing convention hall with a new appreciation for the president. After giving sixteen of his students a month to experience the arts in New York, the headmaster of exclusive Landhaven School in Camden, Maine, had driven his pupils to the convention to expose them to the on-the-ground happenings of election season. At least one of the boys was impressed with Truman's performance. "He's really quite dynamic," he told a *Time* reporter. "I hadn't realized it before."[124]

Though the Republican Party slammed Truman, with Iowa congressman Ben Jensen claiming "he is reaching for the last straw and is not fit to be President" and another Republican saying the Turnip Day session was "the last act of a desperate man," some in the media, until now almost unanimously dismissive of Truman's chances, gave the president credit this time.[125] "It was a great speech for a great occasion," declared liberal columnist Max Lerner, while Clayton Knowles, writing in the *New York Times*, thought that "President Truman got in the first good punch of the 1948 campaign."[126]

Bill Batt, watching from Washington, was ecstatic.[127] Just hours after Truman arrived back at the White House at 4:10 a.m., the Research Division director cabled Clifford this breathless message:

> Congratulations to you, and Charlie, Dave and George. Entire speech was superb. Best yet. You were 100 percent right on off the cuff decision. Special session idea electrified convention. Illinois delegate, Philadelphia committeeman, Harvard student, everyone we quizzed returning from convention unanimously enthusiastic about special session.
>
> I am completely confident the Boss has hit the comeback trail and we will see a reversal of today's Dewey Truman standings within six weeks. Taking weekend off unless you need me before Monday. Regards,
>
> Bill[128]

Certainly, Batt was blowing his own horn over the success of the special session proposal in Democratic circles, with two mentions in as many sentences. And yet all his anecdotal evidence and press reports agree that Truman's very-late-night address had indeed continued the momentum gained from the speeches of Hubert Humphrey and Alben Barkley, while showing Thomas Dewey that if he wanted the White House, he would have to fight to get it.

The next day, Batt sent a second message to Clifford with several press clippings that reacted favorably to Truman's acceptance speech. Doris Fleeson of the *Washington Star* believed that Dewey was put in an uncomfortable position by the special session, as Batt himself had predicted in his June 29 memo. Batt went on to write, "As for the second column by Lowell Mellett [it] indicates that the Southern revolt smells less of magnolia than it does of crude oil."[129]

Indeed, the walkout of thirty-five southern delegates during the Democratic Convention was only the beginning of the fallout from below the Mason-Dixon line. It had been bad enough for the Dixiecrats when Truman had spoken to the NAACP on June 29, 1947, and far worse when he had spoken of the results from the Civil Rights Committee's report during his 1948 State of the Union address. But now, with the events of Philadelphia, the issue had been elevated from what some Democrats in the South had considered the harmless folly of a president doomed to electoral defeat to the official platform of their party, with a seemingly resurgent Truman at its head. Though his odds for victory in November were still long, Truman had won the nomination comfortably, defied the "draft Eisenhower" dissidents, and captured the imagination of the delegates, large sections of the press and, arguably, the nation.

Truman, of course, had not acted in isolation. The minority report introduced by Vaughan and the Dawson address that followed had put kindling in the grate, and the rousing civil rights speech from Hubert Humphrey, prompted by Biemiller and his ADA crew, had added the logs needed to sustain a roaring fire. But it was the president who had tossed in the match to set the tinder ablaze and then blown the bellows.

Thurmond was under no illusion that he and the rest of the Dixiecrat leaders could frighten Truman into caving on civil rights. After the NAACP address, the president had seen the ecstatic reaction of the ten thousand who had gathered on the steps of the Lincoln Memorial, which was not a coincidental choice of venue. It had further convinced him of the rightness of his position, so when he turned to NAACP executive secretary Walter White and told him he had meant "every word of it—and I'm going to prove that I do mean it," he had not been pandering.[130] If he was going to back down, Thurmond knew, it would have happened before the convention. When a reporter asked Thurmond if Truman was proposing going beyond FDR's civil rights agenda, the 103rd Governor of South Carolina noted the distinction, unwittingly echoing the president's pledge to White: "Yes—but Truman really *means* it."[131]

But whatever the president's resolve, the southern Democrats were eager to show that they meant what *they* said about never allowing Truman or any other president to end segregation in the South. On July 17, Alabama governor Jim Folson and Theophilus Eugene "Bull" Connor, the Birmingham commissioner of public safety (a post that gave him control of the city's police) and the man who had led the Mississippi and Alabama walkout at the convention in Philadelphia, welcomed more than six thousand people to the Municipal Auditorium in Birmingham, Alabama.[132] They had answered Mississippi governor Fielding L. Wright's call for "every man and woman who believes in states' rights and who opposes Harry S. Truman and the things he stands for" to attend.[133] Once there, this boisterous crowd waved Confederate flags, held up portraits of Robert E. Lee, and sporadically launched into the refrain of "Dixie." Frank M. Dixon, Folson's predecessor, accused Truman of wanting to use his civil rights program against whites in the South, "to reduce us to the status of a mongrel, inferior race."[134]

Some prominent southern Democrats refused to take part in this breakaway movement, including Richard Russell, who had been the region's protest candidate in Philadelphia. Harry F. Byrd, the Virginia senator, had vocally criticized Truman's supposed meddling in states' rights before the convention, but he refused to align himself with Wright, Connor, Thurmond, and the other rebels who gathered in Birmingham.[135] A group of Mississippi students were not so loyal to their president or the Democratic Party as Byrd and Russell, chanting "To hell with Truman" over and over.[136]

In vowing to defeat Truman and Dewey, both of whom supposedly wanted a "police state," the newly formed States' Rights Democratic Party created a "Declaration of Principles," which slammed the president for his "infamous and iniquitous program [of] equal access to all public accommodations for persons of all races, colors, creeds and national origins."[137] The raucous attendees nominated Thurmond as their first presidential candidate and Wright—who after Truman's 1948 State of the Union address had called the president's ten-point civil rights program "a stab in the back" for the South—as Thurmond's running mate. With his close-cropped, side-parted silver hair, and round-rimmed glasses, Wright physically resembled Truman, but other than their appearance and Democratic affiliation—which for Wright, it seemed, was now at an end—the similarities between the two ended.

Though he did not formally accept the breakaway party's nomination that evening, Thurmond gave what sounded like an acceptance speech. Just days before, he had cautioned his fellow delegates against holding such a meeting so soon after the Democratic National Convention. But now that his status had, at least in notion, changed from Strom Thurmond, governor of South Carolina to Strom Thurmond, would-be president, the forty-six-year-old (who was younger than Tom Dewey by just nine months) got caught up in the fervor of the occasion. Continuing Dixon's defiant tone, he told the wildly cheering crowd, "Truman has forced himself upon the Democratic Party but he cannot force himself on the people of this great country."[138] Then, the adrenaline from the applause urging him on like a bolting horse, he went even further, asserting that "there's not enough troops in the army to force the southern people to break down segregation and admit the nigger race into our swimming pools, our homes, and into our churches."[139]

If the states' rights crowd thought they had Truman on the back foot with such aggressive rhetoric or after nominating Thurmond and Wright and continuing to disparage the president in the press, they were soon disabused of this overly optimistic notion. On July 26, the same day he opened the Turnip Day session of Congress, Truman acted decisively on two of the ten civil rights points he had outlined back in February.

Thumbing his nose at Thurmond and his States' Rights Party backers, Truman issued Executive Order 9980, which stated that "the principles on which our Government is based require a policy of fair employment throughout the Federal establishment, without discrimination because of race, color, religion, or national origin . . . it is desirable and in the public interest that all steps be taken necessary to insure that this long-established policy shall be more effectively carried out." Going on to outline these steps, Truman included that all personnel decisions would be based on merit, each government department head would be held accountable for fair employment practices, and each department would have a Fair Employment Officer to ensure discrimination was eliminated.[140]

By no means done for the day, Truman also issued Executive Order 9981, which desegregated the US armed forces with a single bold statement: "It is hereby declared to be the policy of the President that there shall be equality of treatment and opportunity for all persons in the armed services without regard to race, color, religion, or national origin."[141] To ensure this principle was implemented, the order also established the Committee on Equality of Treatment and Opportunity in the Armed Forces. Truman issued a firm statement about why he had taken such decisive action, saying that he issued the regulation "in order to make the guarantees of the Constitution real and vital." He then told Congress, "I believe they are necessary to carry out our American ideals of liberty and justice for all."[142]

The orders, which were the most significant concerning civil rights in a generation, received a rapturous reception from black leaders, with Harlem politico Herbert L. Bruce pledging to raise a million dollars to help Truman win in November, which would "serve as the Negro's contribution in the fight to make the Truman civil rights program a living reality."[143]

Predictably, the anti-civil-rights contingent in the South was mortified at the adoption of such orders and took the opposite position to Bruce's. It was not just the decrees themselves, but also Truman's use of presidential edict to breathe them into being, which the Dixiecrats saw as yet more justification for branding him an authoritarian who shunned democratic process and imposed federal mandates on the South by decree.[144] Richard Russell, who had won 263 votes as the South's protest candidate against Truman at the Democratic National Convention and who on the day of Truman's declaration was meeting with nineteen southern senators to discuss the next steps of their rebellion against the president, channeled Churchill as he told a reporter, "We will never surrender." Truman, on the other hand, had given in, Russell thought, with the executive orders being proof that the president had issued an "unconditional surrender" to Henry Wallace's progressives.[145]

The Dixiecrats were not alone in their criticism of the president. His Republican opponents quickly accused him of political opportunism, with GOP Senate leader Kenneth S. Wherry saying that Truman "knows he can't get a civil rights bill, so he's making these gestures to get the Negro vote" and Wisconsin junior senator Joseph McCarthy wryly declaring, "You can certainly tell the campaign has started."[146] Even General Omar Bradley chimed in, stating that he supported segregation in lower Army ranks: "The Army is not out to make any social reforms," the World War II hero said. "The army will put men of different races in different companies. It will change that policy when the nation as a whole changes it."[147]

Whatever his indignation may have been in reaction to such comments, Truman could not allow the South's condemnation or his general's defiance to distract him from his pressing business on Capitol Hill. He had taken a much-needed welcome jaunt down the Potomac on the presidential yacht *Williamsburg*, on which he spent a lazy weekend and was so tired he "slept almost around the clock" from Friday to Saturday lunchtime.[148] But once back on shore, Truman was determined to press the Eightieth Congress into either acting to pass reform on housing, Social Security, health care, education, and the other main issues on his domestic agenda or admitting that their liberal platform was but an imitation of his own, a sleight of hand designed to confuse undecided voters to abandon the president. In a statement to the press following Truman's opening remarks to Congress, Howard McGrath eloquently encapsulated the Research Division's reasoning for advocating a special session: "What is done to achieve the President's recommendations will be a testing of our patriotism. What is not done will be a proof of our partisanship."[149]

Certainly, Truman did not show much faith in his fellow politicians to put patriotism above partisanship or, in a rare gloomy moment, his own prospects when he wrote to his sister, Mary, the day that he signed the executive orders and opened the Turnip Day session:

> It's all so futile. Dewey, Wallace, the cock-eyed Southerners and then if I win—and I fear I will, I'll probably have a Russian war on my hands. Two wars are enough for anybody and I've had two.
>
> I go to Congress tomorrow and read them a message requesting price control, housing and a lot of other necessary things and I'll in all probability get nothing. But I've got to try.[150]

At least the Democratic congressmen who would push Truman's proposals to their recalled peers would be well-equipped. The weekend before the special session began, Matt Connelly called Bill Batt from the White House, telling the already overworked Research Division chief that he needed talking points for all the legislation pitches by 10 a.m. on Monday, July 26. Kenneth Birkhead pulled an all-night work session and his colleagues nearly matched him as they raced to meet the deadline, which was ambitious even by the demanding standards of their day-to-day assignments. They worked through Sunday as well, and then dictated their work to their frantically scribbling secretaries, who couriered the packages to Connelly's office just in time.[151]

It soon became apparent that their hard work would be in vain if passing meaningful legislation was the goal and that the divide between the traditional and reformist wings of the Republican Party would indeed complicate matters. Though moderate Republicans, including Warren, Dewey, and Arthur Vandenberg, tried to convince the old guard element of the party to make some concessions, Robert Taft, in keeping with his position that the Republican Party must provide strong opposition to Truman's liberalism, refused to flex even one millimeter. "No! We're not going to give that fellow anything!" the Ohio man blustered when his colleagues advised that the GOP pass just a couple of conciliatory bills.[152]

And so it went. Truman, as Batt had recommended to Clifford, called for the GOP-controlled Congress to do something about each of the domestic plank issues, saying in the opening remarks, "The urgent needs of the American people require our presence here today."[153] In urging Congress to take "positive action" on every point he had outlined in the State of the Union—and which the Research Division was focusing its Files of the Facts—he tempted the GOP to prove that it was serious about enacting the liberal reforms it had proposed just weeks earlier in Philadelphia. And he did so with an elegant ending to his speech on the 26th, telling those in the chamber, "The vigor of our democracy is judged by its ability to take decisive actions—actions which are necessary to maintain our physical and moral strength and to raise our standards of living. In these days of continued stress, the test of that vigor becomes more and more difficult. The legislative and executive branches of our government can meet that test today. The American people rightly expect us to meet it together. I hope that the American people will not look to us in vain."[154]

But despite the opportunity to work constructively with Truman for the first time and, more importantly with the election looming, the potential of inflicting yet another embarrassing public relations defeat on the president by confounding him and actually ratifying meaningful legislation at the Turnip Day session, the GOP backed Taft's demand for resistance.[155] The Research Division had planned for the Democrats to try a few tricks, Johannes Hoeber revealed to his wife in a letter: "60 Democrats will march to the speaker's table to sign the discharge petition for the T-E-W [Taft-Ellender-Wagner] Bill. That may be the only bill that passes."[156] But contrary to Hoeber's hopes, there would be no meaningful bills coming out of this less than special session.

Dewey, for his part, wanted to avoid Truman's linking him with congressional inaction and so wanted passage of a few token bills. But Dewey couldn't risk further widening the gap between himself and the more conservative wing of the party by publicly criticizing them or opposing their opposition in the House and Senate.[157] And besides, for all his good intentions, Dewey wasn't a congressman. So he remained on the periphery, largely mute in the media and focusing on campaign planning for his own train tour, which would follow parts of Truman's route and would soon be dubbed the Victory Special.[158]

As Dewey was taking a back seat, another would-be president, Henry Wallace, was receiving widespread criticism as the third political convention to come to Philadelphia, that of the Progressive Party, wound down. In his July 24 speech to accept the fledgling group's nomination, with Idaho senator Glen Taylor as his running mate, Wallace had urged that the United States withdraw from Berlin, calling the western occupation zone "a colony."[159] The Progressive platform also demanded an end to the Marshall Plan and Truman Doctrine. In its place would be a peace plan based, ambitiously, on Wallace's recent conversation with Stalin in Moscow. At home, Wallace and his supporters asked for some of the same things Truman had demanded of the Eightieth Congress, including widespread provision for low-income housing, racial equality, and more labor-friendly legislation to replace the Taft-Hartley Act. But Wallace went further left than Truman domestically, proposing the nationalization of American industry and vowing, as the supposed political heir to Thomas Jefferson, to eradicate the "ghosts of the Great Depression, the banking house boys and the oil-well diplomats" that Truman had let infiltrate the government.[160]

If the mainstream press was still largely against the president, it was even harsher on Wallace in the wake of his speech to twenty-five thousand in a muggy Shibe Park, the Philadelphia baseball stadium. Joseph and Stewart Alsop said he had given a "ghoulish performance" that was not befitting of a former vice president, and they dismissed the third party as nothing more than "a Communist front organization."[161] An editorial in the *Milwaukee Journal* insisted that Wallace's domestic policies were "a masterpiece of political insincerity, fraud and contradiction" and charged that "the Wallacites stand for a craven and abject peace at any price policy" that would "go to any lengths to appease Soviet Russia." [162] In his *New York Times* column, Arthur Krock dismissed the Progressive caucus as a "tragi-comedy" put on by "the Communist engineering corps" and lamented that the party seemed to lack any real policies but was instead basing its platform on a "cunning play on everyone's grievances." [163]

Truman should have been able to capitalize on the media's cruel indictment of Wallace, but instead he was soon bedeviled by yet another calamity that threatened to hinder his campaign planning or put him further behind Dewey in the polls. On July 30, Elizabeth Bentley, a former communist spy, told a congressional subcommittee that she had received classified information from more than thirty government officials. To make matters worse, she repeated this explosive testimony less than twenty-four hours later in front of the House Un-American Activities Committee (HUAC). Those implicated included William W. Remington, a Treasury Department official, and Harry Dexter White, formerly in that department and more recently a US emissary to the International Monetary Fund. And with many more witnesses scheduled to appear in front of the HUAC in the coming weeks, Washington was abuzz with rumors and scuttlebutt on who might be next on the list of "pinkies." [164] The press had a field day, with the *New York World Telegram* boasting the most sensational headline: "Red Ring Bared by Its Blond Queen." It was also the least factual, as Bentley was actually a brunette. [165]

Truman knew that the fallout from the communist scandal was likely to go on well into the election campaign, despite any attempts he made to divert attention by red-baiting Wallace and the Progressives. [166] Yet on the last day of July, the calendar promised a welcome break from the controversy, the frustrating gridlock of the Turnip Day Congress session, and planning for the Whistle Stop Tour. The occasion was the dedication of the new Idlewild International Airport in New York City. Whatever the president's newfound comfort behind a microphone, the Research Division could not risk Truman delivering a speech without notes at this high-stakes event. It was likely to be the only meeting between the president and his would-be usurper, and Truman had to be on top form to upstage Dewey in his backyard. If he could do so in this crucial battleground state, he could gain vital votes over the governor of New York, who was the firm favorite to defeat Truman there.

So Bill Batt went to work, drafting a full, three-page address for Truman, which he rushed to Clark Clifford in plenty of time for him, Elsey, and Chapman to review it.[167] Batt also attached a compare-and-contrast piece on the differing tactics of Truman and his Republican challenger. In his opening lines, the Research Division director appraised Dewey's difficulties with the Turnip Day and any domestic legislation it may yield:

> They keep him out of the limelight, he is forgotten. The limelight is
>   on a battle between the President and the Congress.
> Dewey suffers because in this special session, the Republicans are
>   damned if they do and damned if they don't.
> Dewey is in a horrible dilemma. If he speaks, the Congress
>   Republicans resent it. If he doesn't, the country resents it.[168]

Batt concluded that because of these factors, Dewey would seek to frighten voters by implying that Truman and Marshall's foreign policy was increasing the risk of war. Truman could avoid "playing into Dewey's hands," Batt believed, by stating his commitment to the maintenance of peace and then turning the focus back on domestic issues. He then listed the issues that were at the heart of the special session and, in a larger sense, of Truman's campaign, which he thought would appeal to New York voters.[169]

For minorities, Truman's civil rights plans and intent to increase foreign immigration to four hundred thousand would be key. Price controls and housing provisions were also essential messaging points due to the lack of affordable homes in New York City and the state as a whole. A tenth of the population were "depressed people," Batt stated, so Truman's push for broadening Social Security and increasing the minimum wage would hit home. A congressional loan to build the UN headquarters in the Big Apple would give New Yorkers a sense of renewed pride. The president would do well to also mention foreign aid through the international wheat agreement and link this to domestic farming policy to win over the state's substantial agricultural population.[170]

In closing, Batt affirmed that these points would not just appeal to the crowd at Idlewild, but also to the nation. "And they can be emphasized in the place where television and movie cameras show Dewey listening, jammed right in a corner he cannot escape from."[171]

Dewey would have seven minutes to speak to New York and the nation (via radio), followed by ten for Truman, and Fitzpatrick believed these "could very easily be the most important ten minutes in the entire campaign. I hope he will take advantage of the occasion." The author of the memo summarizing and commenting on Fitzpatrick's missive thought that not only would Truman's airport dedication speech enable him to go on the offensive against Dewey, but it would also raise questions in voters' minds about the reserved, vague address that the Republican candidate would likely deliver at the same venue. Chief among these, the writer bluntly predicted, would be, "What does that timid, super-cautious apotheosis of silence think about the President's views?"[172]

On July 31, Truman took the fifty-two-minute flight from Washington to Idlewild in his plane, *The Independence*. There to greet him were some friends and foes from Congress, delegations from thirty nations and, perhaps more importantly on this occasion, a grinning Thomas E. Dewey. As Truman descended the metal steps, clad in a flawless double-breasted tan suit and holding his fedora with his left hand to prevent the mischievous wind from whisking it across the tarmac, he used his right to grip Dewey's outstretched hand. As the two men, who were roughly the same height, stood eye to eye, they spoke in the cordial yet clipped tones that rival politicians are expected to perfect for such occasions. "I'm glad to welcome you here," Dewey said, making it clear who was on familiar ground. "It's nice to see you again," Truman replied, matching Dewey's smile.[173]

As the afternoon moved forward, the analysis of Batt and Fitzgerald proved to be correct. Truman received a twenty-one-gun salute and watched with Dewey from a steel observation deck as US Air Force fighters and bombers (including the new and formidable B-36) flew in formation overhead for thirty minutes in what was billed as the biggest display of air power since the end of World War II.[174] The president then listened as his Republican opponent used his usual combination of vague statements and unimaginative imagery, albeit delivered in a pleasingly sonorous timbre. Dewey called the airport "a symbol of peace" and then repeated himself moments later, saying it was "a powerful implement for peace."[175]

Following Dewey to the microphone, Truman invoked similar sentiments, though his term for the new airfield was a little more original: "the front door of the United Nations." As Batt had suggested, the president not only focused considerable time on New York being the permanent home of the UN, but he also told the 215,000 in attendance at the five thousand-acre site and the audience listening across the country by radio that one of the keys to maintaining international peace through the world organization was economic recovery.

Though he did not go into the specific Democratic plank details that Batt had hoped for, Truman did include a couple of the Research Director's points about agriculture and industry:

> The American people are doing their best to bring about recovery by sharing the products of our factories and fields, and by lending the money necessary to revive industry and agriculture in other countries.
>
> We welcome Idlewild Airport because it will help so greatly in the free and rapid exchange of goods. This is the essence of international trade and prosperity.
>
> Once the devastation of war has been repaired, the countries of the world can produce enough for everybody. With the knowledge we now have about medicine, and agriculture, and the many other sciences, the danger of war which comes from mass poverty should vanish forever.[176]

Dewey's performance, though dull and repetitious, had not been a disaster. He had also played the role of gracious host and had come across as the gentleman that he undoubtedly was. But Dewey was also, for all the media hype, still the candidate in waiting. Truman had spoken on behalf of his nation in a statesmanlike address that had defused the election campaign attacks that Bill Batt predicted Dewey would mount over foreign policy.[177] It was Truman, not Dewey, who had taken the bold action that ended the war. Though Dewey had welcomed the legion of foreign dignitaries, it was Truman they had greeted as head of state. And it was Truman who, as commander-in-chief, had presided over an aerial show of strength that not only wowed the crowd but also sent a message to Moscow that although the American armed services had demobilized, they were far from diminished.

With a pivotal speech that eclipsed Dewey's behind him and the start of the fall Whistle Stop Tour ahead, Truman flew directly from Idlewild to Missouri. There he would vote in the Democratic primary the following Tuesday and then spend a last few relaxing days at home in Independence before returning to Washington to finalize his plan for the unrelenting, sixty-three-day war for the White House that he would unleash from the rails on September 1.[178]

July had seen Truman punctuate his party's nomination with arguably his finest presidential speech. He had also issued two executive orders that achieved meaningful advances in civil rights, and, with the Turnip Day session nearing almost certain stalemate, was well on the way to proving that the Republican Congress had no intentions of sticking to the Republican platform. And yet, as the last muggy days of July passed away, Truman was mired in the communists-in-government scandal, further derided by the States' Rights, Progressive, and Republican Parties, and trailing Dewey by double digits in all major polls. With just one month to go until Truman's train, the Last Chance Special, took the campaign to the nation, could he use the August intermission to plan a successful comeback, even as he tried to keep a lid on the boiling pot of Berlin and prevent the Democratic Party from splintering yet further?

August

Truman began August as he had ended July, presiding over a Congress chamber full of disgruntled members who, Democrats and Republicans alike, would rather have been enjoying their summer break and, in the case of the GOP old guard, who were determined to end the special session with less than special results. Frustrated, tired, and thoroughly sick of the fractious atmosphere in Washington, the president flew to Independence to spend the first weekend of the month with his family and away from his opponents.

As Truman journeyed to his home state, the Research Division team was holed up for another long weekend's work. Within days the skeleton crew would be bolstered by the arrival of another skilled wordsmith and rhetorician, thirty-seven-year-old Harvard Law School graduate David Lloyd. In addition to his distinguished academic career, this witty, well-groomed New Yorker—who while working sported fashionable Clubmaster eyeglasses and a trim black suit—had proven his worth as counsel to several Senate committees, the Mission for Economic Affairs in 1945 and 1946 and as director of research and legislation for the ADA.[1] In addition to wanting Lloyd's expertise on economics, Batt also welcomed the lawyer's input on civil liberties.[2]

But on this weekend, as Batt awaited Clifford's approval of his petition for Lloyd and the Research Division staff beavered away without Lloyd in their sweaty, cramped, and noisy offices, the Batt group was blown off course—for at least a few hours—by some unwelcome attention. Anthony Leviero, the veteran reporter who had been with the *New York Times* since the Wall Street crash and had taken over the White House beat in late 1947, somehow got wind of the Research Division's role in Truman's campaign planning.[3] It was no secret that the Republican National Committee had such a team as part of Dewey's highly structured election machine, but the DNC had tried its best to keep its own more secret weapon under wraps. It was not to be. Leviero filed a story titled "Something New Is Added at the White House," and now the world would know how Truman was getting the information for each of his tour stops.

"They are zealous liberals, part of a new crop of New Dealers," Leviero wrote in the story, which Research Division assistant director Johannes Hoeber later called "a bombshell."[4] Leviero continued, "The research group has been doing spade work to produce materials that has found its way into the Party's and the Administration's pronouncements on such issues as the anti-inflation program and housing. These are the men and means that will assist Mr. Truman in his aim to reach the people. Mr. Truman believes that all he needs to do to win is to talk plainly to the average voter."[5]

On August 3, Truman was himself just an average voter, at least for a few hours. He was, predictably, the first one up in his fourteen-room, Victorian-style whiteboard house on the leafy, everyone-knows-everyone Delaware Street in Independence that he had called home for almost thirty years. Leaving the house quietly a little after 7 a.m. so as not to wake Bess or Margaret, who didn't share her father's fondness for rising with the sun, Truman walked a block and a half to Memorial Hall to cast his ballot in Missouri's Democratic primary election. He then drove to the Fairfax airport in Kansas City, Kansas, and his DC-6 plane was wheels up before 8 a.m., bound for Washington. One reporter asked if he had a lunchtime appointment at the White House. "I might have," he replied coyly.[6]

Whatever Truman's social plans were, his attention was soon wrenched back to the unpleasant business at hand. The same day that he returned from his weekend trip home, the House Un-American Activities Committee invited testimony from *Time* editor Whittaker Chambers. Hunched over the microphones in the committee chamber, sweat on his wide brow, the short, jowly newsman admitted being a former member of a communist group in Washington. This was bad enough, but Chambers then proceeded to identify Nathan Witt and Alger Hiss as two of several government insiders who had spied for Moscow. The mustachioed, tousle-haired Witt followed degrees from New York University and Harvard Law School with a position at the National Labor Relations Board and was promoted to chairman in 1937, a post he held for three years before resigning following accusations of communist sympathizing. As a State Department director, Hiss (who like Witt was also a Harvard man) had helped organize American involvement in the Yalta Conference, contributed to planning the San Francisco council of foreign ministers, and coauthored the UN Charter.[7] These revelations could only be bad for Truman and his hopes of winning the election.

Chambers went on to reveal to the lawmakers, who looked on in dismay from behind their long table opposite the witness, that Harry Dexter White, former assistant secretary of the treasury and now a US representative to the nascent International Monetary Fund, was "certainly" a communist who had, like Hiss, resisted Chambers' efforts to pull him away from the subversive organization. Chambers had tried to reveal the extent of the communist web in 1939, he claimed, but was ignored by Roosevelt's officials.[8]

Chambers' testimony was a full-blown catastrophe for Truman. Communism in government had been an issue since the previous presidential election, during which an uncharacteristically harsh Thomas Dewey claimed that the administration of his opponent, FDR, "has been taken over by the combination of big city bosses, Communists and fellow travelers."[9] And since Roosevelt's passing, the Republicans had also accused Truman of looking the other way as communists infiltrated his administration, claims that increased in frequency and harshness during the runup to the 1946 midterms.

Republican National Committee chairman Carroll Reece had insisted that there were "pink puppets in control of the federal bureaucracy," and Joseph Martin, the pugilistic GOP leader in the House, swore up and down that his party would do better than the Democrats at "cleaning out the Communists, their fellow travelers and parlor pinks from high positions in our Government."[10] The GOP's stinging campaign rhetoric was just the beginning. The Seventy-Ninth Congress had overseen just four investigations into communism in government, but the Eightieth had done far more than "nothing" on the issue, launching twenty-two probes into it.[11]

Truman himself had stoked the anticommunist fire. He could handle being dismissed as dumb or inexperienced, but he would not abide accusations of weakness or inaction. Motivated by the Republican barbs and a desire to look like he was in control, he set up the Temporary Commission on Employee Loyalty shortly after his party lost both houses to the GOP in the 1946 midterms. As a result of this body's findings, Truman announced a new loyalty program in March 1947 to investigate every federal employee.

His executive order merely spurred on the HUAC to intensify its investigations into possible "reds." It also prompted the creation of other committees charged with uncovering "disloyalty," issuing disciplinary measures, and hearing appeals. In addition, Truman's measure authorized relentless FBI director J. Edgar Hoover, who hardly needed encouragement to expand the powers of his organization or stoke his own ego, to investigate any federal employee suspected of being disloyal to the United States. Hoover and the HUAC also saw Truman's mandate as justification to not only compile dossiers on more than two million government staffers, but also to investigate Hollywood and just about any other area of American society in which "disloyal" threats to the nation might lurk in the shadows.[12]

To some critics, this was an unquestionable abuse of power, unparalleled since John Adams' congressional allies passed the wildly controversial Sedition Act in 1798, which prompted outrage from James Madison, Thomas Jefferson, and others worried about the federal government overstepping its boundaries. Jefferson claimed that the Sedition Act proved his Federalist rivals "mean to pay no respect" to the Constitution, while Madison worried that it removed the "right of freely examining public characters and measures, and of free communication among the people."[13] Now, 150 years later, David Lilienthal, head of the Atomic Energy Commission and later himself a target of the HUAC, worried that Truman's so-called "loyalty" scheme meant that "the usual rule that men are presumed innocent until proved guilty is in reverse."[14]

Charges that the Democrats, despite Truman's measures and his commitment to a strong, anticommunist foreign policy, were still being "soft on Communism"—as Truman's nemesis Robert Taft put it—were not just leveled at the Democratic Party.[15] By mid-1948, it was also widely believed that "reds" were driving Henry Wallace's Progressives to the far left. Certainly, communists and "fellow travelers" were vying for control of some of the most powerful trade unions in the country with those noncommunist progressives who supported workers' rights and still believed in capitalism.[16] But Chambers' incendiary accusations weren't leveled at Wallace or the leaders of the CIO, Teamsters, or AFL (communist or not), but rather at people connected to the White House, both during FDR's presidency and Truman's. And though he had admitted his own temporary "disloyalty" and worked for Henry Luce, a longtime Truman critic, Chambers' standing as an editor at one of the nation's most widely read publications gave his claims credence, as did the fact that Elizabeth Bentley, an alleged communist spy, had also accused Dexter White, the US representative to the IMF. Certainly the gloating HUAC chairman Karl Mundt—a Republican congressman from South Dakota and a longtime Truman belligerent who had proposed an Adams-like bill demanding that the Communist Party and its affiliates in the United States register with the attorney general—thought so. After the hearing he told reporters, "Slowly and surely we're piecing together this pattern of Communist conspiracy to a gullible and rather indifferent America, to show it is a fact that 'it can happen here.'"[17]

Two days after Chambers spilled his dirty secrets to the HUAC, Hiss appeared before the committee and emphatically refuted the editor's accusations. With his sharp, handsome features and his lean frame clad in a trim-fitting khaki suit that accentuated his ramrod-straight posture, Hiss was the opposite of the husky, slouching Chambers in appearance and manner. Looking at the committee members unflinchingly, he said, "I am not and never have been a member of the Communist Party. I do not and never have adhered to the tenets of the Communist Party. I am not and never have been a member of any Communist-front organization. I have never followed the Communist Party line, directly or indirectly. To the best of my knowledge, none of my friends is a Communist."[18]

The HUAC had not yet become the House equivalent of the Senate's Government Operations Committee witch hunters later led by Joseph McCarthy, who began his anti-red crusade in earnest in 1950. But the group, dominated by arch-conservative Republicans, was far more high-profile than the wartime Truman Committee had been, and whereas Truman had warned his fellow committee members to avoid grandstanding as they uncovered abuses in military spending, the leaders of HUAC courted publicity as they tried to smoke out communists.[19] So McCarthy and his cohorts were unwilling to let the Hiss matter drop, despite Truman's refusal to hand over what he called "government loy-alty papers" and his assertion that the investigation was "a red herring" designed to mask the failures of Republican lawmakers to address hous-ing, inflation, and the other major issues facing the campaign and the country.[20]

HUAC committee member John McDowell, a Republican from Penn-sylvania, was convinced otherwise, claiming that atomic material had been flown from the United States to Russia as part of communist ac-tivities on domestic soil in 1943, which he insisted were still rampant.[21] Truman's myriad opponents outside the committee chamber were no more forgiving than was the HUAC. Senator Homer Ferguson of Michi-gan, never a friend of Truman, was the president's harshest critic. Slam-ming Truman's intention to hang onto the loyalty scheme records instead of giving them up to McCarthy's men, he fumed that the Missourian was trying to put up "an iron curtain between Congress and the public busi-ness." Truman was steering the country toward "centralized executive dictatorship," Ferguson said, and threatened to impeach him if things didn't change in a hurry.[22]

The problems that the domestic communism fracas posed for Truman overshadowed the rare good news he received about communism abroad on August 5. Following a visit to the Kremlin by US diplomats, the Red Army stopped enforcing the Berlin Blockade, allowing food, raw materi-als, and aid to enter and leave the American, British, and French zones for the first time in weeks. Furthermore, the Soviets also unfroze the bank accounts of the anticommunist Berlin city government, enabling it to make last-minute payments needed to keep the public sector going in the fractured German capital.[23]

If Truman gained temporary satisfaction from the improved situation in Berlin, he could afford no such ease with his own household affairs on Pennsylvania Avenue. When he first assumed the presidency he had "felt like the moon, the stars, and all the planets had fallen on me."[24] But now it wasn't the celestial bodies that were menacing him, but the ground be-neath his feet. Or, more specifically, Margaret's feet. Early in the second week of August he wrote to his sister, Mary Jane: "The White House is still about to fall in. Margaret's sitting room floor broke in two but didn't fall through the family dining room ceiling. They propped it up and fixed it.

Now my bathroom is about to fall into the Red Parlor. They won't let me sleep in my bed or use the bath. I am using Old Abe's bed and it is very comfortable."[25]

Truman likely wished that the floor *would* swallow his opponents in Congress.[26] With just forty-eight hours to go until the two-week Turnip Day gathering dissolved, Truman had given the Republicans one last chance to act, saying, "There is still time for the Congress to fulfill its responsibilities to the American people. Our people will not be satisfied with the feeble compromises that are apparently being concocted."[27] Yet such compromises were all that he or the nation would get from the obstinate GOP Congress. This despite Truman's note to himself stating that he'd made a last-gasp effort "to get some fighting spirit into them" and DNC chairman Howard McGrath challenging Dewey to stop "assiduously saying nothing" and persuade his fellow Republicans to pass a strong anti-inflation bill.[28]

Truman wasn't surprised by the lack of action. Other than securing a loan for the permanent home of the United Nations in New York and boosting sales of turnip seeds in his home state, calling Congress back had, at least on the surface, achieved little in terms of legislation.[29] Truman wrote to his sister, Mary Jane, just after the "do-nothing" group dissolved, and he seemed glad to be rid of it: "My special session turned out to be a dud as I was sure it would. They are just fooling around doing nothing as I expected. It is a crying shame for them to act like that when the country sorely needs action."[30]

Though he wrote of regret, Truman recognized that his choice to put the Republicans and, indirectly, Dewey and Warren's liberal platform in the dock had been the right decision, as they had both been found wanting. The fact that the Eightieth Congress failed to address the nation's myriad social and economic problems—as Truman defined them—gave him more ammunition for the verbal barrage he had begun on the June "inspection" tour, and it had vindicated Bill Batt's argument in favor of calling the Turnip Day gathering. Truman was still convinced that direct government intervention was needed to cure the nation's problems. Not enough affordable homes? The government should build more. Prices too high? The government should extend price controls. Health care inadequate? The government should provide nationwide coverage. Now that the Republicans in Congress had solidified their insistence on limited federal intervention, Truman could again portray himself as a man of action. He could also drive a wedge between the Republican old guard and Dewey's comparatively liberal election manifesto.[31]

In his desire to stymie Truman at every turn and to "not give that fellow anything," Taft and his allies had proved to be not only pigheaded, but also shortsighted. Unable to check his animosity toward the man he still regarded as the "senator from Pendergast," Taft had indulged his obstructionist impulse with a blinkered view that only saw the special session as a head-to-head between himself and Truman. Indeed, Taft stated in a nationally syndicated editorial that "The only reasonable way to work out a Republican program . . . is in cooperation with a Republican President."[32] The Ohioan should have instead looked beyond his pride to the wider picture of the election campaign and refreshed his memory by re-reading Truman's comments from the June tour about the Eightieth Congress. Then he might have seen that a rigid stance that blocked Truman's proposed legislation point by point gave his foe even greater cause to call out the Republican Party as the party of special interest, of status quo, and of inertia when he returned to the rails in September. Certainly, Taft was correct that the Republican Party needed to present a strong position to potential voters, but his decision to advise a shutout in the Turnip Day session was to yield a bitter harvest in the weeks to come.

Truman wasn't the only one wanting to tarnish the GOP's reputation. Upon accepting the States' Rights Party's nomination for vice president in a clammy city coliseum in Houston, Mississippi governor Fielding Wright slammed Dewey's party and Truman's, declaring that "the present Democratic and Republican parties are philosophically bankrupt" to wild cheers from his nine thousand supporters. "They veer from point to point without regard for principle, but only with an insensate desire to pander to any minority for votes," Wright added. He also had sharp words for his other opponent for the presidency, Henry Wallace, saying that the States' Rights group was running against "the Communist Progressive Party." The Democratic and Republican parties were almost as bad, Wright claimed, and supported "the fundamentals of a police state." Ironically, several rows of armed officers stood watch over the gathering as Wright spoke.[33]

In accepting the Houston delegates' nomination for president, J. Strom Thurmond agreed with his running mate, claiming that Truman, Wallace, and Dewey were steering America toward "the rocks of totalitarianism." All three backed a policy of "misnamed civil rights," Thurmond said, which was "a shameful betrayal of our nation's charter." The antilynching bill was, the governor of South Carolina believed, nothing more than "a federal seizure of police powers," and he called on "States' Rights Americans" to form an alliance that would block Truman's unconstitutional and unbidden extension of the federal government. Insisting that each state should be able to set its own agenda on racial equality or inequality, Thurmond said, "If the interests of New York are better served under laws prohibiting segregation, then they should have the right to prohibit segregation. If the people of Georgia are better governed under segregation laws, then they should have the right to enact segregation."[34]

Less than forty-eight hours after the Houston gathering, Henry Wallace took to the radio to reject the assertions of Wright and Thurmond. In his first nationwide broadcast of the campaign, Wallace insisted, "I do not believe in Communism and the Progressive Party does not believe in Communism." He then set out to explain the difference between his supporters' philosophy and a communist stance: "Most Progressives, while still distrustful of monopoly capitalism, still think it is possible . . . to develop a Progressive capitalism that will prevent war, scarcity and depression." He fully backed democratic processes and would "not tolerate anyone in the Progressive party who preaches the overthrow of the Government by force and violence."[35]

Regardless of whether or not Wallace advocated violent measures, Truman knew that he would have to fight the Progressive Party nominee hard on farming issues. Wallace had been instrumental in developing high-yield hybrid corn in 1923, which had helped farms recover from the Dust Bowl. The resulting popularity in the Midwest had influenced FDR's selection of Wallace as his running mate of choice in 1940, before the president's confidants convinced him that Wallace was a liability. The main reasons were that Wallace had feuded with several high-ranking Democrats, had taken a controversial, highly publicized trip to Russia, and, in the words of DNC secretary Ed Pauley, "was making too many pro-Soviet statements."[36] Now, four years later, Wallace threatened to further dent the Democrats' chances in the Midwest, even with Truman promising extended price supports.[37]

However, on August 12, fortune handed Truman's team a way to gain the upper hand over Wallace, Dewey, and Thurmond on the farming issue. As Clark Clifford worked in his office late on the hot, sunny afternoon of August 12, peering at the papers on his desk in rapt concentration, he was interrupted by a loud knock at the door. The lawyer lifted his gaze to see W. McNeil Lowry, Cox Newspapers' Washington bureau chief standing there with an envelope in his hand. The thirty-five-year-old Lowry had been working on an investigative article for the past few weeks since receiving a tip from one of his stringers, *Dayton Daily News* farming editor Jesse Garrison.

Through typically detailed follow-up research, Lowry had found evidence that a crisis was brewing in rural America that had gone unnoticed in Washington D.C. His mission this day was simple: to alert Clifford and thereby Truman to a loose plate in the seemingly impenetrable Dewey armor.[38]

The two men sat down and Lowry handed his host an envelope. Clifford slit it open and pulled out two copies of a story which had run that week under the dynamite headline "Congress Acts to Force Down Farmers' Prices at Behest of Grain Lobby." Despite the serious implications, the piece failed to resonate in Washington because it was in the relatively obscure Dayton newspaper. Clifford realized that Lowry really had *something* here. He began gesturing excitedly in the air, pretending to write with an index finger the speech that Truman would deliver once he fully grasped the magnitude of the story Lowry had gift-wrapped for him.[39]

While Truman, as chief executive, had overseen agricultural policy since he took the mantle from FDR, it was a Republican-dominated congressional committee chaired by Truman's old adversary, Republican congressman Jesse Wolcott, that had sent recommendations for the most recent policy on pricing controls, supply, and distribution to Capitol Hill. The recommendations seemed reasonable on the surface, extending pricing support to keep farmers profitable and consumers happy, yet there was a potentially calamitous provision, Lowry's article revealed: Whatever the harvest yield of 1948, farmers were not allowed to receive another cent in government funding for new storage facilities.

This had been fine for the past couple of years, as output had been consistent. But if fall 1948 yielded a bumper crop of corn and grain, as Jesse Garrison had heard it would from Ohio corn farmers, the surplus would not be eligible for government-set pricing unless it was housed in certified facilities built at the farmers' expense, either on their land or at third-party, off-site silos. Many farmers could ill afford such an outlay, particularly on short notice, and so faced the lose-lose scenario of either borrowing thousands of dollars to finance extra storage or selling off their yields at rock bottom, nonsupported prices.

Neither scenario, Lowry and Clifford knew, would be acceptable. The farmers would want someone to swing for this, and in this election year it would be either the incumbent or the challenger. Truman, the two Democrats resolved, would certainly not be the focus of their ire. Rather, it would be Dewey who would take the fall for his colleagues' calamitous policy.[40] And, Clifford quickly schemed, as Robert Taft and many other Republicans dismissed price support as heavy-handed, big-government meddling that they had vowed to stop, it shouldn't be too hard to make the case that the brewing grain storage storm was deliberate GOP weather making. It mattered little that Dewey was in favor of ongoing price support; Clifford and his team could, if they positioned the story correctly, tar the entire Republican Party with this same brush.[41]

If the story had ended there, it would have been bad enough for the GOP. But the ever-diligent Lowry had found further evidence in the Congressional Record and through friends in the Agriculture Department that grain lobbyists and speculators had pushed through the legislation and stood to make big money from selling discounted produce for bargain prices. And this was made possible by the actions of a Republican-dominated committee in a Congress that Truman had opposed at every opportunity.[42]

Though not wanting to gloat over the likely misfortune of the nation's farmers, Clifford knew that Lowry had handed him a new bundle of logs to stoke Truman's fire. He quickly set about assembling the kindling.

Clifford's first strike was to send a copy of the article to US attorney general Tom C. Clark. The blunt, no-nonsense Texan wasted little time ordering the seizure and sealing of files belonging to the North American Export Grain Association, Minneapolis Grain Exchange, the Chicago Board of Trade, and the Kansas City Board of Trade, all of which were implicated in the possible price-rigging and lobbying scandal that Garrison and Lowry had unearthed.[43]

Next, Clifford put in a call to Dupont Circle. Once Bill Batt and Johannes Hoeber found out about the farming fiasco, they immediately put Dave Lloyd to work. The articulate and precise lawyer had finally become a member of the Research Division despite a holdup when the DNC treasurer squawked that there was no money in the coffers to round out Batt's team. Now he put his skills to work in articulating the farmers' plight, Truman's concern, and the folly of the Republicans. Within days, Lloyd had expanded his white paper on agricultural policy, and in reviewing a list of whistle stops at which Truman could unleash yet another domestic policy invective against Dewey and the GOP, Batt, Charlie Murphy, and Clifford settled on a single, pivotal appearance: Truman's speech at the National Plowing Match in Dexter, Iowa.[44]

The Research Division boys were by now used to getting rush requests from Clifford and Murphy that required action in hours, or at best a few days, not least due to the sheer number of speeches that Truman was delivering. So having more than a month to draft, revise, and redraft the Dexter address—with Clifford also paying close attention to each iteration—was a luxury they were going to use to its full potential. No matter what gains the Republicans had made in the Midwest in 1944 and again in the 1946 midterms, or how popular Henry Wallace was there, it was going to be Harry Truman who positioned himself as the decisive leader who had the region's best interests at heart. The grain storage controversy fit perfectly with the Research Division's narrative that positioned the Democrats as the champions of the working class and the Republicans as their enemies.[45]

As well as spurring the Batt group's fact finding, Clifford sought Lowry's help in composing several key messaging points. Through his in-depth reporting, the journalist knew the issue better than anyone and understood how politically toxic it was for the Republicans and Dewey, who was soon to be guilty by association if the Dexter speech resonated as expected.[46] At first, Lowry felt conflicted. True, he was a Democrat and had gone out of his way to bring the matter to Clifford's attention because he, as a Kansan, felt a sense of duty to his farmers in the Midwest who were getting a raw deal from lobbyists and, he believed, from the GOP. But he was also a journalist rather than an opinion columnist and was therefore obliged to report the facts impartially. After mulling the matter, the first line of argument won out: Lowry reasoned that he had gone this far and now should bring the issue to its logical conclusion.[47] Another speechwriter who contributed to the speech was Albert Z.

Carr, usually called "Bob" by his colleagues, a battle-tested former FDR staffer who had been brought in to whip up talking points for certain key speeches in Truman's 1948 bid.[48]

Clifford also sought the counsel of Charles Brannan, Truman's secretary of agriculture. He provided suggestions for the Dexter speech and details of exactly how much money had been taken out of Iowa farmers' pockets by the Republican congressional committee. Oscar Chapman was amazed by the scope of the problem, later recalling, "It was really cutting very deeply, and therefore we pressed that issue hard in that section of the country." Brannan also provided Chapman, Clifford, and the other campaign staff with logistical guidance for the Midwest section of the Whistle Stop Tour, including where exactly the president should stop and speak, and when.[49]

In addition to taking the Republicans to task over the grain storage bins debacle, Truman wasn't about to let the country forget his foes' misdeeds on other domestic issues either. On August 16, he issued a statement criticizing the shortcomings of the price control legislation he had just reluctantly signed:

> This bill represents the feeble response of the Congress to the demands of our people for strong, positive action to relieve us from the hardships of exorbitant prices and to protect us from the inflationary dangers which threaten our prosperity.
>
> The failure to take adequate measures in this critical situation is final proof of the determination of the men who controlled the 80th Congress to follow a course which serves the ends of special privilege rather than the welfare of the whole nation. The record is clear.[50]

The GOP wasted little time in firing back at the latest evidence that Truman wanted to expand the role of the government even beyond its role in FDR's day in extending price controls indefinitely. Less than twenty-four hours after Truman's address, Colorado's Eugene Millikin, chairman of the Senate Finance Committee, held nothing back as he told reporters: "The Congress did not give the President the right to re-impose allocations, rationing, inventory and price control, and excess profits taxes. This parcel of egregious error was misdirected to a peacetime America devoted to its economic and political freedoms."[51]

Whoever was in the right, it's questionable whether America was paying much attention on this particular day, as the country was in mourning for the iconic sportsman of the era, the beloved Babe Ruth. Following a long battle with cancer, the Yankees' home run king, who held sixty-two big league baseball records, finally succumbed to the illness at New York's Memorial Hospital. He was fifty-three.[52]

★ ★ ★

"THE PRESIDENT HAS PUT HIS NECK ALL THE WAY OUT FOR US"

As the Red Scare continued to build at home, communism also continued to pose problems abroad. Though the infusion of funds from the Marshall Plan had helped the Greek government stave off a communist takeover and force rebel leader General Markos Vafiadis to flee to Soviet-dominated Albania, his band of rebels still proved to be a determined foe, particularly in the mountains. Vafiadis' men dug into their positions and refused to concede defeat even though surrounded by loyalist troops.[53]

Anticommunist forces faced a much grimmer picture in China, where, AP writer James D. White reported, "The Communists are not only winning the civil war, but their progress is steady and thus far has not been stopped by military means."[54] There was also renewed tension in Berlin. The Soviets had offered hope in the first days of August by lifting their blockade and economic lockdown, but on the eleventh day of the month they abandoned their promise to unblock the funds needed for the city council to continue functioning. In response, the Truman administration and British and French governments issued a ban on banks in their sectors transferring funds to the Red Army–policed zone. Now that the blockade was back, American pilots resumed their aid flights despite Soviet aircraft maneuvers between the occupied zones. Undeterred by this display of intimidation, bullish US Air Force secretary W. Stuart Symington declared that the Russians would "not stop us from doing our job" and promised West Berliners that the flights—now involving one hundred repurposed four-engine C-54 bombers—would continue indefinitely.[55]

The news from Asia was somewhat better. Though North Korea was still dominated by communists, Truman officially recognized the new government of Syngman Rhee in the south, which General Douglas McArthur's forces still occupied to help stave off possible communist destabilization. "It will be a signal honor to participate in the birth of your national freedom, a momentous event," McArthur cabled Rhee.[56]

Back home, Truman was also determined to finally deliver freedom to black residents of Jim Crow states. The Rowe-Clifford memo, "The Politics of 1948," had made it clear that if Truman was to have a chance in the election, he would have to dominate voting among ethnic minorities. In his April note to Clifford, Bill Batt had focused on the need for the president to appeal to black voters in urban areas and to steer them away from Henry Wallace, a longtime proponent of civil rights who had planned a series of campaign speeches to integrated audiences in the South, and from Tom Dewey, who also advocated ending southern segregation and could potentially undermine Truman's leadership on the issue.

To ensure that black voters saw Truman as the true champion of civil rights, the DNC had sent members of the black press on Truman's train, distributed press releases and other promotional material to black newspapers several times a week, and courted influential community leaders to rally their residents around Truman. In mid-August, one of these leaders, Herbert L. Bruce, reported that the strategy was paying off despite the best efforts of the Dixiecrats to hold the desertion of the southern voting block over Truman's head.

Bruce told reporters, "Since the National Convention, when President Truman refused to offer a single concession on his civil rights program to the South, there has been a swell of sentiment to him among my people. The people of Harlem are beginning to appreciate that the President has put his neck all the way out for us . . . and the least we can do is support him." [57] It seemed Truman had made progress to secure the backing of at least one of the three main groups Clifford identified in an August strategy memo to the president—the other two being labor and farmers.[58]

Truman's support for what Bill Batt rightly called "a powerful Civil Rights plank" was not, as some of his detractors claimed, some publicity stunt nor a stance he just maintained in public. On August 18, Truman had his secretary, Rose Conway, type up a letter to Ernie Roberts, a longtime friend the president had met during his artillery service in World War I.[59] A few days earlier, Roberts had written to his fellow Missourian advising him to drop the civil rights plank before it lost him the election, positing, "You can win the South without the 'Equal Rights Bill,' but you cannot win the South with it." He continued, in lines that wouldn't have sounded out of place coming from Strom Thurmond's pen: "Harry, let the South take care of the Niggers, which they have done, and if the Niggers don't like the Southern treatment they can come to Mrs. Roosevelt. . . . Harry, you're a Southerner."[60]

It would have been understandable for Truman to ignore this note given how busy he was just two weeks before starting the autumn leg of the Whistle Stop Tour, or to put off his reply until after the election. He did neither, instead laying out his position on civil rights to Roberts in stark terms that echoed Lincoln:

Dear Ernie:

I appreciated very much your letter of last Saturday night from Hotel Temple Square in the Mormon Capital.

I am going to send you a copy of the report of my Commission on Civil Rights and then if you still have that antebellum proslavery outlook, I'll be thoroughly disappointed in you.

The main difficulty with the South is that they are living eighty years behind the times and the sooner they come out of it the better it will be for the country and themselves. I am not asking for social equality, because no such thing exists, but I am asking for equality of opportunity for all human beings and, as long as I stay here, I am going to continue that fight. When the mob gangs can take four people out and shoot them in the back, and everybody in the country is acquainted with who did the shooting and nothing is done about it, that country is in a pretty bad fix from a law enforcement standpoint.

When a Mayor and a City Marshal can take a negro Sergeant off a bus in South Carolina, beat him up and put out one of his eyes, and nothing is done about it by the State Authorities, something is radically wrong with the system.

On the Louisiana and Arkansas Railway when coal burning locomotives were used, the negro firemen were the thing because it was a back-breaking job and a dirty one. As soon as they turned to oil as a fuel it became customary for people to take shots at the negro firemen and a number were murdered because it was thought that this was now a white-collar job and should go to a white man.

I can't approve of such goings on and I shall never approve it, as long as I am here, as I told you before. I am going to try to remedy it and if that ends up in my failure to be reelected, that failure will be in a good cause.

I know you haven't thought this thing through and that you do not know the facts. I am happy, however, that you wrote me because it gives me a chance to tell you what the facts are.

Sincerely yours,

Harry S. Truman[61]

The next day, August 19, Truman turned his attention from a key domestic and personal issue to an increasingly troublesome foreign one, as he chaired a meeting of the National Security Council. The main topic of conversation was the renewed stalemate in Berlin. Here, despite the hope inspired by a brief lifting of the blockade in the first week of August, Stalin's military commanders were once again preventing traffic by road, river, or rail between their eastern zone and the western zones.[62] Four-party talks dragged on, but while the Soviets were willing to parley, they were not in any mood to make concessions, a frustrated Secretary Marshall revealed.

In an effort to show that the blockade would not force America to desert the city or the German people, the daily airlift continued, with yet more American, British, and French aircraft being diverted to help — most of them repurposed US Air Force planes now dropping medical supplies, food, and, as the nickname "candy bombers" suggests, even confectionary to grateful West Berliners. These provisions averaged 3,300 tons a day, and the city now had a thirty-two-day store of food and twenty-five days worth of coal in reserve. The talks would continue, with the Americans hoping that the Moscow delegates would see that as more and more supplies made it over the east-west line, the notion of a true blockade became ever more ridiculous. But with the Soviets, even irrefutable facts were not always enough to prompt a change of heart or of policy if Stalin thought otherwise, particularly not with the Red Army still greatly outnumbering American, British, and French forces in Germany.[63]

As the foreign policy experts deliberated over the Berlin situation, Truman's advisory team continued to finalize logistics for the imminent campaign. Acting on the suggestions of the Research Division,

Clark Clifford recommended three distinct legs for the fall Whistle Stop Tour: the first in the Midwest, the second in the West, and the third in the East. Truman agreed, and with that, Clifford sent word to the Batt group, prompting Bill Batt to assign a thorough fact sheet on every possible stop to his six staffers. These contained everything from typical political fare such as voting histories, demographics, and key local industries to interesting trivia that Truman might use in an introduction from the rear platform of his rail car. As the Research Division staffers completed each one, Batt scribbled an "x" next to the name of the town—from Little Falls, New York, to Monett, Missouri, to American Fork, Utah, and everywhere in between.[64] Truman would make the most stops in Texas—twenty-two, where he would try to nullify the growing influence of the States' Rights Party, with nineteen talks in Oklahoma and seventeen apiece in the Midwest swing states of Ohio and Indiana. Whether the president would approve Clifford's notion of a "short trip into the South" to take the fight to the States' Rights Party remained to be seen.[65] The Research Division would have more than enough work on its hands, either way.

As Batt and company toiled at Dupont Circle on the seemingly endless list of the local fact sheets, Truman's inner circle did the same ten minutes away at the White House, fine-tuning campaign messaging for "the Boss." Chief on their minds was the appeal to the crucial labor vote, not least because this demographic had helped FDR win all four terms and because Truman would launch his fall campaign with a speech to a largely working-class audience in Detroit's Cadillac Square on September 6, which was, appropriately, Labor Day.[66]

Truman needed to secure the backing of the major unions, their millions of members, and influential and respected leaders such as the UAW's Walter Reuther, but despite his veto of the Taft-Hartley Act and his provisions for a higher minimum wage, more federally funded low-income housing, and extended unemployment benefits—built on components of FDR's New Deal—such support was by no means guaranteed. Wallace was courting the labor vote, the powerful Teamsters union was still flirting with the GOP, and Truman had had a testy relationship with labor since he had signed an executive order for reconversion on August 18, 1945. In doing so, Truman's statement had made clear his goal: "To move as rapidly as possible without endangering the stability of the economy toward the removal of price, wage, production and other controls and towards the restoration of collective bargaining and the free market."[67]

Despite Truman's best intentions, the US economy was anything but stable during the ensuing three years—in fact, it was convulsive, turbulent, and at the worst of times seemingly on the brink of collapse. In the wake of World War II, labor leaders had demanded "catch up" pay increases for the war years, when such raises had been capped by FDR's legislation. Their members, they argued, had been the pistons in the wartime production engine room and should be compensated accordingly. Management, predictably, opposed major increases. The owners of coal mines, steelworks, railroads, and other union-dominated industries proposed modest pay boosts, but their attempts to appease the union bosses fell short, insultingly short if one believed the fiery rhetoric of John L. Lewis. He was the talismanic president of the United Mine Workers union (UMW) and someone Margaret Truman believed was "an arrogant man whose ambitions were almost boundless," who the 1946 *Harvard Crimson* editorial labeled "a dictator" and a "scrofulous nuisance to the public at large," and who Truman had called "a son of a bitch."[68]

Trying to force the hands of industrial bigwigs and government mediators, the bellicose Lewis and his fellow union bosses initiated the most devastating and financially crippling walkouts in American history.[69] Some of these, such as the 113-day General Motors strike that saw one hundred thousand workers leave their posts, halted production at just one company, but others, like the train workers' strikes and the April 1946 walkout of four hundred thousand mine workers, threatened the entire US economy.[70] At one point, a million workers deserted their posts.[71] Without staff to churn out raw materials, fashion these into finished goods, or transport them, no major industry could function. Worse still, White House advisers warned Truman that the delay of grain shipments would not only lead to domestic food supply issues, but could also result in the hunger and potential starvation of millions in Europe who depended on US exports. No airlift could be successful in Berlin if there was nothing to transport.[72]

Truman had since repaired some relationships with labor leaders, such as the one with A. F. Whitney, the head of the influential Brotherhood of Railway Trainmen, whom he had once threatened with "the gun" in a White House negotiation if Whitney refused to cancel a railroad strike that threatened to bring the US economy to its knees. Truman bristled at the demands of the trainmen and, in his fury at being dictated to by labor bosses, told a joint session of Congress on May 24, 1946, that he would draft strikers into the army if they didn't relent. The strike ended at the last minute, but Truman had made his point that the president would not be bent to the will of the unions. To emphasize this position to the other heads of organized labor, Truman had also banned John L. Lewis from the White House.[73]

Perhaps this history of confrontation with Whitney, Lewis, and the rest explains why Truman's veto of the Taft-Hartley Bill in June 1947 (an unsuccessful veto that the Republican-controlled Congress overrode) failed to convince many union chiefs that he was a friend of labor. In the runup to the 1948 election, William Green (AFL), Philip Murray (CIO), Daniel Tobin (Teamsters), and Jack Kroll (CIO-PAC) wanted a new man in the White House who was more malleable than Truman. So in the weeks before the Democratic National Convention these influential men tried to rally support for William Douglas (Truman's VP pick, who rejected a place on the Democratic ticket), General Eisenhower, or anyone else not named Harry Truman.[74] Eisenhower's refusal to seek political office that year and Truman's nomination helped quiet the dissent, but the president needed more than begrudging union support. He was desperate to secure the financial backing of Green, Murray, Tobin, and Kroll and the labor vote windfall that would result from their public endorsements. On the other end of the equation, Truman feared that failure to secure such backing could lead to labor going over to Wallace's Progressive Party, with disastrous consequences come November 2.

This desperation led to the decision to open Truman's fall campaign with a speech in Detroit's Cadillac Square, where he had addressed two different union rallies almost four years previously, on September 4, 1944, while campaigning as FDR's running mate.[75] Not merely the Motor City (and therefore the UAW's back yard), Detroit was also a hub for steelworking, milling, and other core manufacturing industries. As with all the major speeches that year, the Research Division played a part in selecting the site, researching the issues, and providing speech fodder for the president.[76]

Given the trouble that labor had given him since he became president, Truman couldn't afford any slip-ups in the Detroit address.[77] He needed to convince his doubters among the union rank and file that he was their champion and the Republican Party their enemy. Certainly he would once again accuse the GOP of being the party of big business and special interest, and he would use the Taft-Hartley Act as his main justification for such a claim, regardless of how this legislation had strengthened his hand. But people had heard this before, and Truman needed more.

So he called on a team of experts to assist Charlie Murphy, Dave Bell, Clark Clifford, and George Elsey in writing the speech, even as the Research Division continued to gather facts he could use to underpin their copy.[78] John Gibson, assistant secretary of labor, was the first of the economic policy veterans Clifford summoned to the White House. Meeting with Truman, Clifford, and Murphy, Gibson gave the group information on the current mood among blue-collar workers and offered to write the first outline for the Cadillac Square address, a proposal the group accepted.

A few days later Gibson sent his talking points to Murphy and Bell, who combined them with some Trumanisms to create a second draft. Truman also pulled in FDR's veteran speechwriters David Noyes and Albert Carr to contribute to this pivotal address and the shorter supporting ones the president would deliver in Flint, Pontiac, Grand Rapids, and Lansing as he took to the rails for the first leg of the fall tour.[79]

Truman then worked late into the night preparing his own third draft from the materials his advisers had provided. He had certainly ad libbed a lot during his rousing acceptance speech at the Democratic National Convention the previous month, so none of his speechwriters balked at this hands-on approach. He read his version aloud to Murphy, Carr, Noyes, and Bell, and then told them to tinker with it while he went to meet Margaret's train, ever the doting dad. And so they did, putting it in a more usable, piecemeal form that Truman could read easily to the massive crowd that was expected to show up in Detroit on Labor Day weekend to see him kick off the most frenetic, intense, and, arguably, important two months of his political career.[80]

Whether reading over Clifford and Elsey's reports from the Research Division, meeting with the Joint Chiefs over the continuing impasse with the Soviets in Berlin, or raising funds, Truman continued to work long hours in August. Yet, recognizing how thoroughly exhausting the Whistle Stop Tour would be in September, October, and right up until the polls closed on November 2, he also made time to take several breaks with his family and inner circle of advisers. As had been his way since the water-loving Truman moved into the White House, these took the form of cruising the Potomac on the presidential yacht, the Williamsburg.

First launched as the private vessel ARAS in 1930, the 243-foot vessel was acquired by the navy and renamed the USS Williamsburg after the famous May 1862 Civil War battle, and it saw naval service off the coast of Iceland in World War II. The boat performed diverse roles for the US Navy, including merchant ship escort, submarine observer, and troop transport. Following the war, it was reconverted back into a civilian vessel and put at Truman's disposal. The twin Winton diesel engines propelled the president to his beloved Key West when he could take longer breaks, but with the election campaign about to get underway, shorter trips closer to Washington would have to suffice.[81]

Though the Williamsburg was, like Truman's train, outfitted with the latest communications equipment that enabled him to talk with his advisers in D.C., the president knew that to gain the full benefit of time away he must resist the temptation to use the vessel as a mobile White House. So when he took to the water, he slept late, ate plenty, and exerted most of his energy on swims performed with the awkward sidestroke he had perfected as a boy in Missouri swimming holes.[82] Back on the boat, he relaxed in a wicker chair under a canvas veranda that shaded the fantail from the unrelenting sun, often eschewing his usual three-piece suit for a short-sleeved shirt, khakis, and a driver's cap as he read a book or chatted with old friends and members of the so-called "Missouri Gang" of insiders, including John Snyder, secretary of the treasury; Charlie Ross, press secretary; and Major General Harry Vaughan. Truman was cordial and sometimes even playful with the reporters who borrowed or charted boats to scribble about and photograph his every move, waving to them from the foredeck and bantering back and forth.

Truman's previous trip on the yacht that month had been a brief, overnight one on August 7, when, with the Eightieth Congress reaching its meager end, he had taken little time to relax and had instead read over the day's reports. But now that the tension of the Turnip Day session was behind him and the full rigors of the campaign trail a few days ahead, the president decided that a longer and more leisurely getaway was needed. Not least to escape from the stinging comments of Republican House majority leader Charles Halleck, who turned up the pre-election heat by claiming that "President Truman is a confused, bewildered, perplexed man swamped by the tremendous responsibilities of the Presidency." Halleck charged that Truman had "degraded his high and respected office" by calling Congress back from its summer break in an "obviously desperate political maneuver." Still not done, the Indiana congressman praised the GOP-led HUAC for uncovering communist spy groups that were "running through the Truman administration like water through a sieve" and warned that these "alien-minded forces seek to destroy our republic." [83]

Looking to put such vitriol out of his mind, Truman boarded the *Williamsburg* on August 20 for a nine-day cruise that would take him down the Potomac to Chesapeake Bay, where, after a couple of days of puttering around, the yacht would continue its voyage through the Chesapeake-Delaware canal and into Delaware Bay. Then the yacht would take Truman and his team—which included Clark Clifford, Charlie Ross, and all the other usual shipmates—down the Atlantic coast to Hampton Roads, Virginia, before heading back up Chesapeake Bay and the Potomac. [84]

During Truman's first two days on the water, reporters on the White House beat failed to borrow, hire, or commandeer a vessel to get close to him, and they begrudgingly followed the *Williamsburg's* eastward course on land. They caught a break, though, on August 22, securing the use of the small yacht *Wanderer*. Truman was in a jovial mood as he addressed them by radio later that day and threatened to leave the smaller vessel behind and take the *Williamsburg* into deeper water. "Will it rock enough to justify our crossing the Gulf Stream?" he asked. [85]

Despite Truman's best intentions, the trip could not provide a complete rest. After all, there was the running of the country to attend to, an election to finish planning, and a three-way party split to fret over. As the White House press corps got used to their new, temporary berth, Charlie Ross radioed to tell them that Truman was working on his Labor Day address as the *Williamsburg* headed northeastward up Chesapeake Bay with the *Wanderer* in pursuit. [86]

Truman also dealt decisively with a new tangle in the Gordian knot of Soviet relations, revoking the diplomatic credentials of Soviet consul general Jacob Lomakin and instructing General Marshall to close the US Consulate in Vladivostok, as the Soviets had demanded. The spat was caused by the Soviets trying to force three schoolteachers who sought refuge in New York to return to Russian soil against their will. One of them, Oksana Kasenkina, leapt three stories from the Soviet consulate onto the unforgiving concrete below, landing her in Roosevelt Hospital for several days. When the State Department raised a stink and threatened to cut consular relations, the Soviets countered by asking the United States to close its consulate and to abort plans to build another on its territory as agreed during postwar negotiations. This was a setback for American and British negotiators hoping to end the Berlin Blockade once and for all, and the fact that a Soviet policeman had shot and killed a German intelligence agent who fled into the US zone certainly didn't help matters. Truman, it seemed, just couldn't catch a break.[87]

Meanwhile, Truman's announcement of a draft exemption for married men caused many applicants who wanted to avoid fighting the Red Army to crowd into marriage license bureaus across the country. The rush on the Brooklyn bureau was so overwhelming that officials called the police in to help restore order.[88]

On August 29, with just hours remaining until Truman returned to dry land and the pressure cooker of the election, he took two refreshing swims near windswept Blakistone Island, under the shadow of the now-dim tower of the white stone lighthouse, which had been decommissioned in 1932. As Truman splashed around, the ever-vigilant White House reporters were observing and likely wishing they could escape the heat of the Maryland summer day, abandon their posts, and join the president in the cool water.[89]

On deck, it was left to Charlie Ross—Truman's steady pressman, confidant, and the only member of his staff who called him "Harry" instead of "Mr. President" or "the Boss"—to brief the reporters who were not on the boat watching the tanned and relaxed Truman get his exercise. "The President is looking forward to the campaign with a great deal of zest," the press secretary told them. "It is going to be an extensive one, as you know."[90]

Indeed it was, and Bill Batt's Research Division was determined to be ready. As the time approached when their diligence would hopefully yield dividends, they placed calls, wrote messaging points, and updated reports. Everything at Dupont Circle was directed toward helping Truman establish "continuous close contact with the people," as Frank Kelly put it.[91]

Despite all their hard work, however, the Batt group would never be working more than a couple of days ahead of Truman's train because of the sheer number of speeches he was to deliver, more than 280 compared to the 70 he had given during the June "shakedown cruise," as Charlie Murphy called it.[92] Time was now up. As soon as the White House calendar flipped from August to September, the fall leg of the Whistle Stop Tour would be on.

September

Looking out at the white stone arches of Washington's Union Station on September 3 from the rear platform of his seventeen-car train—from which he would try to admonish, joke, and persuade his way back into contention—Harry Truman saw several familiar faces among the modest contingent that had gathered to see him off. One was that of his running mate Alben Barkley, whose wrinkles belied a vigor that almost outstripped that of the indefatigable president. As a farewell, the veteran Kentucky politico, who had 250 speeches of his own planned for the ensuing weeks, told Truman how to rhetorically treat the Republicans in his speeches: "Mow 'em down, Harry!"

"I'm going to give 'em hell!" Truman responded emphatically, echoing the cheer he had heard from the crowds during his June train tour.[1]

Margaret, standing beside her father, chided him with mock outrage. "You ought not to say 'hell,'" the president's daughter said.[2]

Waving good-bye to Barkley and the rest of the well-wishers, the Trumans went out of the sunshine's glare and into the shade of the Ferdinand Magellan's well-appointed dining room, where the president would meet with Clifford, Elsey, and the others around the long mahogany table to continually tweak speeches and strategy during the sixty-three days on the track. The fall campaign was now officially underway. Either Harry Truman would win four more years in the White House or his presidency would be over in just sixty-three helter-skelter, speech-filled, train-bound days.[3]

Barkley had told Truman that it would be "a victorious trip," but there was trouble from the start.[4] The radio networks had gotten wind of the fact that Truman's campaign finances were flagging. Now, radio bosses at the Mutual Broadcasting System wanted their fee, a princely $50,000, the equivalent of half a million dollars in today's currency, up front or they would refuse to broadcast Truman's speech from Detroit's Cadillac Square to the nation. Imagine, an incumbent president denied the chance to address the people via radio in an election because the campaign cupboards were bare.

The petty cash on the train certainly wouldn't come close to such a sum, nor were Truman or any of his advisers able to cover the shortfall. Each person on the team was a generalist in some ways, with a fluid job description that ebbed and flowed as needs dictated. Somehow the responsibility to pay the network fell to, or fell on, undersecretary of the interior Oscar Chapman.

Campaign finance manager Louis Johnson was in charge of raising funds for the campaign, at least officially. Yet with Truman on his way to Detroit to give the big kickoff speech for the fall Whistle Stop Tour and Johnson doing the rounds in Washington, it was Chapman who was tasked with rustling up the radio networks' ransom so that the nation would hear Truman's speech from Cadillac Square. Despite the growth of television, radio was still the dominant medium, with 94.4 percent of American households owning one or more sets. The Truman campaign could ill afford to let such a vast audience hear nothing of the president's first major campaign speech.[5]

Clifford and Charlie Murphy had learned from the fiasco of the near-empty stadium in Nebraska during the June tour, and they now had staff out beating the bushes in front of the Truman train days before he arrived for a major address. For this reason, Johannes Hoeber was there meeting with staff at the local Democratic offices and reporting back to Bill Batt any details he could pass along to Clifford for fine-tuning the president's Labor Day address and the other upcoming speeches in Michigan.[6] Oscar Chapman had also been in Detroit all week, sweet-talking the unions, meeting with local Democratic Party bigwigs to ensure they would be in Cadillac Square, and double-checking that everything from the motorcade route to media coverage to seating on the podium was in order. But despite his proximity to the venue and his proven versatility, the quick-minded, broad-shouldered undersecretary of the interior was no financier.[7]

Thrust unwittingly into the role of fund raiser, Chapman had moved from concern to fretting to near panic as his attempts to get the cash fell flat. From his participation in high-level campaign planning sessions, Chapman knew that Dewey was not only dominating Truman in the opinion polls but also in fund raising. On the June tour, Truman had bashed the GOP for being controlled by big money interests, but now that Wall Street backers were making this rhetoric a reality by bankrolling Dewey, Truman would gladly have traded balance sheets with his opponent.

Whether he would have wished it or not, with just two and a half days remaining before Truman took the microphone in Cadillac Square it was up to Chapman to answer a simple, yet seemingly impossible question: Where on Earth was the radio broadcast money going to come from?

After failing in his initial attempts to obtain extra funds from Democratic backers, Chapman's next step was a logical one: he called Howard McGrath at DNC headquarters. But the party chairman had bad news. There was no war chest for this type of expense, although publicity director Jack Redding had asked McGrath to allocate $10,000 to it back in August.[8] "My God, Oscar, we haven't got that kind of money!" the exasperated, overworked McGrath told Chapman.[9]

The big labor unions were starting to come around to Truman, but he needed a convincing performance in Detroit to make them believe he could defeat the Republican "dream ticket" and that they were better off supporting the president than Henry Wallace, who was aggressively courting labor votes. Abe Feinberg, business executive, philanthropist, and friend of Harry Truman, was trying to use the president's early recognition of Israel to shake loose money from wealthy Jews, but he had only just started these efforts. With McGrath out of answers and the list of East Coast backers exhausted, to whom could Chapman now go?

Salvation came from an unlikely source more than a thousand miles away from the factories and warehouses of Detroit. Genial, neatly coiffed Roy Turner had been governor of Oklahoma for just a year, but he had been friends with Truman since 1944, when they had met during the then senator's trip to the Sooner State to address the Democratic Committee as keynote speaker. At the time of this first meeting, Turner had already made millions from his oil company and cattle ranch.[10] Since then, he had become national president of the Truman-Barkley Clubs, which had sprung up across the nation since the Democratic Party convention and were raising money, distributing pro-Truman leaflets, posters, and pamphlets, and trying to encourage a high turnout on November 2.[11]

Despite his wealth and admiration for the president, Turner was taken aback when Chapman called him unexpectedly less than seventy-two hours before Truman's Cadillac Square address with a request for an emergency donation. "Governor, I'm in the tightest spot I've ever been in in my life," Chapman admitted as he sat anxiously in his room at the grand and aptly named Book Cadillac Hotel. If he didn't raise $50,000 by midnight, the Truman team would be forced to cancel the national radio broadcast of the fall campaign's opening speech.[12]

Even for a man of means, such an amount was not small change. Still, Turner soon realized the gravity of the situation and the disastrous consequences if Truman's words did not make it to radio sets in homes across the nation.[13] "Of course you can't cancel," the Oklahoma governor insisted.

Knowing that there was, as Truman's train rolled toward Michigan, nobody else who would come to the president's aid, Turner told a grateful and relieved Chapman that he would take the matter in hand.

"Stay in your room and I'll call you back in an hour," he said.

But as Chapman looked at his watch and sweated in the Detroit heat, an hour came and went. Another thirty minutes. And thirty more. Still no call.

Then, two hours after Turner had given his assurance, Chapman's phone rang.

"You're in business, Oscar," he said. "I've just cleared the whole thing with the network. I've laid down $50,000 with their station here, and everything is checked out all the way up the line. You tell those sons of bitches that if they don't put this show on the air on Monday, I'll wreck this damn station of theirs before sundown."[14]

There was more good news for Truman that weekend. Americans for Democratic Action (ADA), more than a third of whose chapters had lobbied furiously for Dwight Eisenhower to take Truman's place atop the Democratic ticket, finally pledged their support to the party's cause rather than declaring their allegiance to Henry Wallace. In a statement released after its leaders conferred in Chicago, the organization's press release stated, "ADA is deeply concerned with the election of a liberal majority in both houses of Congress. It is clear that the majority of liberal candidates are running on the Democratic ticket and we will exert every effort, locally and nationally, to insure their election." This was not a ringing endorsement of Truman personally, but with chapters across the country, he could but welcome ADA's support, despite his dubious relationship with the organization's top brass.[15]

Whatever some remaining doubters in the ADA thought about Truman and however much the combination of the ADA's pluck and Hubert Humphrey's brave oratory had forced his hand, the Man from Missouri *had* made the boldest civil rights stand in a generation at the Democratic National Convention. This won many ADA leaders over, just as it had Eleanor Roosevelt. Writing in her nationally syndicated "My Day" column on September 4, the former first lady asserted, "President Truman has made a courageous fight for civil rights."[16]

Forty-eight hours later, it was time for Truman to put such moxie to the test before the American people. On the morning of September 6, he warmed up for the Detroit address with a speech at a rain-soaked Grand Rapids rally and a rear platform talk in Lansing, where the downpour stopped and the sun reasserted itself. During his opening remarks in Grand Rapids, Truman, seemingly unperturbed by the rain soaking his suit, let Michigan know what the state and the nation were in for during the Whistle Stop Tour, his voice ringing true from the three speakers mounted to the roof of his train car. "I am just starting on a campaign tour that is going to be a record for the President of the United States, and when I get through you are going to know the facts."[17] Echoing his rhetoric from the June trip, he then laid out the voters' options on polling day (conveniently neglecting to mention the Progressive or States' Rights Parties):

> You just have two parties to choose from in this election: the Democratic Party which stands for the peace and the welfare of the people and the little man, and the Republican Party which stands for special interests.
>
> The record proves conclusively that the Republican Party is controlled by special privilege; and that the Democratic Party is responsive to the needs of the people.[18]

Speaking again less than two hours later, he urged the residents of Lansing to make it clear which option they wanted by casting their ballot: "If you really have the welfare of this country at heart, and want to prevent the country from being turned over to special privilege, you must vote on November 2nd." And while the pollsters and most media outlets were against him, Truman aired his conviction that he wasn't touring the country in vain, declaring boldly that if there was a high voter turnout, "I shall be perfectly satisfied with the result. I know what that result will be."[19]

Several hundred had greeted the president at the Lansing station, but that was little preparation for the scene that awaited him in Detroit. Though the crowd didn't get close to the three hundred thousand he had hoped for (and goodness knows he would exaggerate the numbers at every stop in letters to friends and family throughout the campaign), press and police estimates all later agreed that more than one hundred thousand crammed Cadillac Square to see the first major speech of the fall Whistle Stop Tour. After waiting a couple of minutes for the cheers, whistles, and yells to subside, Truman began by acknowledging Walter Reuther and Frank Martel—the head of the Detroit Federation of Labor—who were seated behind him on the platform in a show of support. He then promised the audience that he wasn't going to give them any platitudes or flowery phrases but would instead "speak plainly and bluntly." And, true to his word, he got right to the matter at hand:

> These are critical times for labor and for all who work. There is great danger ahead. Right now, the whole future of labor is wrapped up in one simple proposition:
>
> If, in this next election, you get a Congress and an administration friendly to labor, you have much to hope for. If you get an administration and a Congress unfriendly to labor, you have much to fear, and you had better look out.[20]

To show them that this fear was justified, Truman used data provided by the Research Division in their Files of the Facts on labor, charging that the Republican Party had presided over three depressions within the previous forty years—in 1907–1908, in 1921, and, of course, the Great Depression that began in 1929.[21] Truman preferred to call this "the Republican panic" and accused that party of failing to fix it: "There was no unemployment compensation under the Republicans. There was no floor under wages under the Republicans. Average hourly earnings in 1932 were only 45 cents under the Republicans. From 12 to 15 million workers were out of work and unemployed under the Republicans."

In contrast, FDR returned a steady hand to the wheel in 1933, and during fifteen years of oversight the Democrats had not only supported a strong labor movement that was, Truman said, our best bulwark against communism," but had also:

> Passed the Wagner Act to assure fair collective bargaining, abolished the sweat shop, provided unemployment compensation, passed the Social Security Act, saved millions of workers' homes from foreclosure, brought the average wage from 45 cents to $1.33 per hour.
>
> You all remember how a Democratic administration turned the greatest depression in history into the most prosperous era the country has ever seen. Sixty-one million people are employed today.[22]

These achievements were under threat though, Truman said, from the Republican congressmen he called "spokesmen of reaction," for whom the Taft-Hartley Act—which, Truman reminded them, he had vetoed as "a shocking piece of legislation" only to see his veto overridden—was merely "a foretaste of what you will get if the Republican reaction is allowed to continue to grow."[23] A GOP victory in November would lead to a "steady barrage of body blows" against labor as Dewey's party took the side of big business. The typical Republican did not care about the worker, Truman insisted, but instead "is a man with a calculating machine where his heart ought to be." And this heartlessness put workers in danger, the president warned, not only of another "boom and bust" fallout, but also of losing "our Democratic institutions of free labor and free enterprise." The unions and their members must fight, not at the picket line, but at the ballot box, he urged.[24]

As Truman reached the final stage of his speech, he quickened his pace, the words spilling out like an Oscar-winning actor anxious to thank everyone before the stage orchestra cuts him off. In Truman's case, he was not trying to thank but admonish, and it was not a band but those pesky radio broadcasters he was concerned about. Yes, Roy Turner's connections and deep pockets had been enough to get nationwide coverage, but only for the allotted time slot. ABC had threatened to cut him off if he ran over, which would be a disastrous start to a last-ditch campaign that allowed no leeway for such missteps.[25] So, wary of the ever-ticking clock, he rattled off his final, populist, GOP-bashing rallying cry for the afternoon:[26]

All of labor stands at the crossroads today. You can elect a reactionary administration. You can elect a Congress and an administration which stands ready to play fair with every element in American life and enter a new period of hope. The choice is yours.

Do you want to carry the Taft-Hartley law to its full implication and enslave totally the workingman, white-collar and union man alike, or do you want to go forward with an administration whose interest is the welfare of the common man?

Labor has always had to fight for its gains. Now you are fighting for the whole future of the labor movement. We are in a hard, tough fight against shrewd and rich opponents. They know they can't count on your vote. Their only hope is that you won't vote at all. They have misjudged you. I know that we are going to win this crusade for the right![27]

Waving good-bye to the cheering throng that had jammed Cadillac Square and the surrounding streets, Truman quickly made his way by car to the idling Ferdinand Magellan. Speaking for three minutes later that afternoon in Hamtramck, Truman pulled out a Research Division tidbit to endear himself to the crowd: "I understand that you are 97 percent Democratic. Now I wonder what's the matter with that other 3 percent? See what you can do about that in November!"[28]

His next stop was Pontiac, where he reminded the audience, reclining in the hazy, late afternoon sun, of the transformational labor legislation he and FDR had passed:

The Home Owners' Loan Act which saved millions of homes from foreclosure.

The Federal Deposit Insurance Act to protect banking deposits. There has not been a single loss to a depositor in a bank in 3 years. That is the greatest record in the history of the country.

The Fair Labor Standards Act which established a minimum wage and prohibited child labor.

Social security laws which provided protection for those who needed it most.[29]

These achievements were the opposite of the dubious record of his Republican opponents, who Truman said had "passed a law that weakened labor unions. They have taken social security benefits away from more than 700,000 people. They have given tax relief to the rich at the expense of the poor. They have passed a rich man's tax law. They refused to pass a law to control prices. They refused to provide adequate housing. They refused to provide aid for education."

If voters stayed away on November 2, as Truman claimed they had when the Democrats were humbled in the 1946 midterms, they would "get a continuation of this Taft-Hartley backward-looking Congress." It was only by casting their ballots that the country could get "back on the road to progress."[30] After a fact-packed talk to a crowd Charlie Murphy thought was "very friendly and responsive" in Flint, Michigan, Truman made an impromptu stop in Toledo, Ohio, at 11:55 p.m., almost seventeen hours after his waking time that day.[31] "Who wants to see the President?" he asked the five thousand or so night owls. "I do, I do, Mr. President!" yelled an enthusiastic boy, his high-pitched voice rising above the clamor as Truman beamed down from the rear platform. Truman vowed that "before this campaign is over I expect to visit every Whistle Stop in the United States."[32] He then cracked a joke about the local baseball team—a typical Research Division tidbit—before returning to the serious business at hand:

This may be the end of Labor Day, but I am just beginning the most important labor of my life. I am going to make the most important campaign that this country has witnessed since the Lincoln-Douglas debates. I intend to cover the length and breadth of this land, and take to the American people a message of the utmost significance. I am going to tell you the facts. The message concerns November 2nd. The question before you people is whether you want to go forward with the Democratic Party, or whether you want to go back to the past, go back to the horse and buggy days of the Republican Party.

The guest of honor got a little way further down the outline that Murphy had prepared when a man shouted out his assurance that Truman could be sure of getting the labor vote. Truman quick-wittedly abandoned his talking points and launched into an off-the-cuff salvo about the "do-nothing" Congress and what they hadn't done for the people, later prompting an editorial in the *Pittsburgh Press* to contend that he was "running against Congress" instead of fighting "the man to beat," Thomas Dewey.[33]

After confidently assuring the crowd that once the ballots were counted "we will have a Congress that will work in the interests of the people, and I will still be in the White House," Truman introduced his daughter, Margaret. Wearing a two-orchid corsage on a fitted navy blue blouse, the vivacious twenty-four-year-old brunette threw petals from six red roses into the crowd. They cheered and their hands stretched out for more, but she said shyly, "There just aren't enough to go around."[34] As her father turned to go back into his train car, a man in the crowd—who a *Toledo Blade* reporter later claimed was "considerably confused by stimulants"—yelled up at the rear platform, "Come again, Wallace!"[35]

More than a hundred guests, including local politicians, union leaders, and journalists who *did* know their president then boarded the seventeen-car train to get a closer look at the man who was trying to retain his slippery grip on the White House.[36] They talked, talked, and talked some more as night soon became morning. For Truman, sleep would have to wait until he got back to Washington, where he and his team would return to finalize their preparations for the next stage of the tour, to commence on September 18 in Iowa.

Truman likely expected a Republican response to his fighting words in Michigan and Ohio, but these would not be from his challenger. Tom Dewey would not make his opening remarks of the campaign until he spoke in Des Moines, Iowa, on September 20, less than forty-eight hours after Truman addressed thousands of farmers at the National Plowing Match.[37] Back in June, Robert Taft had dubbed the president's speaking odyssey the Whistle Stop Tour. It would have been fair for the Democrats to respond that Dewey, with his follow-my-president campaign agenda, was on the Copycat Tour.

It was left to one of the men Dewey had beaten for the nomination, Harold Stassen, to speak out for the GOP. Addressing a far more modest crowd in Detroit than the one Truman had spoken to the previous day, the University of Pennsylvania president chided Truman for having "dishonored labor with an extreme demagogic appeal to set class against class." Truman could not "furnish the essential leadership" America needed, Stassen said to the cheers of his three thousand supporters, and in desperation was resorting to "scolding, threatening, complaining speeches."[38] But whatever Stassen's criticisms, Truman was in the arena, fighting for all he was worth, while Dewey remained on the sidelines. At this early stage, was the New York governor demonstrating the "essential leadership" Stassen talked of, or merely the complacency of a man who believed his victory was a sure thing?

In a campaign potholed with difficult days, September 9 proved particularly tricky for Truman to climb out of. That morning, veteran pollster Elmo Roper announced that his organization would stop feeling the nation's pulse because, he believed, the president's campaign had suffered a fatal cardiac arrest. Writing in a nationally distributed column, Roper asserted, "Thomas. E. Dewey is almost as good as elected to the Presidency of the United States." Though he went on to write that a Truman comeback was not statistically impossible, Roper reasoned that "Mr. Truman's campaign is not likely to evoke any electoral miracles and Mr. Dewey is not rash. So this is not a hare and tortoise race, and neither is it a race between two closely matched thoroughbreds—it is a very ordinary horse race in which one horse already has a commanding lead over the other."[39]

There was also little in the way of comfort for the president during his morning White House press conference. Though the US military was still successfully conducting the biggest peacetime airlift in history to defy the Soviet blockade of Berlin, tensions were still running high, and, horrifyingly, Red Army troops had fired into an angry crowd of civilians who were staging a huge, 250,000-person rally against communism. Truman tried to divert the panicky press corps' attention elsewhere, but they understandably kept coming back to the subject. Was war with Moscow imminent? What could America do with so many opposing forces massed against it? And seven other questions that Truman could do little to answer convincingly, as he himself didn't know how the tense situation would play out.[40]

That afternoon, the Washington beat writers were given fresh material about the Berlin crisis by the president of the International Ladies' Garment Workers Union, David Dubinsky, whom Truman had summoned to the White House in an effort to garner more labor support. When asked for his prediction about America's role in postwar Berlin, Dubinsky candidly shared his fear that the US military would be "pushed out." Dubinsky told the scribbling journalists that he was gravely concerned about the future of his worker counterparts in Germany. "Hitler put the trade union leaders in concentration camps, but Stalin will chop their heads off. I told the President that in the event we are pushed out of Berlin we should protect them." If Dubinsky didn't have their full attention before, he certainly had it now with such a forthright replay of his Oval Office conversation. How did Truman respond, the writers wanted to know. Dubinsky told them: "He said, 'We will not be pushed out of Berlin.'"[41]

After his meeting with Dubinsky, Truman was right back in the thick of the campaign. Despite the impact of Truman's Detroit speech, the creaky Democratic fund-raising machine was still in need of some grease, so finance manager Louis Johnson invited some of FDR's old backers to dinner with the president. After he had made the grins-and-handshakes rounds in the Red Room, Truman abandoned dignity for pragmatism. Climbing onto a chair to make sure he was heard, Truman made it known in no uncertain terms that unless his guests reached deep into their wallets, the Whistle Stop Tour wouldn't make it past Pittsburgh. "I am appealing for your help," the president told the assembled Who's Who of well-heeled Democratic backers. "Help to carry my message to the American people. We just haven't got the money to buy radio time. In Detroit on Labor Day we had to cut out one of the most important sections of my speech because we didn't have the money to stay on the air."[42] Though stunned for a few seconds by the strange nature of such a request, and from the president, of all people, the attendees honored their host as he had asked, with two pledging $10,000 apiece and more following their lead. So the Last Chance Special would, at least for the time being, take to the rails again.[43] Still, some journalists were shocked by the spectacle, with Drew Pearson lamenting Truman's "appalling" performance and stating that the chief executive looked "pathetic and alone" as he stood atop the quilted chair begging for money.[44]

The next afternoon, Truman sought some much-needed R&R on the water after spending the morning seeing "customers," as he called White House guests who wanted something from him. He rounded up Clark Clifford, Charlie Ross, Matt Connelly, and some of the other usual suspects, and together they went for an overnight jaunt down the Potomac to Quantico on the *Williamsburg*. Though he devoted a few hours to working on campaign speeches, the most eventful happenings of that evening were, according to Truman's diary, a nap followed by a long massage to ease away the mounting tension. The president, who had suffered a bevy of anxiety and overwork-related complaints in the past, could ill afford to let stress derail his fall campaign when it had only just begun.[45]

On September 11, Truman recorded, "The next day we go to Blakistone Island, anchor and enjoy sunlight . . . spend a most pleasant day talking of world affairs, western trip, speeches and prima donnas in government."[46]

Truman would have preferred to stay longer with his friends, but world events would not allow it. Reluctantly returning to the "great white jail" at 4:30 p.m. on September 13, Truman listened to his top military advisers' proposal to send an emissary to London, with the goal of talking with British prime minister Clement Attlee, foreign secretary Ernest Bevin, and other officials about building storage "huts" for bomb components at B-29 bomber airfields should the Berlin crisis escalate beyond the limits of diplomacy and into armed conflict with the Soviets. The president expressed his desire to avoid ever repeating the atomic bombings of Hiroshima and Nagasaki, but he said grimly that if the Soviets pushed him far enough he would again sanction the use of such terrible force. To try and avoid this, he approved the diplomatic trip to London. Meanwhile, other leading American negotiators would continue with their plan to present the Berlin blockade issue to the United Nations, with the aim of the international body issuing a strong reprimand to Russia.[47] Truman ended the day on a pessimistic note, scribbling in a pad on his desk, "I have a terrible feeling . . . that we are very close to war. I hope not."[48]

The next day Truman wrote on a notepad that he "had another hell of a day." He had a broad range of appointments, including a "sitting for an old Polish painter. And I don't like to pose—but it's part of the trial of being President." After a full day he worked on into the evening, revealing, "Had the gang in at 6:00 pm and worked on the farm speech for Des Moines."[49] He would have liked to get back to the solace of the *Williamsburg* or to visit his family in Missouri, but with the pivotal Iowa farming speech just four days off, his campaign team and schedule dictated otherwise.

Foreign affairs also continued to move fast. On September 15, British foreign secretary Ernest Bevin told a packed House of Commons that the impasse in Berlin was just a small part of the threat that communist expansionism posed to democratic societies worldwide. Communists wanted to take over Southeast Asia, he cautioned, and were trying to instigate civil wars on every continent. "No one can see the end of it," the foreign secretary concluded glumly.[50]

It seemed that on the day Bevin spoke of ill tidings abroad, all of Truman's doubters and critics at home had coordinated verbal attacks against him. The president claimed that Robert Taft was making a printers' strike worse by trying to "put the heat on" the National Labor Relations Board. Never one to duck a challenge, particularly from Truman, the fearless Ohio senator sniped back. "President Truman's charge only shows that we have reached the silly season in politics," Taft said. "The truth is that President Truman, by the veto message accepted largely from the Communist Party sympathizer Lee Pressman [another of those identified as "disloyal" by Whittaker Chambers] . . . has encouraged the open defiance of the law now engaged by some of the more radical labor bosses."[51]

Taft was not the only one to criticize Truman that day or to pooh-pooh his election chances. In his nationally syndicated column, veteran political observer Thomas L. Stokes proclaimed, "If President Truman is reelected he will thereby become the miracle man of this crazy era." Stokes went on to summarize the main obstacles daring the president to "just stay home," including Republican control of key states, the ongoing tensions in Berlin, Dewey's huge polling lead, and the Democratic Party's fund-raising woes and three-way split. "Yet with all this, the man just fights harder," Stokes concluded. "You have to admire his spunk."[52]

All too soon it was time to go. As Truman said his good-byes and prepared to board his train on September 17 for a fifteen-day slog during which he would speak 128 times in seventeen states, the Associated Press republished a sobering *Editor & Publisher* survey. It found that 69 percent of daily US newspapers supported Tom Dewey, 16 percent wanted Truman, 4 percent favored Thurmond, and just 0.28 percent wanted Wallace, with 11 percent undecided. These numbers looked bad for Truman—and what polls in this campaign cycle didn't?—but 61 percent of the dailies backed Dewey in the 1944 contest, and it mattered not a jot on polling day, as FDR prevailed.[53] It was voters, after all, who decided elections. Brien McMahon, Democratic senator from Connecticut, declared that if more than a million of them turned out for Truman and Barkley then they would carry his state on November 2.[54] But before Connecticut came the next swing, which would take Truman through Ohio, Pennsylvania, and Iowa, which were all up for grabs if Truman could put in a stronger performance there than his challengers.

Truman quickly settled into a campaign routine. He rose every day between 5:00 and 6:00 a.m., had a breakfast of toast, eggs, orange juice, and coffee, and perused the talking points for the first couple of rear platform talks that day. Then, if time allowed, he got off the train to take a brisk walk with Secret Service agents in tow, often taking a couple of his aides with him for company and conversation as they tried to keep up with his military pace of 120 steps per minute.[55] Then it was back to the Ferdinand Magellan to freshen up and make the first appearance of the day to the crowds. Even unexpected mishaps couldn't shake Truman out of his forward momentum. As the train came to an abrupt halt at one station, brakes squealing, Truman spilled a bottle of soda all over his trousers. He got out of his wet seat and started for the bedroom to get a clean pair of slacks, but, realizing that he only had a few minutes to talk from the back platform before the train started up again, he turned on his heel and, unashamedly, walked out to greet the crowd, wet trousers and all.[56]

Between each stop, Truman looked over another Research Division fact sheet with Clifford and Elsey, reviewed the agenda with Charlie Ross and Matt Connelly, and read briefings from General Marshall and other cabinet members, while also trying to flick through a few newspaper articles so he could keep up with the comings and goings at home and abroad. After a brief lunch, he gave between two and five more speeches from the train, then delivered an address at a larger venue either before or just after a hastily consumed dinner, which was often little more than a ham sandwich and glass of buttermilk.[57] Next, he spoke to a further three or four audiences until 10:00 or 11:00 p.m., before talking some more with senators, congressmen, city mayors, and other local dignitaries who boarded the train. These late night bull sessions would often go on long after midnight, leaving the president with between four and seven hours of repose before he got up and repeated the process. Sunday, in accordance with Truman's faith, was usually a rest day, though several times on the Whistle Stop Tour he broke with this practice to deliver a few talks to round out the week.[58] One news report condensed a typically madcap day aboard the Last Chance Special into a single sentence: "Between breakfast and midnight that day, Harry Truman traveled 500 miles by train, 141 by automobile and bus, made 11 speeches in 15 different towns, changed his clothes eight times and met 250 politicians, labor leaders and civic dignitaries."[59]

The campaign machine also ran on a set pattern, based on the lessons learned during the June "inspection" tour and modified to accommodate extra demands placed on Truman's staff by the sheer scope of the fall leg. During breakfast and morning breaks, Clark Clifford and his deputy George Elsey discussed the day's talking points with the president and gave their feedback on the previous days' happenings. Every two days they sent a runner from the train to the local municipal airport to collect a pouch sent from the Research Division via the White House, which contained four- or five-page fact sheets on each of the upcoming whistle stops. Elsey, his dark hair always neatly combed into a high side part no matter how busy or tired he was, distilled the Batt group's fodder into several talking points for the president and supplemented these with real-time information based on current events. Meanwhile, Clifford, his long legs contorted awkwardly under one of the too-short desks in his car—which was just in front of the president's accommodations—added annotations and strike-throughs to the final draft of the next major address and changed any lofty prose into "simple sentences and simple words."[60]

Charlie Ross sent press releases down to the correspondents' cars at the front of the train several times a day, and the reporters and photographers jumped from their cars and hustled back to hear Truman speak at each scheduled stop. Once they had jostled their way to a suitable spot on the teeming platform, they scribbled away on notepads or in the margins of the press releases they received moments before Truman's voice crackled into life through the train's speaker system. Once the president was done, the newsmen (and, barring a few exceptions such as Alice Dunnigan, the first female African American reporter to ride a presidential train, they were men) scurried back to the front of the train, filing their hastily assembled reports from the radio-equipped media cars, which had Western Union operators at the ready. Many of those who switched back and forth between Truman's Last Chance Special and Dewey's Victory Special preferred the courage and zest of the president

Bess (far left) and Margaret (center) Truman join the president on the rear platform of his Ferdinand Magellan train car on its way to Washington D.C. following his election victory. *Harry S. Truman Library and Museum*

Truman holds up the *Chicago Tribune* with the erroneous headline "Dewey Defeats Truman" at Union Station in St. Louis, Missouri, on November 3. *Harry S. Truman Library and Museum*

Truman and India Edwards, executive director of the DNC Women's Division, talk tactics aboard the whistle stop train. *Harry S. Truman Library and Museum*

The Santa Fe train used by the president on his western "inspection tour" to California in June 1948. *Harry S. Truman Library and Museum*

Truman inspects a horse at a campaign stop in Oklahoma on September 29, 1948. Proving his farming credentials, Truman correctly guessed the horse's age. *Harry S. Truman Library and Museum*

15

Truman speaks to a group of young boys from his train during his 1948 campaign. *Harry S. Truman Library and Museum*

A Democratic Party campaign poster featuring Truman (right) and Alben Barkley (left). *Harry S. Truman Library and Museum*

Truman talks with reporters on his campaign train on October 16, 1948.
Harry S. Truman Library and Museum

Reporters crammed into the small press car on Truman's train type up
their stories on the president's latest speech. *Harry S. Truman Library and
Museum*

Truman (L) shakes hands with rival candidate Thomas Dewey
at the dedication of Idlewild Airport, New York, on July 31, 1948.
Harry S. Truman Library and Museum

A Clifford K. Berryman cartoon shows Thomas Dewey (right) asking Truman about the wisdom of him continuing his 1948 presidential bid. *Clifford K. Berryman Political Cartoon Collection, United States Senate Collection, Center for Legislative Archives*

Standing with several aides, Truman waves to the crowd that
gathered to see him speak in Crestline, Ohio, on September 17, 1948.
The Crestline Historical Society

(opposite)
Truman winks at photographers and reporters
from the rear platform of his train car during the
1948 Whistle Stop Tour. *Library of Congress Prints
and Photographs Division*

Truman hails a crowd during an evening speech on September 29, 1948. *Mr. George Webb*

Truman holds a boy as he speaks into radio microphones, probably at the dedication of a statue in Bolivar, Missouri, on July 4, 1948. *National Archives and Records Administration. Office of Presidential Libraries. Harry S. Truman Library*

The armor-plated Ferdinand Magellan presidential train that carried Truman across America during the Whistle Stop Campaign. *Michael Hall, Gold Coast Railroad Museum*

The Ferdinand Magellan train car dining room that Truman ate in nightly with his family and aides during the 1948 campaign. *Michael Hall, Gold Coast Railroad Museum*

A telegram to Truman from a southerner who vows
not to vote for the president because he is a "negro lover."
Harry S. Truman Library and Museum

The July 27, 1948, issue of the *Chicago Defender* announces Truman's bold plan to desegregate the US armed forces, which he had declared in Executive Order 9981 the previous day. *Library of Congress*

Bill Batt and Frank Hoeber are reunited fourteen years after they worked together in the DNC Research Division. Here Batt swears in Hoeber as his deputy in President John F. Kennedy's Economic Development Administration in 1962. *Hoeber Family Archive, Philadelphia PA, Francis W. Hoeber, Custodian*

to the "stuffed shirt" opponent, according to Clifford.[61] Dewey's team may have been more organized, but the Republican's comparatively few speeches, plus the fact that he stuck to his speechwriter's prose so faithfully and displayed what historian Irwin Ross called "quiet reasonableness" in contrast to Truman's bluster, meant that the writers on the president's train had more to write about.[62]

Behind the scenes, advance man Don Dawson would be out ahead of the president by several days, meeting with local Democratic leaders, rustling up extra funds when he could, and ensuring that all the logistics for Truman's major speeches were running smoothly. On the train, Charlie Murphy and Bill Boyle, the man who would take over from Howard McGrath as DNC chairman after the election, backed up Dawson's efforts by reaching out to Truman supporters at upcoming stops by phone.[63]

★ ★ ★

"AGAINST A MAN ARMED WITH BRASS KNUCKLES ... IT IS POOR JUDGMENT TO DEFEND ONESELF WITH A POWDER PUFF"

The biggest speech on the mid-September leg of the Whistle Stop Tour would be in Iowa on the 18th, but Truman would have a few smaller ones first to rehearse some of his main points. On the 17th, his train rumbled into Pittsburgh, where he transferred temporarily to another train—the Freedom Train. The year before, this red, white, and blue train pulled by a modern diesel locomotive began crisscrossing the nation on a tour that would almost rival the president's. The Freedom Train made 300 stops across the country between 1947 and 1949, where visitors crowded the carriages to peer through bullet-proof glass displays at one hundred documents of historical importance, including the Declaration of Independence, the United States Constitution, the Gettysburg Address, the Bill of Rights, and, fittingly for the 1948 election, the Truman Doctrine. People who clambered aboard would also be treated to Americana coming through the overhead speakers, including the song "Freedom Train," a Top Thirty hit written by Irving Berlin and performed by Bing Crosby and the Andrews Sisters.

The most apt part of the refrain, given Truman's appearance on September 17, was:

You can shout your anger from a steeple
You can shoot the system full of holes
You can always question "We the People"
You can get your answer at the polls.[64]

With hundreds of people jostling for position on the small platform below him and several thousand more listening outside the station via an army PA system, Truman had some words of his own to add to Berlin's simple, patriotic lyrics. Lacking the eloquence of Thomas Jefferson or Abraham Lincoln but matching them in spirit and vigor, he said:

> We have a system in which we believe that the Government is for the benefit of the individual. There are other systems which make the individual subject to the whims of the Government. We've been fighting for that ever since 1776, for the welfare and the benefit of the individual.
>
> We have the greatest Government in the world. We have the greatest country in the world. We have the most powerful country in the world. Let's live up to our ideals and keep working for that peace which all of us want so badly. We want peace in the world and justice to every individual in every nation in the world. That's what we fought two world wars for. I'm hoping, and I've always been hopeful, that we would eventually reach that ideal condition where the United Nations would represent the world as the United States represents the Government of the United States.[65]

Thurmond, Dewey, and Wallace would have applauded such an exhortation for liberal democracy, even if they may have questioned Truman's methods for upholding it. But the Pittsburgh crowd needed no caveats, cheering the president and Margaret, who stood beside her father on the rear platform waving at the well-wishers below. Also with him were Pittsburgh mayor Dave Lawrence and county commissioner John Kane, both of whom had vocally supported Truman for the vice presidency back in 1944.[66]

After shaking hands with as many people as time would allow and smiling broadly as a man further back in the multitude yelled, "You're on the road to victory!," Truman went back to his own train, which trundled down the track to Crestline, Ohio.[67] There, in the same spot where he had opened the June trip, Truman delivered some ill news to the 1,500 train workers and their families who had stayed up until 10:25 p.m. to hear him speak: "I have just received a confirmation of a very sad incident. The United Nations Mediator in Palestine was assassinated today. His death emphasizes again the difficulties in our efforts to secure liberties under law to all the peoples in the world. We know that through orderly world organization we must seek liberties like those we hold precious in towns such as this beautiful city in Ohio."[68]

The same day, Soviet Russia had cast another shadow on peace by insisting that the communist countries would block Western attempts to put the Berlin standoff before the United Nations meeting in Paris. The East German military newspaper *Tagliche Rundscha*, a mouthpiece for the Politburo used to test opinions, stated that it was in fact the United States, not Russia, that was jeopardizing the world "in sharp contradiction to United Nations statutes." Despite such warnings and accusations, the America-led airlift set a new single-day record, delivering almost five thousand tons of coal and other supplies with 581 flights.[69]

With night now enveloping the Ferdinand Magellan, Truman switched his working attire—which that day included a wide-lapel black suit accented with a natty black polka dot tie and white pocket square—for pajamas and retired to his bedroom, where he could, at long last, spend a few hours alone and in silence. Or so he thought. Just a couple of hours later, the president's repose was unceremoniously interrupted by a rapping at his door. Another international incident? Strikers back in the picket lines? A security threat to the train? No. It was a sheepish-looking aide, who told the bleary-eyed president that Illinois political boss Jake Arvey had boarded at the last stop and wanted a word. At 3:00 a.m. A few minutes earlier, Arvey's county commissioner, Arthur X. Elrod, had warned the Chicago kingmaker that "the big wheel's asleep." Elrod had apparently forgotten, however, that the Truman wheel, like those of his train, rarely stopped, particularly not when there was a little less than six weeks left in the campaign that would either extend or derail his career. So Truman, shaking off his slumber, had someone put on a fresh pot of coffee and talked for as long as Arvey wanted. The former army colonel, whose expansive personality was barely contained by his short frame, had been influential in nominating Adlai Stevenson for the Senate, and he wanted to discuss this and Truman's prospects as the train rolled across Illinois and on into Iowa.[70]

Many politicians would have allowed themselves to sleep in a little later than usual after a 3:00 a.m. tête-à-tête. Just as well, then, that Truman barely considered himself a politician. He rose before dawn as always, raring to go for a potentially decisive appearance at the National Plowing Match. His enthusiasm was such that one *Time* reporter wrote that he and his fellow writers who were jammed into the media cars at the front of the train "were frankly horrified at Harry Truman's endless cheerfulness and energy. Despite a sore throat and his 64 years he leaped out of bed at 5 every morning, apparently unable to wait for another exhausting day."[71]

Truman had spoken to 55,000 people at the University of California, Berkeley when he delivered the June 12 commencement address and to as many as 125,000 in his Labor Day speech in Detroit. Another huge audience awaited him on the afternoon of September 18 at the Iowa fields just outside Dexter, eighteen miles east of Des Moines. This was the same day that Alben Barkley made his first campaign speech in Wilkes-Barre, Pennsylvania, which would be followed by 249 more addresses as the intrepid Kentucky senator defied his seventy-one years and flew back and forth across the country in a chartered DC-3 plane.[72]

For the previous two weeks, Truman had traversed the Midwest, making his case that he, the president of the United States, was not some aloof intellectual blueblood like many of his predecessors in the White House. On the contrary, Truman was out to prove that he alone— not Dewey nor Wallace nor Thurmond—truly understood the daily challenges of the farmer because, heck, back home in "Missour-uh," he *had been one*.[73] This campaign was by no means the first time Truman had leaned on his agricultural background to woo potential voters. It was actually the continuation of his campaigning to farmers during Senate elections back in Missouri, during which he had used his land-tilling credentials to his advantage.[74]

Such an appeal had helped him squeak by his Senate primary challengers in 1934 by just 8,400 votes in what Truman later called "the most bitter, mud-slinging campaign in Missouri's history of dirty campaigns."[75] Now, fourteen years later, the president knew that to have any chance of overcoming Dewey's massive polling lead, he must carry Iowa,

Missouri, and most of the other Midwest states. And he was prepared to again sling some mud to do it. Winning the Hawkeye State would not be easy, though, as Iowa's governor, Robert D. Blue, was not, as his name suggested, a Democrat, and all of the state's eight senators and congressmen were also Republicans. To make matters worse, another presidential rival, Henry Wallace, was a native son.

Whatever Taft and the rest of his GOP opponents would say about Truman's farm policy, the swing of the agricultural vote toward the Republican Party had begun long before he became president. In 1936, Franklin Roosevelt had garnered close to two-thirds of farmers' support at the polls, with 59 percent voting for him. Eight years later, in 1944, with Truman now on the ticket with him, the percentage of farmers supporting FDR dropped precipitously to 48 percent.[76] What would the tally be this time around?

Just as Cadillac Square had been for the labor vote in the first week of the fall campaign, the National Plowing Match was to be a test of a key component of Truman's vote-getting strategy. If he could win over a potentially hostile audience, in a state in which Dewey was leading the polls by fourteen points, perhaps he could recapture the farmers who had bolted from the New Deal coalition in FDR's final election in 1944.[77] To try and do so, Truman would condense the evolution of his agricultural message, with its many facets, into a single, fact-packed address, one that the Research Division, Clark Clifford, Dave Lloyd, W. McNeil Lowry, and Charlie Brannan had been working on for the past month, going through draft after draft, edit after edit.[78]

And now was also the time for Truman to really call out the Republicans on their disastrous grain storage policy, which, with the bumper crop, was threatening farmers with fire-sale prices at best, and bankruptcy at worst. With curly-haired Bess—at Truman's side now that her annual summer visit to Missouri was over—and Margaret watching from the wings, both wearing hats that helped shield their faces from the insistent sunshine, Truman took to the podium. Just before he was ready to go on, Bess realized that he was without a boutonnière, so she hurried forward, looked at her husband in mock reproach, and pinned a red carnation on his buttonhole before going back to Margaret's side. With his outfit now complete and a giant, two-story blackboard towering behind him listing the scores from the plowing match, Truman gazed out at the sea of faces in front for a few moments and then looked over his notes one last time.[79]

He started off in positive fashion, lavishing praise on the multitude that had braved the dust and heat to come to hear him speak: "It does my heart good to see the grain fields of the Nation again. They are a wonderful sight. The record-breaking harvests you have been getting in recent years have been a blessing. Millions of people have been saved from starvation by the food you have produced. The whole world has reason to be everlastingly grateful to the farmers of the United States."[80]

Truman then connected the farmers' efforts to foreign policy. "In a very real sense, the abundant harvests of this country are helping to save the world from communism. Communism thrives on human misery. And the crops you are producing are driving back the tide of misery in many lands."[81] This was a tenuous link, perhaps, but logical enough at its essence as American grain exports were still helping European nations get back on their feet after the war.

But what Truman had really come there to do was to again blast the GOP and, in his now tried and tested "guilty by association" rhetorical style, Thomas Dewey. To set the scene, Truman started off with a history lesson, blaming greedy banks and the Republicans for the loss of almost a quarter million farms in the wake of the Great Depression. In contrast, he insisted, FDR's agricultural policy had returned this livelihood to many, reduced interest rates on agricultural loans, and almost eradicated farm foreclosures.[82]

He then continued to tie the GOP to the selfish interests of bankers, lobbyists, and industrial tycoons in a broad-sweeping attack that appealed to farmers and laborers alike to sit up and take notice of the Republican agenda before it was too late:

> Republican reactionaries want an administration that will assure privilege for big business, regardless of what may happen to the rest of the Nation. The Republican strategy is to divide the farmer and the industrial worker—to get them to squabbling with each other—so that big business can grasp the balance of power and take the country over, lock, stock, and barrel.
>
> To gain this end, they will stop at nothing. On the one hand, the Republicans are telling industrial workers that the high cost of food

in the cities is due to this Government's farm policy. On the other hand, the Republicans are telling the farmers that the high cost of manufactured goods on the farm is due to this Government's labor policy.

That's plain hokum. It's an old political trick. 'If you can't convince 'em, confuse 'em.' But this time it won't work. The farmer and the worker know that their troubles have been coming from another source.[83]

The grain storage debacle was, Truman asserted, just one more example that showed that the Republicans were "gluttons of privilege" who cared little, if at all, for the common man and more for the kickbacks from their lobbyist and grain speculator backers who stood to reap millions of dollars in profit from the wholesale of cheap crops. With their failure to provide adequate housing for the harvest, which, as Lowry predicted, had been a bumper one for oats, wheat, and corn, the Republican Congress "stuck a pitchfork in the farmer's back." Truman, on an emotional and rhetorical roll, followed this indelible image with a dramatic plea: "I'm not asking you just to vote for me. Vote for yourselves. Vote for your farms. Vote for your future."[84]

After Truman left the stage to appreciative but far from rapturous applause, Oscar Chapman got in among the farmers to see what they thought of the president's stance. He also asked what they had expected from the Eightieth Congress and how this expectation aligned with the harsh reality they now faced. Chapman later encapsulated their sentiments in this way: "Why didn't Congress let us have a little money to build storage tanks to save our crops when they were giving money to every industrial plant in the United States to increase their industrial capacity and efficiency and everything else?"[85] Up to this point, Chapman had been convinced that Dewey would win Iowa. Now he thought that Truman might be able to pull off an upset.

And what if Iowa was only the beginning in the Midwest? Chapman knew better than to draw decisive conclusions from a few offhand comments, but many farmers from surrounding states had joined their Iowa brethren that day, and with more than a dozen speeches in the area over the coming days, perhaps Truman could gain some real momentum.[86]

Clark Clifford thought that the speech had demonstrated Truman's fighting spirit to Iowa's farmers, the media and Dewey, but he wondered if the president had gone too far in his attacks on the Republicans. Had the zeal of the president's approach—which Thomas Stokes, writing in the *New York Times*, called "raw, harsh, demagogic slogans"—backfired and actually turned people off?[87] Like Chapman, Clifford loped around the fairground with long-legged strides for a while after Truman left the stage, wiping the sweat from his brow and trying to gauge the overall reaction, but his brief, informal survey failed to yield any conclusive results.[88]

Whatever the impact of portraying the Eightieth Congress as callous toward rural areas and linking Dewey to it by implication (he again did not mention his opponent by name), Truman had little time to assess his performance. The pivotal speech—and the plowing demonstration he gave afterwards, just in case further proof was needed that he could indeed create a straight furrow—were just more items on that day's crowded itinerary.[89]

But while the rails called him back, Truman would not be denied a good meal to see him through the rest of a packed schedule. With Bess and Margaret at his side, he ducked under the awning of a marquee and into the merciful shade. This offered some relief from the sun, which sent the mercury soaring past 105 degrees, but Truman still needed more of a cool down, so he took off his jacket and rolled up his shirtsleeves. The president loaded his plate in the buffet line with fried chicken, mashed potatoes, baked beans, buttered corn, cheese, tomatoes, and relish. He managed to get the heaping helping back to his table and set it down with a clunk on the red-and-white checked tablecloth.[90]

After Truman worked his way through the many layers of his lunch and made small talk with the thirty farmers who pulled up folding chairs to join him in the country feast, he ushered Bess and Margaret into a waiting car and their driver took them back to the train, past an estimated fifty thousand people who had lined the back roads to see the motorcade pass by.[91] The Trumans and their entourage then continued their southward journey, with the president resisting the temptation of a feasting-induced nap as he reiterated his attacks on the Republican's farming failure at each successive stop. By the time his train passed over the Iowa-Missouri border and Truman retired for another inadequate night's sleep, he had been up for almost twenty hours and had given thirteen speeches. It was hard, Margaret Truman recalled, not to be "swallowed in a maelstrom of roaring voices, waving hands and swirling faces."[92]

To compound Truman's weariness, the dusty Iowa farm tracks, relentless summer heat, and his forceful delivery had given him a bad sore throat, just days after he had recovered from the effects of a cold that assailed him when the train left Washington for the Midwest swing. To help his voice endure the strain of talk after talk from the back platform in the coming days, his physician Wallace Graham applied a medicinal spray when "the Boss" was out of the range of the press photographers who dashed from the media cars to cover the scene at each stop. "Dr. Graham just sprayed, mopped and caused me to gargle bad-tasting liquids until the throat gave up and got well," Truman later wrote his sister.[93] He wouldn't have felt any better if he had read popular columnist Joseph Alsop's reaction to his Plowing Match address. Alsop believed that Truman had done little to solve his "well-nigh hopeless political problem" and in following a populist course was "hopelessly miscast in the role of William Jennings Bryan."[94]

At least there was some positive news to cheer the weary, croaky president: the US-helmed airlift in Berlin had its most successful twenty-four hours to date to coincide with Air Force Day (the celebration of that service's independence from the US Army), with bombers delivering 7,000 tons of supplies. This effort, and the fact that it boosted the daily average for the month above 4,500 tons (up from 3,855 in August), prompted the ever-defiant General Clay to declare that Americans "can last indefinitely in Berlin" despite the continued Soviet blockade.[95]

For the good of his throat and in accordance with his strong faith, Truman would respect the Sabbath and take the next day off.[96] This time, to his delight, this welcome and much-needed break would be back home in Missouri.[97] As Truman was struggling with his voice, Alben Barkley was finding his. At a rally in Wilmington, Delaware, the vice presidential candidate, who had earned the nickname "Iron Man" for his relentless campaigning over forty years in office, showed that he still had more than a little fire left. He told the one thousand people who were crammed into the Young Democrats building that the Republican-controlled Congress had "set labor back a generation" with the Taft-Hartley Act and were "sitting idly by while the prices of food and clothing mounted to unprecedented heights."[98] Later that day in Dover, Barkley jokingly told the crowd, which had braved a coastal squall to see him, that he would give them an abbreviated speech. "I don't want you to get your feet wet," he said. "In fact, I don't even want you to get Dewey."[99]

Going into the third week of September, Dewey still had the majority of media support and led Truman in the polls by double digits. Columnists across the country fawned over the New York governor as if describing a general marching into ancient Rome at the head of a triumph procession. Drew Pearson proclaimed that Dewey was running "the most skillful and astute campaign in recent history," and *Time* insisted that "Barring a miracle, [Dewey and Warren] could not fail to sweep the Republican Party back into power."[100] Pollster George Gallup wholeheartedly agreed with the inevitability of a Dewey victory, asking a friend, "Why does the Republican committee want to spend any money? The results are a foregone conclusion."

So what was it about Dewey that earned him such praise? Certainly the New York governor was younger, more polished, and, when he felt like it, a better public speaker than Truman, having honed his rhetorical skills as a prosecutor and district attorney before getting into politics. Perhaps there was another, more tangible reason. As reporters on the Truman train slept in cramped quarters and provided much of their own food, the ninety-two writers and photographers on Dewey's so-called Victory Special enjoyed spacious accommodation and the same fine meals enjoyed by the Republican candidate and his entourage, with roast beef a regular favorite.[101]

But despite all the glowing endorsements of the Republican candidate, some close observers recognized that Truman's aggressive, relentless campaigning and what *New York Times* columnist Cabell Phillips called the president's "warmly personal, straightforward manner" was starting to have an impact that the editorials and polling numbers didn't reflect.[102] And not all these observers were in the president's camp. E. F. Hutton was one of the financiers who had helped secure Dewey's nomination and had since enabled him to build an insurmountable funding lead over Truman. But despite this funding advantage, Hutton questioned Dewey's ability to halt the building momentum of Truman's Whistle Stop Tour. On September 20, he wrote to Dewey's campaign manager, Herbert Brownell, in a panic: "Against a man armed with brass knuckles, well-schooled in the art of eye-gouging, biting and kicking, it is poor judgment to defend oneself with a powder puff."[103]

Whether or not Dewey would follow the pattern from his failed 1944 campaign and discard the powder puff in October in favor of a cudgel remained to be seen.[104] What seemed certain is that Truman would continue his street-fighting tactics against the Republican-controlled "do-nothing" Congress as his train crisscrossed the country. Harsh words, biting, brass knuckles—he was committed to using whatever tools and tactics were needed to defeat Dewey and Warren and finally put to rest the notion that he was an accidental president. Staring at the harsh reality that he may have just one month left in his career, Truman had no option but to fight for every vote he could get. He would also keep running hard day after day, predicted one *Washington Post* writer, who compared the president to a racehorse who ignored the handicappers and "has been told before that he can't win and has been singularly undampened and unimpressed by the information."[105]

On the same day that the big-money Republican backer was warning Dewey's campaign against complacency and the *Post* columnist was commending Truman's racing pedigree, the president gave another major speech, this time in Denver. But first he took time to visit a local veteran's hospital, despite his aides' warning that this would throw off the day's schedule.[106] When he eventually bounded up the steps of the State Capitol he again sang the tune of president of the people and contrasted that with his GOP opponents, who he said were "curiously deaf to the voice of the people. They have a hard time hearing what the ordinary people of the country are saying." Not so when it came to certain other audiences, Truman said: "But they have no trouble at all hearing what Wall Street is saying. They are able to catch the slightest whisper from big business and the special interests." Truman then made a distinction between those who would vote for Dewey and the party they wanted to put in office. "Most Republicans are fine people," he said, but in contrast, "The Republican Party today is controlled by silent and cunning men who have a dangerous lust for power and privilege."[107]

And what did this mean for the people of Colorado? "I predict that they will turn back the clock to the day when the West was an economic colony of Wall Street," Truman warned. "That is terrible even to contemplate." Using Research Division material, Truman then gave the crowd a snapshot of what he viewed as conservatives' failures to conserve western states' resources over the previous thirty-five years:

> You live in a region whose whole future depends on its wise use of the rich resources that Nature has provided. Early in this century, a unique Republican President, Theodore Roosevelt, fought for conservation, only to be repudiated by his party.
>
> All through the Republican administrations from 1921 to 1933, the big business pressure groups prevented adequate conservation measures from being put into effect. They wanted quick profits, the easy way. And so western forests were logged off and left barren. Range lands were grazed off and ruined. Farmland was worked to the point where its fertility was gone. Precious water ran unused past barren land. There was no soil conservation program, no range conservation program.
>
> The Nation lost tremendous quantities of its most valuable resources. The West continued to bow to Wall Street furnishing raw materials at low prices and buying back finished goods at high prices.[108]

These failures came to an end, Truman contended, when FDR took the helm:

> Under his leadership, conservation was made a living reality. You know better than anyone how much it has meant to the West. The Democratic administration won its fight for conservation and for western development against the bitter opposition of Wall Street and the special interests. You of the West see the results of our victory every day. You see those results in bigger and better crops; in new industries; in the growing national parks and forests and the tourists who visit them; in the rising standards of living of the people of the West; and in the stronger economy of the whole Nation.

FDR's stewardship was not a permanent solution, though, and the West faced serious challenges, Truman reminded his listeners: "We are still using our timber faster than we grow it. Thousands of acres of land are still being washed away every year. Disastrous floods are still frequent. Conservation in the West is of first importance to the whole country."

He then went on the offensive against his favorite target for abuse and ridicule, stating:

> The Republicans in Congress consistently tried to cut the ground from under our conservation program. Last year, the Republican-dominated House of Representatives voted to cut the agricultural conservation program in half in 1947, and to end it entirely by 1948.
>
> The Democrats in the Senate led, and finally won, a fight to save the life of that program. They saved it, but they could not completely restore it. The program was seriously damaged by the Republican 80th Congress.[109]

It was not just conservation in the West that concerned Truman, but also the region's industrial present and future. He framed this issue in a curious way—tribalism: "I know that all of you recognize the importance of creating new industries in this region, using the resources of the West, so as to reduce your industrial dependence upon the East."[110] Being from the heart of the Midwest, Truman could claim impartiality between East and West, and he was certainly no part of East Coast elitist circles, as FDR had been.

The president continued:

> For my part, I am convinced that rapid and sound industrial development in the West will make a vital contribution to the living standards and the well-being, not only of the people of the West, but of the whole Nation.
>
> The heart of the western industrial development program is hydroelectric power. Coupled with the irrigation projects and flood control, electric power is of fundamental importance to your future.

The issue of western economic and industrial development was not just a matter of regionalism to Truman, but also one subject to the differing visions, words, and actions of the two main political parties:

> The Democratic Party, for the past 15 years, has been energetically developing the great dams, irrigation projects, and power systems which have contributed so much to the prosperity of the West.

But as soon as the Republican Party gained control of the Congress, it began to tear down the whole western development program. The Republicans slashed funds right and left. They cut back projects to bring water to the land and electric power to industry.

Right here in this State, the Colorado-Big Thompson project is under way. It is an inspiring project, involving the transfer of water from one side of the Continental Divide to the other. The Republican Congress sharply reduced the funds for that project. When I pointed out the danger of that action and requested them to restore those funds, they refused to do it.

Wherever you turn, no matter what field of activity, you find the same story. In the light of the evidence, I say flatly that the Republican leaders have been working against the interests of the people. I say they have been eager agents of the big business lobbies and the most reactionary elements in American economic life. They jump for these lobbyists, but they won't do anything for the people.

In the last 16 years, Democratic administrations have built a firm foundation for a new and greater West. We restored grazing lands for the sustained production of livestock. Millions of cattle and sheep feed today where only prairie dogs and rattlesnakes existed before. We restored forests for a sustained yield of timber. Trees stand for the future where exploiters would have wiped them out. We established a sound conservation policy to prevent land erosion and restore the fertility of the soil.

We built the Federal system of hydroelectric and irrigation projects which are now providing water for more than 5 million irrigated acres in the West and for better living for millions of people. We have been leading the fight for decent housing, effective reduction of the cost of living, and a rise in living standards—all for a better Nation of happier people.

That is the Democratic record—a record of which I am exceedingly proud.

There is more to do, much more. What we have done so far is only the beginning. This is no time to permit progress to be checked, when you can foresee great new developments of your agriculture, your industry, and your commerce, if you have the aid and support of the Federal Government.[111]

As he often did at the end of addresses in large arenas and whistle stop speeches alike, Truman wrapped up his most significant speech of Western conservation and development by issuing his listeners a challenge and letting them know that for all his words and Dewey's it would be they, the people, whose votes determined the future of their state and region:

> Your need is to insure the election of an administration pledged
> to give you that aid and support—in other words, you need a
> Democratic administration. There is a hard fight ahead. We shall
> have to fight the slick political propaganda of the special interests
> and the Republican leadership.
>
> We shall have to fight the millions of dollars that Wall Street is
> pouring into the treasury of the Republican Party. We shall have to
> fight the Republican undercover sabotage of the West.
>
> But we of the Democratic Party are eager for that fight. In fact,
> I am taking it to them right now. We believe that we owe to future
> generations the bequest of a strong America, mighty in its resources
> and wise in its use of them.
>
> We are firmly determined to leave after us a land that is better
> than we found it.[112]

Truman's opponents were concerned with different domestic and foreign policy issues on the night of September 20. Arriving in New York for the opening speech of his campaign, Henry Wallace told a national radio audience that on that evening, "as never before in our history the United States . . . is in the hands of incapable and dishonest men." The Progressive Party candidate blamed Democrats and Republicans for bringing the country "to a crisis that is fantastically dangerous to America and to the world." The wind now in his sails, Wallace moved into perilous waters of his own, where he risked sinking his presidential ambitions by giving just cause to those who accused him and his party of harboring communist sympathies. "The Cold War has expanded on all fronts," he said. "We must make it clear where the responsibility lies."[113]

To the Republicans, the Democrats, and even the States' Rights Party supporters and their political hopefuls, the answer lay at Stalin's door. But not to the former vice president, who charged, "Russia has made mistakes, many mistakes. But the men of the bipartisan bloc—Dewey, Truman, Dulles and Forrestal—started the Cold War." Without caring how many savage editorials his comments would inevitably trigger or what his rivals would say, Wallace went on to say that the leaders of the Democratic and Republican Parties were following "an approach which if permitted to come to full fruition, will completely destroy the civilization of the last 2,000 years and may destroy all human life on this planet."[114] Wallace's attack went against the unwritten code of bipartisanship that Truman and Dewey had subscribed to for talks on foreign policy during the campaign and to which Democrats and Republicans had adhered since the United States entered World War II. Evidently the Progressive candidate thought that he had to say whatever was necessary, on any topic, to pull votes away from his opponents.

Nothing the former vice president could utter would convince a group of Utah schoolchildren to abandon their favorite in the race. After speaking for a few minutes in Price, with the spectacular Wedge Overlook and Nine Mile Canyon carving a dramatic swath through the mountainous scenery beyond the station, Truman realized that a group of youngsters who had come with their teachers had been unable to see him as they craned their little necks in vain. Even the tightest schedule wasn't going to stop the president from righting this wrong. He bounded down the steps from the back platform, made his way through the crowd, and, with a big smile on his face, bent down to gently shake the tiny hand of each first grader in the line.[115] Then, back on the rear platform, he received a gift that would help if protesters chose to throw eggs and fruit, as Dixiecrats had at Henry Wallace in the South as retribution for the Progressive candidate welcoming blacks to his talks.[116] Photographers snapped pictures of a grinning Truman posing in a coal black miner's hard hat, complete with a front-mounted spotlight, presented by local union officials. Inside the hat was printed an apt dedication: "Wear this to protect yourself from hard knocks."[117]

Whatever sympathy he may have felt for Wallace's rough treatment at the hands of the people who opposed the civil rights legislation both candidates supported, Truman had little choice but to take his predecessor as vice president to task over his renewed attacks on American foreign policy. The president chose a packed City Hall in San Francisco to defend his record and reiterate his desire for peace. He did not dignify the remarks from his former commerce secretary and now rival for the presidency—who a *Pittsburgh Post-Gazette* editorial said was "debasing himself by saying such outrageous things" — by mentioning his name, but rather focused on the big picture issues.[118] This was fitting, as the Soviets had just announced their intention to pull Red Army units — more than two hundred thousand troops — out of North Korea by January 1, 1949.[119]

Truman reminded the crowd in San Francisco that it was in their city that he had signed the United Nations Charter on August 8, 1945. Truman then reiterated the three founding aims of the UN: economic conditions for peace, enabling countries to "settle their differences peacefully without shooting each other," and providing collective security for member nations who were under threat. Though there was turmoil in many places, Truman asserted that he still believed that the UN was putting these principles into practice.[120]

Contrary to Wallace's claims that the United States had started the Cold War, Truman was quick to point out how the actions of the Soviet Union continued to hamper the effectiveness of the world organization. Truman then defended the bipartisan stance that had led to the passage of the Marshall Plan (and, of course, to Wallace's criticism): "It has been the policy of the United States under this administration to keep foreign policy out of politics; that is, politics within the United States. It is necessary for us as a nation to go to the water's edge with a solid front."[121]

On foreign policy the Republican and Democratic parties were united, but not so on domestic issues, Truman stated. He recapped the main points he had made about labor in his Cadillac Square speech, about farming in Des Moines, and about western development and conservation in Utah (the latter was in the same in spirit as his Denver address but was perhaps less effective since Truman had spent most of the day with Frank Spina, his barber and longtime friend from Battery D, instead of working on his speech).[122] Truman then painted a grim, fear-inducing picture of what would happen if a majority chose Dewey instead of him on November 2: "If you get Republican control of this Government, you might just as well turn it over to the special interests, and we will start on a boom and bust cycle, just like we did in 1920. We will end up with a crash which in the long run will do nobody any good but the Communists."[123]

This was not the first time during the campaign that Truman had used fear as a motivator for people to vote for him, nor to claim that a strong domestic economy was a bulwark against communism. In case this wasn't enough to convince San Franciscans, Truman turned to a now-familiar populist appeal, imploring his audience to "Vote for your own interests. Vote for the interests of the laboring man. Vote for the interests of the farmer. Vote for the interests of the white-collar worker. Vote for the interests of the little businessman. Vote for the interests of California. Vote for the interests of the nation as a whole, and you can't help but elect a Democratic Congress with a Democratic President."[124]

This was Truman's sixth speech of the day, below his average but still more than given by Tom Dewey, who gave just one as the Victory Special continued to languidly follow the Last Chance Special westward.[125] Dewey promised to restore unity to the United States and provide competent leadership that the nation had not enjoyed under Truman's reign. In Carmi, Illinois, Dewey's running mate, Earl Warren, echoed Dewey's call for unity, highlighting the divisions with Democratic Party ranks.[126] Truman was less than impressed by such talk, believing that "unity" was just another in the long line of hollow Dewey platitudes. Before he gave his address in San Francisco he had told a small audience in picturesque Sparks, Nevada, against the red-rock backdrop of the Carson and Virginia mountain ranges, "I stand for Democratic principles, and everybody knows where I stand. You don't get any double talk from me. I'm either for something or against it, and you know it. You know what I stand for. I hope you can find out what the other people stand for when the time comes. I very much feel that it will be a long time before you know exactly what they believe."[127]

Back in Washington, the Research Division read the reports of Dewey and Warren's recent comments, as they did virtually every other campaign story by the Associated Press, United Press, and major newspapers. Bill Batt thought that the Republicans' unity call presented an opportunity that went beyond Truman's "double talk" criticism. "What would you think of the possibility of taking this unity theme and using it as a stick to beat the Republicans with?" Batt wrote to Clifford. "Sure we are all for national unity. But you can't have unity in a vacuum. How about a little unity for federal aid to education? Or public housing? Or price control? Or any of the other wonderful issues we have?"[128]

It didn't take Truman long to put the rhetorical stick that Batt offered to good effect. At Gilmore Stadium in Los Angeles on a warm September

23 evening, he took Dewey to task for failing to engage and say what he and his party believed in:

> I have come here tonight to tell you where I stand on the big issues before the country in this campaign.
>
> This is a championship fight. And I am convinced of one thing: the American people are sold on the idea that nobody deserves to win a championship fight by running away. I do not believe that anybody is going to win this fight by running away from the record or ducking the issues.
>
> In our system, the people have a right to know exactly what our two major parties stand for on specific issues. They have a right to know who is for them and who is against them.
>
> The decisive battle has arrived. The people are going to have to choose one side or the other. The Democratic Party and I have nothing to conceal. We are proud of our record. The underlying struggle in this campaign is a struggle between two sets of ideals.[129]

Dewey and the Eightieth Congress were not the only targets of Truman's ire on this evening. For the first time in the fall campaign, he also went after the Progressive Party and its supporters. He was eager to ensure that the group didn't repeat Robert LaFollette's 1924 feat of securing 16 percent of the popular vote. While the thirteen electoral votes the bouffant LaFollette secured did not impact the verdict in that election—incumbent Republican president Calvin Coolidge handily dispatched his Democratic challenger John Davis 382 votes to 136—a similar showing by Wallace could derail Truman's chances of staying in the White House. With the Democratic Party also split to the right by the Strom Thurmond's Dixiecrats, whom Truman's advisers thought were sure to win at least several southern states, Truman needed to prevent Wallace from further eroding his support.[130]

To those liberals who believed that backing Henry Wallace was the best way ahead for the nation, Truman had a simple riposte on this balmy California night: "Think again." He had come under fire for supposedly being soft on communism at home, but it was not the Democratic ranks that had been infiltrated, Truman asserted. In fact, "Communists are guiding and using the third party," and as such it was the president's "party which truly expresses the hopes of American liberals, and which has the power to fulfill those hopes." Casting a ballot for anyone other than him would, Truman insisted, merely strengthen the Republican cause. His advice to those who were tempted to support Wallace? "Don't waste your vote."[131]

After the California swing, the Truman train turned around and headed back east into Arizona. His last whistle stop of the day on September 25 was in Phoenix, where he spoke until after 11:00 p.m. to seven thousand people who were enjoying the cool nighttime temperature in the desert.[132] Truman expanded on his plans for harnessing the might of the Colorado River to provide power, irrigation, and more to the people of Phoenix and the other states it flowed through. If they voted for him five weeks hence, Truman promised that his administration would complete such projects by 1950.

And what of his Republican opponent's plan for Arizona and other western states? Truman turned to the language of the memo that Bill Batt sent to Clark Clifford back in July to advocate for the Turnip Day session: "In their platform for this year—1948—they say they 'favor progressive development of the Nation's water resources for navigation, flood control, and power, with immediate action in critical areas.' They also said they favored a comprehensive reclamation program. When it comes to making promises, they come right along saying, 'Me, too.'" If Arizonans helped Dewey win, Truman assured them that it would be a disaster, saying, "God help the country." Rather than following through on their promises, Truman insisted, the Republican Party would be content "throwing more monkey wrenches into the machinery," as they ignored the West and focused on their plan to "move the capital from Washington to Wall Street."[133]

It was another early start the following morning as Truman rose before dawn, wolfed down a quick breakfast, flicked through a stack of newspapers, and reviewed the talking points for that day. At 7:35 a.m. he ventured out onto the back platform in little Lordsburg, New Mexico, the seat of Lincoln County, where celebrated, elaborately mustached sheriff Pat Garrett, the man who claimed to have killed Billy the Kid, had protected the citizens from outlaws. Truman didn't have a Billy the Kid story for the townspeople, but he did let them know that although it was unusually early for a politician to be up, it wasn't for him. "Of course, 7:30 is not nearly so early in New Mexico as it is in Washington," he said. "Washington people, you know, have a habit of not getting up until along toward mid-day, and they can't understand why the President of the United States gets up at 5:30 every morning."[134]

Then he turned to some Research Division facts, stating, "In 1932 the residents of New Mexico had an income of less than $100 million. Do you know what it was in 1947? It was $500 million, which is 5 times what it was under the Republicans. Thirteen times as many farms in New Mexico have electricity now as had electricity in 1932. And the farmers are earning about eight times as much money as they did in 1932." This was proof, Truman insisted, that the country could go one of two ways depending on who it elected come November: "If there is any farmer or miner or workingman who is foolish enough to want to turn the clock back, he ought to vote the Republican ticket. Otherwise, he had better vote for himself when he votes for me."[135]

His campaign was not an exercise in political vanity, Truman assured his listeners, but rather, echoing the language Henry Wallace had used that summer, "a crusade." Their participation was vital in determining its success or failure, and their own. Truman finished up with some of his harshest rhetoric since he had accused the Republicans of having "stuck a pitchfork in the farmer's back" during his Plowing Match speech in Iowa. Now, three weeks on, he said, "On election day, don't stay at home, don't do like you did in 1946, when you elected that good for nothing 'do-nothing' 80th Congress. When you study the record of that Congress, it is staggering the things they did to you, and the things they did not do that they should have done. They tried to cut the throat of the West, and I had to come out here and tell you about it."[136]

Meanwhile, Truman's main challenger, Tom Dewey, was speaking in less violent terms to a packed auditorium in San Francisco. He alleged that Truman and FDR before him had been "deliberately discouraging production and trying to raise prices," which took money from the wage earner's wallet. Dismissing Truman's plans to curb increased prices through government controls, the New York governor offered a different approach: "A large part of the answer to inflation is to produce more and more of the things our people want and need."[137]

The following morning of September 26, Truman broke his rule of avoiding political activity on the Lord's Day to indulge merrily one of the seven deadly sins—gluttony. The reason for these uncharacteristic transgressions was the jovial John Nance Garner, who had served as FDR's vice president from 1933 to 1941. Though Truman's views were almost invariably further left than the conservative Democrat Garner, he, like FDR, appreciated the Texan's quick wit, political savvy, and irrepressible joie de vivre.

And boy, did Garner know how to put on a show. He arranged for the local high school band to noisily greet Truman's train with cymbals, drums, and horns as it rolled into Uvalde, Texas. The town's main distinctions, other than being home to Garner, was as the self-proclaimed honey capital of the world and, supposedly, the only bottler of cactus juice, which was fitting as Garner's nickname was "Cactus Jack." Once Truman had worked his way past the band and through the four thousand residents who were up unusually early to hail the arrival of their president, he was presented with an equally atypical welcome gift: a goat wearing a gold blanket with "Dewey's Goat" emblazoned across it. This was the perfect opportunity for Harry to go hokey, and he did not disappoint. "I'm going to clip it and make a rug, and then let it graze on the White House lawn for the next four years," he said.[138]

Whatever Truman's plans really were for the goat, he certainly wasn't about to eat the beast, though by this time he had already been up for some time and was more than ready for the day's opening meal. And Garner was more than happy to oblige, laying on what Margaret Truman referred to as "the most tremendous breakfast in the history of the Truman family and, I suspect in the history of any American family. There was white wing dove, bacon, ham, fried chicken, scrambled eggs, rice in gravy, hot biscuits, Uvalde honey, peach preserves, grape jelly and coffee." In return for the feast, the musical welcome, and the goat, Truman gave Garner two bottles of fine Kentucky bourbon, which he told him was "medicine, only to be used in case of snakebite."[139] Garner saw no sense in putting off sampling the smoky drink, replying conspiratorially, "This is something I'm going to save until you are elected," he said. "But come on, Harry, and let's you and I go strike a blow for liberty."[140]

Arguably it was Truman who needed the antivenom, if the toxic bites of the press and his opponents were anything to go by. Speaking in Alben Barkley's home state of Kentucky, a typically outspoken Strom Thurmond bashed the president for "again desperately seeking political support, feels it to his advantage to turn on the principles which he said he believed in all his life, and to yield to the pressure of the ignorant Eastern minority groups." But could Truman be undone by the States' Rights split in his party? Certainly, according to Thurmond. "The prospects of the states' rights ticket in the electoral college are better than the prospects of electing either the President or Governor Dewey. We are the only ticket on which a compromise can be reached."[141] It was clear, then, that Thurmond's aim was not winning the popular vote, but forcing a stalemate that would lead to his breakaway group's victory in the Senate following gridlock in the Electoral College. The governor of South Carolina left the means for such a result to the imagination of his listeners.

In Asheville, North Carolina, Harry Truman's running mate saw the November 2 result going a different way. Braving a relentless rain so cold that it threatened to turn into sleet or snow at any moment, he implored an umbrella-wielding crowd of around one thousand at the ballpark to support him and Truman on polling day, as a vote for Thurmond or Wallace "was a vote for the Republican party." Contrary to the claims of Thurmond and Fielding Wright that the president had betrayed everyone below the Mason-Dixon line, Truman was treading the path of Franklin Roosevelt, who "knew and loved the South," Barkley said. Dewey, on the other hand, would not act in the region's best interests if he was elected, as shown by his statements "in sympathy with" for-profit ownership of the government-run Oak Ridge nuclear plant in Tennessee.[142]

Back in Texas, Truman's administrative assistant Donald S. Dawson had taken over from Oscar Chapman as the de facto campaign "advance man," with Chapman returning to other duties on the campaign. Dawson had been holed up in the luxurious, wood-paneled penthouse of the Adolphus Hotel—paid for by rich Texas Democrats including attorney general Tom Clark's brother, Bob—ensuring that Truman had more to look forward to in Texas than just Cactus Jack Garner's big breakfasts.

One of Dawson's tasks in the state, as it would be in every other, was to ensure that Truman had a higher profile going into polling day than Strom Thurmond. The States' Rights candidate had powerful advocates who were trying to convince Democrats and independents to desert Truman and vote for Thurmond instead. And unlike in some other states, the governor of South Carolina would appear on the ballot on November 2 in Texas.[143] Though the Texas Democratic Convention had seen five pro-Dixiecrat leaders ousted for "disloyalty," Arthur Krock declared in a *New York Times* column that "Texas Democrats . . . are split deeper and more bitterly than they were in 1928, with the consequence that Governor Thurmond or even Governor Dewey may carry the state."[144] The fact that a Dewey victory was even mentioned is surprising, as there was just one Republican in the state legislature and leading figures in the state's Republican office, including their chief financier, were fund raising for the States' Rights Party.[145]

Dawson had also discovered that some of Texas's longtime supporters of the president were feeling left out of his plans for the Whistle Stop Tour. Dawson spent hours on his hotel room phone, ensuring that the allies of Clark, Senator Sam Rayburn, and other leading Democrats would be in what Dawson called "places of prominence" at each appearance Truman made in the Lone Star state.[146] Dawson's efforts were rewarded. He later recalled with satisfaction the scene in El Paso: "The railroad station was at the end of a long street that had another street coming in at an angle. The President spoke from the back platform of the train. When he arrived, both of those streets were filled with crowds backed up for two city blocks trying to see the President and wanting to hear him speak."[147]

And speak Truman did. Armed with a bevy of "hard cold facts" assembled by the Research Division, Truman informed his audience that the Rio Grande reclamation project kick-started by FDR and continued by his administration to the tune of more than $20 million to "irrigate 4½ million acres of land and provide more than 3 million kilowatts of power" in Texas and other western states. Such initiatives, however, were under threat from "backward looking Republicans" who had voted to cut funding by 50 percent in 1948, Truman claimed. And when the GOP's chairman of the Committee on Public Works responded to protests over reclamation provisions he said "the West is squealing like a stuck pig."[148]

Another Republican-dominated body, the Committee on Public Works, opposed government ownership of public power utilities in western states, arguing they would be better off in the hands of private companies. This was, Truman believed, because the Republicans "want to turn this electric power over to the hijackers; so they can stick you with high prices." Texas voters had to make a simple choice, Truman said: "You can vote for the party that will slow down—or maybe even stop—the construction of Federal reclamation and power projects; you can vote for the party which promises to give the benefits of Federal power to the private utility interests so they can get rich at your expense . . . or you can vote for the party which promises continued development of the West for the benefit of the whole country."[149]

A little further down the line, Senate candidate Lyndon B. Johnson, the tall, ambitious, forty-year-old from Stonewall, joined the president's train in San Antonio. There, Truman said that achieving lasting peace "is much more important than whether I am President of the United States."[150] Nonetheless, Truman would do anything to ensure the latter, and he proved it when he dropped a penny into a wishing well during his parade before an estimated crowd of three hundred thousand in the city.[151] Arriving at San Marcos, Johnson came out onto the rear platform with Truman and, towering over the president, introduced him to the cheering throng waiting below. Truman saw a large sign that read, "World government means world peace." Thinking for just a second, the quick-witted president pointed toward the banner and said, "Well, if the United Nations is supported as it should be, that will mean world peace."[152]

Achieving this was easier said than done, though. As Truman was speaking, talks between American, British, French, and Soviet diplomats reached a stalemate every bit as portentous as the standoff on the ground in Berlin. The Western democracies had offered to allow Soviet currency to extend into their occupation zones under four-power oversight in exchange for the Russian administration quashing "all transport restrictions"—that is, ending the blockade, as Stalin had promised more than a month before. However, according to US mediator Walter Bedell Smith and other State Department officials, Soviet military commanders didn't think the arrangement was favorable and insisted that they have sole control over transport in Berlin *and* the Soviet currency in the German capital. This was anathema to Smith, George Marshall, and their British and French compatriots, who decided that the only remaining option was to bring the matter before the United Nations Security Council. So much for world peace.[153]

★ ★ ★

"ALBEN BARKLEY AND I ARE ENGAGED IN A TOUGH, HARD FIGHT. AND WE ARE GOING TO WIN THAT FIGHT, BECAUSE WE ARE RIGHT."

During the first full month of the fall campaign, the Research Division didn't just gather facts, write white papers, and provide speech fodder to Charlie Murphy, George Elsey, and Clark Clifford. Batt and the others also made recommendations on what Truman should and shouldn't say, where and when.

Batt wrote to Clifford in mid-September strongly suggesting that the president should not deliver his first major speech on communism in Los Angeles like some of his advisors had suggested. To win Clifford and Charlie Murphy over, Batt laid out his case logically, an approach Clifford, as a detail-oriented lawyer, favored over emotional appeals. "Communists have had a great deal of influence in California," Batt wrote. "Communist participation in labor activities and strikes . . . far exceeded before the war anything I ever saw in other parts of the country."[154]

The potential trouble for Truman was that California Republicans had claimed communist activities were not confined to labor action but had also seeped into the Democratic Party organization in this state. And, unfortunately for California Democrats, an investigatory committee "found quite a bit to justify its contentions."[155] This led to legislation excluding communists from city government, which Batt worried Republicans "would use to show that their anti-Communist measures have been more effective than the federal government's," should Truman speak about communism in Los Angeles. Batt also predicted "attacks from the Wallaceites," who he believed would "attempt to drive liberal Democrats away from the Democratic ticket."[156]

As was the case elsewhere, not least in Philadelphia where he and Research Division colleague Johannes Hoeber lived, Batt knew the ADA and other organizations were under considerable pressure from those who leaned a lot further left: "Non-communist liberals in California have had an up-hill row . . . freeing their organizations from Communist influence," according to Batt.[157]

Batt's reasoned and thorough argument struck a chord with Clifford, and Truman moved his major communism-related address to the more accommodating Oklahoma.[158] And, as Batt also suggested in his memo, the appearance came "early in the campaign," during the first of Truman's fall trips, rather than in the last few days of October, as had been the original intention.[159]

But, for once, Thomas Dewey had the first word on an issue, and an atypically forceful one at that. Speaking in Los Angeles on September 25, the presidential hopeful said that there was a better way to get rid of communists in governments than giving Truman the $25 million he had asked for to do it: voting Republican. "We will keep informed and we'll keep the American people informed," he promised. Then Dewey took aim at Truman's controversial "loyalty" investigations, stating that if he won the White House, "we'll have no thought police. We will not jail anybody for what he thinks or believes. So long as we keep the Communists among us out in the open, in the light of day, the United States of America has nothing to fear."[160] It was his strongest stump performance of the month, and one that dared Truman to answer the charge that his policies on tackling communism were jeopardizing freedom of thought and expression.

Three days later it was time for Truman's retort. The train rolled into Oklahoma City on September 28, and Truman, Bess, Clifford, Elsey, and the rest took several cars past the city limits and several miles down dusty roads to the sprawling Oklahoma State Fairgrounds. While Margaret and Bess's driver dawdled, Truman's driver abused the gas pedal, as the president noted that he could again be cut off by the radio networks if he ran over, and being on time would help avoid this. So the limousine sped along the back roads, so fast that onlookers couldn't see him waving to them.[161] Truman was introduced by none other than Oklahoma governor Roy Turner, the man who had gotten the president's Labor Day speech on the air. Squinting as the sun reflected harshly on the thick lenses of his glasses, the president warmly shook his friend and backer's hand, and then took the podium to enthusiastic applause.[162]

As with any unfounded criticism of his policies and his character, "give 'em hell" Harry wasn't going to tolerate even the suggestion from Tom Dewey, the HUAC, or anyone else that he was swayed by communists or that he approved of their subversive system. Truman was eager for the facts, as he saw them, to once again speak for themselves about the actions of his administration and those of his Republican opponents: "The record is plain for all to see. Republican politicians have contributed nothing against the fight on communism in this country. The Democratic Party has steadily improved the well-being of the American people, the best defense against communism, and we have successfully prevented the spread of communism in this world."[163]

He was also quick to point out the difference between a liberal democratic agenda and a nonrepresentative communist approach to government, insisting, "The Democratic Party is for free government and against totalitarianism."[164] Truman was confident that he had delivered a solid message that would take the sting out of his opponents' charges about the White House being soft on communism at home and abroad. But long before the morning newspapers showed whether Truman had hit his mark with the media, there was trouble. And, predictably, money trouble. Again.

Like the radio networks, the railroads were by now well aware of the Truman campaign's hand-to-mouth subsistence. And, unfortunately for Truman, the seventeen-car Last Chance Special didn't run on goodwill. So when railroad administrators realized that the president's fuel bill and other expenses had gone unpaid for one whistle stop too many, there was the very real chance that they would keep the Ferdinand Magellan and its companion cars in Oklahoma City overnight, if not indefinitely. With another full speaking schedule starting early the next morning, this was unthinkable. But once more in this underfunded trip, there was no money.[165] Wallace's group had diverted funds from some liberal backers, and still more were reluctant to risk their money on what more than two-thirds of media outlets—of both the Democratic and Republican persuasion—were all but guaranteeing a Dewey victory.

Luckily for Truman, his old pal Roy Turner was among the party who had come to the station to see him off. Turner, by now well used to playing the role of deliverer, and with his oversized personality likely relishing it, invited some wealthy friends onto the train for a chat with the president in the temporary club car that had been attached to provide more space for the meet-and-greet sessions that followed many stops. A chat that led to an impromptu fund raiser, which garnered more than enough money to pay off the Rock Island Railroad and get the Whistle Stop Tour rolling again.[166]

As his campaign got a much-needed financial boost, Truman also seemed to be reinvigorated. The next day he delivered sixteen speeches.

Starting at 7:35 a.m. in Shawnee, Oklahoma, he spoke to six audiences before noon and another four before dinner. After polishing off what was more like a snack than a full meal, he got right back to it, finishing his Oklahoma tour with brief remarks in Vinita and Afton. Then it was on into his home state, where Truman spoke to two groups mid-evening and ended his marathon day a few more miles further down the Missouri tracks after an 11:10 p.m. talk in Marshfield.

The biggest turnout that day had been in Tulsa. Local newspapers estimated that more than one hundred thousand people lined the route from Union Depot into the heart of the city, showering paper streamers and confetti on the president and his entourage. As the motorcade crept along Boston Avenue, Bess Truman leaned over to *Tulsa World* reporter Yvonne Litchfield, who was riding with the first lady and Margaret in the back seat of the open-topped limousine, and said above the din, "There won't be a soul left to fill the stadium."[167]

Once the cars had gone through the city and to Skelly Stadium, her concern proved unfounded: fifteen thousand had packed the bleachers to see Truman. He started off with a little of the "local color" that Charlie Murphy said the Research Division provided for every whistle stop, stating, "I know that you are looking forward with me, and not backward with the Republican Party. Now, if that's the case—and I believe it is—you can't help but send Dixie Gilmer to the Congress, and you must send Bob Kerr to the Senate, and then we'll be well on the road to curing that 'do-nothing' Congress."[168]

He then added an anecdote of his own, in typical Truman fashion: "Oklahoma in the First World War was the training ground for the 35th Division, of which I was a member, over here at Fort Sill. I spent one of the coldest winters in my life at Fort Sill, Okla. And when it wasn't cold, why, it was blowing Texas up one day and blowing Kansas down the next. But I still like Oklahoma and always shall like it, because I've been coming here all my life."

Truman went on to praise the resilient farmers of Oklahoma, who he said would reach $1 billion in production by the end of 1948, a far cry from the troubles of the Dust Bowl. It was not their resolve alone that had made this transformation possible, Truman claimed, but also New Deal farm programs that FDR had started and he wanted to extend, if his opponents in the Republican Party would let him.

After touting his administration's investment in energy utilities—which he said had increased hydroelectric output in the West from 78,000 kilowatts in 1932 to more than 2.5 million kilowatts in 1948—Truman vowed to fight for continued improvements. He could only deliver these if Oklahomans voted for him instead of "the candidates who threaten to reverse the established policies and turn the clock back to the boom-and-bust Republicanism of the twenties."[169] A few hours later, Truman showed that he was even more relatable in small groups. An Oklahoma cowboy struggled to rein in his boisterous Palomino colt in Ardmore, and several onlookers stepped back nervously from the horse. Truman was unfazed and went right up to it, observing the animal's open mouth and quickly declaring to the rider that his mount was six years old. "Correct!" came the reply, to the delight of the president and the crowd.[170] As Truman's train was leaving Oklahoma and heading into Missouri later that day, Governor Turner told reporters, "Undoubtedly, more people saw the president and he spoke to more people than any man before in the history of Oklahoma."[171]

The same day as Truman wrapped up his Oklahoma appearances, Tom Dewey made some of his most telling comments to date on foreign policy, telling five thousand people in Great Falls, Montana, that even if the United States elected a new administration, it would not alter the country's position in Berlin. "The totalitarian states must not misunderstand what is happening here," the New York governor said. "They must not make the error of believing that because we are exercising our constitutional right to change our government, this nation is at all split or divided." If he took over in the White House, Dewey said, his party would act abroad on the mantra of "peace with honor," and, with an eye on Moscow, he warned "let no dictator or trigger-happy militarist anywhere make any mistake about that purpose."[172]

The next night, September 30, Dewey followed up on these comments as he addressed a packed house at the Mormon Tabernacle in Salt Lake City. During a carefully worded speech that his team had worked on with the Republican Party's two experts on the topic, John Foster Dulles and Arthur Vandenberg, Dewey stated that as "the decisive world power" the United States had the responsibility to respond to aggression with "firm but even-tempered resistance" as it helped establish "a just and lasting peace" in Europe and beyond.

Echoing the call of Winston Churchill at Fulton in March 1946 in his warm baritone that was easier on the ears than Truman's flat, midrange delivery, Dewey called for his country to secure such peace by maintaining military strength. He asserted, "The best way for us to get along with Soviet leaders is to deal with them as strong equals and by doing so to restore their respect for us." While this implied that Stalin and the Politburo had come to underestimate the United States during Truman's watch, Dewey avoided criticizing the president. In fact, Dewey outlined a nine-point blueprint for peace and called for "wholehearted" support of the Marshall Plan and armed forces "so strong that no nation will again risk attacking us," which mirrored Truman's stance.[173] Though the president continued to denigrate the Republican Congress, and Dewey disagreed with him on many domestic points, the GOP's standard bearer recognized that world peace and national security were too important to jeopardize with partisan bickering.

Meanwhile, Truman was making a speech of his own in Louisville, Kentucky, one of his only appearances in Dixiecrat territory as Clifford focused his efforts on states they believed were not yet lost to Strom Thurmond. Instead of talking about foreign affairs this time, he went to war on everyone who was against price controls, including the National Association of Manufacturers and his favorite target, the Eightieth Congress.

In a speech that Research Division assistant director Johannes Hoeber had worked on all night the previous Saturday, Truman said, "Since they killed price control in 1946, the Republican Old Guard have given ample proof that they were quite satisfied with prices going higher and higher and with profits of big business getting bigger and bigger."[174] Truman justified to his running mate's home state the harsh words that he used so far on the campaign, saying, "Alben Barkley and I are engaged in a tough, hard fight. And we are going to win that fight, because we are right." Though Dewey had supported his foreign policy record and only hinted that a Republican administration would do better, Truman again implied that his would-be foil wasn't saying anything of substance. "In this fight we are bringing out the facts of a shameful record—a Republican record," Truman said. "And the Republicans don't like it one bit. They say it isn't polite. They want us to confine the campaign to undisputed generalities, so the people will lose their big chance to find out what the real issues are."[175] Truman went on to claim that "there never was a more vicious or a better organized campaign to mislead and deceive the American people" than the National Association of Manufacturers, who were in cahoots with "the party of special privilege."

Far from done with the Republican Congress, Truman assailed it for failing "to bring more good housing at lower prices and lower rents" as he had asked. "As a result the Government today can do nothing to help the cities and towns build low-rent housing, nothing to help cities and towns clear their slums, and nothing to bring better rural housing," Truman went on. The GOP had also stymied benefits, Truman claimed, and had "passed a law—over my veto—actually taking away social security rights from nearly a million people who already had them." In addition, the eightieth session had done nothing to bust up monopolies that removed choice and competition, and therefore the chance of lower prices, from the market. Truman then issued a series of challenges to his listeners that left little doubt of his intentions to continue and extend New Deal interventionism in domestic affairs:

> Give us a Democratic Congress and we will get action against high prices. That will be a change.
>
> Give us a Democratic Congress and we will get action for more housing at lower prices. That will be a change.
>
> Give us a Democratic Congress and we will take action against monopoly. That will be a change.
>
> Give us a Democratic Congress and we will move forward for the benefit of all the people, toward better housing, better medical care, better education—all the things that mean a happier and more secure life for the average American family.
>
> That is the sort of change we Democrats propose. That is the kind of change the American people need and want, and you can get that change, if you'll do your duty and vote on Election Day.

Truman and Dewey were not the only ones to deliver speeches that day. Speaking at the United Nations gathering in Paris, Soviet deputy foreign minister Andrei Vyshinsky claimed that America was pursuing "war aims" with its action in Berlin and dismissed Truman and Dewey's belief in a US monopoly on nuclear power as a "dangerous miscalculation." The Soviet warned that his government would reject any rulings from the

UN or the Atomic Energy Commission regarding nuclear material because "it is not an international organization—it is an American organization." Vyshinsky also criticized Truman's comments about advances in nuclear weapons, scoffing, "Apparently the President of the United States describes as 'progress' a bomb which will kill half a million people."[176]

Truman did not waste his breath on a response to such a diatribe. Instead, as Tom Dewey returned to his New York base after a week stumping up and down the West Coast, the president went back to Washington, where he would rest for just four days before returning to the rails for a final push. This last leg of the Whistle Stop Tour would prove to be more frustrating, tiring, and arduous than even he could anticipate.

October

With exactly one month to go until the election, Truman viewed reports of the latest Soviet malfeasance with bemusement. As the United Nations considered publicly admonishing Russia for the Berlin blockade, Soviet military commander Vasily Sokolovsky's office sent a press release to world media outlets audaciously claiming that "no blockade exists or has existed" and blaming any tension on Western attempts to meddle with financial operations in the Soviet zone. Stalin's tenacious foreign minister, Vyacheslav Molotov, whose full mustache and round-rimmed glasses gave him at first glance a vague resemblance to Theodore Roosevelt, insisted that because the partitioning of Germany had been a Western idea, the Americans, British, and French had forsaken any claim to Berlin. He also rejected the UN's right to say or do anything about the impasse in Germany. How could American diplomats hope to broker a settlement with such unreasonable and blatantly duplicitous men?[1]

The Research Division and its support staff worked extraordinarily long hours, pausing only for meals, a few beers, and, if they were really lucky, a few hours' sleep or the odd weekend back at home. Their meager accommodations in the upper room of the American Veterans Committee lodge on New Hampshire Avenue would have offered little respite in a normal work situation, let alone the toil-around-the-clock environment that Batt and his team found themselves in. Though he had bunked up in many less-than-luxurious rooms when on assignment, Frank Kelly was taken aback when he first saw the sparse room he would be sharing with Batt, Hoeber, Lloyd, Birkhead, Barriere, and Dreyer. "There was a row of beds in a big open space," he later recollected. "It was like a monastery."[2]

Clifford let Batt know in a laudatory memo the impact of his team's work in helping Truman slam Congress and champion his brand of populism:

> Dear Bill,
>
> As our first trip comes to an end, I want to express my deepest appreciation for the fine work that you and your staff have done. Your support and assistance have been invaluable and are appreciated by us all.[3]

During the early days of October, Truman kept up his specific attacks on what he considered the failures of the "do-nothing" Congress, backed up with facts still supplied daily by Bill Batt's team via air courier dispatches prepared by Charles Murphy back in Washington. As *Time* put it, echoing Truman's sentiments for perhaps the first time in his presidency, "Whatever hell may be to others, hell to Harry Truman seems to be a world populated by the Republican members of the eightieth Congress."[4]

As the president's Last Chance Special maintained a frenetic, desperate pace from town to town, state to state, Dewey's Victory Special "moved through the country with leisurely assurance," according to *Time*. "Because he was ahead, he could keep to general terms, imply Administration failures without committing himself to specific remedies of his own. He gambled nothing."[5] Some could have judged the GOP candidate's laid-back approach harshly when comparing it to the vigor of the incumbent as he rattled down the rails for mile after mile. But not most newspaper and magazine editors and publishers. In endorsing the New York governor for higher office, a statement from the Scripps-Howard executive team praised him for "competence, wisdom, understanding of basic issues and . . . firm and skillful leadership."[6]

Certainly, this was not the first time that a Dewey campaign had been praised for solid organization or criticized for a lack of originality. Writing about his failed 1944 bid, James Weschsler of the *Nation* had lauded Dewey's team for "a magnificent display of efficiency," but also took issue with him for consistently delivering "monotonous, un-inspired" speaking performances.[7] Perhaps the latter was the result of Dewey's dislike of impromptu, unscripted speeches and his preference for the safe confines of press conferences and windy talks in which he stuck to his prepared notes almost verbatim.[8] Though another former New York governor, FDR, prevailed in that election despite being understandably preoccupied with the war effort, he did not capitalize on Dewey's lackluster stumping with the kind of barnstorming campaign that Truman was mounting. Indeed, by October 5, 1944, FDR had made just two speeches. On the same day four years later, Truman had delivered more than two hundred.[9]

Despite Truman's intrepid campaigning, he was gaining little if any traction, at least if the polls were anything to go by. The *New York Times* predicted that Dewey would win fourteen Western states and garner 153 electoral votes to Truman's 71.[10] The news was little better for Truman in the other half of the nation. When asked by Gallup, "If the Presidential election were held tomorrow, how would you vote—for Truman, for Dewey or for Wallace?" the majority of respondents in eleven of twelve eastern states chose the New York governor. Only Rhode Island, of little value in the Electoral College in the event of a close vote, chose Truman. But the news wasn't all bad for the president. "It would take a comparatively small shift of sentiment to give President Truman the lead in three other states—Connecticut, Maryland and West Virginia," George Gallup reported to the nation on October 6. Henry Wallace was losing ground in several states, including New York, and was, at least according to the pollster, a nonfactor in the other eleven states surveyed. Neither was Strom Thurmond, readers were led to assume, though Gallup's omission of him from the voting question made it difficult to tell what people thought of the States Rights' Party. Gallup agreed with Truman's assertion that a small turnout on Election Day would harm the president's chances and enhance Dewey's. But as the bulk of Truman's Whistle Stop Tour speeches in the region were still to come and so many states were in the balance, he had a chance of getting out the vote in his favor.[11]

October 7 brought the Truman family some unexpected and unwelcome extra drama, more incendiary than the facts and figures of Gallup's latest report. After leaving the train for a few hours, the president was heading into New Jersey by car, preparing to deliver several speeches. Curly-haired Bess rode in another open-topped car with Representative Mary T. Norton, the first female Democrat to represent her party in the House.

As the motorcade passed by, some fireworks that overenthusiastic local Truman supporters set off sent sparks raining down on the two startled women, threatening to set their clothes ablaze. The car screeched to a halt and Mutual Broadcasting System reporter Chester Heslep jumped out of his seat in the third car in the procession, ran over to the screaming first lady and Norton, and helped Secret Service agents beat the sparks out. With the women's brief ordeal over and his place in campaign lore secure, Heslep didn't want to miss an exclusive. He abandoned his place in the car, forced his way through the massing crowd and into the nearest phone booth, and placed an out-of-breath call to the Mutual Broadcasting System newsroom in New York to relay the incident. The station included it in that night's "All the News" program, and Heslep went back to following the Truman train as it moved into Dewey's New York. Despite being a state that typically voted Democratic, New York would be closely contested because of the governor's second run at the presidency. Truman hoped to steal Dewey's home court advantage by giving twenty-one speeches there at both ends of October, almost running the entire alphabet with addresses from Albany to Oneida to Yonkers.[12]

Thankfully, the next day held no fire hazards for the presidential party, but things were not going smoothly. Truman's usually prompt schedule had unraveled on this fourteen-stop day and his train pulled into New York Central Terminal at 7:30 p.m., at least fifteen minutes late. Perhaps such a delay wouldn't be a problem for a politician who, like Dewey, made just a couple of appearances a day, but for Truman, who was still averaging at least ten, it was. Around five thousand people had gathered in the light rain to see him, but whispers and mumbles quickly flew among the disappointed onlookers that as he was late for that night's big talk in Buffalo, he would only stay a couple of minutes. Truman had other ideas, telling the local Democratic Party chairman, "These people came to hear me and I won't disappoint them."[13]

So he stepped up to the microphone and spoke from the rear platform for fifteen minutes, again criticizing the "do-nothing" Congress and concluding by telling the crowd that they had the choice to elect either the Democratic Party, which represented "the people," or the GOP, which was beholden to "special interest." Once he was done and had once more introduced Bess, who was wearing a blue dress, as "the boss" (no doubt to her chagrin, given her disdain for the phrase on the June tour), Truman enjoyed a local drum corps' rendition of "Over There" in recognition of his World War I service before the train left for Buffalo.[14] Another group of percussionists from nearby Le Roy gave him a rhythmic farewell, playing "America" and, appropriately, the World War I favorite "There's a Long, Long Trail A-Winding," the music competing with the growl of the train's engines as the seventeen-car vehicle started off down the line.[15]

The news was less welcoming elsewhere. That same day, the *Chicago Tribune*, a paper with a long history of animosity toward Truman, splashed its front page with news of the president's plan to send Chief Justice Frederick Vinson to Moscow to try to negotiate an end to the Berlin blockade. This was a direct affront to General Marshall and further increased the tension between the secretary of state and his boss. Did Truman not think the former army hero capable of brokering a settlement? Why was Vinson, a man of the law and not of the battlefield or the State Department, better suited to the task? What were the president's reasons for holding this news back, only for it to be leaked to the media? John Foster Dulles, considered the favorite to be Dewey's secretary of state, stayed out of the fray, refusing reporters' requests for comment.[16]

Many others were less restrained. Never one to miss the chance to take Truman to task, Strom Thurmond said, "His incompetency endangers the peace of the world. It is another attempt of the President to appeal to the followers of Henry Wallace."[17] And to Wallace himself, the debacle was another sign that America should do what Stalin wanted and leave Berlin for good. Speaking in Minneapolis, the Progressive Party candidate claimed that Winston Churchill had hijacked American foreign policy with his Sinews of Peace speech at Fulton, Missouri, in 1946, and that ever since, Truman's stance toward the Soviet Union had been "based on hatred."[18]

To columnist David Lawrence, the president had "committed one of the most serious blunders of his whole career."[19] Popular pipe-smoking writer and novelist Paul Gallico quoted an unnamed Republican as describing discord between the president and his secretary of state thus: "Marshall does not know half the time where he stands. They didn't consult Marshall but asked the networks to line up time on the air. Then they put it to Marshall at Paris and naturally he raised Cain."[20] Even foreign newspapers joined in the criticism, with London's *Liberal News Chronicle* describing for its readers "the havoc of Truman's unhappy scheme."[21] Regardless of Truman's motivation or the opinions of his opponents and doubters, one thing was clear: he had no choice but to cancel the Vinson trip and try to repair the damage with Marshall, who was planning to leave the Paris talks for Washington at the earliest opportunity. Truman's aim had been noble: to advance the stop-start talks with the Soviets and ultimately to broker a lasting settlement that would end the Berlin blockade. Yet in calling in an outsider in Vinson, Truman had slighted his secretary of state and made himself look like the novice president his many detractors had long claimed he was. Some critics also claimed that Truman was undermining the very fabric of American democracy with his Vinson plan. A stinging letter from "Oldtime Democrat" to the *Pittsburgh Post-Gazette* reminded readers that as chief justice, Vinson was head of the judicial branch of government and that Truman's scheme was "belittling to the dignity of his office and an affront to his position."[22]

For all the trouble that his hastily abandoned Vinson plan had stirred, Truman could hardly sit on his hands and wait in the Oval Office for the return of the miffed general. There was, after all, the matter of a presidential election to attend to. So at 6:00 p.m. on October 11 he was back on board the Ferdinand Magellan, off on a six-state, seven-day swing through Ohio, Illinois, Indiana, Wisconsin, Minnesota, and West Virginia, where he would give a total of forty-two speeches. Laughing off the strain of the previous few days, a smiling Truman told the White House press corps that he felt "perfect" as the train got underway. Certainly Louis Johnson's campaign finance team had given him a much-needed reason to smile, revealing that Truman's uncompromising style had led to a tenfold increase in small donations to his campaign since the fall leg of the Whistle Stop Tour began.[23]

The first state Truman visited as he looked to carry this momentum into mid-October was Ohio. In his first talk of the day at a fancy buffet breakfast in Cincinnati's Netherlands-Plaza Hotel, Truman again assailed Dewey for offering the country nothing more than platitudes: "We are in the middle of an election campaign right now. The Republican candidate for President has made a good many headlines with clever talk about unity. He claims that if he is elected there will be unity. I don't know what he means by that. I am going to try to analyze it the best I can. Of course, we don't know what he means by unity because he won't tell the country where he stands on any of the issues in which the American people are so deeply interested."[24]

In Robert Taft's home state, Truman also took the veteran senator to task over the Taft-Hartley Act, saying, "Senator Taft said about that bill, and I quote him: 'This bill is not a milk-toast bill. It covers about three-fourths of the things pressed on us very strenuously by the employers.' I don't think labor was very carefully listened to when that bill was passed. I wish every one of you could read the veto message which I sent to Congress on that bill."[25] This was even though in private he had told National Labor Relations Board member James Reynolds that "I'm convinced that Taft-Hartley is a pretty good law."[26] Indeed, the act had helped him avoid a repeat of the crippling strikes of 1946 and 1947, which had resulted in millions of lost work days and Truman's desperate threat to draft striking railroad workers into the armed forces if they didn't relent. Such are the incongruences of a presidential campaign.

Truman then went on to claim that the Eightieth Congress had failed to meet the needs of "thousands and thousands of young men and women who are thirsting for an education," had taken "social security away from at least a million people," and "consistently opposed a sound national health program." This was evidence, Truman claimed, that the GOP favored "narrow-minded class legislation."[27]

This was becoming a textbook message for the campaign: that the Republican Party favored the rich, while the Democratic Party, in true Robin Hood fashion, upheld the cause of the poor. Truman certainly felt that Taft practiced the former philosophy, saying, "Now, I served in the Senate with Bob, and I like him personally. There is one thing I do like about him: You know where he stands; that is more than you can say of some of the Republican candidates. Bob is frankly—he is frankly conservative. He believes in the welfare of the top ahead of the welfare of the bottom. But he is frank about it, and I can understand that. While he and I are personally on the friendliest of terms, we are as far apart as the poles on what we think is best for the welfare of the people of this country."[28]

All talk of friendship aside, Robert Taft was not one to meekly let such accusations slide by from any opponent speaking in any location, least of all from a president he loathed deriding him in Taft's beloved Buckeye State. And so on October 13, he responded to the president's remarks during a speech in St. Petersburg, Florida, where he was stumping for Dewey. There, Taft lived up to his billing of speaking "frankly," declaring that Truman wanted to establish a federal entity to "fix wages, fix prices, and ration all commodities, and subject the life of every family to direction from a federal bureau," a plan that was "far from the ideas of most

Southern Democrats." The Ohio senator then said that "the remedy of the New Dealers for every problem is to create a federal bureau, give it un-limited power and money and take over from the states functions granted to them by Congress." Truman sought to cure economic ills through ex-pansion of the centralized government, but Dewey and the GOP were try-ing to spur growth and development, he said, "while maintaining the lib-erty of the individual and the liberty of the local community to live their own lives and work out their own problems."[29]

While Taft delivered his pointed rebuke, the Last Chance Special left Wisconsin and crossed into neighboring Minnesota. In Minneapolis, Truman had another of the personal encounters that typified the Whistle Stop Tour. As his motorcade wound its way past the teeming sidewalks, ten-year-old Bette Bunker shook free of her father and rushed out into the street to hail the president. Ever vigilant, the Secret Service agents who jogged alongside the slow-moving procession stepped between the girl and Truman's open-topped car. Truman, recognizing that there was no danger, shooed them away and motioned to his driver to stop the vehicle. He leaned over the side of his door, asked Bette's name, gently shook her hand, and told her to ask her parents to vote for him. Little did Truman know that the girl's father, Martin, a strapping, six-foot-tall appliance salesman who had served in the US Navy during World War II, was a life-long Republican and would no more vote for the Man from Missouri than would Robert Taft.[30]

Clark Clifford had been on the job for as long as he could remember without a break, cramped up in what he called "a tiny stateroom where I slept and ate and wrote" for forty of the previous fifty days.[31] So after he joined Truman's motorcade, in which the presidential entourage paraded through jam-packed streets in Duluth with Hubert Humphrey, the star of the Democratic National Convention, he decided to seek a welcome break from the confines of the train, even if just for a couple of hours. As Truman went to St. Paul's Municipal Auditorium to deliver the speech he and Clifford had worked on between seven speeches that day, the special counsel visited friends in Minneapolis for dinner. Though Clifford later wrote that he drank infrequently because "alcohol didn't agree with me," the group consumed several welcome beverages before dinner, and then a few more with their meal as they listened to the president's address on the radio.

Through the haze, Clifford realized that he could no longer hear Truman's voice. This meant the speech was over and the president was on the way back to the rail yard. With such a tight schedule, the train wouldn't wait for anyone, even an essential staffer. The worse-for-wear Clifford recalled the frantic scene that followed as the clock approached midnight: "Driving wildly, we made it to the station just in time, but as I lingered, making prolonged and fond farewells about fifty or sixty feet from the train, it began to pull out. Running directly behind it on the tracks, I clambered onboard at the last possible moment, in full view of several amused and cheering local reporters. If the President was aware of the incident, he never mentioned it."[32]

The evening had been less eventful for Truman, but he had used his time at the Municipal Auditorium to again take Dewey to task over his lack of precision and clarity and overusing "unity" in speech after speech. "Unity . . . cannot be produced by mealy-mouthed political speeches," he said. "Unity on great issues comes only when the voice of the people has been heard so clearly, so strongly, so unmistakably that no one . . . can doubt what the people mean." An unusually complimentary *Time* magazine report stated that the talk, which he delivered to a packed house of fifteen thousand people with six thousand more listening outside, "was Truman's best since his acceptance speech in Philadelphia, and it noted that in his final swing across the Midwest the president "had consistently outdrawn Dewey" in attendance both at whistle stops and large venues. Truman certainly was living up to prospective Illinois governor Adlai Stevenson's label of "a scrappy little guy."[33]

As his main opponent was assailing him, Dewey was unusually aggressive in his criticism of the president on the same evening. Speaking in Alben Barkley's Kentucky, the Republican nominee took a rare pot shot at Truman's decision making. Though he didn't refer to the Vinson affair by name, Dewey echoed Taft as he told an audience of four thousand in Lexington that "These are too serious times to trifle with incompetence and blunders in positions of high importance." Moving on to Louisville, Dewey claimed that while the Republicans and Democrats standing together to tackle world problems had been a force for good, cooperation on Capitol Hill only occurred "whenever the Administration has permitted it." On Truman's watch, Dewey believed that "we have not seen the gains the American people had a right to hope for." For all his criticisms of his opponent, however, the would-be president conceded that Truman was up against a formidable foe. No doubt referring to the on again off again Berlin blockade, Dewey said, "A band of frantic zealots is striking at the ramparts of freedom with all means short of war." Unlike Henry Wallace's charges that Truman and Marshall's actions were jeopardizing peace, Dewey believed that the real problem was "the aggressive designs of the ruthless, ambitious leaders of the Soviet government."[34] It seemed, then, that whether Truman remained in his post or Dewey took over, Stalin and company could expect a continuation of a strong, unyielding stance from Washington.

The US delegate to the United Nations, Warren Austin, a seasoned seventy-year-old former senator from Vermont who had been an FDR loyalist and whom Truman had hand-picked to speak for America to the world organization, shared a similar view of international affairs when he addressed the UN General Assembly in Paris. The stout Austin, who had honed his speaking skills as a state attorney and special counsel before entering politics, claimed that the Soviet postwar slogan of "work and production" should be abandoned and that Moscow should adopt one that better fit its actions: "wreck and destroy." The Berlin blockade was evidence that the communists were determined to ensure a "state of constant turmoil and economic chaos" and that therefore neither America nor its allies would even consider scaling back their arms by one-fifth, as Vyshinsky had called for. And it was not just Germany that was experiencing the ill effects of Moscow's bitter medicine, Austin charged. "Is it necessary to go into details regarding the domination of Romania, Poland, Hungary, Albania, Bulgaria, Czechoslovakia, and Yugoslavia?" he asked the committee. "Recent events, in truly impressive detail, have disclosed that the price of Soviet friendship is complete subservience to Soviet policy."[35]

Not so, Vyshinsky replied. In fact, "We are yearning to cooperate," the Russian said, peering through his round, black-rimmed spectacles. The man who had lorded over the Moscow purge trials, in which thousands were either sentenced to death or condemned to years of brutal hardship in the Gulag, was not about to be intimidated by the claims of an American diplomat.[36] Instead, Vyshinsky continued to assert—with no regard for the facts of what was happening in Berlin and across Eastern Europe—that Russia was the injured party. While America hid behind "the atomic bomb," the Soviet Union was just trying to maintain its security as best it could. But despite the best intentions of Vyshinsky and his Politburo colleagues, "whatever we do is wrong" and America "showers blame on us."[37]

Truman responded not to these unsupported Soviet claims but to the harsh reality faced by Berliners as the weather got colder. He approved a US Air Force proposal to intensify the airlift operation by activating hundreds of reserve pilots and sending huge Douglas Globemaster transport planes to Germany to deliver even more medical supplies, raw materials, and food. This would be critical to the survival of West Berlin residents as the Soviet transport embargo deprived them of coal for heating their homes.[38] Perhaps reading American newspaper reports of this new action, Radio Moscow urged Americans to vote for Henry Wallace, who would give both nations the best choice of averting conflict.[39]

The president did not think Wallace could handle the Soviets and he certainly didn't believe Dewey was up to the task, either. Speaking to a large crowd at Botcher Field in Milwaukee on October 14, Truman slammed his Republican opponent for bringing up the issue of atomic energy when "he displayed a dangerous lack of understanding of the subject." The matter was not something to be taken lightly, Truman insisted, as "This is a force which holds great danger of catastrophe in the wrong hands. At the same time, it holds great promise of a better life in the right hands." While Dewey sat on the sidelines, it had fallen to Truman to decide how to use this devastating weapon, the president said:

> As President of the United States, I had the fateful responsibility of deciding whether or not to use this weapon for the first time. It was the hardest decision I ever had to make. But the President cannot duck hard problems—he cannot pass the buck. I made the decision after discussions with the ablest men in our Government, and after long and prayerful consideration. I decided that the bomb should be used in order to end the war quickly and save countless lives— Japanese as well as American.
>
> But I resolved then and there to do everything I could to see that this awesome discovery was turned into a force for peace and the

advancement of mankind. Since then, it has been my constant aim to prevent its use for war and to hasten its use for peace.[40]

But while he was working for the safe control of atomic energy within the framework of the United Nations and "developing atomic energy for peaceful uses" that could usher in "a whole new age of creative abundance," the Republicans had other ideas. Dewey's speech in Arizona on September 23 implied that "the peacetime uses of atomic energy should be taken from the Government and turned over to private corporations." This was illustrative, Truman believed, of "the basic conflict between the Democratic and the Republican parties. Here again is the vital issue between the people and the selfish interests. I believe that atomic energy should not be used to fatten the profits of big business. I believe that atomic energy should be used for the benefit of all the people." While the Truman administration oversaw atomic energy for the common good, "It is clear from the comments of the Republican candidate that powerful, selfish groups within the Republican Party are determined to exploit the atom for private profit." Truman was not going to let this happen, he assured his listeners, insisting, "I shall fight this effort with all the strength I have."[41]

It was not just Dewey who was going to test the president's mettle. George Gallup's column that day informed the nation that "the breaking up of the traditional political pattern of the South this year is dramatically shown" in his organization's latest test of opinion in the region. This showed that "Three states which Democrats have been able to count as 'absolutely safe' in most past elections have moved out of the Democratic column and are today under the banner of the anti-Truman States' Rights Party." The situation looked grim for the incumbent in South Carolina, Mississippi, and Alabama, and remarkably, the names "Harry Truman" and "Alben Barkley" were *not even on the ballot* in the latter. It also wasn't looking good for Truman in Louisiana, where he also trailed Strom Thurmond. Virginia and Florida were turning into battlegrounds for Truman, too, as support for Dewey surged there. These developments meant, according to Gallup, that Truman stood to lose up to forty-nine electoral votes in the South, a setback that could cost him the election.[42]

And yet Truman's team refused to alter his itinerary to divert the president below the Mason-Dixon line. His schedule had been planned on an exacting minute-to-minute basis, and the thought of disrupting this was anathema to the Last Chance Special campaign managers, even though they recognized that the November 1947 assertions about the Solid South by James Rowe and Clark Clifford were likely to be proved wrong.[43]

Another reason for standing pat was the focused information gathering that targeted every region of the nation *except* the South. Though they were only working forty-eight hours in advance of Truman's train, Bill Batt and his Research Division team were supplying fact sheets and talking points for every one of the whistle stops, while Clifford, Sam Rosenman, and the other speechwriters were working round the clock on drafts for the president's talks at larger venues, which Truman reviewed with them line by line around the small dining room table in the Ferdinand Magellan, providing commentary such as "Let's not weasel-word it, let's say it like this" when the ghostwriters got a little carried away by their own clever prose.[44] All this work and strategy could hardly be shoved aside for Truman to go tilting at windmills in Dixiecrat-supporting states where, in all likelihood, he would lose to Thurmond even if he did head south. Instead, the president and his team kept their sights firmly trained on regions that were still up for grabs during the final weeks of the campaign: the Midwest and Northeast. If Truman could secure contentious states in these regions, the thinking went, he could offset the expected successes of the States' Rights Party in the South.[45]

Indeed, Truman remained steadfast in such self-belief. Despite the gloomy predictions of George Gallup, Elmo Roper, and the other pollsters, he was convinced that the American people would keep him in the White House after hearing his populist appeals in person and on the radio. The day before Gallup's poll on the South appeared in newspapers, George Elsey sat across from Truman at the Ferdinand Magellan dining room table, writing as the president called out his state-by-state predictions for November 2. When Elsey finally put down his pen, the ledger showed a tally that nobody else thought possible. The president had pegged 340 Electoral College votes for himself, 108 for Dewey, and 42 for Wallace, with 37 labeled "doubtful."[46] "George, how many do I have?" Truman asked his aide. "340, Mr. President." Truman said nothing, just smiling like a man who had already achieved such a decisive result. Clark Clifford had a different reaction, shaking his head when Elsey revealed the president's optimistic forecast.[47]

Arguably the only staffer on the train who didn't share Clifford's skepticism was India Edwards. Beginning her political career as a volunteer on FDR's 1944 campaign after serving as a *Chicago Tribune* journalist and editor from 1918 to 1942 (ironic given the paper's hatred of Truman), the now fifty-three-year-old Edwards, who always pinned her brown hair up into a beehive, had risen quickly through the ranks.[48] By the time the Whistle Stop Tour got underway, her vim, unflagging optimism and proven expertise on garnering female votes for Truman had earned her the job of DNC Women's Division Executive director and an invitation to accompany the president's troupe across the nation.

She believed that Truman was committed to putting more women in positions of influence, and he proved it by acting on her recommendations to promote several female staffers to more important posts. In addition to speaking on Truman's behalf, working with Jack Redding on female-focused radio programming, and dispatching "Housewives for Truman" trucks packed with common household goods labeled with before-and-after price tags to illustrate the daily impact of inflation, Edwards served as an encourager to the president.[49] One morning, the Trumans asked Edwards to join them for breakfast. This was an unusual invitation, but she went to the dining room in the Ferdinand Magellan car all the same. "You know sometimes, India, I think there are only two people in the United States who really think I'm going to be elected President," Truman said. "They're both sitting at this table and one of them is not my wife."[50]

It was not only Truman who was buoyed by Edwards' upbeat outlook. At regular intervals she would stride through the seventeen-car train to the press compartment and implore the few lazy journalists who didn't dash down to the rear platform to see Truman interact with the crowds to "have sense enough to get off the train and circulate a little bit. If you'd see the reaction of the people, you'd know that they are going to vote this man into office."[51] Regardless of whether this prediction came to pass, Truman was certainly giving the ever-growing press contingent plenty to write about. According to George Elsey, Truman "never would use the same subject twice in one day. So, that there was a continuing flow of stories off the train." This was in contrast to Dewey's canned talks, in which, according to reporters who hopped back and forth, the New York governor would "say the same darn thing day in, day out." So even without the admonition from India Edwards, most of the press men would "scamper through the cinders" to hear Truman speak at most stops, knowing he would have something quotable, and probably controversial, to say.[52]

★ ★ ★

"WE'VE GOT 'EM ON THE RUN AND I THINK WE'LL WIN"

Delivering all these speeches was dominating the president's time, but he could not simply abandon his duties as chief executive. Indeed, packets of official documents sent from the White House by Charlie Murphy accompanied the Research Division talking points picked up at local airports en route, and Truman still reviewed and signed up to six hundred pages per day by his estimate.[53] He was also determined to continue creating directives, even if he had but days left as president. He issued an executive order on October 15, stipulating increased training for reserves in the armed forces. The order closed with a call to volunteers to "take an active part in building up the strong and highly trained reserve forces which are so vital to the defense of the United States."[54] This edict was the culmination of plans Truman and his secretary of state, George Marshall, had formulated before the end of World War II to engage the nation's young men in universal military training (UMT) to ensure that America was well prepared to face the challenge of potential future conflict. Marshall had seen how unready most young men were to enter the fray against the Axis powers in 1940 and was determined that this would not happen again, particularly if Soviet Russia proved to be as adversarial as its land grab in Eastern Europe and long and tarnished history of eliminating opposition suggested.[55]

The scheme Marshall and Truman proposed had met with strong opposition from within and outside the Democratic Party. Predictably, one of its chief foes was Robert Taft, who as late as April 7, 1948, had said, "UMT is a return to the New Deal belief that results can only be accomplished by Government compulsion, and power given to Government bureaus."[56] The Ohio senator had, however, been willing to vote for a compromise bill that passed both Houses on June 24 that required men between the ages of eighteen and twenty-six to register. This meant that those aged nineteen to twenty-six could be called up for twenty-one months' active service and then five further years of reserve duty. Though this fell short of the far-reaching implications of UMT, the combination of the act and the October 15 executive order for ramping up reservist training still went a considerable way to making sure the United States had enough battle-ready troops should the situation with the Soviet Union deteriorate beyond the possibility of peaceful settlement. It also sent a message to Moscow that Stalin would not catch his ideological foe unawares should he attempt to muscle America out of Berlin. This was compounded by Britain and America combining their airlift operations under American command. US military governor General Lucius Clay told reporters from both countries that the arrangement would go smoothly "as we learned to work so closely with the British together during the war."[57] The "starvation measure" of the blockade that aimed to force America out of the German capital would fail, Clay believed. "By continuing this airlift indefinitely and maintaining our position in Berlin we will have assured people who do want freedom that they will not be abandoned," he concluded.[58]

The Politburo's actions, though, made it clear that either the American message didn't get through or the iron-willed Stalin simply didn't care. Hours after Truman issued his decree and Clay made the Anglo-American arrangement known, the Soviet military administration released a statement of its own, insisting that from now on all highway traffic into Berlin would have to pass through the Russian zone. In the Soviet-run province of Brandenburg, Red Army troops had shuttered forty train stations to prevent entry into the British, French, or American zones by rail, and passengers in the few stations that still operated were inspected by stern-faced, Kalashnikov-wielding soldiers. They snatched any packages containing more than eleven pounds of food as "smuggled" goods, a term also applied to the contents of German trucks halted at gunpoint as they tried unsuccessfully to move westward through the Brandenburg Gate that divided the Allied and Soviet zones.[59] The US delegate to the United Nations, Philip Jessup, stated that the Western Allies would not negotiate any more with Moscow until the blockade was lifted. His French counterpart, Alexander Parodi, who had served the French liberation movement during World War II even after Paris fell, declared that the Soviets were "less interested in solving the question of Berlin than in prolonging indefinitely . . . conversations . . . to permit agitation."[60]

As the Soviets let soldiers at armed checkpoints do the talking, Truman finally shared his feelings with the world about the Vinson-to-Moscow fiasco on October 18. Speaking candidly in his old artillery uniform in a humid Miami as guest of honor at the national American Legion convention, Truman defended the idea that had proved so controversial in a month where he should have avoided tipping any more apples off the already tilting cart. "At this time I want to make it clear that I have not departed one step from my desire to utilize every opportunity to work for peace," the president said. "Whenever an opportunity arises, I shall act to further the interests of peace within the framework of our relations with our allies and the work of the United Nations." Reiterating a line from previous whistle stops, Truman avowed that achieving lasting world peace was more important to him than retaining the presidency.[61]

Though he spoke of the world situation, Truman's dual purpose that day was to show solidarity with military veterans. This was one of the second-tier domestic issues of the Democratic plank and the subject of one of the eleven Files of the Facts prepared by Bill Batt's group. Despite his fondness for pushing his train's speed to its limit—unlike FDR, who preferred a more leisurely pace—the president knew that even the most ambitious crew could not have taken the seventeen-car procession all the way from Washington to south Florida overnight. So he had journeyed to Miami in his presidential plane (a forerunner of the more official-sounding Air Force One) at 6:00 a.m. on the 18th, with Bess and Margaret, Clifford, Elsey, and a bevy of other aides. Arriving at Miami International Airport, Truman walked through a guard of honor from the 82nd Airborne Division, among whose number his States' Right opponent Strom Thurmond had served with distinction in World War II.[62]

Then it was on to a waiting open-topped car, its cream-colored paintwork buffed and polished, American flags fluttering proudly on either side of the silver front grille. As the scream of Hellcat jets mixed into a cacophony with the sub-bass rumble of Superfortresses and the whoops and hollers of more than thirty-five thousand American Legion members and sixty-five thousand Floridians who lined the streets, Truman sat on top of the rear seat, waving with one hand while trying to retain his dark blue legion cap in the stiff breeze with the other.

After lunch at the red-tiled, Mediterranean revival style Roney Plaza Hotel, there was more waving and smiling as the Truman party drove another eight miles to his keynote address at the legion event in Dinner

Key. There, eight thousand Legionnaires crammed into a makeshift arena fashioned from two cavernous aircraft hangars to hear the president. He opened up by reminding his audience that he was one of them, saying: "I am glad to be here today as a delegate from Missouri first, as a comrade-in-arms, and as Commander in Chief of the Armed Forces of the United States." [63]

Next, Truman spoke about the importance of the American Legion in the post–World War II world: "I am happy to see the younger men of World War II joining and strengthening our organization, which has never failed to be vigilant for the welfare and security of this great country of ours. I have looked forward to this opportunity of counseling with you as veterans." [64] While he valued the sacrifice of active servicemen, Truman said, "It's an altogether different task to secure good men after the shooting stops than it is to secure them while the fighting is going on." [65]

The president then took issue with those who abandoned bipartisanship and questioned his foreign policy with "loose and irresponsible talk to the effect that the United States is deliberately following a course that leads to war. That is a plain and deliberate lie." He was taking a shot at Henry Wallace without mentioning the name of his Progressive Party rival.

Whatever the criticisms of Wallace and the provocations of the Soviet Union, Truman made it clear that he would not be swayed from the course of securing lasting peace through strength: "We have taken, and we will continue to take, a firm position, where our rights are threatened. But our firmness should not be mistaken for a warlike spirit. The world has learned that it is weakness and appeasement that invite aggression. A firm position on reasonable grounds offers the best hope of peace, and we have been open to reason at every point."

Despite his overriding desire for peace, Truman assured his listeners that he was not and would never be another Neville Chamberlain, stating, "We recognize the principle of mutual conciliation as a basis for peaceful negotiation, but this is very different from appeasement. While we will always strive for peace, this country will never consent to any compromise of the principles of freedom and human rights. We will never be a party to the kind of compromise which the world sums up in the disgraced name of Munich." [66]

Eager to show, with Election Day less than three weeks away, that he had been a solid steward of American's power in peacetime, Truman then laid out his record, point by point:

In the past 2 years, the United States has made three major moves of foreign policy in the European area. Each move has been tied in with the work of the United Nations. Each move has been designated to reduce the dangers of chaos and war.

The first move was made in March 1947, when we offered economic and military aid to Greece and Turkey, then threatened by Communist aggression.

Three months later, we began our second major move—the great program for European economic recovery. With American help under this plan, 16 European nations are making a joint effort, unprecedented in history, to overcome heavy economic losses suffered in the great war.

A number of these countries have already increased their production and improved their financial stability. It is not too much to say that this plan holds the key for the economic future of Europe and the world.

Our third major move was the joint action of the United States, Great Britain, and France in establishing a working, but by no means final, economic organization for the Western Zones of Germany, under allied military control. This step was undertaken to encourage the economic revival of Germany, under proper safeguards, so as to aid the recovery of all Western Europe and promote stability.

We have also been giving support and encouragement to the organization of the Western European Union.

These actions were not outward-looking at the expense of America's best interests, Truman said, but rather, "This country was at the same time protecting its own interests. No nation can afford to disregard self-interest. I think it is fair to say that American policy has revealed an unusual degree of enlightenment. We have taken it as a first principle that our interest is bound up with the peace and economic recovery of the rest of the world. Accordingly, we have worked for all three together—world peace, world economic recovery, and the welfare of our own Nation." [67]

Truman then set out the defining question of the early Cold War period, wondering aloud, "Can we so reconcile the interests of the Western powers and the interests of the Soviet Union as to bring about an enduring peace?"[68] This question could not be answered satisfactorily when there was a lingering "fog of distrust" between the Soviet Union and its Western counterparts. He would try to help lift this by continuing to seek opportunities to parley with Moscow, by exercising "patience," and by continually strengthening the UN. As he brushed away sweat from his forehead on that clammy Florida afternoon, Truman finished on a determined yet hopeful note. "I would only add that our Nation has never failed to meet the great crises of its history with honor and devotion to its ideals. My friends, and fellow Legionnaires, we shall spare no effort to achieve the peace on which the entire destiny of the human race depends."[69]

A letter that Truman wrote to his sister, Mary Jane, the next day on October 20 reveals the extent of Truman's self-belief, which was being restoked every day by the large crowds he encountered on train platforms, in stadiums, and in conference halls across the country, not to mention the endorsement that had finally come from Eleanor Roosevelt:[70]

> We arrived in Miami at 10 o'clock and I had one of the most enthusiastic receptions in the campaign on the streets. There must have been 200,000 people out and it was eighty in the shade, and no shade for me. The Legion gave me an ovation. There were at least 80,000 in the audience and that many outside.
>
> We took off at 4:15 and arrived in Raleigh two hours and thirteen minutes later. Went to the hotel and stayed all night. There were people all along the way from the airport, which is fifteen miles out of town. It was cold too. Yesterday I spoke to 50,000 people from the Capitol steps and as many more at the fairgrounds in the afternoon.
>
> We've got 'em on the run and I think we'll win.[71]

Just saying that he would win didn't make it so. Instead, Truman had to channel this bravado into relentless action during the final two weeks of the campaign. And so he did. He began by defending the principles of the New Deal and attacking his Republican opponent during a White House radio address on October 21. Before Truman took the microphone at 10:05 p.m., the country heard an introduction from wavy-haired actress Tallulah Bankhead, whose sultry tones were piped in from her dressing room at New York's Plymouth Theater, where she was taking an intermission break during a starring turn in *Private Lives*. With no regard for the Republican producer who had green-lighted her participation, the glamorous Broadway star said that her family had served in the House and Senate for sixty years, and that in honor of their memory, "I'm for Harry Truman, the human being. By the same token, I'm against Thomas E. Dewey, the mechanical man with a synthetic smile on his face."[72]

The president could hardly have asked for a better introduction. Riding the momentum, he said the agenda ushered in by FDR and continued after his passing "is a program for going forward. True liberalism looks to the future. True liberalism is more than a matter of words. It cannot hide behind the catch phrases of the Republican candidate for President—catch phrases like 'unity' and 'efficiency.' Unity for what? And what kind of efficiency?"

Truman claimed that Dewey, whom he again didn't mention by name, "is the chief prosecutor against the New Deal. He has spoken against it, he has campaigned against it. He wrote a book called 'The Case Against the New Deal.' And now he wants to come to Washington and destroy it." He then focused his derision on the Taft-Hartley Act, which he said "converts the Wagner Act from a charter protecting the basic rights of workers into an instrument for union busting by anti-labor employers." And what was the president proposing to halt the "grave danger" posed by this act and its proponents? He laid out an eight-point program that mirrored the Files of the Facts compiled by Bill Batt and the Research Division:

> We should repeal the Taft-Hartley Act.
> Then we should increase the minimum wage from 40 cents an hour to at least 75 cents an hour.
> Social security insurance should be extended to the large groups of people not now protected.
> The insurance benefits should be increased by approximately 50 percent.
> We should expand our facilities for looking after the Nation's health.
> The Federal Government should provide aid to the States in meeting the educational needs of our children.
> The Congress should provide aid for slum clearance and low-rent housing.
> We should do something, at once, about high prices.

Truman finished on a positive, populist note, declaring, "Our program is for the people. And that's why we're going to win this election on November the second."[73]

Before he returned to the Ferdinand Magellan for the final eight-day push, Truman allowed himself one more rest day at the White House, if one can call a full day of planning, going over whistle stop notes, and adding remarks and redlines to the major addresses planned for Pittsburgh, Chicago, and New York "rest." Then, early on the morning of October 23, Truman, Ross, Clifford, and the rest rode in a motorcade of black limousines that snaked its way along the dawn-lit streets of the capital to Union Station, bound for nine eastern and midwestern states before reaching a fitting end point in Truman's beloved Missouri. Margaret and Bess would be with him on the rails for the first few days and then would fly back to Independence to prepare for what they hoped would be a victory celebration.[74]

While Truman continued his hard-hitting remarks at Pennsylvania whistle stops that acted as a warm-up for the Pittsburgh speech, Dewey was proclaiming his desire for the country to move forward after the election "without scars and without bitterness"—an election he, his advisers, and more than two-thirds of media outlets expected him to win handily. In these last days before the American people voted, Dewey vowed that he would not resort to "vituperation or abuse" as had the president.[75]

He may have been savage, Truman retorted in Johnstown, Pennsylvania, but he was merely "talking plainly to people about the issues . . . the only way I know how to do business. I want you to know where I stand." Meanwhile, all they were getting from Dewey was hot air, the president said. Then he quipped, "You know what G.O.P. stands for these days? It stands for 'Grand Old Platitudes.'"[76]

If it wasn't clear what Dewey stood for, Truman was pretty certain what the Republican Party was about: fulfilling the greedy aims of its "special interest" backers. He said, "When the war ended, big business decided to torpedo price controls." Because of the Eightieth Congress's hostility toward the price controls proposed by the White House, "Prices have gone up 30 cents on the dollar. Food has increased in price almost 50 on the dollar. We have had to spend our wartime savings to pay the grocery bill." Truman then told his listeners the destination for this extra cash: "It has gone just where big business and the Republican Party planned for it to go—into higher profits. Corporation profits after taxes have increased 70 cents on the dollar since price control was killed." This excess was being funneled back into Republican campaign funds, Truman insisted.

If voters chose him over Dewey, Truman promised, "Then we can bring prices down to where your weekly pay envelope will not only keep your family going for the week, but you will be able to put something aside for all the fine things you hoped to buy after the war and haven't been able to buy.

"Then we will have a Government for the people. We will have Federal aid to education. We will have slum clearance, and half a million new low-rent houses. We will have a 75-cent minimum wage. We will have extended social security for every working man and woman in the United States. We will have health insurance to help pay the doctor bills of every American family."[77] In many ways, the contents of this speech did more to outline the Democratic Party platform than the address Truman gave later that day in Pittsburgh, in which he again slammed the labor record of the Republican-led Eightieth Congress. The turnout in that city was remarkable, though, as more than one hundred thousand people "piled out of theaters, taverns, stores, apartments, homes, autos, all along the route," and welcomed the president with "flares, placards and shouts" all along the ten-mile parade route.[78]

After a day taking the much-needed rest that the Sabbath offered the next day, Truman was back on task on October 25. He warmed up for his big evening speech in Chicago with rear platform talks in Indiana and Illinois. Speaking in the town of Garrett, Indiana, the president summarized his relentless efforts in the fall campaign and the contrast between his approach and Dewey's: "It has been a good campaign for me. It has been a hard campaign. I have traveled from one end of the country to the other, telling millions of people about peace, prices, and places to live, and the other issues which face the Nation today. My opponent has talked a great deal too, but he said almost nothing about where he stands on the major issues facing the American people today."[79]

Truman then assailed the "Third Party" of Henry Wallace, which had been "taken over" by communists "in a vain attempt to split the Democratic Party." These dubious elements were in cahoots with the GOP, Truman said, stating that "The Republicans financed the Third Party to get on the ballot right here in Indiana in a number of counties. We have got straight-out evidence on that, and I can prove it." It's unclear whether Truman really had proof of this outlandish claim, but he gave his audience little time to ponder its validity before he moved onto his next point. Showing off his literary knowledge, Truman referred to Aesop's fable of The Ass and His Purchaser as he said of the GOP, "By their friends ye shall know them."[80]

A few miles down the line in Gary, Truman opened up in a softer stance, going back to hokey Harry as he shared a joke with his audience in the Municipal Auditorium:

> I heard a story not long ago about an elderly man who was driving into Gary, and he gave a lift to a young fellow who was going his way. During their talk, the older man asked the young fellow, "What takes you to Gary?"
>
> The young man kind of hesitated, put his head down, and finally said: "I am working for the Republican State Committee. They are sending me to Gary to see what I can do to get the people there to vote the Republican ticket."
>
> The old man was silent for a while, and then he said: "Son, I've listened to a lot of sad stories for the last 50 years, but that's the saddest one I've heard yet."[81]

Once the laughter died down, Truman reverted to attack mode. While he was fighting for the working man, Truman said that the Republicans "don't want you to have good wages. They don't want the farmer to have good prices." Digging into his Research Division–provided figures, Truman reminded them how much better off they were in 1948 than sixteen years previously, before FDR took the helm: "[T]he average hourly rate of pay in industry is $1.33 an hour, instead of 45 cents as it was in 1932. More than three times as much . . . under Democratic administrations. Average weekly earnings are $52.96, instead of the measly $17.05 that you got in 1932." Farmers were also better off, too, but not for long if the GOP prevailed. He then compared the smooth-sounding Dewey to an ill-intentioned physician, saying, "The special privilege boys are at work throughout the land, crooning 'unity,' hoping you will open your mouths, shut your eyes, and swallow that soothing syrup, and go to sleep and not go to the polls. That's what they are trying to do. Don't be deceived, my friends. They took you to the cleaners in 1929. They want to do it again.

They love labor and the farmers in October, but it's a little bit different after election." [82]

While Dewey and his running mate, Earl Warren, talked about change, Truman said, "It's time for them to change. It's time for them to change their habit of opposing everything that is done in the interests of the people. It's time for them to change the Taft-Hartley Act—and repeal it. It's time for them to change, and support us in raising the minimum wage to at least 75 cents an hour." If his opponents wanted to talk about "cooperation," Truman had some suggestions for them on that front, too: "I say it's time for them to cooperate with us in trying to do the right thing. They ought to cooperate in widening social security protection, increasing unemployment benefits and raising old-age payments. I say it's time for them to cooperate to bring down those Republican high prices." [83]

The GOP could waffle all they wanted, but Truman distilled the campaign to a simple choice, "It is the people against the special interests." He was in no doubt which side would prevail: "I trust the people. Every good Democrat does. I trust their common sense, their decency, and their sense of justice. That's why I'm talking with you right now. We beat this Republican outfit in 1932. Beat them in 1936. We beat them in 1940. And we beat them 4 years ago. We'll do it again." [84]

Though he was building on by-now familiar themes, this was one of Truman's most effective speeches. He successfully tore down three of Dewey's favorite buzzwords—"unity," "change," and "cooperation"—while reiterating the improved quality of life the nation enjoyed under FDR and his time in the White House. Truman also demonstrated his fighting spirit with a rousing conclusion.

And yet just when it looked like his luck might begin to change, he tripped over his own tongue. Buoyed by a tumultuous reception from the estimated 750,000 people who lined the streets of the Windy City later that day to see Truman and a gaudy, noisy parade of brass bands, floats, and standard bearers, the president arrived at Chicago Stadium in high spirits. [85] Despite problems with Russia in Berlin and a communist-inspired strike in France, the president was feeling confident that he was gaining momentum as the campaign reached its final stage.

Yet instead of capitalizing on the momentum, Truman let his enthusiasm and passion get the better of him. He had included a fear-based element in his Gary talk and at many whistle stops, but now, with just a week to go until Election Day, he turned up the dial to a fever pitch, saying, "if the antidemocratic forces in this country continue to work unchecked, this Nation could awaken a few years from now to find that the Bill of Rights had become a scrap of paper."[86]

He continued, "What are these forces that threaten our way of life? Who are the men behind them? They are the men who want to see inflation continue unchecked. They are the men who are striving to concentrate great economic power in their own hands. They are the men who are setting up and stirring up racial and religious prejudice against some of our fellow Americans."[87]

There were three groups of ne'er-do-wells who had put America in "danger," Truman told the audience of twenty-five thousand, and all three of them were "working through the Republican Party." These allies of big business were a threat, he believed, because "Again and again in history, economic power concentrated in the hands of a few men has led to the loss of freedom."[88]

Getting up a full head of steam, Truman surged ahead into his most dramatic allegations of the campaign and, arguably, of his political career:

> When a few men get control of the economy of a nation, they find a "front man" to run the country for them. Before Hitler came to power, control over the German economy had passed into the hands of a small group of rich manufacturers, bankers, and landowners. These men decided that Germany had to have a tough, ruthless dictator who would play their game and crush the strong German labor unions. So they put money and influence behind Adolf Hitler. We know the rest of the story. We also know that in Italy, in the 1920s, powerful Italian businessmen backed Mussolini, and that in the 1930s, Japanese financiers helped Tojo's military clique take over Japan.[89]

While he had not minced words at any point of the campaign and had been far more stinging in his attacks on the GOP than Dewey had been in his statements about the Democratic Party, Truman had only mentioned his opponent by name twice and had concentrated most of his fire on the "do-nothing" Eightieth Congress. But now, as the governor of New York continued to abide by Queensbury rules, the president had put on the "brass knuckles" that one writer had previously referred to and begun throwing punches that would earn him disqualification in a true gentleman's contest. Just when Truman could ill afford even a minor setback, he had made his biggest blunder since his ill-conceived comments about Joe Stalin being "alright" back on the June tour. Certainly, Clifford, Rosenman, and the other speechwriters may have come up with the Dewey-as-Hitler analogy, but they operated behind the scenes, and it was the man who once kept a sign stating "The Buck Stops Here" on his desk who must now reckon with the consequences.

And they were quick in coming. As Truman entertained Chicago boss Jake Arvey late into the night—he didn't even board the train until 2:00 a.m.—outraged reporters put their pencils to work.[90] The next morning's early editions were almost unanimous in their criticism. "President Likens Dewey to Hitler as Fascists' Tool," blared the front page of the *New York Times*. The Chicago address was "one of the bitterest speeches he has yet delivered," wrote *Pittsburgh Post-Gazette* copublisher Paul Block Jr., who also noted that while Truman had gone for a crowd-stunning knockout, "words intended to bring down the house were listened to in polite silence."[91]

Oblivious to the furor that his ill-conceived comment about Dewey had caused, Truman was happy with his performance in Chicago, writing to his sister that former mayor Kelly and current mayor Kennelly "both said that the demonstration was better than any ever held here, including FDR." The president then laid out the itinerary of his campaign's final madcap week: "We go from here to Cleveland tomorrow. From Cleveland to Boston . . . to Providence, R.I., to New Haven to New York. Then to Brooklyn and on Friday night we leave for St. Louis. Saturday night . . . I'll be winding up the campaign with all I have in the old conservative Mo. Metropolis." Then, providing insight into the fatigue that he stoically refused to show to anyone outside his inner circle, Truman predicted, "I expect to sleep all day Sunday."[92] Truman told reporters on his train that the "tide was rolling" in his favor and predicted that on November 3 "some of the reddest-faced people the country has ever seen will be the pollsters."[93]

But even an all-out, exhaustion-causing effort wouldn't put Truman over the top, most journalists still predicted. James Hagerty, writing in the *New York Times*, insisted that, contrary to Truman's defiant statement, the GOP's "dream ticket" of Tom Dewey and Earl Warren "appear certain to defeat President Harry S. Truman and Senator Alben W. Barkley . . . by a large plurality."[94] The only consolation for the Democrats, Hagerty believed, was that the latest polls indicated that the Democrats might achieve a tie in the Senate, or maybe even a narrow majority. To this end, some reporters contended that Truman might have given up trying to claw back Dewey's seemingly insurmountable lead and was focusing his energies elsewhere. In an op-ed piece for the Associated Press, J. Frank Tragle wondered if Truman's remaining whistle stop appearances were "not aimed more at helping Democratic congressional candidates than aiding him."[95] And veteran Washington beat writer Thomas L. Stokes reported that in Alabama "they really fixed up Harry Truman good and proper. There is no way to vote for the President of the United States on Nov. 2." As a result, Stokes assumed that Strom Thurmond would easily carry the state.[96] The *Atlanta Journal-Constitution* extended this prediction to the entire nation, stating "Harry Truman is defeated" and asserting that such a result "is what the Southern revolt wanted."[97]

Such defeatism was all well and good for the naysayers, but the Man from Missouri refused to listen to it. Regardless of what the candidate list was in Alabama, what the Dixiecrats would achieve, or what gloomy forecast the polls still held, Truman continued to "pour it on" as the Ferdinand Magellan propelled him across the final leg of the Whistle Stop Tour. Despite the late night after the Chicago speech, Truman bustled out of his bedroom right on time on the morning of October 26, with another five speeches on the day's schedule, again planned down to the smallest detail by Matt Connelly.[98]

During the first one, at 9:35 a.m. in South Bend, Indiana, Truman steered away from making more accusations about fascism, but he delivered some of his strongest points to date about immigration. For months, his team had been working with foreign-language newspapers to disseminate positive reports about the Democratic Party's pledge to increase the quota for those who wanted to flee hardship in postwar Europe and the president's efforts to turn the proposal into reality. This was another of the suggestions in the Rowe-Clifford policy manifesto from the previous year, which Chapman, Clifford, Murphy, and the rest had put into action almost point for point.[99]

Truman told his listeners that "South Bend is one of the great melting pots of this country. Families of a great many races and religions work here together side by side as Americans, for the welfare of this great Nation of ours. You know that being an American is more than a matter of where you or your parents came from. It is a belief that all men are created free and equal and that everyone deserves an even break. It is a respect for the dignity of men and women without regard to race, creed, or color. That is our creed. That is the creed of the Democratic Party."[100]

He then explained how recent experience had opened his eyes to the need for an open-armed immigration policy in the United States: "When I was in Potsdam in 1945 I paid a visit to the displaced persons camps over there and I found about 1,200,000 displaced persons in those camps. They were from all the countries of Europe which had been overrun—they were Poles, Latvians, Lithuanians, and Romanians—people from Austria and France and other countries in those camps. They were so arranged that I suggested that we send 100,000 Jews to Palestine, that we take 400,000 people in this country—400,000 of those people in this country—send 400,000 to South America, and let the British colonies take another 400,000."

However, yet again, the Eightieth Congress had failed. Truman claimed that "they said, 'oh, no; 400,000 is too many'—and they waited 3 years. And so the 80th Congress passed a law to admit only 202,000 people. They did that grudgingly, at the end of the present session. And to make it worse the Republican leaders wrote so many restrictions into the law which discriminate against people of certain religions—and will serve to keep them out of the United States."[101]

This inaction had grave consequences, Truman revealed. "This means that we will be leaving at least 200,000 homeless people in Europe—people whom we ought to have working right here in the United States, now." This was simply not good enough for the nation that should be showing an example. "If this country is to move ahead in our position of world leadership, we must demonstrate to the world that we practice what we preach," Truman said. And how could those who had crammed onto the platform help ensure a better deal for immigrants? They simply needed to show up on November 2 and "elect a Congress and an administration that believes in the principles that have made this Nation great."[102]

That evening Tom Dewey, who had rolled into the Windy City mere hours after Truman's train had rolled out, told another packed house in Chicago Stadium that his opponents "have now, I am sorry to say, reached a new low of mud-slinging." Rather than sitting back and taking abuse, Dewey insisted that "The time has come to rebuke those who preach the doctrine of fear."[103] The Democratic Party had been, Dewey said, "openly sneering at the ancient ideal of a free and united people" and stoking "antagonism and prejudice." Finally sounding like Thomas E. Dewey, the courageous attorney-at-law, the New York governor then took aim at Truman, stating that, "We all know the sad record of the present administration. More than three years have passed since the end of the war and it has failed to win the peace." Gathering steam as he approached his summation, Dewey told his audience that "millions upon millions of people have been delivered into Soviet slavery while our own administration has tried appeasement one day and bluster the next."[104] Where had this fiery, forthright Dewey been the entire campaign, and why had he waited until mere days remained in the campaign to respond to Truman's constant baiting and criticizing?

Regardless of how late in the game Dewey had waited to unleash his oratorical prowess on the president (though, it should be noted, he never mentioned Truman by name), most of the news media still believed he would waltz into the White House. The *Boston Globe* reported that Dewey's wife, Frances, had never been there, but Republican staffers were convinced that "the prettiest First Lady in years" wouldn't have long to wait before she became intimately familiar with 1600 Pennsylvania Avenue.[105] Writing for the United Press, White House beat reporter Lyle C. Wilson laid out the extent of the challenges facing the chief rival of Mrs. Dewey's husband: "Mr. Truman is running against the states' rights candidate, J. Strom Thurmond, in the south. He is running against Henry A. Wallace in some of the great industrial states with sizable left wing concentrations. He is running against Dewey pretty much all over. It looks like Mr. Truman will be outrun."[106]

Wilson had overlooked another pressing worry for the president: the knife-edge standoff with Russia in Berlin. George Marshall met with French foreign minister Robert Schuman and British foreign secretary Ernest Bevin and issued a statement asking Russia to withdraw its veto of the UN's compromise proposal, which would see a single Soviet currency in Berlin (albeit with four-power oversight) and the end of the blockade. In the same meeting, Marshall, Schuman, and Bevin also discussed plans to bolster their alliance through a North Atlantic "security pact," which Canada would be invited to join.[107] Certainly the Western democracies needed to work together to counter the continuing strong-arm tactics of the Soviets in Germany, where, according to British military governor Sir Brian Robertson, there were now between two hundred and four hundred thousand police in the eastern sector, trained by and sympathetic to their Russian overlords. "You can guess as well as I can what its purpose is," Robertson said at a press conference.[108]

There was even more bad news in the fight against communism much further east, in China. There, Mao Zedong's rebel forces overran ever-weakening loyalist resistance in the strategically vital city of Mukden in southern Manchuria, a development the AP described as "the most stunning government loss in the three-year civil war." If American, British, and French administrators faced an uphill struggle in Germany, Nationalist Party leader Chiang Kai-Shek was in danger of slipping ever further down an Everest in China. For Truman, another AP dispatch noted, the deteriorating situation in the pivotal Asian nation was "the first major reverse of the Cold War." If China succumbed to Mao's communist take-over attempt, what next for the continent, where Japan was still in the early stages of rebuilding after World War II, and Korea was already split between democracy and totalitarianism?[109]

October 27 gave Research Division staffer Frank Kelly another opportunity to see the campaign up close when he traveled to Boston for a meeting with his publisher, Atlantic Monthly Press, about the forthcoming publication of his book on the Iranian crisis of 1946, *An Edge of Light*. As luck would have it, this trip coincided with Truman's campaign stop in Boston, where he would deliver a major address that was a key part of the final Whistle Stop Tour leg. If the president was to come back at Dewey, he needed the voters in Beantown and other urban centers in the Northeast to back him.

Though there was little letup at the Research Division offices, George Elsey gave Kelly permission to extend his stay by a few hours after the meeting with his editor and got him a security pass from the Secret Service. This gained Kelly admission into the Hotel Statler, where Truman and his entourage would be staying for one night after he paraded through downtown Boston and met with local Democratic candidates.[110] These included the thirty-one-year-old John F. Kennedy, the rising star congressman from Massachusetts's eleventh district. Kenneth Birkhead, who was making twenty to thirty calls a day to gather research for speeches and the Research Division fact sheets, had called the up-and-coming Democrat in the buildup to the Boston trip, and the president was eager to confer with the son of the former British ambassador as he made his swing through Beantown.[111]

On the morning of October 27 Frank Kelly used his security pass to get past Secret Service agents and approach Truman's suite, eager to see how the president was handling the ceaseless pressure on him. As he walked along the hall, Kelly, whose family back in Kansas City knew the Trumans, heard a spirited piano waltz emanating from behind the doors of the president's room.[112] Walking in, Kelly watched as Truman's hands nimbly picked up the pace on the keys to bring the piece to a close. The music at an end, he jumped up from his stool and said, "Let's go, boys. We can't keep a crowd of good Democrats waiting." Then, perhaps sensing that not everyone in the room shared his optimism, he gave them a few words of encouragement for the final push: "It won't be long now before we are finished with all this traveling."[113]

Truman bounded out of the hotel for the short drive to the red-brick Mechanics Hall, at Huntington Avenue and West Newton Street near the Boston and Albany Railroad yard, where he would address a labor audience. Or, it would be more accurate to state, he tried to leave. "I've never seen such a mob in a lobby," Kelly said later. "They had to fight to get him through, and people were just cheering madly. Elsey got me into a car with Dr. Graham; it was right behind the President's." The crowd was so big and pressed so close to the vehicles, however, that the motorcade couldn't gain any momentum. All around there were cheers for the incumbent and, despite all his efforts, still the underdog: "Keep it up, Harry," "You're going to win, Harry." Now it was Truman's turn to be encouraged.[114]

Kelly continued: "The policemen were trying to get the caravan of cars to move, and I looked over at this big Irish cop next to me on a motorcycle and I said, 'How does this crowd compare with what Roosevelt drew when he came through Boston?' This cop looked at me and said, 'Roosevelt never drew a crowd half as big as this in Boston. We like Harry better up here.'"[115]

Beat writers from Boston and those from the Truman train later estimated that up to 250,000 had turned out to see the man who hoped to win another four years in the White House. Such reports were filed in double-quick order after each speech. There were just a few minutes between whistle stops, and so once writers had jotted down a few spider-scrawls in notebooks now dog-eared from overuse and being jammed wherever there was space in the overcrowded, clammy press quarters, they pushed through the crowds and sprinted back down the platform. Clambering up the metal steps into their compartment, the hacks picked away on portable Remingtons, rushing to bang out a couple hundred words in time to hand to the telegraph operator at the next station stop. Even this madcap pace was sometimes not fast enough, so the writers just pulled down a sliding train window and flung envelopes of copy to Western Union reporters who were waiting below with open arms, ready for more airborne missives.[116] It was not all work for the press corps, though. To pass the time when the train kept going for several hours without pausing, they made up little ditties, such as this one set to the tune of "I'm Looking Over a Four-Leaf Clover":

> I'm looking over a well-warmed-over Dewey from '44;
> One for the money and two for the show; Halleck was promised but
>   Warren will go.
> No use complainin'; I'm still maintainin'; we'll get what we had
>   before:
> Harry or Dewey, the same old hooey, again and again and more.[117]

The day after receiving the emotional boost in Boston, Truman gave his first address in Quincy, Massachusetts, where father and son presidents, John and John Quincy Adams, had been born (when the town was known as Braintree). Despite the event starting several hours before the usual early service time, a full crowd had packed the pews of the First Parish Church long before Truman took the lectern at 7:30 a.m. Truman didn't need a Research Division fact sheet for his opening (though Elsey had, of course, received one), in which he recounted the town's connection to both the Adams family and to Thomas Jefferson.

Truman then praised the quality of Boston's shipyards, which, he told the audience, had proved competent during his investigatory work on the Truman Committee during World War II. Now, though, it was peacetime, and he was working hard to "win the peace," he assured them. "It is much harder to win the peace than it is to win a war, because everybody is behind you when you have to fight for the welfare of your country."[118] Indeed, his approval rating had climbed to as high as 87 percent during his first few months as president and wartime commander-in-chief, and slumped into the mid-thirties in May 1948.[119]

He wasn't just battling for peace now, Truman revealed, but was also trying to end "the menace of Communism." Truman then positioned himself as the leader of the anticommunist struggle, saying, "I have fought communism here in the United States, and I have led in the fight against communism all over the world. Communists don't like me very well. They are all against me, and I am glad of it. I don't want them for me. I hate communism, and because I have fought so much to prevent its spread, the Communists hate me. They are doing their very best to prevent my election."

And how would he continue to combat communism if his opponents failed to get him out of the White House? By implementing the social programs that the Eightieth Congress had stymied. He told the audience, "I know that the best way to stop communism in this country is to make sure that every citizen has a good standard of living, and a job all the year round, a decent place to live, and good schools with medical care for his family."

Truman elaborated on his planned domestic agenda for 1949 and beyond, and then reiterated the call for his listeners to cast their votes in his favor to ensure that he could deliver on the issues most important to them:

Vote for the control and lowering of prices.
Vote for decent housing.
Vote for the repeal of the Taft-Hartley Act.
Vote for the party that knows that the way to beat communism is by keeping this Nation strong and prosperous.[120]

After three more speeches in Massachusetts that morning and one in Rhode Island just after lunch, Truman rolled into Connecticut. Truman spoke from the rear platform in New London and New Haven, but delivered his most significant off-the-cuff address of the afternoon in Bridgeport. Batt and his Dupont Circle boys had outdone themselves with the opening local anecdote, which Truman effortlessly tied to his past and then used to introduce his forward-thinking plans for the next four years, if only the voters would have him:

> You know, when I was a kid, about 17 or 18 years old, I saw the first horseless carriage in Independence, Mo., and there were just about this many people out to look at it. And that was a Locomobile that was made right here in Bridgeport, and it was a horseless carriage. It looked just like an old buggy, and it ran with steam. But there is quite a change now in that automobile business from what it was in those days, and that's true of the age in which we live. We are living in an age with which we haven't yet caught up, and I am doing everything I can to keep the country going forward instead of trying to turn the dock back to that old steam horseless carriage we had in 1902.[121]

This was the eighth of Truman's fifteen speeches that day. But he would have been forgiven for quickly forgetting it following a parade in New York the likes of which put even Boston's rousing procession to shame. His train pulled into Grand Central Station at 4:20 p.m. and embarked on a nine-mile parade through Gotham, with 101 police motorcycles—the largest escort in city history—accompanying him. Ticker tape and confetti floated and twirled in the gathering dusk like unseasonably early and colorful snowflakes. Truman—with Margaret and Bess, both wearing elaborate orchid corsages and beaming at the reception that greeted "Daddy" as they trundled along five and six cars behind him—waved to the estimated 1.4 million New Yorkers who cheered him through the streets. The screams for the president's popular daughter—"Margaret, Margaret!"—seemed to eclipse even the welcome for her father, and she held first one black-gloved hand and then the other aloft to acknowledge their adulation.[122] Oscar Chapman described that with the Truman ladies standing beside him on the rear platform of the train, the president made people think, "Here's one of our neighbors with his wife and daughter." The reaction in New York on this day was even more enthusiastic for the whole family, hopefully a sign of things to come.[123]

After Truman met local government workers at City Hall and spoke for a few minutes, the motorcade continued to wind its way past whooping and hollering onlookers, who seemed undeterred by the gathering gloom. Arriving at Sara Delano Roosevelt Park, he was greeted by a towering white, layered cake with a golden Statue of Liberty on top in recognition of the sixty-two-year anniversary of the monument. It was fitting, then, that he chose to talk of freedom and world peace, which, he said in a nod to FDR's mother, for whom the park was named, was "the greatest gift we can give our mothers." His greatest goal, he said, was not winning the election, but avoiding war. Invoking his military service in World War I, he declared, "Peace is what I've been working for all my life." As his listeners in the park focused on him and residents of the tenement blocks behind strained to hear the words broadcast from the PA system, Truman echoed Churchill's Sinews of Peace speech he had attended in March 1946 as he said, with a Politburo audience in mind as much as the New Yorkers who had turned out to see him, "Peace is within the reach of mankind, but there is no peace in weakness. There can be peace in strength. I never shall give up trying to get world peace."[124]

As he enjoyed the applause, a local organizer asked Truman to do the honors of slicing the cake. "It's such a pretty cake, I hate to cut it," the president replied. After a few moments he relented, cutting deep into the dessert and cramming a large piece into his mouth. This would be the only food he was likely to get until a very late dinner hours later.[125]

Returning to his car, an overcoat now backing up his suit in its fight against the evening chill, Truman again rode high on the back seat next to New York mayor O'Dwyer and DNC chairman Howard McGrath. As the car made its way to its next stop at Union Square, speakers blared, "Happy Days Are Here Again." Someone brought a microphone to the slow-moving lead car, and the president called out, "We are winning this election! Don't let them tell you any different."[126] Then it was onto the Democratic Club at Thirty-Seventh St. and Madison. There he continued to be contagiously optimistic, saying, "We are going to win because everyone is against us—except the people. And, my friends, the people have the votes. The special interests are against us, the exploiters of labor, the monopolists, the lobbies, and most of the newspapers—nearly 90 percent of the newspapers are against us. Those are the ones that are against us. I repeat, the only ones that are for us are the people."[127] Truman walked out of the club, flanked by Margaret and Bess, who carried rainbow-hued bouquets of flowers, while he busied his right hand shaking with every club member and onlooker who halted his progress every few feet.[128]

After relaxing during a couple of hours' downtime at the Biltmore and giving an unremarkable dinner address at the Waldorf-Astoria, Truman moved on to the celebrated entertainment and boxing venue, Madison Square Garden. Once again, it would be up to campaign advance man Donald Dawson to smooth out a potentially embarrassing situation for the president: Madison Square Garden had been double-booked.

On the June trip, Truman had made a few slipups, but the chief calamity was the lack of promotional work in Omaha, which resulted in the president speaking in a stadium that was less than half full, with the national media on hand to capture the "acres of empty seats," as a caption in a gloating *Life* magazine pictorial put it.[129] With just days to go before the country went to the polls to cast their votes in a referendum on Truman's presidency, the same could not happen again at New York's premier venue. So many media outlets were against him and would gleefully show the scenes if there was an empty arena. The only thing worse than a small audience would be no audience at all, and that's just what would happen if Dawson couldn't secure the president top billing at Madison Square Garden.

Though the New York Democratic Party had attempted to book the venue in keeping with Truman's precise, stop-by-stop campaign schedule, the Liberal Party had already reserved it for that evening. Its most enthusiastic supporters had booked seats, and Dawson was having a devil of a job convincing Liberal Party bigwigs such as David Dubinsky, head of the biggest garment workers' union, and the Madison Square Garden promoter to allow Truman to speak and the public to come in without buying the remaining tickets in advance and paying the same booking fee as the early bird ticket holders.[130]

Eventually the promoter, Dubinsky, and the other Liberal Party leaders caved and agreed to cede the stage to the president and to allow general admission. But when Dawson drove over to the arena, he was shocked to see so many empty seats. It was Omaha all over again. Dubinsky, who was one of the few Truman fans in his party and had offered to help with his Madison Square Garden event, didn't believe it was that bad until a frantic Dawson took him by the arm and marched him up to the balcony, giving them both a bird's-eye view of the debacle. Improvising to avert crisis, Dawson and Dubinsky bounded back down the concrete steps, opened the doors, and ushered in as many people as possible from a parade that had accompanied Truman from the Biltmore Hotel. And so, by way of Dawson's improvisation, Truman spoke to an almost-full house that night.[131]

The Madison Square Garden speech was significant as a blue-ribbon event at a historic venue, but it paled in comparison to the lasting significance of the one he delivered the following day in Dorrance Brooks Park, Harlem, New York. On that chilly afternoon, Truman received a warm reception from the large crowd and the Franklin D. Roosevelt Memorial Brotherhood Medal from Dr. C. Asapansa-Johnson, president of the Interdenominational Ministers Alliance.[132]

The roots of the speech Truman delivered to a largely black audience went back to the Committee on Civil Rights that he had established in late 1946. Since then, civil rights had become more and more prominent in his domestic agenda, and, with the southern Democrat revolt now in full swing in fall 1948, also more controversial and politically hazardous.

There was an important background to the Harlem speech. Back on April 20, Batt sent a memo to Gael Sullivan and Clark Clifford, in which he relayed a "shocking report on the Negro vote in New York City" delivered by Jack Ewing. Polls in 1948 were typically down on the president's election chances, but in the case of the black vote, they had understated Truman's woes. The numbers predicted that between 20 and 30 percent would vote for Henry Wallace in November, but Ewing's conversations with ward leaders in Harlem and Brooklyn suggested that the actual figure in these districts was 70 percent.[133]

Despite this gloomy outlook, there was yet time for a turnaround, Batt believed. Having spoken at length with black leaders, including influential educator George Weaver, Batt proposed a four-point plan of action. First, the campaign managers needed to announce the appointment of "Congressman [William L.] Dawson or whoever you have in mind to head up the Negro group for the campaign."[134] Dawson was the Democratic Illinois congressman who fought for equal opportunity rights, opposed the poll tax voting requirement for black would-be voters, and declared in a memorable 1945 speech to Congress, "The right to work is the right to live."[135]

In addition to quickly choosing Dawson or someone equally qualified to coordinate campaigning in predominantly black wards in New
York City, Batt urged Sullivan and Clifford to also create a press liaison
position to ensure Truman-focused coverage in black-owned and black-
read newspapers. This person would not only ensure White House press
releases were printed, but also "that feature stories be dug up, written
up and planted showing the things the Administration is doing for the
Negroes."[136] One such story would be on housing, which Batt lamented,
"has never gotten adequate play."[137]

Third, Batt proposed that Truman issue the executive order acting on
the recommendations of the Committee and Civil Rights Committee to
end segregation in the armed forces and ensure equal pay and conditions
for all civil servants. Truman had issued this order on July 26, and, as Batt
predicted in this April note, it had led to "another Southern revolt."[138] At
the time of writing, though, the Research Division director had told Sullivan and Clifford that such a consequence was worth the risk.

The final point of Batt and Ewing's plan was for Truman to continue
to appoint black men and women to government positions if they were
qualified, particularly to high-profile posts. Were there any openings,
Batt wondered, for appointments "in the large metropolitan areas where
the depredations of the Wallaceites are particularly severe"?[139] He then
mentioned the potential creation of a new federal judgeship in his home
state of Pennsylvania and inquired as to whether there was the potential
for a black appointee.

Since Batt wrote this memo in April, Truman had acted on the first
three of his recommendations, with Dawson becoming deputy chairman of the DNC Negro Division and responsible for drafting the party's
civil rights plank at the convention, as well as communicating with the
black press.[140] Truman's campaign team had, in fact, gone one step further than Batt, Nash, and Ewing had advised regarding press relations,
making Alice Allison Dunnigan the first black correspondent ever to accompany a president on a campaign trip in June 1948, as well as inviting
two black male reporters on that West Coast jaunt.[141]

In New York, Truman would heed the advice of Oscar Ewing's Monday Night Group, by way of Bill Batt and Clark Clifford. Despite Wallace's
projected dominance in New York City and Dewey's likely strong showing in the state he had governed since 1943, Truman believed he had a

real chance to capture the black vote and, if he got labor and other minorities on board too, to win New York. He was the one, not Wallace or Dewey, who had become the first president to address the NAACP, who had established the Committee on Civil Rights, and who had acted on its recommendations despite warnings about the southern revolt. Indeed, this rebellion seemed to have the opposite effect that some Dixiecrats had hoped. Instead of forcing Truman to cave on the issue, he had merely become more resolute to see his civil rights program through. And as Thurmond and his band continued their hate-filled diatribes against the government, against Truman, and against the oppressed minority he sought equal rights for, Truman's standing with the ADA and other liberal groups improved.[142] Now, as his campaign reached its final act, Truman would deliver a definitive address to solidify this support and turn the tide in inner city New York and other cities with large black populations.

Dave Lloyd was the Research Division expert on civil rights, and Batt assigned him to work closely with Clifford, Murphy, and Chapman on Truman's Harlem address, assisting longtime Truman staffer and speechwriter Philleo Nash. When Batt was evaluating Research Division staffing and saw his team was missing a civil rights point man, he immediately reached out to Lloyd. The two knew each other through the ADA, and the industrious young lawyer, who was making quite a reputation for himself in liberal circles, fit the Research Division profile: a topic expert, a young guy who would work hard, and a known entity. So Lloyd came to Dupont Circle and immediately dove into preparing fact sheets, speech material, and more.[143]

As was typical of young, politically active liberals in the late 1940s, several other members of the Research Division also had backgrounds advocating civil rights. In addition to heralding the growing Nazi and communist threats to democracy in the 1930s, Kenneth Birkhead's father, Leon Milton Birkhead, had been a leading member of the American Civil Liberties Union in Kansas City and later New York and had passed along his contempt for segregation and discrimination to his son.[144] Like many other members of the ADA, Batt and Hoeber were staunch supporters of equal rights for all, and they provided Dave Lloyd with valuable input while he gathered information for the Truman train.

As Truman's Harlem speech loomed, Lloyd finished the Research Division's Files of the Facts #8—Civil Liberties.[145] He then picked parts out of this comprehensive dossier as potential talking points for the president. Philleo Nash then beavered away on six revisions of the final speech version that Truman would take to the podium. When Nash, whose supply of white hair had dwindled to a small clump on either side of his head, brought Truman the final draft, the president told him, "Well, I've been waiting a long time to get this taken care of. We should have done it sooner!" Then he read each page slowly through his thick-rimmed glasses. Once finished, Truman looked up at the speechwriter and exclaimed, "Anybody who isn't for this ought to have their head examined."[146]

Truman carried this viewpoint all the way to the tenements and high rises of Harlem. As the president looked over his notes, the man who had compiled them, Philleo Nash, observed the scene around him to see why the crowd had gone quiet after shouting support for Truman moments earlier: "Almost everybody in that crowd was praying, either with his head down or actually was kneeling . . . they were praying for the President, and they were praying for their own civil rights. And they thought it was a religious occasion."[147]

With such unusual calm making it clear that the rows of police officers and Secret Service agents who protected the platform wouldn't see any action that afternoon, Truman placed his notes on the podium, and began one of the most important addresses of his career:[148]

> Dr. Johnson, and members of the Ministerial Alliance which has given me this award:
> I am exceedingly grateful for it. I hope I shall always deserve it. This, in my mind, is a most solemn occasion. It's made a tremendous impression upon me.
> Franklin Roosevelt was a great champion of human rights. When he led us out of the depression to the victory over the Axis, he enabled us to build a country in which prosperity and freedom must exist side by side. This is the only atmosphere in which human rights can thrive.
> Eventually, we are going to have an America in which freedom and opportunity are the same for everyone. There is only one way to accomplish that great purpose, and that is to keep working for it and never take a backward step.

I am especially glad to receive the Franklin Roosevelt award on this day—October 29. This date means a great deal to me personally, and it is a significant date in the history of human freedom in this country.

One year ago today, on October 29, 1947, the President's Committee on Civil Rights submitted to me, and to the American people, its momentous report.

That report was drawn up by men and women who had the honesty to face the whole problem of civil rights squarely, and the courage to state their conclusions frankly.

I created the Civil Rights Committee because racial and religious intolerance began to appear after World War II. They threatened the very freedoms we had fought to save.

We Americans have a democratic way of acting when our freedoms are threatened.

We get the most thoughtful and representative men and women we can find, and we ask them to put down on paper the principles that represent freedom and a method of action that will preserve and extend that freedom. In that manner, we get a declaration of purpose and a guide for action that the whole country can consider.

That is the way in which the Declaration of Independence was drawn up.

That is the way in which the Constitution of the United States was written.

The report that the Civil Rights Committee prepared is in the tradition of these great documents.

It was the authors of the Declaration of Independence who stated the principle that all men are created equal in their rights, and that it is to secure these rights that governments are instituted among men.

It was the authors of the Constitution who made it clear that, under our form of government, all citizens are equal before the law, and that the Federal Government has a duty to guarantee to every citizen equal protection of the laws.

The Civil Rights Committee did more than repeat these great principles. It described a method to put these principles into action, and to make them a living reality for every American, regardless of his race, his religion, or his national origin.

When every American knows that his rights and his opportunities are fully protected and respected by the Federal, State, and local governments, then we will have the kind of unity that really means something.

It is easy to talk of unity. But it is the work that is done for unity that really counts.

The job that the Civil Rights Committee did was to tell the American people how to create the kind of freedom that we need in this country.

The Civil Rights Committee described the kind of freedom that comes when every man has an equal chance for a job—not just the hot and heavy job—but the best job he is qualified for.

The Committee described the kind of freedom that comes when every American boy and girl has an equal chance for an education.

The Committee described the kind of freedom that comes when every citizen has an equal opportunity to go to the ballot box and cast his vote and have it counted.

The Committee described the kind of freedom that comes when every man, woman, and child is free from the fear of mob violence and intimidation.

When we have that kind of freedom, we will face the evil forces that are abroad in the world—whatever or wherever they may be—with the strength that comes from complete confidence in one another and from complete faith in the working of our own democracy.

One of the great things that the Civil Rights Committee did for the country was to get every American to think seriously about the principles that make our country great.

More than 1 million copies of the full text of the civil rights report have been printed in books and newspapers.

More than 30 different pamphlets based on the report have been printed and distributed by private organizations.

Millions of Americans have heard the report discussed on the radio.

In making its recommendations, the Civil Rights Committee did not limit itself to action by the President or by the executive branch. The Committee's recommendations included action by every branch of the Federal Government, by State and local governments, and by private organizations, and by individuals.

That is why it is so important that the Civil Rights Committee's report be studied widely. For in the last analysis, freedom resides in the actions of each individual. That is the reason I like to hear that scriptural reading from the Gospel according to St. Luke. That's just exactly what it means. It means you and I must act out what we say in our Constitution and our Bill of Rights. It is in his mind and heart—and to his mind and heart—that we must eventually speak to the individual.

After the Civil Rights Committee submitted its report, I asked Congress to do ten of the things recommended by the Committee.

You know what they did about that.

So I went ahead and did what the President can do, unaided by the Congress. I issued two Executive orders.

One of them established the President's Committee on Equality of Treatment and Opportunity in the Armed Services.

The other one covered regulations governing fair employment practices within the Federal establishment.

In addition to that, the Department of Justice went into the Supreme Court and aided in getting a decision outlawing restrictive covenants.

Several States and municipalities have taken action on the recommendations of the Civil Rights Committee, and I hope more will follow after them.

Today the democratic way of life is being challenged all over the world. Democracy's answer to the challenge of totalitarianism is its promise of equal rights and equal opportunity for all mankind.

The fulfillment of this promise is among the highest purposes of government.

Our determination to attain the goal of equal rights and equal opportunity must be resolute and unwavering.

For my part, I intend to keep moving toward this goal with every ounce of strength and determination that I have.[149]

As he moved away from the microphone, the sixty-five-thousand-strong crowd was no longer silent, but instead roared its approval.

Truman's bold Harlem address did not just reach the district's black voters. Eleanor Roosevelt, long skeptical of Truman's nomination as vice president and ability to be a worthy successor to her late husband, was in attendance that afternoon. Whatever their past differences, she could hardly fault Truman's commitment to racial equality now. And Truman was asking millions more, listening to the speech on national radio just seventy-two hours before they went to the polls, whether they could doubt him or ignore their consciences when they cast their votes.

Being so close to the election, the speech was bound to attract even more attention than if Truman had delivered it earlier in the campaign. In addition to being a last-ditch attempt to secure black votes in New York and other large urban areas, it was his final thumbing of the nose to the Dixiecrats. Truman, they must now be aware, was not using civil rights as a cynical electoral tactic to garner votes. He had repeatedly made the case for equality on the national stage, had flat out refused the calls of the Dixiecrats to abandon this position, and had issued two momentous executive orders that integrated the armed forces and ended pay discrimination for federal employees of color.[150] In addition, he had defended his position to friends and family members with no fear of offending even the most backward-looking of them. Now, with just three days to go in one of the most decisive weeks of his life, Truman had made his strongest declaration that he and the Democratic Party he represented believed in implementing a bold civil rights program, regardless of the potentially ruinous political fallout in the South.

Writing in the *New York Times*, Anthony Leviero declared that Truman had "lifted the controversial issue that split the Democratic Party out of limbo" and had spoken "words that appeared to foreclose any possibility of compromise between Mr. Truman and the States' Rights Democrats."[151]

While Dewey refused to criticize Truman's Harlem speech, Henry Wallace just could not help himself. Though he was a longtime proponent of racial equality and had endured egg throwing and catcalling from Thurmond supporters as he took the bold step of addressing mixed-race rallies, Wallace accused his former boss of making "hollow, shallow, worthless promises." Speaking in the Golden Gate Ballroom in Harlem just hours after Truman's address, the Progressive Party candidate also suggested that Truman had previously "invited the Dixiecrats, the race-haters, the lynch boys and the poll-taxers right back into his camp."[152]

Thurmond, of course, went much further in his denunciation, tarring the president as both a communist and a coward. He claimed that Truman's "campaign talks were tinted with red in Harlem and his actions were yellow when he stumped the South." The South Carolina governor went on to say in his statement given to the press in Longview, Texas, where he was resting after finishing his campaign the night before: "What more can you expect from a tight rope artist who has lost his balance on a thin political wire and is desperately grasping at handfuls of votes in the most deceitful campaign ever waged by a presidential aspirant?"[153] This was the States' Rights hopeful's final salvo.

Like Thurmond, Dewey finished his campaign the next night on October 30, with the Republican candidate delivering his final speech, fittingly, in a packed Madison Square Garden.[154] But as his GOP opponent hung up his gloves early at the famous boxing venue, Truman continued to punch right up until the final bell. While Dewey was preparing for his New York signoff, his Democratic opponent's train had left New York and headed southeast, bound for his home state of Missouri. On the way, Truman gave three speeches—one in Ohio, the second in Indiana, and the third in Illinois. This comparatively small number—at least by Truman's standards—was not an indication that the president was tiring, but was rather a matter of time and space; the Ferdinand Magellan had to cover 950 miles in just a few hours.

On that final day aboard the Last Chance Special, a physically, emotionally, and rhetorically drained Truman took an afternoon nap, the first such siesta that Clark Clifford could remember the hitherto indefatigable president taking during the ultra-marathon Whistle Stop Tour.[155] As his train pulled to a halt in St. Louis, Truman spoke briefly to the crowd that had jammed the beautiful Romanesque-style, red-roofed Union Station to see him before he rode by car to Kiel Auditorium.[156] Coming for the last time out onto the rear platform from which he had spoken at more than 350 whistle stops, during a campaign that had taken every ounce of his resolve, determination, and energy, Truman told his fellow Missourians who had braved the evening chill:

I have been from one end of the country to the other—north and south, east and west—and none of them has been any better than this. And that is the way it ought to be in Missouri.

I was born and raised in the "show me" State, and I learned how "show me" works, and I have been showing them—the Republicans are on the run.

On Tuesday there is only one thing I want you to do, and that is to go out and vote for yourselves. If you will vote for yourselves, you will vote the straight Democratic ticket, and everything will be safe for the world, and for Missouri, and for the United States.

Now, don't forget that. Just do a little thinking.

I am going to discuss the whole campaign tonight, and I hope you will listen to me. Then, if I am convincing, just go and vote for your own best interests.[157]

Preparing to address a rapturous crowd at 9:30 that evening, Truman ditched the notes he had worked on with David Noyes, Charlie Ross, and Clark Clifford to give an impromptu and fiery speech that was more reminiscent of one of the whistle stop talks than his major addresses.[158] Truman began by recounting what had happened during "the most momentous period in the history of the world," as he called the three and a half years since he succeeded FDR:

Twenty-six days after I became President, Germany surrendered unconditionally. Four months and 21 days after I was sworn in as President of the United States, Japan folded up and surrendered unconditionally, thus ending the greatest war in the history of the world. I succeeded to the Presidency after one of the greatest Democrats that ever lived in this world had been there for nearly 12 years. I was nominated in Chicago with Franklin Roosevelt in 1944 on the Democratic platform, and I have tried to carry out that platform since I have been President of the United States.

One of my first and greatest decisions after becoming President of the United States was made just 2 minutes after I was sworn in, and that was the order that the conference to form the United Nations should go forward in San Francisco on the 25th day of April. That conference went forward to a successful conclusion, and the United

Nations is working for the peace and welfare of this world, right now.

Though so much had changed, Truman informed his audience that he was "still for Roosevelt's New Deal." This was despite the actions of "saboteurs and character assassins" whose words and deeds had, Truman insisted, led to the Democratic Party's calamitous showing in the 1946 midterm elections.

He also had something to say about Elmo Roper, George Gallup, and the pollsters who had written him off months before. "The smart boys say we can't win," Truman said. "They tried to bluff us with a propaganda blitz, but we called their bluff, we told people the truth. And the people are with us. The tide is rolling. All over the country, I have seen it in the people's faces. The people are going to win this election."[159]

He also took issue with the journalists who had given him no chance of victory and took a dig at the St. Louis Post-Dispatch, which maligned him ever since his first run at the Senate in 1934, when he defeated Roscoe Patterson. "I've been all over the United States from one end to another, and when I started out the song was 'Well, you can't win; the Democrats can't win,'" he said. "Ninety percent of the press is against us, but that didn't discourage me one little bit. You know, I had four campaigns here in the great state of Missouri, and I never had a metropolitan paper for me that whole time. And I licked them every time."[160]

And Truman wasn't done with his list of grievances. He moved on to Thomas Dewey, saying, "Of all the fake campaigns, this is tops so far as the Republican candidate is concerned. He has been following me and making speeches about home, mother, unity and efficiency. He won't talk issues but he let his foot slip and endorsed the Eightieth Congress."[161]

Speaking of which, it was about time for Truman to launch one final, all-out assault on that "do-nothing" group and its Republican chieftains. He went down his domestic agenda point by point, stating, per the Research Division's format, what Franklin Roosevelt had done to turn the country around after the Republican's lax stewardship, what he had tried to do, and how the Eightieth Congress had stymied him.

On farming, Truman said, "One of the first things that this Republican, "do-nothing" Eightieth Congress did was to hamstring the Commodity Credit Corporation, so they couldn't make price support loans to the farmers." Regarding labor, he slammed the Taft-Hartley Act, which, he reminded his listeners, had only passed after Republicans had overridden his veto. "They wanted to take the bargaining power away from labor, so it could not deal with industry on a fair basis," Truman said.

Truman's next item was the minimum wage, which he had tried to raise to seventy-five cents an hour. Once again, the GOP had shut him down. And Congress had also failed the nation on housing, Truman believed. Instead of voting for the Taft-Ellender-Wagner bill, which Truman said, in a rare acknowledgment of Robert Taft's capacity for reform, would have created much-needed low-rent housing and cleared slums, "They passed a fake housing bill, a housing bill which was intended to build no housing. And they are trying to make you believe they 'passed a housing bill.'"

He gave the eightieth session another failing grade on taxation, saying that its members refused to create meaningful legislation to help middle- and lower-class families. "But they could pass a rich man's tax bill, a tax bill that benefited the fellow at the top income bracket, but didn't do the poor boys any good." Republicans did no better on education, Truman said, and failed to pass a bill that would have sent $300 million to states because "They are not interested in whether teachers have good pay or not. They are not interested in whether the kids get a proper education or not. They don't care if there are 75 or 80 kids in one room and one teacher to look after them at a salary that is not a living wage."

The last issue that the White House failed to budge GOP congressmen on was health care insurance, Truman told the packed hall: "I wanted an insurance program that would work, so that a fellow would have a little money saved up, when it came time to pay medical and hospital bills, and the doctor and the hospital would get paid promptly. But the Republicans are against that. They say that's socialized medicine. Well, it isn't. That's just good common sense."

All of this proved, Truman asserted, that there was a divide between the two main political parties: "The Republicans stand for special interests, and they always have.

The Democratic Party, which I now head, stands for the people—and always has stood for the people."

Truman finished with one last plea for people to turn out and cast their ballot. If there was a high turnout, he again predicted a Democratic victory that would work in their favor: "People are waking up that the tide is beginning to roll, and I am here to tell you that if you do your duty as citizens of the greatest Republic the sun has ever shone on, we will have a Government that will be for your interests, that will be for peace in the world, and for the welfare of all the people, and not just a few."[162]

It was, wrote Anthony Leviero in the *New York Times*, Truman's "angriest speech" of the campaign. Certainly, Truman had held nothing back as he gave his last in-person address, and why should he? This was a time for winning, not for trying to repair the many bridges he had burned as he crisscrossed the country "blackguarding Congress at every whistle stop," as Taft had memorably put it.[163]

The next day, Halloween, saw Truman back at home, finally, in Independence. Despite the benefits of being with Bess and Margaret, he couldn't fully relax, and he toiled away at his desk on the radio address he would give the following night via four national radio networks. But at least for one evening he could enjoy the treat of uninterrupted sleep in his own bed, away from the clatter, dust, and ceaseless effort of life aboard the train. In less than seventy-two hours, he would find out if it had all been worth it.[164]

November 2, 1948

On November 1, Truman finally got to make a speech from the comfort of his own home. Addressing the nation at 9:37 p.m., he recounted his whistle stop exploits, which had, he said, seen him talk to "millions." And now, after all the miles, all the talking, and all the late nights and early mornings, it was decision time, he said:

> From the bottom of my heart I thank the people of the United States for their cordiality to me and for their interest in the affairs of this great Nation and of the world. I trust the people, because when they know the facts, they do the right thing. I have tried to tell them the facts and explain the issues.
>
> Now it is up to you, the people of this great Nation, to decide what kind of government you want—whether you want government for all the people or government for just the privileged few.
>
> Go to the polls tomorrow and vote your convictions, your hopes, and your faith—your faith in the future of a nation that under God— can lead the world to freedom and to peace.[1]

In their final predictions that evening, the pollsters cemented the view they'd projected all along: that Truman was toast. Archibald Crossley put the figures at 49.9 percent to 44.8 in the Republican's favor, while Gallup had Dewey at 49.5 and Truman at 44.5. Roper, who had taken a break from polling since early September because he believed a Dewey win to be a foregone conclusion, gave Truman the gloomiest outlook of the three major forecasters, putting the New York governor at 52.2 percent while the president languished at a paltry 37.1.[2]

Still, Truman was undaunted. He knew that, like the epitaph he had admired in Tombstone, Arizona, during the June tour, that "He done his damndest."[3] With the notable exception of the southern states he had all but conceded to Thurmond, the intrepid president had been to every corner of the nation. Including the "nonpolitical" trip to California, which was really the first stage of the Whistle Stop Tour, he had logged a staggering 31,700 miles, speaking 352 times to audiences large and small.[4] From New York to Iowa to California and just about everywhere in between, Truman had given the crowds a combination of precise, rational argument, invective against the Republican Congress, and the numbers to back up both. Thanks to Batt, Hoeber, and the other four tireless staffers in the Research Division offices, he had also tailored his message at every stop to the local populace, making it clear that he cared about what was going on in their towns, their lives and—whether he won or not—their future. And he urged them to improve that future by showing up at the polls to vote for him. For it was only a high Democratic turnout, he knew after the humiliating rout of the 1946 midterms, that could keep him in the White House.

He was, Truman kept reminding them, one of their own, a hardworking, no-nonsense guy who just happened, for at least a little while longer, to occupy the highest office in the land. And by heavens, he was going to fight for them on civil rights, housing, agricultural policy, price controls, and more. In contrast, he kept reminding those who filled the stadiums, crowded the town halls, and lined the railway platforms that the Republicans were the party of special interest, of big business, and of obstruction. If the people elected Dewey, they'd get what they deserved, four years of rolling back the New Deal, of an uncertain foreign policy, and of a domestic program that made their day-to-day lives harder. "Give me a chance, a chance to fight for you," Truman was effectively telling each person who came out to see him: "you won't be sorry." He had been a farmer, a small business owner, a soldier, a worker. So when he told them he knew their problems and how to fix them, he had credibility.

And just to prove his mettle, Truman had risen between 5:00 a.m. and 6:00 a.m. every day, talking to the early birds in his pajamas in a way that he and they knew the aloof Dewey never would or could. Even in this late stage of the proceedings, Truman had "the bounce of a rubber ball," an impressed Charlie Ross observed.[5] Unfazed by making eight or ten, twelve, or even, on a couple of occasions, sixteen speeches in one day, Truman had also come out late at night to give one more defiant address from the back platform, day after day. And what the crowds didn't see, behind the scenes, were the extra hours that followed of Truman poring over the Research Division's innumerable fact sheets, when his body and mind told him to go to bed but his will wouldn't let him. The hurried discussions and revisions with his advisers kept him on message, but he could and did add his own flourishes, speaking to the people with an endearing, down-to-earth Midwest delivery that he was now, at last, comfortable with on any stage—even when it got him into trouble and he went too far, saying something foolish about Stalin or comparing Dewey to a Nazi.[6]

Now there was nothing more Harry Truman could do, only wait. After spending a few hours at their home in Independence on November 2, the president and Bess arrived by car at the resplendent Elms Hotel in Excelsior Springs as the afternoon slipped away. The advisers who accompanied him and those staked out at his favorite old political headquarters in the Hotel Muehlebach knew that "the Boss's" political career, and possibly theirs too, could be over in mere hours.[7] Soon enough, the world would know whether Truman's stupendous effort, his unwavering confidence, and his many, many speeches would be enough to retain the presidency.

Since his "nonpolitical" tour in June, Harry Truman had worked tirelessly. He had on several occasions in his career pushed himself too hard, triggering stress headaches and chronic exhaustion.[8] Yet on this most crucial of campaigns, Truman had not allowed his body to give in to the unrelenting pressure he put on it, nor his self-belief to entertain any eventuality other than victory. This, even as his party split three ways, as the Soviets continued their blockade of Berlin, and as his Republican opponent was lauded as a shoo-in by the majority of the media.

Now on November 2, after giving his all, there was nothing more he could do. He had spoken his mind, in his own way, at every stop, whether addressing eighty thousand people at the National Plowing Match or a handful at one of the many stations well off the main line. If his efforts had been sufficient to pull off the unlikeliest of comebacks he would be delighted, and if he fell short he could rest easy knowing, in the tireless spirit of his father, that there was no more to give.[9] And rest easy he did, finally, on this cold late fall night, taking a Turkish bath and then consuming a supper that was as straightforward as the man himself: a ham and cheese sandwich and glass of buttermilk. He then retired for the evening at 9:00 p.m., the earliest bedtime he had allowed himself in months.[10]

On this night, though, with his political career in the balance, he would not sleep soundly as he usually did. At midnight he woke with a start, and, after fumbling on the nightstand for his glasses so he could see in the gloom, turned on the bedside radio. If he was searching for encouragement, he picked the wrong station: NBC. H. V. Kaltenborn, one of the distinguished reporters Ed Murrow had brought to the network, stated that though Truman was leading the popular vote by 1.2 million votes, his margin would soon evaporate and was still "undoubtedly beaten."[11] Truman had heard this prediction countless times by now and wouldn't let it shake his unshakeable confidence in victory. He turned the radio knob, returned his spectacles to the stand, and went back to sleep, fully expecting better news when he next awoke.

Such tidings would come sooner than he thought. Typically, nobody on the presidential staff would entertain disturbing their chief during the night except for a national emergency, but at 4:00 a.m. Secret Service agent Jim Rowley could contain himself no longer. "The Boss," as most of his team called Truman, had to hear the big news. Rowley shook Truman awake and declared, "We've won." Truman turned the radio back on and heard Kaltenborn somewhat reluctantly say that he was now ahead by two million votes. The president dismissed the commentator's caution over the as yet uncounted farm vote and, now wide awake, agreed with Rowley, "We've got 'em beat."[12]

Truman jumped out of bed, dressed hurriedly, and got in a car. By 6:00 a.m., he was at the Muehlebach Hotel in Kansas City, where he had spent the night of his Senate re-election playing the piano. There to greet him at the campaign's seventeenth floor headquarters were Matt Connelly, who had so efficiently marshaled the president's chaotic campaign, and Bill Boyle. Soon enough, Truman's press secretary and childhood friend Charlie Ross got up, as did Truman's other key advisers who were getting a few minutes of rest after a long night manning the phones. Ross, who had heart trouble and was exhausted from the rigors of the campaign, was uncharacteristically nervous, and others paced anxiously around the presidential suite as the returns came in, the air heavy with cigarette smoke and the aroma of freshly brewed coffee.[13]

Truman, in contrast, was serene, convinced that he would maintain and even extend his lead. Frank Spina, his longtime barber and 35th Division comrade, came to give Truman a haircut and shave, and then the president, ever fastidious about his appearance, changed into a white shirt, blue polka dot tie, and blue suit. At 8:30 a.m., it was official— Truman was still president of the United States. An hour later, word came to him that the Democrats had recaptured the House with a stunning seventy-five-seat turnaround that gave them a 263 to 171 advantage. They also beat the GOP in the Senate, winning nine Republican seats to achieve a 54–42 margin.[14] Perhaps, with the Eightieth Congress no more, Truman could at last pass his ambitious domestic program. At 10:30 a.m. came a congratulatory telegram from his vanquished opponent Tom Dewey, who was as gracious in defeat as he had been classy (if ineffectual) throughout the election cycle.[15]

But this was not the speech the country wanted to hear, not least the people of Independence, Missouri. At 8:00 p.m. that evening, as the president, *their* president, bounded up the white stone steps of the Jackson County courthouse that he had worked so hard to finance, forty thousand of them whooped, whistled, and hollered with reckless abandon. Truman waited a few minutes before taking the podium, savoring the adulation from his friends, neighbors, family members, and others who had believed in him when nobody else, save Truman himself, had.

Then he spoke:

> Mr. Mayor, and my fellow townsmen and citizens of this great county named after Andrew Jackson:
>
> I can't tell you how very much I appreciate this turnout to celebrate a victory—not my victory, but a victory of the Democratic Party for the people.
>
> I want to inform you, Mr. Mayor, that protocol goes out the window when I am in Independence. I am a citizen of this town, and a taxpayer, and I want to be treated just like the rest of the taxpayers in this community are treated, whether you extend the city limits or not.
>
> And I thank you very much indeed for this celebration, which is not for me. It is for the whole country. It is for the whole world,

for the simple reason that you have given me a tremendous responsibility.

Now, since you have given me that responsibility, I want every single one of you to help carry out that responsibility, for the welfare of this great Republic, and for the welfare and peace of the world at large. And I am sure that is what you are going to do.

I can't begin to thank the people who are responsible for the Democratic Party winning this great election. Of course, I am indebted to everybody for that win, and I will have to just say to every single one of you individually that I am going to do the very best I can to carry out the Democratic platform, as I promised to do in my speeches over this country.

And we have a Congress now, and I am sure we will make some progress in the next four years.

Thank you all very much.[16]

From there, the Truman motorcade snaked its way along the darkened Missouri streets to the Kansas City train depot, where he reboarded the Ferdinand Magellan car that had carried him across the nation and to victory. The train stopped briefly in St. Louis and the president came out onto the rear platform to greet his home state faithful once more before resuming his journey back to Washington. Someone handed him a copy of the *Chicago Tribune*'s early edition. On his California "inspection tour" back in June he had declared that along with the *Spokane Spokesman-Review*, this was "the worst in the United States."[17] So it is no surprise that as he regarded the erroneous headline "Dewey Defeats Truman" in all its folly, he cracked a wide grin, reveling in the humiliation of his old media foe. Holding the paper aloft like a prizefighter raising his championship belt after a bruising twelve-round contest, Truman told the reporters, pencils scribbling furiously in their notebooks as photographers' flashbulbs burst all around, "that is one for the books." As the crowd, several thousand strong, clustered behind the press contingent to make sure they heard their president, Truman continued, "It's been a tremendous fight." In his final rear platform speech of the campaign he had asked them to "vote for your interests," and now, with the election behind him and his first full term ahead, he once again called for his fellow Missourians to pledge their support. "Stand by me," he said, his breath visible in the chilly evening air as the cheers echoed around the cavernous station, "because I've got the biggest job in the world now."[18] And with that, he bade them good night, walked back into the quiet confines of the train, and slept the sound sleep of a man who had finally proved that he belonged as president of the United States of America.

7

The World According to Harry Truman

When Research Division chairman Bill Batt reflected later on why Truman faced such a battle in 1948, he said, "They hadn't seen anything like President Truman. Wilson looked and talked like a President. Hoover was a world figure. Even Harding looked more like a President, than President Truman."[1]

And yet, if a president is measured by grit, determination, and grace under pressure, Truman's remarkable come-from-behind victory indicates that he was one of the most capable men to ever hold the office and lead the nation. In the 1948 campaign, his approach and Thomas Dewey's were a study in contrasts. Truman was relentless, Dewey was languid. Truman was precise and forthright, Dewey relied on what one editor called "pleasant-sounding generalities."[2] Truman got down and scrapped in the gutter, Dewey took the high road. In the end, the American people decided that Truman's approach and message were preferable to Dewey's. As Clark Clifford later put it, "He fought, and fought, and fought; he worked like a dog. He worked sixteen hours a day, day after day, week after week, and month after month. And at no time during the whole campaign did I ever hear him utter a word which indicated that he had the slightest doubt that he was going to win."[3]

Whatever the merits of Truman's positive, plainspoken, New Deal–focused approach, there were external forces that contributed to his come-from-behind victory. The Soviets' continued bellicosity in Berlin gave the president the opportunity to prove again his resilience and toughness. Although the airlift was the ingenious idea of others such as General Clay, it was Truman's backing that enabled it to successfully supply Germans in the Western zones. It did not help Dewey that bipartisan foreign policy put an area of typical political debate among presidential candidates off limits, with the exception of Dewey's one stinging attack on the administration during the last week of October. What a contrast to today, when seemingly every move made by the State Department is second-guessed on Capitol Hill, the secretary of state's words and actions are scrutinized in minute detail, and American standing abroad is undermined by interparty bickering.

At home, too, Truman was helped by factors outside of his control, though he may not have viewed them as beneficial before Election Day. It was the ADA and Hubert Humphrey who forced Truman to push the most ambitious civil rights plank in a generation. It had been the president, however, who commissioned the landmark committee that preceded their maneuvers at the Democratic convention, and it was he who boldly signed the two executive orders to desegregate the armed forces and eliminate a two-tier system for government employees. These bold strokes and the DNC's shrewd courting of black journalists and municipal leaders—again on Bill Batt's recommendation—had the intended effect, with Truman gaining more votes from northern blacks than he lost from southern whites. It was on the fractious issue of civil rights, his speechwriter Philleo Nash said, that Truman "first showed he was master of his own party."[4]

And Truman's bold stance on civil rights in the South was only part of the strategy to gain minority backing. Jewish voters, heeding their leaders' calls to support the president who had courageously recognized Israel before any other world leader, backed Truman with their votes and their pocketbooks, and the president's push for immigration reform that would allow more Europeans to enter the United States legally found its mark among voters of Eastern and Central European descent.[5] The combination of Truman garnering 75 percent of the black vote and successfully courting white ex-Europeans more than compensated for the loss of more than 1.1 million votes and four southern states—South Carolina, Louisiana, Mississippi, and Alabama—to Strom Thurmond. The States' Rights candidate's message did not resonate outside his southern stronghold, as he gained just 2.4 percent of the nationwide vote. This was the same percentage as another would-be president whose bid fell flat, Henry Wallace. The former vice president and his so-called "Gideon's Army" failed to win a single state, not least because they failed to win the backing of the groups they so desperately needed, including big labor and

Americans for Democratic Action, both of which plumped for Truman. This even though Wallace had campaigned bravely in the South, braving an airborne assault of eggs and rotten fruit thrown by Dixiecrat supporters when he spoke at racially integrated venues.[6]

When the votes were tallied, Truman won twenty-six states to Dewey's eighteen. The president's decision to focus his campaign on the West and Midwest (as James Rowe had suggested in his influential memo "The Politics of 1948") was validated, as he won all but one of the western states, with only Oregon preferring Dewey. Truman's big push also worked in the Midwest, where his impactful wins included Missouri, Ohio, Wisconsin, Illinois, and Iowa, where his attack on the Republican's failure to provide adequate grain storage evidently hit home. Dewey's strongest showing was in the Northeast, where he beat Truman in nine states, including his backyard of New York. Truman had an important triumph in the region: Massachusetts.

Alben Barkley played an underrated role in Truman's city-by-city, state-by-state victories. Though many journalists mocked the small crowds he drew, the energetic seventy-one-year-old certainly spoke to plenty of them, totaling 250 speeches in thirty-six states that he flew to on a chartered DC-3 paid for by rich friends.[7] Only his white hair betrayed the fact that Barkley was in his eighth decade, as the "Iron Man" proved every bit as energetic as he had when he first earned that nickname campaigning in Kentucky at the start of his storied career. The stellar work of Truman's loyal, never-say-die team—including Clifford, George Elsey, Oscar Chapman, Donald Dawson, and Charlie Ross—was also a factor, as were the prescient tactics they followed from James Rowe's playbook, "The Politics of 1948." This had not only helped in defining the main plank issues, but it had also urged an improved local Democratic Party organization, a Young Democrats recruiting drive, and better relations with minority-owned media outlets—all recommendations the White House acted upon with great success. And goodness knows the trip took its toll on all involved, particularly those staffers holed up on the train for days on end. Clifford suffered an attack of boils that he attributed to being "run down" and recounted the sleepless nights that plagued him intermittently following Truman's most unlikely, come-from-behind victory: "For years afterwards I'd sometimes wake up at night in a cold perspiration thinking I was back on that terrible train. It was a real ordeal. I don't know quite how I got through it except I was young at the time and strong and vigorous."[8]

Though the Research Division—which Clifford understatedly said was of "considerable value" in saving Truman's presidency—was disbanded after the election and its members went their separate ways, its work set the fact-finding pattern for future elections.[9] As Charlie Ross put it later, the "little speeches" that their material fueled were "more important than the big speeches—they got him close to the people."[10] George Elsey, whose job it was to distill the four or five pages prepared by Batt, Hoeber, and company believed that the organized material produced around the clock by the Research Division lifted a burden from Truman: "All the President's whistle stop speeches were delivered from outlines of salient points, so that the President didn't have to just stand on his hind legs on the rear platform and shoot from the cuff," Elsey later said. "That would have been an impossibly difficult situation for him and would have put him under impossible pressure."[11]

Of the seven tireless young men hastily assembled in Dupont Circle, only Dave Lloyd and Frank Kelly went on to serve the federal government after the 1948 election, both as speechwriters. However, the contributions of each of the six young men helped Truman localize his 352 speeches to connect with the public and center his appeals and attacks—however outlandish the rhetoric became at times—on a solid bedrock of facts that further illuminated Dewey's vagueness. The Batt group also provided invaluable advice on the president's delivery, where he spoke, and on what issues. From 1948 on, no longer could a campaign be waged successfully on the type of platitudes that Dewey delivered time and again. The voters now expected what they'd gotten from Truman by way of the Research Division: statistics and figures to provide credibility during even the folksiest of campaign speeches.

While these numbers were helpful to the president, the erroneous, flawed, and inflated polling statistics that had predicted his doom all along were certainly not. The *Chicago Tribune* editorial staff may have caught the majority of the postelection flak for their jump-the-gun front page that hailed Dewey as the victor, but it was Gallup, Roper, and the other pollsters who should have been equally humbled for failing to predict, or even sniff, Truman's comeback win. Truman had poured scorn on the polls in his final campaign speech as the supposed "smart boys," and he was right — they turned out to not be so smart after all. While polls did, of course, make a resurgence and in some later cases become too influential (such as when Bill Clinton's political adviser Dick Morris conducted a poll asking Americans where the Clintons should go on vacation), the Truman vs. Dewey debacle did show that numbers *do* sometimes lie.[12]

For all the strands that made up the web of Truman's victory, three stand above the rest: his rugged determination to pull off the biggest electoral upset in US history; his ability to be himself as he talked with voters; and that the issues he viewed as important — what the Research Division's Frank Kelly summarized early in the campaign as "peace, prices and places to live" — lined up with the values of the people in 1948. Though he offered strong solutions to postwar problems that FDR did not live to see and took bolder steps in civil rights than his predecessor had, Truman staked his political career on continuing and extending the central policies of the New Deal.[13]

Truman wagered that people cared that they were paying a lot more for meat, eggs, and milk than in preceding years, and that the dearth of affordable accommodation, which had plagued the country since the end of World War II, was impacting American families. Truman's solution to this, as had been Roosevelt's, was direct government intervention. Any administration under his control would be active and involved, with price controls to lower inflation, low-cost accommodations to address the housing crisis, and government health care to improve access to quality medical care. If there was a pervasive domestic problem of any kind, Truman believed it was the government's duty to step in and create a solution — a stance that directly conflicted with the small-government rhetoric of Robert Taft and, though it took a more extreme form with the Dixiecrats, Strom Thurmond.[14] With his populist stance, Truman convinced the three key New Deal demographics — farmers, laborers, and ethnic minorities — that his party had their best interests at heart.[15] For a president who largely ignored opinion polls, he had his fingers well and truly on what Research Division director Bill Batt called "the pulse of the nation."[16]

In contrast, the Republicans bet that the country was ready for a change after fifteen years of Democratic rule. The ballot box proved them wrong, as Truman won 49.5 percent of the popular vote to Dewey's 45.1 percent, and 303 electoral college votes to Dewey's 189. This was despite the fact that the New York governor won his state, dominated the Northeast, and captured the midwestern states of Kansas, Ohio, Nebraska, and Michigan.

Truman was certainly not a political mastermind, as had been predecessors John Adams, Abraham Lincoln, and, in the minds of the electorate during that 1948 campaign, Franklin Roosevelt. As his lifelong friend and press secretary Charlie Ross recalled in an article for *Colliers*, "There were no deep-laid schemes, no devious plans, nothing that could be called . . . 'high strategy.' The President's strategy was to go out all over the country and talk to the people in plain terms about the issues as he saw them."[17] Rather, the game plan of the 1948 campaign was the result of opinions and counsel from a diverse team of advisors.[18]

Certainly Ross, Murphy, Clifford, and the rest of Truman's team was talented, undoubtedly the Research Division supplied him with localized, current information much like a primitive Internet, and without question the languid campaign of Dewey and Warren failed to capitalize on the real and imagined failings of Truman's White House tenure. And yet, without the thirty-one thousand miles, the 352 speeches, and the grind of day after day on the trail, giving ten, twelve, sometimes eighteen addresses, it would have been impossible for Truman to win. Almost everyone around him doubted, or even scoffed at, his chances for re-election. He faced the specter of expansionist communism abroad, a three-way split in his own party, a hostile press, a Republican "dream ticket," and the continued challenges of the turbulent postwar economy at home.

Whatever his obstacles, he insisted on climbing over or barging through them to prove to himself, his myriad opponents inside and outside the Democratic Party, and the American people that he deserved to remain in the White House and that he was no accidental president. Ross believed that the turning point came not during Truman's nomination or the rousing acceptance speech that followed, not on the rails, and not during the pivotal addresses in Iowa or Harlem, but rather in the staff meeting following the July Democratic convention, when "the Boss" looked his team in the eye and insisted, "We *are* going to win."[19] It was this spirit that drove him, that kept his staff going in the cramped confines of the train day after day, and that endeared him to the American people.

Despite his newfound off-the-cuff speaking approach, Truman was still never going to be FDR's equal at the podium or in the minds and hearts of the country. Yet in the end what he was—a whip-smart, principled, and passionate man who cared deeply for the people of his country and believed he would do right by them—was enough. There was no muddling over where he stood on each issue. In the vein of Robert Taft, the Republican whom he believed would have given him a sterner test than Dewey, Truman came out and spoke his mind each and every time he was in front of a microphone. This forthrightness was much needed in a year that saw the Democratic Party torn asunder, with Progressive and States' Rights Parties adding competing voices that confused the electorate and threatened to drown out the liberal narrative that Truman was trying to continue after FDR had written the opening chapters.

To counter the opposition on left and right and give the voters a clear view of what it meant to be a Democrat in 1948, Truman put everything into a values-based, fact-backed strategy that, despite the innumerable predictions to the contrary, resonated with the American public.[20] Truman understood their interests better than Dewey did and articulated them well, and, as the president had implored at every whistle stop, the people voted for those interests on November 2. The Truman camp had feared that a low turnout would derail his campaign, but although the total was down 2.9 percent from FDR's last election victory in 1944, 53 percent of eligible voters still cast a ballot.

That a majority of these voters effectively said "yes" to a continuation of New Deal principles is the true legacy of Harry Truman's Whistle Stop Tour, a supreme effort that holds timeless lessons for the leaders of today as they attempt to not only best each other in elections, but more so to craft meaningful legislation in our own partisan, divisive, and obstructionist political scene. Any campaign would benefit from the clarity, conviction, and concision that Truman displayed in this, the defining election of his career. No longer an "accidental president," he had persevered in the face of strong opposition inside and outside his party and against the backdrop of the Berlin crisis and the communist takeover in China, refusing to stop his relentless trek across the nation until he had earned the victory that so many thought beyond him.

Dewey's defeat carries a lesson. Had the Republican nominee followed the line of his party mate Robert Taft and presented a strong vision of conservative values and policy that contrasted those of the New Deal, things may have turned out differently. Instead, he spoke in generalities and tried to ape Truman on policies that he thought would appeal to the widest possible voter base. What did Dewey really stand for? And why should voters choose conservatism over the liberalism that Harry Truman was clearly enunciating? These questions were never really answered on the campaign trail, to Dewey's shame.

The New York governor also succumbed to the fatal flaw of hubris, thinking victory was assured. This led not only to complacency at the microphone, lazy use of canned speeches, and an overreliance on buzz-words such as "unity." Dewey's failure to match Truman's speaking schedule meant the New York governor reached far fewer people as his Victory Special made its leisurely way across the country while Truman's Last Chance Special sprinted ahead. Not every election can be won by hard work, but Dewey's example shows that plenty can be lost by the lack of it.

Afterword

THE LEGACY OF TRUMAN'S TRIUMPH
AND DEWEY'S DEFEAT

As Harry Truman celebrated his successful election campaign, his rivals commiserated their losing efforts. Perhaps the disappointment was the greatest for Truman's main challenger, Tom Dewey. Four years earlier he had also lost to the Man from Missouri when Truman had been the undercard on FDR's final winning ticket. Though he and his running mate, John Bricker, had fallen to Roosevelt and Truman, Dewey had come closer to unseating FDR on the national stage than any Republican challenger. That Dewey had pulled in a commendable twenty-two million votes—just three and a half million shy of Roosevelt's total—had undoubtedly given the former attorney hope that the electoral jury would find in his favor as he made a second bid for the White House. They did not, and Dewey would not get a third attempt. Though he declined to contend at the 1952 Republican convention, however, Dewey once again drove a dagger into the heart of his ideological rival Robert Taft, as the former New York governor saw his choice, General Dwight Eisenhower, beat Taft for the nomination.[1] Eisenhower's routing of Truman's successor-in-waiting, Adlai Stevenson, that November—with Ike winning 442 electoral votes to Stevenson's 89—validated Dewey's centrist philosophy. Taft died the following year.

If Dewey was better suited to being a behind-the-scenes producer than a star under the bright lights, his fellow 1948 candidate J. Strom Thurmond was quite the opposite. Though he never again ran for president, Thurmond took all of his gladiatorial rhetoric to Capitol Hill in 1954, beginning forty-nine years of fiery representation for South Carolina in the Senate (the second longest run in the Senate, next to West Virginia's Robert Byrd). The former States' Rights Party candidate continued to be a thorn in the side of civil rights, punctuated in 1957 when he delivered the longest one-man filibuster in Senate history. Despite his twenty-four-hour, eighteen-minute feat of endurance and bloviating, Thurmond failed to stop passage of the 1957 Civil Rights Act, which continued Truman's work by granting voting rights to all citizens.[2] Thurmond also courted controversy (and, his many detractors contended, publicity) in the arena of foreign affairs when he launched investigations into the censoring of military personnel in the early 1960s, and while serving on the Preparedness Investigating Subcommittee he roundly criticized John F. Kennedy for being too soft on communism.[3] Later in his career, after he became a member of the Republican Party, Thurmond helped bolster Richard Nixon's support among southern delegates at the 1968 Republican Convention and collaborated with Teddy Kennedy to pass extensive criminal law reform while he was head of the Judiciary Committee in the mid-1980s. Though he became one of the first senators to hire a black aide in the 1970s and continued to assert that he blocked integration laws only because they overreached the boundary of federal laws, Thurmond never publicly retracted the incendiary comments he made about "the Negro" when leading the States' Rights Party during the 1948 campaign.[4]

Henry Wallace, in keeping with his eccentric persona, had a less dramatic influence on politics after his underwhelming 1948 election showing. Following his defeat, Wallace switched his focus from politics to agriculture, and he came up with a new breed of chicken that became the choice for 75 percent of farmers that raised the birds. He also cowrote a book on the history of corn, in which he had made his fortune through development of high-yield varieties. In the political arena, Wallace continued to ruffle feathers with his seemingly inconsistent statements and contrarian views. He shocked many of his far-left supporters by backing Truman's decision to embroil the United States in the Korean War in 1950, and he backed Eisenhower in the 1956 election. While Dewey and Thurmond maintained their political positions in the latter stages of their careers, Wallace repented, at least of his soft stance on the Soviet Union, even writing an article for *Time* entitled "Why I Was Wrong." Despite this sea change, he remained committed to nuclear disarmament and the importance of a strong world organization in preserving peace.[5]

After the 1948 campaign, the DNC dissolved the Research Division. Following his time as the group's director, Bill Batt served as assistant to the secretary of labor, a post he held for four years. During this time, he was one of the US emissaries to the United Nations Economic and Social Council Conference on Full Employment in 1950, and from 1953 to 1954 he served as senior economist on the President's Commission on Foreign Economic Policy. In 1961, thirteen years after so ably serving Harry Truman, Batt accepted a post from another Democratic president, John F. Kennedy, who nominated him to the Area Redevelopment Administration.[6]

One of Batt's colleagues at Dupont Circle had a much faster ride to the upper echelons of the political scene. After he was reassigned to Truman's speechwriting team midway through his summer, David Lloyd worked with Clark Clifford, Jonathan Daniels, and other key members of the president's brain trust. He provided not only the type of facts and figures he had assembled for the 1948 campaign but also entire speech drafts for Truman. He kept the connection going with the Man from Missouri when he later became director of the Harry S. Truman Library in Independence.[7]

Though he took up a post teaching English a month shy of Truman's November 1948 victory, Lloyd's Research Division colleague Frank Kelly also found his way back into speechwriting, for Senators Ernest McFarland and Scott Lucas, who was Senate majority leader from 1948 to 1950. After his service on the Hill, Kelly later became vice president of the Center for the Study of Democratic Institutions. He was also an advocate for reducing the proliferation of atomic weapons, cofounding the Nuclear Age Peace Foundation, which honored his legacy with an annual lecture series.[8]

Other members of the Research Division went back to serving their communities. Johannes Hoeber continued his activism in Philadelphia's reform movement, culminating in a new city charter and the election of a reform slate in 1951, the first Democratic administration since the nineteenth century. The new mayor (and later senator), Joseph S. Clark, appointed Hoeber as deputy commissioner of the Department of Public Welfare, now the Department of Human Services, a position he served in for twelve years. In 1962, Bill Batt asked Hoeber to join him as his deputy in the Economic Development Administration. Six years later, Hoeber accepted a position in the State Department heading the Vietnam desk of the Agency for International Development (AID). His role was to ameliorate the suffering of millions of refugees created by the Vietnam War.

Having been a refugee himself, this final job was an appropriate cap to his career.[9]

Phil Dreyer went to the opposite side of the country after the Research Division finished its work, going back home to Oregon in November 1948. In 1950, at the urging of Dave Lloyd, Harry Truman agreed to revive the Research Division in preparation for the fall midterm elections. Dreyer took Batt's place as director and called Kenneth Birkhead, who after the Batt group disbanded in November 1948 had moved back to Truman's home state to finish his bachelor's degree and then obtain a master's from University of Missouri at Columbia. They worked with two others in office space even less ideal than the cramped, hot, noisy quarters at Dupont Cirle in 1948, all jammed into one windowless room at the Washington city news ticker. Birkhead was glad to be working with Dreyer again and enjoyed his tasks, but the DNC was less supportive of the group than it had been two years before, and their efforts were minimized. So when Birkhead was offered a place on Missouri politician Tom Hennings Jr.'s senate campaign, he took it and helped his boss win the election.[10]

After his time in Washington ended in frustration, Dreyer again moved back to Portland, Oregon. He mounted two unsuccessful bids for a seat in Congress—first in Portland and then in California—and later campaigned with Ted Kennedy to help get JFK elected. He served the Kennedy and Johnson administrations, and then returned once more to Portland, where he devoted the rest of his life to serving various political organizations and civic groups.[11]

Picking back up one of the issues that he studied during the 1948 campaign, Dreyer's fellow Research Division member John Barriere served President-elect John F. Kennedy's Force on Housing and Urban Affairs in 1960 as staff director, a position he held until 1964. Barriere's fine work got the attention of Speaker of the House John McCormack, who named him as the first staff policy adviser to that position. He later became executive director of the Democratic Steering and Policy Committee until 1978, helping to complete the work Truman had begun, in the form of the Civil Rights Act of 1964, the Voting Rights Act of 1965, and the Civil Rights Act of 1968.[12]

The successful work of the Research Division was the forerunner to the data-centric political campaigns of today. Bill Batt and his six colleagues used WPA guides, newspaper archives, and other paper-based materials to craft localized talking points for Truman that helped him connect with and convince the crowds that showed up at every whistle stop. Think of how effective these seven young men would have been if given access to the Internet, big data, mobile devices, and the other technological conveniences that staffers in political campaign "war rooms" now possess. Or, indeed, how potent their modern counterparts would be in using such tools if they had honed their skills parsing quickly and selectively through dusty folders, boxes, and dossiers under extreme deadline pressure. Certainly the rise of research as a crucial and widely accepted element of successful campaigning was born in the cramped, airless offices in Dupont Circle in 1948.

When we compare the actions of recent presidential victors to Harry Truman's approach in the 1948 campaign, we see parallels. While there was no repeat of the *Chicago Tribune*'s memorable "Dewey Defeats Truman" gaffe in the 2012 election, many media outlets predicted a Mitt Romney victory right up until voting tallies proved them wrong. Like Thomas E. Dewey more than half a century before, Romney failed to state conservatism's case in convincing terms, came across as aloof, and did not take the fight to Barack Obama. Though Obama's travel schedule did not come close to matching Truman's in intensity, number of speeches per day, or the total number of addresses, he focused many of his appearances on targeted areas that either bolstered his base or convinced undecided voters. While Truman made most of his stops in small towns, Obama gave most of his speeches in large urban centers, with undeniable success; in cities with more than five hundred thousand people the president won 70 percent of the vote. The Truman campaign concentrated on winning votes among blacks, the working class, and farmers, while the Obama team's key demographics were young people, blacks, Asians and Hispanics, and women. The president prevailed in part because his team understood how to communicate with and persuade each of these groups that his was the better option, while Romney followed Dewey's example by trying the "me too" approach with these groups. As a result, Obama secured 55 percent of women, 93, 74, and 69 percent of the vote among blacks, Asians, and Hispanics, and enjoyed a 24-percentage-point cushion among eighteen- to twenty-nine-year-olds. The latter is due in large part to the Obama team's superior use of social media, data mining, and technology, with more than a million people downloading the Democratic Party's election app in the first few days, compared to a paltry forty thousand for the GOP equivalent. Truman was not the greatest orator, but he knew how to talk the talk with the voting blocs who put him back in the White House.[13] Obama did the same in both his election wins; he knew what was important to his audience and communicated this in clear terms. It is difficult to assert that his opponents did likewise.

As Republican candidates look forward, they would do well to not only catch up in social media and analytics, but also to follow Truman's example of taking a stand on key issues, resisting fringe splits in their party, and presenting a clear alternative narrative to that of their opponents. As for the Democratic Party? It has already demonstrated that while America is far different today than it was in Truman's time, the strategic lessons of his Whistle Stop Tour hold true. Let us hope that its policymakers keep in mind the principles of the Man from Missouri, who was in favor of small business, resisted the overreaching demands of big labor unions and big business alike, and fought for the rights of the common voter, of which he was one.

It is also high time that our leaders recognize, as did Truman and his peers, that some issues are bigger than left and right, Republican and Democrat, isolationist and interventionist. Certainly, Truman was hardly a paragon of bipartisanship on domestic affairs while "blackguarding Congress at every whistle stop," as Robert Taft so memorably put it in 1948. Yet Truman understood that the United States was imperiled abroad with the continued spread of expansionist communism, and he worked across the aisle to pass elements of the Marshall Plan that checked this advance and helped get Western Europe back on its feet. At home, the president recognized the grave challenges facing the nation in the postwar period, including a dire housing shortage, a need for increased federal aid to education, and, most significantly, the moral imperative to give American citizens of all colors and creeds equal rights. Though many Republicans rallied behind the latter, most blocked his plans for education and low-cost housing out of sheer stubbornness. And yet somehow that "do-nothing" group passed more than 900 bills between 1947 and 1948. In contrast, the 2012–2013 session had assented to just 50 bills as of December 2013.[14] The success of a congressional session may not be numerical, but when our representatives in the House and Senate vote down bills proposed by their opponents on virtually every issue for the sake of toeing the party line and preventing action, something is fundamentally broken within the Democratic and Republican establishments.

Certainly, Truman's opponent Robert Taft was correct when he asserted the need for our main parties to act as a counterweight to each other and provide the checks and balances that are key to the long-term health of American democracy. And yet it seems that Taft's maxim "The duty of the opposition is to oppose" has been carried too far by Democrats and Republicans in recent times. The United States faces problems different than those Truman tackled in 1948 and following his election victory. And yet our inner-city school systems still struggle, national debt continues to rise to stratospheric heights, and our security is imperiled by terrorism, a resurgent Russia, and belligerent states such as Iran and North Korea. We cannot hope to best these challenges when our main political parties put self-interest above national interest, pander to big money donors and lobbyists instead of listening to the electorate, and favor electoral self-preservation over principles.

It would be idealistic to hope for a "can't we all just get along" political climate. But surely differences of opinion can be put aside for the greater good when there are larger issues at hand at home and abroad. Certainly Republicans in Congress managed this in the arena of foreign policy in the run-up to the 1948 election, when key GOP figures such as Arthur Vandenberg ensured that both parties presented an image of strength and togetherness in the face of expansionist communism (at least over international matters). If Harry Truman's Whistle Stop Campaign shows us anything, it's that the American people support doers, politicians of conviction who speak their mind and put their beliefs into action instead of wasting their breath with "he-said-she-said" finger pointing and Strom Thurmond–like marathon filibusters. As public confidence in elected officials continues to wane as Washington wallows in partisan muck, our politicians must rededicate themselves to debate over quibbling, pragmatism over obstructionism, and give-and-take over gridlock. The stakes are too high, at home and abroad, for them to do otherwise.

Acknowledgments

A book is a collection of words, sentences, and paragraphs, but more than this, it is a collage of people and their stories. This is true of the text and everything that goes on behind the scenes: the research, editing, conversations, brainstorming, and so on.

In my case, it's also part of my family story. Writing this book would not have been possible without the grace and patience of my beautiful wife, Nicole, who is the most creative person I know. And I'm also nothing without the unfailing love of my two talented and wonderful sons, Johnny and Harry, who fill my world with wonder. My parents, Ian and Veronica, helped me get here with unfailing support and encouragement. Without Mum's own love of writing and reading, I would never have picked up a pen, and without Dad's legacy of hard work, I wouldn't be capable of pressing on, day after day (or, more truthfully, night after night). My siblings, Barrie, Jacqui, and Debbie, inspire me to pursue my passion for words, as does the enthusiasm of Janice, Randall, David, Nicole, and Hilde Stephens. Thanks also to the rest of the clans on both sides of the Atlantic, including Lisa, Mike, Molly, and Ollie Flounders, Cherie White, Ira and Debbie Cox and Paul and Nancy Stephens, Mickey Cox, and Leita and Wes Lillibridge.

I'm also lucky enough to have a circle of friends who care about what I put on each page. Brett Chalmers, Henry Worcester, and Tom Seibold shared in the initial coffee-fueled discussions about the book. Dean Nelson and Phil Towle encouraged me to leap into this project with reckless abandon, while the GMC members Mike and Jason Slattery and Sascha Ohler contributed regular stout-based support. Luke Crisell (aka the best feature writer in America), Dan Vanderpool, Justen Wack, Ben Spicer, Jono Lloyd, Antony Spencer, Jon Manley, Paul and Jenny Hunt, Jeremy Snyder, Cory Maxwell, Taylor Johnson, Joey Hockett, Tyler Lucks, "Uncle" Marcus Childs, Mark Johnston, Tim Elliott, Shane Perrin, Tim Keel, Richmond McCluer Jr., Warren Hollrah, Al Cleghorn, Van Brokaw, Lynne Olson, Paul Reid, Rob Havers, Barney Forsythe, O. T. Harris, Marlene Acree, Brian Warren, Erin and Chris Hecker, Tyler Blake, Jeanne Millhuff, Shanti Thomas, Kevin Garber, Coach Rocky Lamar, John and Leatrice Atwood, Nick Whitfield, Crosby Kemper III, Lorenzo Butler, and so many others helped me along the way. I also appreciate everyone who has said something kind about this book, *Our Supreme Task*, and any of my other projects. Just connecting with one reader would be enough motivation to keep going. Connecting with so many more is a blessing.

Writing a book is only part of the publishing journey. Thanks to my agent, Rob McQuilkin, for replying with uncharacteristic all-caps verve to my first e-mail about *Whistle Stop*, and for spending considerable time honing the proposal. Steve Hull at the University Press of New England put in his all as my long-suffering editor, and without him this book would not have been created. I once read that a talented producer makes an album, and the same is true of editors and books. The keen copy editing of Drew Bryan helped catch more mistakes than I believed I was capable of making, and my production editor, Lauren Seidman, pulled pictures and words together wonderfully. Thanks also to Thomas Haushalter for getting the word out (pun intended) about this book. Before the manuscript got to Steve, Lauren, and company, it passed by the wary eyes of Brett, Randall, Richard Marsh, and Francis W. Hoeber, who each provided guidance on what to keep, what to cut, and what to add.

I was fortunate to track down Francis when I started looking for more information on the Research Division. As you may guess from his last name, he is the son of Research Division member Johannes Hoeber, and he kindly shared many gems from his family's archives. This included the delightful story about his sister and Hubert Humphrey doing the dishes after Humphrey had changed the course of the 1948 election with his courageous civil rights speech. David Birkhead also provided a rich biographical sketch of his father and another member of the Batt group, Kenneth. It is this intimate, personal history and the intersection of "ordinary" folk with the "great" figures of history that keeps me up until two in the morning, tinkering with minute details that I hope at least one other person finds as fascinating as I do. That and far too much caffeine.

I found many other valuable materials among the archives of the magnificent Harry S. Truman Library in Independence, Missouri. Archivist David Clark was ever patient with my many requests for information, and each of his colleagues proved more than happy to assist with even the most obscure requests. Kim Ross-Polito, publisher of the *Crestline Advocate*, kindly ran a blurb asking for people who recalled Truman's Whistle Stop Tour there to contact me, and Kris Eckert from the Crestline Ohio Historical Society helped set up an oral interview with Joan Histed and provided a photo of one of Truman's two whistle stops in Crestline. Bette Richards from the Arizona Historical Society was good enough to share her recollections of meeting Truman in 1948. Chad Williams of the Oklahoma Historical Society put the word out in OHS's newsletter, which led to George and Frances Webb kindly sending me their memories, a photograph, and newspaper clippings. Michael Hall from the Gold Coast Railroad Museum took and sent original photos of the *Ferdinand Magellan*, Truman's train car, which you can view at the museum in Miami. The team at MidAmerica Nazarene University's Mabee Library—including Bruce Flanders, Lon Dagley, Glenda Seifert, and Lauren Hays—were typically helpful in securing interlibrary loans and other materials, and I think I crashed the system at the Indian Creek branch of the Olathe Public Library by submitting too many requests. Sorry to anyone I've forgotten to mention.

Last, I'd like to give glory to God for blessing this project and bringing so many wonderful people into my life through it.

Notes

INTRODUCTION: THE ELECTION OF 1948

1. David Jordan, *FDR, Dewey, and the Election of 1944* (Bloomington: Indiana University Press, 2012), 40–48; Lynne Olson, *Those Angry Days: Roosevelt, Lindbergh, and America's Fight Over World War II, 1939–1941* (New York: Random House, 2013), 185.

2. Aida D. Donald, *Citizen Soldier: A Life of Harry Truman* (New York: Basic Books, 2012), 128.

3. Alonzo L. Hamby, *Man of the People: A Life of Harry S. Truman* (Oxford: Oxford University Press, 1995), 430; A. Merriman Smith, *The President Is Many Men* (New York: Harper, 1948), 446.

4. Stanley Weintraub, *Final Victory: FDR's Extraordinary World War II Presidential Campaign* (Cambridge, Mass.: Da Capo, 2012), 40 and 47.

5. Joseph E. Lowndes, *From the New Deal to the New Right: Race and the Southern Origins of Modern Conservatism* (Princeton, N.J.: Yale University Press, 2009), 27–28.

6. Jordan, *FDR, Dewey and the Election of 1944*, 248.

7. "Hague Wants Truman to Ask Gen. Eisenhower to Make Run," Associated Press, July 6, 1948, accessed January 2013 (unless otherwise noted, sources given as "accessed" were accessed from Google News Archive); Hamby, *A Man of the People*, 445–446.

8. Harry Truman to H. H. Brummall, May 24, 1948, Harry S. Truman Library (hereafter HSTL), accessed December 2011.

9. Gary A. Donaldson, *Truman Defeats Dewey* (Lexington: University Press of Kentucky, 1999), 35.

10. Michael Bowen, reader review comment of *Whistle Stop* manuscript, October 2013.

11. Cabell Phillips, *The Truman Presidency* (London: Macmillan, 1966), 161.

12. Harold I. Gullan, *The Upset that Wasn't: Harry S. Truman and the Crucial Election Victory of 1948* (Chicago: Ivan R. Dee, 1998), 53.

13. Robert Taft, quoted by Brian Birdnow, "The Duty of the Opposition Party is to Oppose," *Town Hall*, December 14, 2008, available online at http://townhall.com/columnists/brianbirdnow/2008/12/14/the_duty_of_the_opposition_party _is_to_oppose/page/full/, accessed February 2013.

14. Michael Bowen, *The Roots of Modern Conservatism* (Chapel Hill: University of North Carolina Press, 2011), 73–75.

15. "1948 Truman-Dewey Election," Eagleton Institute of Politics, Rutgers

University, accessed from the institution's website in November 2012; Elmo Roper, "It's Dewey Over Truman by a Landslide," *The Evening Independent*, September 9, 1948, accessed November 2012.

16. Carl Solberg, *Hubert Humphrey: A Biography* (New York: W. W. Norton, 1984), 12–13.

17. "Harry Can't Lose Recalling Congress, Democrats Believe," *Washington Daily News*, July 18, 1948, George Elsey Papers, Box 35, "1948 Pres Campaign Political Clippings" folder, HSTL, accessed November 2012.

18. Joseph Crespino, *Strom Thurmond's America* (New York: Hill and Wang, 2012), 70–71.

19. Donaldson, *Truman Defeats Dewey*, 413.

20. "Testimony of Whittaker Chambers before the House Committee on Un-American Activities," August 3, 1948, University of Missouri–Kansas City Law School, available online at http://law2.umkc.edu/faculty/projects/ftrials/hiss/8-3 testimony.html, accessed November 2012.

21. Andrei Cherny, *The Candy Bombers: The Untold Story of the Berlin Airlift and America's Finest Hour* (New York: Penguin, 2009), 264.

22. "Palestine Truce Broken as Arabs and Jews Clash," *St. Petersburg Times* via the Associated Press, July 7, 1948, accessed January 2013; "Rebels Hold Peak Against Greeks," *Milwaukee Sentinel*, July 5, 1948, accessed January 2013; "Red War Plot Aired in Korea," *Miami News*, July 1, 1948, accessed January 2013.

23. Donald, *Citizen Soldier*, xvi.

24. John Acacia, *Clark Clifford: The Wise Man of Washington* (Lexington: University Press of Kentucky, 2009), 139.

25. Steve Neal, ed., *Miracle of '48: Harry Truman's Major Campaign Speeches and Selected Whistle-Stops* (Carbondale: Southern Illinois University Press, 2003), 3–4.

26. Johannes Hoeber to Elfriede Hoeber, July 21, 1948. Hoeber Family Papers, accessed June 2012; William Batt Jr., oral interview with Jerry N. Hess, July 26, 1966, HSTL, available online at http://www.trumanlibrary.org/oralhist/battw.htm, accessed May 2011.

27. Bill Batt to Clark Clifford, June 4, 1948, Presidential Speech File, Box 33, Clark Clifford Papers, HSTL, accessed November 3, 2012; Frank Kelly, *Harry Truman and the Human Family* (Santa Barbara, Calif.: Capra Press, 1998), 49; George Elsey to Clark Clifford, undated, Clifford Papers, HSTL, Box 21, Batt Correspondence File, accessed August 25, 2012.

28. Samuel L. Popkin, *The Candidate: What it Takes to Win — and Hold — The White House* (Oxford: Oxford University Press, 2012), 156; W. McNeil Lowry, interview with Jerry N. Hess, New York, April 23, 1969, HSTL, accessed August 2012.

29. Harry Truman, Address at Dexter, Iowa, on the Occasion of the National Plowing Match, Public Papers of the Presidents, HSTL, accessed August 2012.

30. Phillips, *The Truman Presidency*, 248.

31. Bill Batt to Clark Clifford, "Dewey's Strategy Vs. The President's," July 27, 1948, Presidential Speech File, Clark Clifford Papers, Box 33, HSTL, accessed November 3, 2012; Bowen, *The Roots of Modern Conservatism*, 172.

32. Paul F. Boller Jr., *Presidential Campaigns: From George Washington to George W. Bush* (Oxford: Oxford University Press, 2004), 71; Roper, "It's Dewey Over Truman by a Landslide."

33. John Gizzi, "1948 and Lessons for 2012," *Human Events*, available online at http://www.humanevents.com/2012/06/23/1948-lessons-2012/, accessed February 2013.

34. David Pietrusza, *1948: Harry Truman's Improbable Victory and the Year that Transformed America's Role in the World* (New York: Union Square Press, 2011), 84.

35. Harry Truman, address at the Colorado State Capitol, Denver, September 20, 1948, quoted by Neal, ed., *Miracle of '48*, 79–80.

36. William E. Leuchtenberg, *The White House Looks South: Franklin D. Roosevelt, Harry S. Truman, Lyndon B. Johnson* (Baton Rouge: Louisiana State University Press, 2007), 206.

37. George Elsey, *An Unplanned Life: A Memoir* (Columbia: University of Missouri Press, 2005), 163.

38. Kristina Peterson and Michael R. Crittenden, "Congress Readies Year-End Dash," *The Wall Street Journal*, December 9, 2013, accessed December 2013.

39. Bill Batt to Clark Clifford, July 9, 1948, Presidential Speech File, Box 33, Clark Clifford Papers, HSTL, accessed November 3, 2012.

40. Frank Kelly, interview with Niel M. Johnson, Independence, Missouri, April 15, 1988, HSTL, accessed June 2012.

1. JUNE

1. H. H. Brummall to Harry Truman, May 15, 1948, HSTL, Independence, Missouri, accessed December 2011.

2. Harry Truman to H. H. Brummall, May 24, 1948, HSTL, accessed December 2011.

3. Ronald T. Farrar, *Reluctant Servant: The Story of Charles G. Ross* (Columbia: University of Missouri Press, 1969), 191.

4. "I Read Your Letter," *Time*, June 14, 1948, accessed December 2011.

5. Alonzo L. Hamby, *Man of the People: A Life of Harry S. Truman* (Oxford: Oxford University Press, 1995), 430; A. Merriman Smith, *The President Is Many Men* (New York: Harper, 1948), 35.

6. John Acacia, *Clark Clifford: The Wise Man of Washington* (Lexington: University Press of Kentucky, 2009), 22–23.

7. "The Rowe/Webb Memo," John F. Kennedy School of Government, Harvard University, available online at http://www.hks.harvard.edu/case/3pt/rowe.html, accessed November 2011.

8. Harry S. Truman, *Memoirs: 1946–1952, Years of Trial and Hope* (Garden City, N.Y.: Doubleday, 1956) 178.

9. Clark Clifford, *Counsel to the President* (New York: Random House, 1991), 199–200.

10. Ibid.

11. James T. Patterson, *Mr. Republican: A Biography of Robert A. Taft* (Boston: Houghton Mifflin, 1972), 312.

12. Zachary Karabell, *The Last Campaign: How Harry Truman Won the 1948 Election* (New York: Alfred A. Knopf, 2000), 88–89.

13. Hamby, *Man of the People*, 435.

14. Harry S. Truman, *Memoirs by Harry S. Truman: Years of Trial, 1946–1952* (New York: Doubleday, 1956), 172.

15. Spencer Warren, "A Philosophy of International Policy," in *Churchill's "Iron Curtain" Speech Fifty Years Later*, ed. James W. Muller, 99 (Columbia: University of Missouri Press, 1999).

16. George C. Marshall, "The Marshall Plan Speech," Harvard University, June 5, 1947, The Organisation for Economic Co-operation and Development, accessed December 2013, available online at http://www.oecd.org/general/themarshall planspeechatharvarduniversity5june1947.htm.

17. Margaret Truman, *Harry S. Truman* (New York: William Morrow, 1973), 391–393.

18. "50 Southern Congressman Declare War on Truman's Civil Rights Plan," *Kentucky New Era*, February 28, 1948, accessed December 2011.

19. Hamby, *Man of the People*, 433.

20. Joseph E. Lowndes, *From the New Deal to the New Right: Race and the Southern Origins of Modern Conservatism* (Princeton, N.J.: Yale University Press, 2009), 27.

21. Ibid., 27–28.

22. Fraser J. Harbutt, *The Iron Curtain: Churchill, America, and the Origins of the Cold War* (Oxford: Oxford University Press, 1986), 153; W. Averell Harriman and Elie Abel, *Special Envoy to Churchill and Stalin, 1941–1946* (New York: Random House, 1975), 294; David McCullough, *Truman* (New York: Simon & Schuster, 1992), 548–549.

23. Hamby, *Man of the People*, 435.

24. Clifford, *Counsel to the President*; Truman, *Years of Trial and Hope*, 178–179.

25. "If I'm Wrong . . . ," *Time*, June 28, 1948, accessed December 2011.

26. David M. Jordan, *FDR, Dewey, and the Election of 1944* (Bloomington: Indiana University Press, 2011), 235.

27. Clifford, *Counsel to the President*, 226; Johannes Hoeber, interview with Jerry N. Hess, Washington, D.C., September 13, 1966, HSTL, accessed April 2012.

28. Francis W. Hoeber, oral interview with the author, June 22, 2012; Johannes

Hoeber, interview with Walter Phillips for the Walter Phillips Oral History Project, Temple University Urban Archive Notes, May 4, 1986, accessed July 2012.

29. "William L. Batt, Jr.," Secretaries of L&I, *PA Manual*, 1957–1958, available online at http://www.psp.state.pa.us/portal/server.pt/gateway/PTARGS_6_2 _73337_10453_552770_43/, accessed January 2013.

30. Clark Clifford to Bill Batt, February 25, 1948, Clifford Papers, HSTL, Box 21 William F. Batt Correspondence folder, March 18, 1948, accessed August 25, 2012.

31. Bill Batt to Clark Clifford, "The President's Address to Congress," March 18, 1948, Clifford Papers, HSTL, Box 21 William F. Batt Correspondence folder, March 18, 1948, accessed August 25, 2012.

32. Bill Batt to J. Howard McGrath and Gael Sullivan, "Report of the Research Division for the Period of March 29 to April 17," April 20, 1948, Clifford Papers, HSTL, Box 21 William F. Batt Correspondence folder, accessed August 25, 2012; Bill Batt to Clark Clifford, April 22, 1948, Clifford Papers, HSTL, Box 21 William F. Batt Correspondence folder, accessed August 25, 2012.

33. Bill Batt to Clark Clifford, March 22, 1948, Clifford Papers, HSTL, Box 21 William F. Batt Correspondence folder, accessed August 25, 2012.

34. Frank K. Kelly, *Harry Truman and the Human Family* (Santa Barbara, Calif.: Capra Press, 1998), 42.

35. David Birkhead, interview with the author, June 21, 2012; David Birkhead, e-mail to the author, June 22, 2012.

36. Edmund Morris, *Dutch: A Memoir of Ronald Reagan* (New York: Random House, 2011), 230.

37. Jim Tuck, *The Liberal Civil War: Fraternity and Fratricide on the Left* (Lanham, Md.: Rowman & Littlefield, 1998), 199.

38. Kelly, *Harry Truman and the Human Family*, 42.

39. Ibid., 21.

40. Ibid., 14.

41. Ibid., 17.

42. Ibid., 14–16.

43. Ibid., 18.

44. Frank Kelly, interview with Niel M. Johnson, Independence, Mo., April 15, 1988, HSTL, accessed September 2011.

45. Kelly, *Harry Truman and the Human Family*, 26.

46. Ibid., 28, 32, 33.

47. Ibid., 34

48. Ibid.

49. Steve Neal, ed., *Miracle of '48: Harry Truman's Major Campaign Speeches and Selected Whistle-Stops* (Carbondale: Southern Illinois University Press, 2003), 95.

50. Ibid., 121.

51. Charles Murphy, "Some Aspects of President Truman's Speeches for the 1948 Campaign," December 6, 1948, Charles Murphy Papers, Confidential File, Box 50, HSTL, accessed December 15, 2012.

52. William Batt Jr., oral interview with Jerry N. Hess, July 26, 1966, HSTL, available online at http://www.trumanlibrary.org/oralhist/battw.htm, accessed May 2011.

53. "Questions on Towns to be Visited by the President," undated, author unknown (likely Bill Batt), "Detroit Speech Preparation" folder, Box 1, John E. Barriere Papers, HSTL, accessed December 1, 2012.

54. Kelly, *Harry Truman and the Human Family*, 35.

55. Batt to Clifford, May 8, 1948, Clifford Papers, Box 22, Batt file, HSTL, accessed August 25, 2012.

56. Matthew J. Connelly, interview with Jerry N. Hess, November 30, 1967, New York, HSTL, available online at http://www.trumanlibrary.org/oralhist /connly2.htm#276; "Truman's Patronage Boss," *Life*, June 27, 1949, accessed December 2012.

57. Connelly, interview with Jerry N. Hess.

58. Felix Belair, quoted in Daniel S. Margolies, ed., *A Companion to Harry S. Truman* (Hoboken, N.J.: John Wiley & Sons, 2012), 84.

59. Franklin D. Mitchell, *Harry S. Truman and the News Media: Contentious Relations, Belated Respect* (Columbia: University of Missouri Press, 1998), 85.

60. Ibid., 86; "Most of Party OKeys Truman's Wallace Ouster," *Kentucky New Era*, September 20, 1946, accessed November 2013; "The Remarkable Opinions of Henry Wallace," *Calgary Herald*, September 20, 1946, accessed November 2013.

61. Clifford, *Counsel to the President*, 199.

62. Truman, *Years of Trial and Hope*, 179.

63. Ibid.

64. Bill Batt to Clark Clifford, "The President's Address to Congress," March 18, 1948, HSTL.

65. Robert H. Ferrell, ed., *Off the Record: The Private Papers of Harry Truman* (New York: Harper & Row, 1980), 135.

66. Ibid., 134.

67. Joseph Alsop to Eleanor Roosevelt, quoted in McCullough, *Truman*, 348.

68. Margaret Truman, *Harry S. Truman*, 221.

69. Matthew Algeo, *Harry Truman's Excellent Adventure* (Chicago: Chicago Review Press, 2009), 71, 220.

70. Warren F. Kimball, "Churchill, Roosevelt and the Reporters," *Finest Hour*, autumn 2011, accessed December 2011.

71. "Truman Is Confident as Train Rolls West," *Tuscaloosa News* via the Associated Press, June 4, 1948, accessed December 2011.

72. "Itinerary and Travel Guidelines, June 1948," Truman Administration File, Charles S. Murphy Papers, HSTL, accessed December 2011; Ernest B. Vaccaro, "Truman Leaves for Missouri," *Tuscaloosa News*, March 4, 1946, accessed December 2011.

73. "Itinerary and Travel Guidelines, June 1948."

74. Kelly, *Harry Truman and the Human Family*, 40; "Rear Platform Remarks in Ohio and Indiana," Harry S. Truman Library and Museum, available online at http://www.trumanlibrary.org/publicpapers/index.php?pid=1643, accessed December 2011.

75. Joan Histed, interview with the author, July 19, 2013.

76. "Truman on Tour," *New York Times*, June 6, 1948; McCullough, *Truman*, 653.

77. "Truman Is Confident as Train Rolls West," *Tuscaloosa News*.

78. "Truman Opens His Campaign for Reelection," *Gettysburg Times* via the Associated Press, June 5, 1948, accessed December 2011.

79. Clifford, *Counsel to the President*, 200.

80. "The Truman-Vandenberg Bill of Goods," *Chicago Tribune*, June 9, 1948, accessed December 2011.

81. Douglas B. Cornell, "Truman Pauses on Trip West to go to Church, Receive Gifts, Including 'Spurs for Congress,'" *Schenectady Gazette*, June 7, 1948, accessed December 2011.

82. "Bay State Delegates Vote to Back Truman," *New York Times*, June 5, 1948, accessed December 2011.

83. Thomas L. Stokes, "Truman Revives Will Rodgers Act," *St. Petersburg Times* via the Associated Press, June 11, 1948, accessed December 2011.

84. India Edwards, interview with Jerry N. Hess, Washington, D.C., January 16, 1969, HSTL, accessed October 2012.

85. Algeo, *Harry Truman's Excellent Adventure*, 61; Myrtle Gaylord, "First Lady Shies from Interviews," *Spokane Daily Chronicle*, June 9, 1948, accessed December 2011.

86. Stokes, "Truman Revives Will Rodgers Act."

87. "Truman Gets a Lift in Idaho," *Daytona Beach Morning Herald*, June 10, 1948, accessed December 2011.

88. "Varied Adventures in the West," *Time*, June 21, 1948, accessed December 2011.

89. "Truman in Bid for Labor Vote," *The Day*, June 6, 1948, accessed December 2011.

90. Richard Norton Smith, *Thomas E. Dewey and His Times* (New York: Simon & Schuster, 1982), 478.

91. Ernest B. Vaccaro, "Truman Puts Price Blame on Congress," *Miami News* via the Associated Press, June 9, 1948, accessed December 2011.

92. Clifford, *Counsel to the President*, 103–104: Gaylord, "First Lady Shies from Interviews"; McCullough, *Truman*, 654, 669.

93. Gaylord, "First Lady Shies from Interviews."

94. Anthony Leviero, "President Tells Union Men it Is Their Fault if Labor Law Is Kept," *New York Times*, June 9, 1948, accessed December 2011; McCullough, *Truman*, 653.

95. "Barrel No. 2," *Time*, June 23, 1948, accessed December 2011.

96. Harry S. Truman, "Rear Platform and Other Informal Remarks in Washington," *Public Papers of the Presidents: Harry S. Truman, 1945–1953*, HSTL, available online at http://www.trumanlibrary.org/publicpapers/index.php?pid=1658&st=&st1= accessed December 2011; "Sunshine Warms Truman for Wallop at Congress," *Spokane Daily Chronicle*, June 9, 1948, accessed December 2011.

97. Leviero, "President Tells Union Men it Is their Fault if Labor Law Is Kept."

98. Anthony Leviero, "Truman Inspects Flooded Vanport," *New York Times*, June 12, 1948, accessed December 2011.

99. "Full Schedule Awaits Truman," *Spokane Daily Chronicle*, June 9, 1948, accessed December 2011; Leviero, "President Tells Union Men it Is their Fault if Labor Law Is Kept."

100. "Address in Seattle Before the Washington State Press Club," June 10, 1948, HSTL, accessed December 2011.

101. "Marshall Says Major Steps Have Been Taken," *Sarasota Herald-Tribune* via the Associated Press, June 9, 1948, accessed December 2011.

102. McCullough, *Truman*, 653.

103. Charles S. Murphy, interview with C. T. Morrissey, Washington, May 2, 1963, available online at http://www.trumanlibrary.org/oralhist/murphy1.htm#28, accessed December 2011; Gaylord, "First Lady Shies from Interviews"; "Wallgren, Monrad Charles (1891–1961)," HistoryLink (Washington State), undated, available online at http://www.historylink.org/index.cfm?DisplayPage=output .cfm&file_id=9246, accessed December 2011.

104. Leviero, "Truman Inspects Flooded Vanport."

105. "Full Schedule Awaits Truman," *Spokane Daily Chronicle*; "Truman Signs Flood Relief Bill," *The News and Courier* (Charleston, S.C.), June 11, 1948, accessed December 2011.

106. McCullough, *Truman*, 653; "Vicious Slur, in Taft's View," *Milwaukee Journal*, June 11, 1948, accessed December 2011.

107. Kelly, *Harry Truman and the Human Family*, 40

108. "Vicious Slur, in Taft's View," *Milwaukee Journal*.

109. "Taft Assails Truman Tactics," *The News and Courier* (Charleston, S.C.), June 11, 1948, accessed December 2011.

110. Ernest B. Vaccaro, "Truman Says 'Uncle Joe's' Hands Tied," *The Florence Times* via the Associated Press, June 12, 1948, accessed December 2011.

111. McCullough, *Truman*, 653.

112. Clifford, *Counsel to the President*, 201.

113. "Russians Get Tough Again in Germany," *Florence Times* via the Associated Press, June 12, 1948, accessed December 2011.

114. Anne Applebaum, *Iron Curtain: The Crushing of Eastern Europe, 1944–1956* (New York: Doubleday, 2012), 218–219.

115. Daniel F. Harrington, *Berlin on the Brink: The Blockade, the Airlift and the Early Cold War* (Lexington: University Press of Kentucky, 2012), 70–71.

116. Applebaum, *Iron Curtain*, 254.

117. Anthony Leviero, "Truman Warns Soviet it Opposes All Free World," *New York Times*, June 13, 1948.

118. "President's Talk on Foreign Policy," *New York Times*, June 13, 1948, accessed December 2011.

119. Ibid.

120. Kelly, *Harry Truman and the Human Family*, 41.

121. "Lynching Bill Approved by Senate Group," *The Day*, June 12, 1948, accessed December 2011.

122. "Court Forbids Shipping Strike," *Portsmouth Times*, June 14, 1948, accessed December 2011.

123. "Truman Raps Critics of His Speaking Trip," *The Day* (New London, Conn.), June 14, 1948, accessed December 2011.

124. "President in Los Angeles for Speech," *St. Joseph News Press* via the United Press, June 14, 1948, accessed December 2011.

125. Clifford, *Counsel to the President*, 202; Kelly, *Harry Truman and the Human Family*, 43.

126. Harry S. Truman, "Address Before the Greater Los Angeles Press Club," Public Papers of the Presidents: Harry S. Truman, 1945–1953, HSTL, available online at http://www.trumanlibrary.org/publicpapers/index.php?pid=1680, accessed December 2011; "Truman Jabs Congress Hard," *Milwaukee Journal*, June 15, 1948, accessed December 2011.

127. Ferrell, ed., *Off the Record*, 141.

128. "Truman Jabs Congress Hard," *Milwaukee Journal*.

129. Ibid.

130. Robert J. Donovan, *Conflict and Crisis: The Presidency of Harry S. Truman* (Columbia: University of Missouri Press, 1996), 401; Margaret Truman, *Harry S. Truman*, 27.

131. "Truman Fights Foreign Policy in Politics, But He Bars No Holds on Domestic Policy," *New York Times*, June 16, 1948, accessed December 2011.

132. "Presidential Job Approval: Harry S. Truman," The American Presidency Project, data compiled from Gallup polls by Gerhard Peters, available online at http://www.presidency.ucsb.edu/data/popularity.php?pres=33&sort=time&direct=DESC&Submit=DISPLAY, accessed January 2013.

133. "Truman Fights Foreign Policy in Politics, But He Has Bars No Holds on Domestic Policy," *New York Times*.

134. "Crack About 'Whistle Stops' Blows up Gale for Taft," *Milwaukee Journal*, June 19, 1948, accessed December 2011.

135. Harry S. Truman, "Veto of Resolution Excluding Certain Groups From Social Security Coverage," June 14, 1948, HSTL, accessed December 2013.

136. "Coronet," *Time*, July 5, 1948, accessed December 2011; "Russians Get Tough Again in Germany," *Florence Times*; Leviero, "Truman Warns Soviet it Opposes All Free World."

137. "Angry Congress Overrides Veto for Third Time," *Lewiston Morning Tribune*, June 17, 1948, accessed December 2011.

138. Smith, *Thomas E. Dewey and His Times*, 455.

139. Michael Bowen, *The Roots of Modern Conservatism* (Chapel Hill: The University of North Carolina Press, 2011), 56.

140. Ibid, 480.

141. Michael Bowen, reader review comment of *Whistle Stop* manuscript, October 2013.

142. Bowen, *The Roots of Modern Conservatism*, 52–54.

143. Harold I. Gullan, *The Upset that Wasn't: Harry S. Truman and the Crucial Election Victory of 1948* (Chicago: Ivan R. Dee, 1998), 54.

144. Gary A. Donaldson, *Truman Defeats Dewey* (Lexington: University Press of Kentucky, 1999), 37.

145. Gullan, *The Upset that Wasn't*, 93.

146. Donaldson, *Truman Defeats Dewey*, 32.

147. Bowen, *The Roots of Modern Conservatism*, 33.

148. Ibid., 483.

149. Ibid., 484.

150. Ibid., 57–58.

151. Patterson, *Mr. Republican*, 409.

152. Sidney M. Shallet, *New York Times*, June 23, 1948; Meyer Berger, "Taft's Elephant Fails to Give Clue as to Who Will Gain Nomination," *New York Times*, June 22, 1948.

153. Drew Pearson, "Washington Merry-Go-Round," *St. Joseph Gazette*, June 24, 1948, accessed January 2013.

154. "Summaries of the Nominating Speeches at GOP Convention," *New York Times*, June 24, 1948, accessed January 2013.

155. Smith, *Thomas E. Dewey and His Times*, 498.

156. Patterson, *Mr. Republican*, 414.

157. Ibid., 378.

158. Ibid., 415.

159. Smith, *Thomas E. Dewey and His Times*, 501.

160. "Truman vs. Dewey," PBS, available online at http://www.pbs.org/wnet/historyofus/web13/segment5_p.html, accessed January 2013.

161. Kelly, *Harry Truman and the Human Family*, 31.

162. "Suggestions on Western Campaign Trip," June 23, 1948. President's Secretary's Files, HSTL, accessed October 2012.

163. Ibid.

164. Ibid.

165. Ibid.

166. "Files of the Fact XII: Thomas E. Dewey," Bill Batt et al., John E. Barriere Papers, HSTL, accessed July 2012.

167. Kenneth Birkhead to Philleo Nash, "Statement on the Negro Voter and Housing," June 29, 1948, Whistle Stop Study Collections, HSTL, accessed September 2012.

168. "Draft, Defense Fund Measures Signed," *Lewiston Morning Tribune*, June 25, 1948, accessed January 2013.

169. "Coal Pact Lifts Fear of Strike," Associated Press, June 25, 1948, accessed January 2013.

170. Dwight Eisenhower to Leslie E. Schwartz, June 15, 1948, quoted in "Truman's Foes Still Plugging for Eisenhower," Associated Press, June 28, 1948, accessed January 2013.

171. "Truman Held Sure of Only 26 Votes Out of 404 in South," *New York Times*, June 30, 1948, accessed January 2013.

172. "'Dixiecrats' to Caucus in Philadelphia," Associated Press, June 28, 1948, accessed January 2013.

173. "Truman Held Sure of Only 26 Votes Out of 404 in South," *New York Times*.

174. "Truman's Foes Still Plugging for Eisenhower," Associated Press, June 28, 1948, accessed January 2013.

175. Ibid.

176. "Thousands Mill in Red Sector for New Marks," United Press, June 29, 1948, accessed January 2013.

2. JULY

1. Peter Edson, "Edson Says Dixiecrat Walkout Would Help Democratic Party; Trust Strangles South," Associated Press, July 8, 1948, accessed July 2013.

2. "Hague Deserts Truman for Ike," Associated Press, July 5, 1948, accessed July 2013.

3. "Truman Sees Nomination on First Ballot," Associated Press, July 1, 1948, accessed July 2013.

4. Frank K. Kelly, *Harry Truman and the Human Family* (Santa Barbara, Calif.: Capra Press, 1998), 33–35.

5. Francis W. Hoeber, oral interview with author, June 22, 2012.

6. Johannes Hoeber, interview with Walter Phillips for the Walter Phillips Oral History Project, Temple University Urban Archive Notes, May 4, 1986, accessed July 2012.

7. William L. Batt Jr. to Clark Clifford, May 11, 1948. Clark Clifford Papers, Box 21, William L. Batt Jr., Director of Democratic National Committee Research Division, Correspondence 1948–1949, HSTL, accessed August 2012.

8. Picked Germans Take Over Ruins," *Spokane Spokesman-Review* via the Associated Press, accessed July 2012; "Taken Into Protective Custody," *Mannheimer Tageblatt*, trans. Francis W. Hoeber, accessed July 2012; Johannes Hoeber, interview for the Walter Phillips Oral History Project; Francis W. Hoeber, "Johannes Höber 'Taken into Protective Custody' by the Nazis, March 13, 1933," available online at http://hoebers.wordpress.com/2012/01/17/johannes-hober-taken-into-protective-custody-by-the-nazis-march-13–1933/, accessed January 2012.

9. Johannes Hoeber, interview for the Walter Phillips Oral History Project.

10. Francis W. Hoeber, "An Affidavit of Support—Key to Escape from Nazi Germany," November 12, 2012, available online at http://hoebers.wordpress.com/. Francis W. Hoeber, interview with the author, May 23, 2012.

11. Johannes Hoeber, "Philadelphia Carries On," *National Municipal Review*, September 1939, accessed July 2012.

12. Johannes Hoeber, oral interview for the Walter Phillips Oral History Project.

13. Ibid.

14. Francis W. Hoeber, interview with the author, June 8, 2012.

15. William L. Batt Jr. to Clark Clifford, May 11, 1948. Clark Clifford Papers, Box 21, William L. Batt Jr., Director of Democratic National Committee Research Division, Correspondence 1948–1949, HSTL, accessed August 2012.

16. Johannes Hoeber to Elfriede Hoeber, July 21, 1948. Hoeber Family Papers, accessed June 2012.

17. Johannes Hoeber, interview with Jerry N. Hess, September 13, 1966, HSTL, accessed March 2011; Frank Kelly, interview with Niel M. Johnson, Independence, Missouri, April 15, 1988, HSTL, accessed June 2012.

18. Bill Batt, oral interview with Jerry N. Hess, July 26, 1966, HSTL, accessed March 2011.

19. Ibid.

20. Shelley Herochik, "A Life of Activism: Initiative Backer Phil Dreyer, From Past to Present," *Portland Business Journal*, September 8, 2002, accessed October 2012.

21. Kelly, interview with Niel M. Johnson.

22. "Current Addresses of Research Division Personnel," 1949, Hoeber Family Papers, accessed July 2012.

23. "Rebels Hold Peak Against Greeks," *Milwaukee Sentinel*, July 5, 1948, accessed January 2013.

24. "Red War Plot Aired in Korea," *Miami News*, July 1, 1948, accessed January 2013.

25. "Palestine Truce Broken as Arabs and Jews Clash," St. *Petersburg Times* via the Associated Press, July 7, 1948, accessed January 2013.

26. "Events Leading to the Blockade of West Berlin," Whistle Stop online collection, HSTL, accessed January 2013.

27. "Truman Backs Marshall's Stand in Berlin Crisis," St. *Petersburg Times* via the United Press, July 2, 1948, accessed January 2013.

28. Daniel F. Harrington, *Berlin on the Brink: The Blockade, the Airlift and the Early Cold War* (Lexington: University Press of Kentucky, 2012), 83.

29. Ibid.

30. Andrei Cherny, *The Candy Bombers: The Untold Story of the Berlin Airlift and America's Finest Hour* (New York: Penguin, 2009), 264.

31. Ibid.

32. Ibid., 265–270.

33. David Sentner, "Berlin Crisis Blamed on Truman's Potsdam Errors," *Milwaukee Sentinel*, July 3, 1948, accessed July 2013.

34. Matt Meyer, "The Stop-Truman Drive," *The Washington Daily News*, July 3, 1948, accessed December 1, 2012, Elsey Box 35, HSTL.

35. Alonzo L. Hamby, *Man of the People: A Life of Harry S. Truman* (Oxford: Oxford University Press, 1995), 446.

36. Ibid.

37. "Hague Wants Truman to Ask Gen. Eisenhower to Make Run," Associated Press, July 6, 1948, accessed January 2013.

38. James A. Hagerty, "Georgia, Virginia Back Eisenhower, Denounce Truman," *New York Times*, July 7, 1948, accessed January 2013.

39. Ibid.

40. Harry Truman to Winston Churchill, July 10, 1948, quoted in Margaret Truman, *Harry S. Truman* (New York: William Morrow, 1973), 17.

41. Nancy Gibbs and Michael Duffy, *The Presidents Club: Inside the World's Most Exclusive Fraternity* (New York: Simon & Schuster, 2012), 60.

42. Ernest B. Vaccaro, "President Honors Bolivar's Memory," Associated Press, July 7, 1948, accessed January 2013; Drew Pearson, "Washington Merry-Go-Round," July 7, 1948, accessed January 2013.

43. Bill Batt to Clark Clifford, June 4, 1948, Presidential Speech File, Box 33, Clark Clifford Papers, HSTL, accessed November 3, 2012.

44. "Why Should Congress Quit," *The Christian Science Monitor*, June 2, 1948, Presidential Speech File, Box 33, Clark Clifford Papers, HSTL, accessed November 3, 2012.

45. Walter Gaston Shotwell, *Life of Charles Sumner* (New York: Thomas Y. Crowell and Company, 1910), 332; James McPherson, *Battle Cry of Freedom: The Civil War*

Era (Oxford: Oxford University Press, 2003), 152–153; David McCullough, *Truman* (New York: Simon & Schuster, 1992), 644.

46. Bill Batt, oral interview with Jerry N. Hess, HSTL.

47. "Should the President Call Congress Back?" June 29, 1948, Box 33, Clark Clifford Papers, HSTL, accessed November 3, 2012.

48. "Cold Figures on Truman Hopes," *U.S. News and World Report*, July 2, 1948, accessed December 1, 2012, Elsey Papers, Box 35, HSTL.

49. Hamby, *Man of the People*, 449–450.

50. Ibid.

51. James T. Patterson, *Mr. Republican: A Biography of Robert A. Taft* (Boston: Houghton Mifflin, 1972), 377–379.

52. Michael Bowen, *The Roots of Modern Conservatism* (Chapel Hill: University of North Carolina Press, 2011), 68.

53. Drew Pearson, "The Washington Merry-Go-Round," *The Washington Post*, July 26, 1948, accessed September 2012.

54. Bowen, *The Roots of Modern Conservatism*, 73–75.

55. George Elsey to Clark Clifford, undated, Clifford Papers, Box 21, Batt File, HSTL, accessed August 25, 2012.

56. "Eisenhower Reiterates Decision to Refuse Presidential Draft," *Montreal Gazette*, July 10, 1948, accessed December 2012.

57. "James Roosevelt Abandons Fight for Eisenhower," *Pittsburgh Post-Gazette*, July 10, 1948, accessed December 2012.

58. Reuven Frank, "1948: "Live . . . From Philadelphia . . . It's the National Conventions," *New York Times*, April 17, 1948, accessed December 2012; Lynne Olson, *The Murrow Boys, Pioneers on the Front Lines of Broadcast Journalism* (New York: Mariner, 1997), 387.

59. David Brinkley, *David Brinkley: A Memoir* (New York: Knopf, 1995), 80–81; James L. Baughman, *Same Time, Same Station: Creating American Television, 1948–1961* (Baltimore: Johns Hopkins University Press, 2007), 131, 139; Mike Conway, *The Origins of Television News in America: The Visualizers of CBS in the 1940s* (New York: Peter Lang, 2009), 249–253.

60. Kelly, *Harry Truman and the Human Family*, 57–59; "New Deal Victory at Democratic National Convention," *U.S. News and World Report*, undated article, Elsey Papers, July 1948 Campaign File, Box 35, HSTL, accessed December 1, 2012.

61. Bill Batt to Clark Clifford, April 20 1948, Batt folder, Box 21, Clifford Papers, HSTL, accessed August 2012; William E. Leuchtenburg, *The White House Looks South: Franklin D. Roosevelt, Harry S. Truman, Lyndon B. Johnson* (Baton Rouge: Louisiana State University Press, 2007), 190–191.

62. Carl Solberg, *Hubert Humphrey: A Biography* (New York: W. W. Norton, 1984), 16.

63. "Barkley Boomed to the Front on Strength of Keynote Talk," North American Newspaper Alliance, July 13, 1948, accessed December 2012.

64. Kelly, *Harry Truman and the Human Family*, 59–60.

65. "Civil Rights Battle Faces Convention," *St. Petersburg Times*, July 14, 1948, accessed January 2013.

66. Nell Dobson Russell, *Minneapolis Spokesman*, July 1945, quoted by Iric Nathanson, "Into the Bright Sunshine—Hubert Humphrey's Civil-Rights Agenda," *MinnPost*, May 23, 2011, accessed January 2013.

67. Solberg, *Hubert Humphrey*, 12–13.

68. Leuchtenburg, *The White House Looks South*, 191.

69. Thomas J. Collins, "Potential Unmet," *Hubert-Humphrey.com*, accessed December 2012, available online at http://www.hubert-humphrey.com/06141998.hhh.

70. Solberg, *Hubert Humphrey*, 1–4.

71. Robert Caro, *The Years of Lyndon Johnson, Master of the Senate* (New York: Knopf, 2002), 443.

72. Ibid.; Solberg, *Hubert Humphrey*, 3–6.

73. Robert Ruark, "Old Alben Drew Convention's Largest Applause," Associated Press, July 14, 1948, accessed December 2012.

74. Alonzo Hamby, "1948 Democratic Convention: The South Secedes Again," *Smithsonian*, August 2008 issue, available online at http://www.smithsonianmag.com/history-archaeology/1948-democratic-convention.html, accessed December 2012.

75. Ibid.

76. Hal Boyle, "'Dear Alben' Brings Unity with Sledge-Hammer Oratory," *Spokane Daily Chronicle* via the Associated Press, July 13, 1948, accessed December 2012.

77. "Truman Praises Barkley Speech," United Press, July 13, 1948, accessed December 2012.

78. Boyle, "'Dear Alben' Brings Unity with Sledge-Hammer Oratory," *Spokane Daily Chronicle*.

79. Eleanor Roosevelt, "My Day," July 14, 1948, United Feature Syndicate, The My Day Project, George Washington University, available online at http://www.gwu.edu/~erpapers/myday/displaydoc.cfm?_y=1948&_f=md001018, accessed December 2012.

80. "Captive Mine Walkout Settled, Contract Signed," *Pittsburgh Post-Gazette*, July 13, 1948, accessed December 2012.

81. "Veteran Kentucky Senator Is Seen as Best Bet to Attract Agreement of Party Majority," United Press, July 13, 1948, accessed December 2012.

82. "Kentuckian Cheered at Convention," *Youngstown Vindicator* via the Associated Press, July 13, 1948, accessed December 2012.

83. Herbert G. Ruffin II, "Vaughan, George L," Blackpast.org, available online

at http://www.blackpast.org/?q=aah/vaughan-george-l-1885–1950; McCullough, *Truman*, 638.

84. McCullough, *Truman*, 638.

85. Leuchtenburg, *The White House Looks South*, 192.

86. Solberg, *Hubert Humphrey*, 17.

87. Hubert Humphrey, 1948 Democratic National Convention Address, July 14, 1948, American Rhetoric, available online at http://www.americanrhetoric.com/speeches/huberthumphey1948dnc.html.

88. Kelly, *Harry Truman and the Human Family*, 60.

89. Caro, *The Years of Lyndon Johnson, Master of the Senate*, 443.

90. Kelly, *Harry Truman and the Human Family*, 60.

91. "Demo Convention Builds up Like Philadelphia in '48," *Sarasota Herald-Tribune* via the Associated Press, August 25, 1968; Jack Bell, "Democrats Vote Down Southern 'Rights' Revolt, Associated Press, July 14, 1948, accessed January 2013.

92. McCullough, *Truman*, 640.

93. Dorothy Thompson, "Wallace's Speech Pure Demagoguery," *The Spokesman-Review*, January 5, 1948, accessed July 2013; Ronald T. Farrar, *Reluctant Servant: The Story of Charles G. Ross* (Columbia: University of Missouri Press, 1969), 196.

94. Francis W. Hoeber, message to the author, July 28, 2013.

95. Francis W. Hoeber, oral interview with the author, June 8, 2012; Francis W. Hoeber, "Celebrating a Civil Rights Milestone in Our Little North Philadelphia Row House—1948," July 30, 2012, available online at http://hoebers.wordpress.com/2012/07/30/celebrating-a-civil-rights-milestone-in-our-little-north-philadelphia-row-house-1948/, accessed July 2012.

96. Anthony Leviero, "Truman to Accept in 'Off-Cuff' Talk, *New York Times*, HSTL, Elsey Papers, Box 35, "1948 Pres Campaign Political Clippings" folder, HSTL, accessed December 1, 2012.

97. Bill Batt to Clark Clifford, July 9, 1948, Presidential Speech File, Box 33, Clark Clifford Papers, HSTL, accessed November 3, 2012.

98. Bill Batt, oral interview with Jerry N. Hess.

99. George Elsey, oral interview with Charles T. Morrissey, February 17, 1964, HSTL, accessed December 2011; George Elsey, *An Unplanned Life: A Memoir* (Columbia: University of Missouri Press, 2005), 164.

100. Matthew J. Connelly, interview with Jerry N. Hess, November 30, 1967, HSTL, accessed December 2011; Charles Murphy, "Some Aspects of President Truman's Speeches for the 1948 Campaign," December 6, 1948, Charles Murphy Papers, Confidential File, Box 50, HSTL, accessed December 15, 2012.

101. "Up From Despair," *Time*, July 26, 1948, accessed October 2012.

102. Ibid.; Frank, "1948: "Live . . . From Philadelphia . . . It's the National Conventions."

103. "'Bolt' Recalls Huge Walkout in 1860," Associated Press, July 15, 1948, accessed January 2013.

104. Murphy, "Some Aspects of President Truman's Speeches for the 1948 Campaign," HSTL.

105. Anthony Leviero, "Departure from Capital," New York Times, July 15, 1948, accessed December 2012; "Up From Despair," Time.

106. "President Waits Call for 4 Hours," New York Times, July 15, 1948, accessed December 2012.

107. Ibid.

108. "Up From Despair," Time.

109. Ibid.

110. McCullough, Truman, 641; Connelly, interview with Jerry N. Hess.

111. McCullough, Truman, 641.

112. Ibid.

113. James Reston, "In a Fighting Mood," New York Times, July 15, 1948, accessed December 2012.

114. Leuchtenberg, The White House Looks South, 192.

115. Elsey, An Unplanned Life, 164.

116. Reston, "In a Fighting Mood," New York Times.

117. Harry Truman, Address in Philadelphia Upon Accepting the Nomination of the Democratic National Convention, July 15, 1948, HSTL, accessed December 2012.

118. Jack Bell, "Truman Challenges GOP," Associated Press, July 15, 1948, accessed January 2013.

119. David C. Bell, interview with Jerry N. Hess, August 20, 1968, HSTL, May 2012.

120. McCullough, Truman, 641.

121. Connelly, interview with Jerry N. Hess.

122. "Harry Can't Lose Recalling Congress, Democrats Believe," Washington Daily News, July 18, 1948, Elsey Papers, Box 35, "1948 Pres Campaign Political Clippings" folder, HSTL, accessed November 2012.

123. "O'Dwyer Promises his Aid to Truman," New York Times, July 25, 1948, accessed December 2012.

124. "School on Wheels," Time, July 26, 1948, accessed October 2012.

125. McCullough, Truman, 644.

126. McCullough, Truman, 643; Clayton Knowles, "Truman Forcing GOP to Say Who Runs Party," New York Times, July 18, 1948.

127. Francis Hoeber, conversation with the author, January 29, 2012.

128. Bill Batt to Clark Clifford, July 15, 1948, Presidential Speech File, Box 33, Clark Clifford Papers, HSTL, accessed November 3, 2012.

129. Bill Batt to Clark Clifford, July 21, 1948, Presidential Speech File, Box 33, Clark Clifford Papers, HSTL, accessed November 3, 2012.

130. McCullough, *Truman*, 570.

131. Richard Wormser, "Harry S. Truman Supports Civil Rights," Jim Crow Stories, PBS, available online at http://www.pbs.org/wnet/jimcrow/stories_events _truman.html, accessed November 2012.

132. This was the same Bull Connor who would become infamous fifteen years later for turning fire hoses and attack dogs on peaceful civil rights demonstrators in Selma.

133. "Former Wright Delegates Plan on Birmingham," *Sarasota Herald-Tribune*, July 15, 1948, accessed December 2012.

134. Leuchtenburg, *The White House Looks South*, 196–197.

135. "Effects of New Deal Victory," *U.S. News and World Report*, August 19, 1948, 1948 Presidential Campaign, July–August 1948 folder, Box 35, Elsey Papers, HSTL, accessed December 1, 2012.

136. "Tumult in Dixie," *Time*, July 26, 1948, accessed January 2013.

137. Ibid.

138. Joseph Crespino, *Strom Thurmond's America* (New York: Hill and Wang, 2012), 70–71.

139. Ibid., 71.

140. "Executive Order 9980: Regulations Governing Fair Employment within the Federal Establishment," signed by Harry Truman on July 26, 1948, HSTL, available online at http://www.trumanlibrary.org/executiveorders/index .php?pid=29&st=&st1=, accessed November 2012.

141. "Desegregation of the Armed Forces," HSTL website, available online at http://www.trumanlibrary.org/whistlestop/study_collections/desegregation /large/index.php, accessed November 2012.

142. John E. Jones, "Message Indicates Civil Rights Program Is Now Closed Issue," *Pittsburgh Post-Gazette*, July 27, 1948, accessed January 2013.

143. "Truman Prods Dixie's Bruises," *The Milwaukee Journal*, July 27, 1948, accessed December 2012.

144. Leuchtenburg, *The White House Looks South*, 207.

145. "Truman Prods Dixie's Bruises," *The Milwaukee Journal*.

146. Ibid.

147. "Bradley Supports Army Segregation," *Spokane Daily Chronicle*, July 28, 1948, accessed December 2012; "Army Is Firm on Race Lines," *The Milwaukee Journal*, July 28, 1948, accessed December 2012.

148. Margaret Truman, *Harry S. Truman*, 17.

149. Jones, "Message Indicates Civil Rights Program Is Now Closed Issue," *Pittsburgh Post-Gazette*.

150. Harry Truman to Mary Jane Truman, July 25, 1948, quoted in Margaret Truman, *Harry S. Truman* (New York: William Morrow, 1973), 17.

151. Batt, interview with Jerry N. Hess, HSTL.

152. Robert J. Donovan, *Conflict and Crisis: The Presidency of Harry S. Truman, 1945–1948* (Columbia: University of Missouri Press, 1996), 411.

153. Harry S. Truman: "Message to the Special Session of the 80th Congress," July 27, 1948. Online by Gerhard Peters and John T. Woolley, *The American Presidency Project*. http://www.presidency.ucsb.edu/ws/?pid=12967.

154. Ibid.

155. Gary A. Donaldson, *Truman Defeats Dewey* (Lexington: University Press of Kentucky, 1999), 170.

156. Johannes Hoeber to Elfriede Hoeber, July 21, 1948. Hoeber Family Papers, accessed June 2012; "A Place to Live," *The Harvard Crimson*, December 14, 1948, accessed January 2013.

157. "A Place to Live," *The Harvard Crimson.*"

158. Bowen, *The Roots of Modern Conservatism*, 72.

159. W. H. Lawrence, "Wallace Accepts, Calling on Allies to Give Up Berlin," *New York Times*, July 24, 1948, accessed January 2013.

160. Ibid.

161. Stewart and Joseph Alsop, "Communists Alone Run Wallace Campaign," *Pittsburgh Post-Gazette*, July 28, 1948, accessed January 2013.

162. "What the Third Party Really Is," *The Milwaukee Journal*, July 26, 1948, accessed January 2013.

163. Arthur Krock, "A Sustaining Element Missing at Philadelphia," *New York Times*, July 26, 1948, accessed January 2013.

164. Donaldson, *Truman Defeats Dewey*, 413; "Ex-Communist Exposes 'Net,'" *Montreal Gazette*, August 4, 1948, accessed March 2013; Douglas B. Cornell, "Spy Hunting House Committee Goes Underground for Quiz of New Witness," United Press, August 6, 1948, accessed March 2013.

165. John Early Haynes and Harvey Klehr, *Early Cold War Spies: The Espionage Trials that Shaped American Politics* (Cambridge: Cambridge University Press, 2006), 72.

166. Richard M. Fried, *Nightmare in Red: The McCarthy Era in Perspective* (Oxford: Oxford University Press, 1991), 9.

167. Bill Batt to Clark Clifford, "Suggested Speech for Dedication of New York's Idlewild Airport," Presidential Speech File, Clark Clifford Papers, Box 33, accessed November 3, 2012.

168. Bill Batt to Clark Clifford, "Dewey's Strategy Vs. The President's," July 27, Presidential Speech File, Clark Clifford Papers, Box 33, HSTL, accessed November 3, 2012.

169. Ibid.

170. Ibid.

171. Ibid.

172. Ibid.

173. "Peace Effort Stressed by President, Dewey," *The Tuscaloosa News*, August 1, 1948, accessed November 2012.

174. Ibid.

175. "Truman, Dewey, Dedicate Huge Field," *Spokane Daily Chronicle*, July 31, 1948, accessed November 2012.

176. Remarks in New York City at the Dedication of Idlewild International Airport, HSTL website, accessed November 2012, available online at http://truman library.org/publicpapers/viewpapers.php?pid=1769.

177. Batt to Clifford, "Dewey's Strategy Vs. The President's."

178. "Truman, Dewey, Dedicate Huge Field," *Spokane Daily Chronicle*.

3. AUGUST

1. Bill Batt to Clark Clifford, August 5, 1948, Batt Correspondence Folder, Box 21, Clifford Papers, HSTL, accessed August 25, 2012.

2. Johannes Hoeber, interview with Jerry N. Hess, Washington, D.C. September 13, 1966, HSTL, accessed April 2012.

3. Anthony Leviero, "From Washington, District of Columbia in 1951," in *National Reporting 1941–1986*, ed. Heinz-Dietrich Fischer and Erika J. Fischer, 61 (Boston: De Gruyter, 2011).

4. Hoeber, interview with Jerry N. Hess, HSTL.

5. Anthony Leviero, "Something New Is Added at the White House," *New York Times*, August 1, 1948, accessed September 2012.

6. "President Votes Early, Flies East," *The Spokane Chronicle* via the Associated Press, August 3, 1948, accessed March 2013.

7. "Testimony of Whittaker Chambers before the House Committee on Un-American Activities," August 3, 1948, University of Missouri–Kansas City Law School, available online at http://law2.umkc.edu/faculty/projects/ftrials/hiss/8-3 testimony.html, accessed November 2012.

8. "Ex-Communist Exposes 'Net,'" *Montreal Gazette*, August 4, 1948, accessed March 2013.

9. Stanley Weintraub, *Final Victory: FDR's Extraordinary World War II Presidential Campaign* (Cambridge, Mass.: Da Capo, 2012), 189.

10. Robert Justin Goldstein, "Prelude to McCarthyism: The Making of a Blacklist," *Prologue* 38, no. 3 (Fall 2006), accessed March 2013.

11. Richard M. Fried, *Nightmare in Red: The McCarthy Era in Perspective* (Oxford: Oxford University Press, 1991), 72.

12. Jack D. Meeks, *From the Belly of the HUAC: The HUAC Investigations of Hollywood,*

1947–1952 (College Park: University of Maryland Press, 2009), 169; Fried, *Nightmare in Red*, 69.

13. Goldstein, "Prelude to McCarthyism"; "The Alien and Sedition Acts," Constitutional Rights Foundation, available online at http://www.crf-usa.org/america-responds-to-terrorism/the-alien-and-sedition-acts.html#.UXh6taKPNNQ, accessed April 2013.

14. David McCullough, *Truman* (New York: Simon & Schuster, 1992), 552.

15. Ibid., 550; Fried, *Nightmare in Red*, 7.

16. Osler L. Peterson, "Henry Wallace: A Divided Mind," *The Atlantic*, August 1, 1948, accessed March 2013; Fried, *Nightmare in Red*, 66.

17. Fried, *Nightmare in Red*, 73; "Ex-Communist Exposes 'Net,'" *Montreal Gazette*.

18. "Testimony of Alger Hiss before the House Committee on Un-American Activities," University of Missouri–Kansas City Law School, available online at http://law2.umkc.edu/faculty/projects/ftrials/hiss/8-5testimony.html, accessed November 2012; Fried, *Nightmare in Red*, 92.

19. Victor A. Navasky, *Naming Names* (New York: Hill and Wang, 2003), 78; Fried, *Nightmare in Red*, 3.

20. "Inquiry Declared Diversion for Inflation Inaction," Associated Press, August 5, 1948, accessed December 2012.

21. "House Prober Gets Track of Air Shipment," *Milwaukee Journal*, August 5, 1948, accessed March 2013.

22. Kent Hunter, "Ferguson Paves Way to Impeach Truman," *Milwaukee Sentinel*, August 7, 1948, accessed April 2013.

23. "Truman Balks Commie Probe," Associated Press, August 6, 1948, accessed March 2013.

24. McCullough, *Truman*, 427.

25. Harry Truman to Mary Jane Truman, August 10, 1948, quoted in Margaret Truman, ed., *Letters Home by Harry Truman* (Columbia: University of Missouri Press, 2003), 222.

26. George Dixon, "Washington Scene," *Milwaukee Sentinel*, August 11, 1948, accessed June 2012.

27. Harry Truman, "The President's News Conference," August 5, 1948, The American Presidency Project, accessed October 2012, available online at http://www.presidency.ucsb.edu/ws/index.php?pid=12973.

28. Harry Truman, August 3, 1948, typed diary of Harry S. Truman, January 6–September 14, 1948, Diaries, Memoirs File, Post-Presidential Files, Truman Papers, HSTL, accessed March 2013; "Dewey Challenged to Beat Inflation," *Lewiston Morning Tribune* via the Associated Press, August 7, 1948, accessed April 2013.

29. Gary A. Donaldson, *Truman Defeats Dewey* (Lexington: University Press of Kentucky, 1999), 170.

30. Harry Truman to Mary Jane Truman, August 1948, quoted in Margaret Truman, *Harry S. Truman* (New York: William Morrow, 1973), 19.

31. Harold I. Gullan, *The Upset that Wasn't: Harry S. Truman and the Crucial Election Victory of 1948* (Chicago: Ivan R. Dee, 1998), 192.

32. "Text of the Taft Statement Upholding GOP Congress," *New York Times*, August 9, 1948, accessed November 2012.

33. Joseph Crespino, *Strom Thurmond's America* (New York: Hill and Wang, 2012), 74–76; "Thurmond Hits Truman, Dewey, Wallace as Leading U.S. to 'Rocks of Totalitarianism,'" *New York Times*, August 12, 1948, accessed August 2012.

34. Ibid.

35. "Wallace Defends Progressive Idea on Radio Network," *The Evening Independent*, August 13, 1948, accessed October 2012.

36. Edwin Pauley, interview with J. R. Fuchs, HSTL, accessed December 2013.

37. Lynne Olson, *Those Angry Days: Roosevelt, Lindbergh, and America's Fight Over World War II, 1939–1941* (New York: Random House, 2013), 187–188.

38. Samuel L. Popkin, *The Candidate: What it Takes to Win—and Hold—The White House* (Oxford: Oxford University Press, 2012), 156.

39. W. McNeil Lowry, interview with Jerry N. Hess, New York, April 23, 1969, HSTL, first accessed August 2012.

40. Clark Clifford, "What Should Be the Main Objectives of the Democratic Campaign," memo to Harry Truman, August 17, 1948, accessed June 2012, Whistle Stop study collection, HSTL online.

41. Popkin, *The Candidate*, 156–157.

42. Lowry, interview with Jerry N. Hess, HSTL.

43. Ibid.

44. Ibid.; Bill Batt to J. Howard McGrath, "Personnel" memo, August 10, 1948, Batt Correspondence file, Box 21, Clifford Papers, HSTL.

45. Johannes Hoeber, interview with Jerry N. Hess, Washington, D.C., September 13, 1966, HSTL.

46. Clark Clifford, *Counsel to the President: A Memoir* (New York: Random House, 1991), 227–228.

47. Lowry, interview with Jerry N. Hess, HSTL.

48. Robert J. Donovan, *Conflict and Crisis: The Presidency of Harry S. Truman, 1945–1948* (Columbia: University of Missouri Press, 1996), 421.

49. Oscar Chapman, interview with Jerry N. Hess, Washington, D.C., April 28, 1972, HSTL, accessed September 2011, available online at http://www.truman library.org/oralhist/chapman3.htm#91.

50. "Statement by the President," August 16, 1948, Elsey Papers, Box 23, HSTL, accessed December 1, 2013.

51. "Truman Signs Bill, Flays Congress," *Daytona Beach Herald*, August 17, 1948, accessed March 2013.

52. "Cancer Takes Life of Babe Ruth, 53," Associated Press, August 17, 1948, accessed March 2013.

53. "Climax in Greece," *New York Times*, August 10, 1948, accessed May 2012.

54. James D. White, "Rebel March in China a Steady One," August 9, 1948, accessed June 2013.

55. "Allies in Berlin Counter-block Soviet Money," *The Pittsburgh Press*, August 11, 1948, accessed April 2013.

56. "Korean Rule Is Recognized," *Milwaukee Journal*, August 13, 1948, accessed April 2013.

57. "Shift of Harlem Voters from Wallace Reported," unknown newspaper, August 10, 1948, J. Howard McGrath Papers, Clippings — Senator — DNC Chairman folder, box 61, HSTL, accessed December 15, 2012.

58. Clifford, "What Should Be the Main Objectives of the Democratic Campaign."

59. Bill Batt to Clark Clifford, July 6, 1948, Batt Correspondence file, Box 21, Clifford Papers, HSTL; Fried, *Nightmare in Red*, 20.

60. Ernest W. Roberts to Harry Truman, August 1948, quoted in Michael Gardner et al., *Harry Truman and Civil Rights: Moral Courage and Political Risks* (Carbondale: Southern Illinois University Press, 2003), 130.

61. Harry Truman to Ernest W. Roberts, August 18, 1948, Teaching American History, available online at http://teachingamericanhistory.org/library/index.asp?document=591, accessed March 2012.

62. "Truman Balks Commie Probe," Associated Press.

63. Daniel F. Harrington, *Berlin on the Brink: The Blockade, the Airlift and the Early Cold War* (Lexington: University Press of Kentucky, 2012), 159–160.

64. "1948 Presidential Campaign Stops for Harry S. Truman's Whistle Stop campaign," HSTL, accessed June 2012.

65. Clifford, "What Should Be the Main Objectives of the Democratic Campaign."

66. Ibid.

67. Bill Batt, Johannes Hoeber, and Research Division staff, Files of the Facts VII: Labor, Batt Correspondence file, Box 21, Clifford Papers, HSTL.

68. Ibid.; Margaret Truman, *Harry S. Truman*, 321, "Truman Versus Lewis," *The Harvard Crimson*, November 19, 1946, accessed April 2013; Robert H. Ferrell, *Harry S. Truman: A Life* (Newtown, Conn.: American Political Biography Press, 2007), 232.

69. Jonathan Daniels, *The Man of Independence* (Columbia: University of Missouri Press, 1998), 326.

70. Aaron Brenner et al., *The Encyclopedia of Strikes in American History* (Armonk, N.Y.: M. E. Sharpe, 2009), xxiii; Alden Whitman, "Harry S. Truman: Decisive President," *New York Times*, undated, accessed April 2013.

71. Clifford, *Counsel to the President*, 88.

72. McCullough, *Truman*, 597.

73. "Whitney Tells How He Made Up With Truman After Dispute," *Toledo Blade* via the Associated Press, February 7, 1949, accessed September 2012.

74. Paul Martin, "Ike Blossomed Late in Life But Never Stopped Until He Reached Presidency," *Niagara Falls Gazette* via Gannett News Service, November 8, 1956, accessed October 2012.

75. Weintraub, *Final Victory*, 115.

76. Detroit, Michigan Folder, Box 1, Barriere Papers, HSTL, accessed December 1, 2012.

77. "Domestic Policy," American Experience, http://www.pbs.org/wgbh/ameri canexperience/features/general-article/truman-domestic/, accessed March 2013.

78. Charles Murphy, "Some Aspects of the Preparation of President Truman's Speeches for the 1948 Campaign," Box 82, 1948 Campaign folder, Charles Murphy Papers, HSTL, accessed June 9, 2012.

79. Ibid.

80. Ibid.

81. "For sale Presidential Yacht—USS Williamsburg used by Harry S. Truman," Agent4stars.com, accessed March 2013.

82. *Dear Harry, Truman's Mailroom, 1945–1953: The Truman Administration Through Correspondence with Everyday Americans* (Mechanicsburg, Pa.: Stackpole Books, 1999), excerpt in the *Denver Post*, undated, accessed March 2013.

83. "Rival Parties Debate Record Set by Congress," Associated Press, August 18, 1948, accessed April 2013.

84. "Truman Cruise to Begin Friday," *Milwaukee Journal*, August 17, 1948, accessed April 2013.

85. "Reporters Pursue Truman's Yacht," *Pittsburgh Press*, August 21, 1948, accessed October 2012.

86. "Truman Is Working on Labor Day Talk," *Lewiston Daily Sun* via the Associated Press, August 23, 1948, accessed October 2012.

87. "Truman Voids Red Consul's Credentials," *Sarasota Herald-Tribune*, August 25, 1948, accessed April 2013; "Recovery Predicted for Mrs. Kasenkina," United Press, August 25, 1948, accessed April 2013; Richard K. O'Malley, "Red Tension Kept Alive by Gunplay," Associated Press, August 25, 1948, accessed April 2013.

88. "Many Speed to Altar to Beat Draft," *Youngstown Vindicator* via the Associated Press, August 23, 1948, accessed April 2013.

89. The United States Lighthouse Society, Chesapeake Chapter, "Blakistone Island Light," available online at http://www.cheslights.org/heritage/blakistone .htm, accessed April 2013; "Truman Readies for U.S. Trip," *Sarasota Herald-Tribune* via the Associated Press, August 30, 1948, accessed April 2013.

90. Ronald T. Farrar, *Reluctant Servant: The Story of Charles G. Ross* (Columbia: University of Missouri Press, 1969), 191; "Truman Readies for U.S. Trip," *Sarasota Herald-Tribune.*

91. Frank Kelly, "How the President Can Reach the People," July 22, 1948, Political File, Box 21: Misc. Clifford Papers, HSTL, accessed August 25, 2012.

92. Murphy, "Some Aspects of the Preparation of President Truman's Speeches for the 1948 Campaign," HSTL.

4. SEPTEMBER

1. Brian Burnes, *Harry S. Truman: His Life and Times* (Kansas City, Mo.: Kansas City Books, 2003), 166.

2. "Mowing 'Em Down," *Time*, September 27, 1948, accessed October 2012.

3. David McCullough, *Truman* (New York: Simon & Schuster, 1992), 653.

4. James K. Libbey, *Dear Alben: Mr. Barkley of Kentucky* (Lexington: University Press of Kentucky, 1979), 97.

5. Franklin D. Mitchell, *Harry S. Truman and the News Media: Contentious Relations, Belated Respect* (Columbia: University of Missouri Press, 1998), 174.

6. Johannes Hoeber, interview with Jerry N. Hess, Washington, D.C., September 13, 1966, HSTL, accessed April 2012.

7. Donald S. Dawson, interview with James Fuchs, Washington, D.C., August 8, 1977, HSTL, accessed May 2012, available online at http://www.truman library.org/oralhist/dawsond.htm; Cabell Phillips, *The Truman Presidency* (London: Macmillan, 1966), 232.

8. Irwin Ross, *The Loneliest Campaign: The Truman Victory of 1948* (Portsmouth, N.H.: Greenwood Publishing Group, 1977), 175.

9. Phillips, *The Truman Presidency*, 232.

10. Harry Easley, interview with J. R. Fuchs, Webb City, Missouri, August 24, 1967, HSTL, accessed November 2012; "Biographical Note: Roy Turner," 100 Years of Oklahoma Governors, Oklahoma Department of Libraries.

11. Arrell M. Gibson, *Oklahoma: A History of Five Centuries* (Norman: University of Oklahoma Press, 1981), 235.

12. Jack Redding, *Inside the Democratic Party* (Indianapolis: Bobbs Merrill, 1958), 263.

13. Margaret Truman, *Harry S. Truman*, 20.

14. Phillips, *The Truman Presidency*, 233.

15. Eleanor Roosevelt, "My Day," September 4, 1948, accessed May 2013; David L. Chappell, *A Stone of Hope: Prophetic Religion and the Death of Jim Crow* (Chapel Hill: University of North Carolina Press, 2007), 34–36.

16. Roosevelt, "My Day," September 4, 1948.

17. "Rear Platform and Other Informal Remarks in Michigan and Ohio," Pub-

lic Papers of the Presidents, HSTL via The American Presidency Project; Monte M. Poen, ed., *Letters Home by Harry Truman* (New York: G. P. Putnam's Sons, 1984), 220.

18. Poen, *Letters Home by Harry Truman*, 220.

19. Ibid.

20. Harry S. Truman, "Labor Day Address in Cadillac Square, Detroit," September 6, 1948. Online by Gerhard Peters and John T. Woolley, The American Presidency Project. http://www.presidency.ucsb.edu/ws/?pid=12988.

21. Barriere Papers, Box 1, Files of the Facts folder, HSTL, accessed November 3, 2012.

22. Truman, "Labor Day Address in Cadillac Square, Detroit," The American Presidency Project.

23. Ibid; Daniels, *The Man of Independence*, 334.

24. Ibid.

25. Murphy, "Some Aspects of the Preparation of President Truman's Speeches for the 1948 Campaign," HSTL.

26. Aida D. Donald, *Citizen Soldier: A Life of Harry S. Truman* (New York: Basic Books, 2012), 9 and 27.

27. Truman, "Labor Day Address in Cadillac Square, Detroit," The American Presidency Project.

28. "Rear Platform and Other Informal Remarks in Michigan and Ohio," Public Papers of the Presidents, HSTL.

29. Ibid.

30. Ibid.

31. Murphy, "Some Aspects of the Preparation of President Truman's Speeches for the 1948 Campaign," HSTL.

32. "Truman to Speak at 'Whistle Stops,'" *New York Times*, September 7, 1948, accessed March 2013.

33. Ibid; "Rear Platform and Other Informal Remarks in Michigan and Ohio," Public Papers of the Presidents, HSTL; "Truman in Michigan," *Pittsburgh Press*, September 8, 1948, accessed March 2013.

34. Carter Townes, Crowd Greets President with Cheers," *Toledo Blade*, September 7, 1948, accessed March 2013.

35. Ibid.

36. Ibid.; List to board President's special train, Toledo, Ohio, September 6, 1948. President's Secretary's Files, Truman Papers, HSTL, accessed March 2013.

37. Press release, speech of Thomas E. Dewey, September 21, 1948, Clipping File, Democratic National Committee Records, HSTL, accessed March 2013.

38. "Stassen Assails Truman Record as a 'Failure,'" *Lewiston Daily Sun* via the Associated Press, September 7, 2013, accessed March 2013.

39. Elmo Roper, "It's Dewey Over Truman by a Landslide," *The Evening Independent*, September 9, 1948, accessed November 2012.

40. Andrei Cherny, *The Candy Bombers: The Untold Story of the Berlin Airlift and America's Finest Hour* (New York: Penguin, 2009), 381–382.

41. Ibid., 382.

42. Drew Pearson, "Washington Merry Go-Round," September 18, 1948, Elsey Papers, Box 35, HSTL, accessed December 1, 2012.

43. Cherny, *The Candy Bombers*, 383; Margaret Truman, *Harry S. Truman*, 21; Ross, *The Loneliest Campaign*, 176.

44. Pearson, "Washington Merry Go-Round."

45. Harry Truman to Mary Jane Truman, September 11, 1948, quoted in Poen, *Letters Home by Harry Truman*, 273; Typed diary of Harry S. Truman, January 6–September 14, 1948, Diaries, Memoirs File, Post-Presidential Files, Truman Papers, HSTL, accessed March 2013.

46. Typed diary of Harry S. Truman, January 6–September 14, 1948.

47. Daniel F. Harrington, *Berlin on the Brink: The Blockade, the Airlift and the Early Cold War* (Lexington: University Press of Kentucky, 2012), 171–173.

48. Typed diary of Harry S. Truman, January 6–September 14, 1948.

49. Ibid.

50. "Asia Seizure Aim of Reds, Bevin Warns," *Pittsburgh Post-Gazette*, September 15, 1948, accessed April 2013.

51. "Truman Invites Law Invasion," *The Pittsburgh Press*, September 15, 1948, accessed April 2013.

52. Thomas L. Stokes, "Despite Tough Sledding Truman Shows Real Drive," *Spokane Daily Chronicle*, September 15, 1948, accessed April 2013.

53. "Text of 1948 Campaign Speeches," Whistle Stop Study Collection, HSTL; "The Roaring Presses," *Time*, September 20, 1948, accessed May 2012.

54. "Truman Starts Today on Long Campaign Tour," *St. Petersburg Times* via the Associated Press, September 17, 1948, accessed April 2013.

55. "Family Life," Miller Center at University of Virginia, accessed May 2013, available online at www.millercenter.org; McCullough, *Truman*, 703.

56. Charles Ross, "How Truman Did It," *Collier's*, December 25, 1948, accessed December 2012.

57. Scott Charton, "Truman Supporter Still Relishes Victory and Handshake," *Kansas City Star*, November 2, 1998, accessed May 2013.

58. Ross, "How Truman Did It," *Collier's*.

59. "Democrats Acres of Folks," *Time*, September 27, 1948, accessed May 2013.

60. William Batt Jr., oral interview with Jerry N. Hess, July 26, 1966, HSTL, available online at http://www.trumanlibrary.org/oralhist/battw.htm, accessed May 2011; George Elsey, interview with Jerry N. Hess, July 10, 1969, Washington, D.C., accessed October 2011, available online at www.trumanlibrary.org; Clark Clifford interview with Jerry N. Hess, HSTL, Washington, D.C., May 10, 1971, accessed September 2011, available online at http://www.trumanlibrary.org.

61. Clifford, interview with Jerry N. Hess.

62. Ross, *The Loneliest Campaign*, 195–196.

63. Donald S. Dawson, interview with James Fuchs, August 8, 1977, Washington, D.C., HSTL, accessed December 2011, available online at www.trumanlibrary.org; Charles Murphy, interview with Jerry N. Hess, May 21, 1969, Washington, D.C., HSTL, accessed December 2011, available online at www.trumanlibrary.org.

64. "The Freedom Train," The Lincoln Highway National Museum and Archives, available online at http://www.lincoln-highway-museum.org/FT/FT-04-Song-Index.html, accessed May 2013.

65. "Rear Platform and Other Informal Remarks in Pennsylvania and Ohio," Public Papers of the Presidents, HSTL, accessed May 2013.

66. "President Re-Dedicates Freedom Train," *The Pittsburgh Press*, September 17, 1948, accessed May 2013; Robert Taylor, "Truman Urges Peace Effort," *The Pittsburgh Press*, September 17, 1948, accessed May 2013.

67. Taylor, "Truman Urges Peace Effort."

68. "Mowing 'Em Down," *Time*; "Rear Platform and Other Informal Remarks in Pennsylvania and Ohio," HSTL.

69. "Berlin Russians Fight to Bar U.N.," *The Pittsburgh Press* via the United Press, September 17, 1948, accessed May 2013.

70. "Mowing 'Em Down," *Time*; Charles B. Cleveland, "Col. Jack Arvey: A Master Politician," *Illinois Issues*, November 1977, available online at http://www.lib.niu.edu/1977/ii771134.html, accessed May 2013.

71. "Democrats Acres of Folks," *Time*.

72. Libbey, *Dear Alben*, 97–98.

73. Steven R. Goldzwig, *Truman's Whistle-Stop Campaign* (College Station: Texas A&M University Press, 2008).

74. Daniels, *The Man of Independence*, 170.

75. "Harry S. Truman: His Life and Times," HSTL website, available online at http://www.trumanlibrary.org/lifetimes/senate.htm.

76. "Effects of New Deal Victory," *U.S. News and World Report*, August 19, 1948, 1948 Presidential Campaign, July–August 1948 folder, Box 35, Elsey Papers, HSTL, accessed December 1, 2012.

77. McCullough, *Truman*, 669.

78. Clifford, *Counsel to the President*, 227–228.

79. "Mowing 'em Down," *Time*.

80. Harry Truman, Address at Dexter, Iowa, on the Occasion of the National Plowing Match, Public Papers of the Presidents, HSTL, accessed August 2012.

81. Ibid.

82. Ibid.

83. Ibid.

84. Ibid.

85. Oscar Chapman, interview with Jerry N. Hess, HSTL, Washington, DC, April 28, 1972, accessed September 2011, available online at http://www.truman library.org/oralhist/chapman3.htm#91.

86. Ibid.

87. Thomas L. Stokes, "Mood of America," *New York Times Magazine*, October 17, 1948, accessed June 2013.

88. Chapman, interview with Jerry N. Hess.

89. William J. Bray, "Recollections of the 1948 Campaign," HSTL, accessed May 2012, available online at www.trumanlibrary.org.

90. Ibid.; "Truman Sheds His Coat to Dine on Fried Chicken," *The Milwaukee Journal*, September 19, 1948, accessed April 2013.

91. "Mowing 'Em Down," *Time*.

92. Margaret Truman, *Harry S. Truman*, 22.

93. Ibid.

94. Joseph Alsop, "Truman Fails to Stir Farm Belt Interest," *Pittsburgh Post-Gazette*, September 22, 1948, accessed April 2013.

95. Harrington, *Berlin on the Brink*, 175, 178.

96. Bray, "Recollections of the 1948 Campaign," HSTL.

97. W. H. Lawrence, "President to Stump All Day in State After Parade Through Denver; Busy Colorado Day Set for President," *New York Times*, September 20, 1948, accessed August 2012.

98. Clayton Knowles, "Barkley Returns 'Had Enough' Jibe," *New York Times*, September 21, 1948, accessed January 2013.

99. Libbey, *Dear Alben*, 97.

100. James C. Humes, *My Fellow Americans: Presidential Addresses that Shaped History* (Westport, Conn.: Praeger, 1992), 178; James David Barber, *The Pulse of Politics: Electing Presidents in the Media Age* (New Brunswick, N.J.: Transaction Publishers, 1980), 58.

101. Gary A. Donaldson, *Truman Defeats Dewey* (Lexington: University Press of Kentucky, 1999), 172.

102. Cabell Phillips, "Truman and Dewey in Trim for the Campaign," *New York Times*, September 5, 1948, Elsey Papers, Box 35, HSTL, accessed December 1, 2012.

103. E. F. Hutton to Herbert Brownell, September 30, 1948, quoted in Michael Bowen, *The Roots of Modern Conservatism* (Chapel Hill: University of North Carolina Press, 2011), 74.

104. David Jordan, *FDR, Dewey, and the Election of 1944* (Bloomington: Indiana University Press, 2012), 281.

105. "Above the Battle," *Washington Post*, September 13, 1948, Box 35, Elsey Papers, HSTL, accessed December 1, 2012.

106. Bray, "Recollections of the 1948 Campaign," HSTL.

107. "Address at the State Capitol in Denver," September 20, 1948, Public Papers of the Presidents, HSTL, accessed October 2013, available online at http://www.trumanlibrary.org/publicpapers/index.php?pid=1822.

108. Ibid.

109. Ibid.

110. Ibid.

111. Ibid.

112. Ibid.

113. "Bipartisan Bloc Hit by Wallace," *The Spokesman Review* via the Associated Press, September 21, 1948, accessed April 2013.

114. Ibid.

115. Stokes, "Mood of America," *New York Times Magazine*.

116. Eben A. Ayers, interview with Jerry N. Hess, Washington, D.C., January 12, 1967, HSTL, accessed June 2012.

117. "Summary of news coverage of campaign trip in Utah," September 22, 1948. President's Secretary's Files, Truman Papers, HSTL, accessed April 20, 2013; Richard Shaw, "1948: A Trifecta of State, Local and National Politics," *Sun Advertiser*, undated, accessed July 2013.

118. "The Opening Speeches," *Pittsburgh Post-Gazette*, September 22, 1948, accessed April 2012.

119. "Russians Revive Plea for End of Occupation," *Montreal Gazette*, September 22, 1948, accessed April 2012.

120. Harry Truman, "Truman Speech at City Hall in San Francisco," September 22, 1948; "Rear Platform and Other Informal Remarks in Nevada and California," HSTL, accessed October 2012.

121. Ibid.

122. Bray, "Recollections of the 1948 Campaign."

123. Truman, "Truman Speech at City Hall in San Francisco."

124. Ibid.

125. "Dewey and Truman Blow Hot As Campaign Moves West," United Press, September 22, 1948, accessed April 2013.

126. Ibid.

127. "Rear Platform and Other Informal Remarks in Nevada and California," HSTL.

128. Batt to Clifford and Murphy, September 1948, Batt Correspondence File, Box 21, Clifford Papers, HSTL, accessed August 25, 2012.

129. "Address at the Gilmore Stadium in Los Angeles," Public Papers of the Presidents, HSTL, September 23, 1948, available online at http://www.trumanlibrary.org/publicpapers/index.php?pid=1955, accessed April 2013.

130. Amity Shlaes, "Calvin Coolidge and the Moral Case for Economy," *Imprimis* (February 2013), accessed February 2013.

131. Ibid.

132. *The Southeast Missourian*, September 24, 1948, accessed April 2013.

133. Harry Truman, "Address at Phoenix, Arizona," September 24, 1948, Public Papers of the Presidents, HSTL, accessed April 2013.

134. Harry Truman, Rear Platform and Other Informal Remarks in New Mexico and Texas, Public Papers of the Presidents, HSTL.

135. Ibid.

136. Ibid.

137. "Dewey and Truman Talk Inflation and Power," Associated Press, September 26, 1948, accessed April 2013.

138. Margaret Truman, *Harry S. Truman*, 33–34.

139. Ibid, 34.

140. Bray, "Recollections of the 1948 Campaign," HSTL.

141. "Thurmond Sees Electoral Victory," *Toledo Blade* via United Press, September 26, 1948, accessed April 2013.

142. "Barkley Seeks Votes in South," *Kentucky New Era*, September 28, 1948, accessed April 2013.

143. Joseph Crespino, *Strom Thurmond's America* (New York: Hill and Wang, 2012), 79; "Thurmond Accepts Texas Nomination," *News and Courier*, September 10, 1948, accessed May 2013; "Anti-Truman Drive Mounting in South Nets 45 Electors," *New York Times*, September 12, 1948, accessed March 2013.

144. Arthur Krock, "Truman Woos Liberals but Wars on Dixiecrats," *New York Times*, September 25, 1948, accessed May 2013.

145. Michael Bowen, reader review comment of *Whistle Stop* manuscript, October 2013.

146. Donald S. Dawson, interview with James Fuchs, August 8, 1977, Washington, D.C., HSTL, accessed May 2012.

147. Ibid.

148. Harry Truman, Address at El Paso, Texas, September 25, 1948, HSTL, accessed May 2013.

149. Ibid.

150. Krock, "Truman Woos Liberals but Wars on Dixiecrats"; "Congress Would Destroy U.S. Rights, Says Truman," *Spokane Daily Chronicle*, September 27, 1948, accessed May 2013.

151. "Congress Would Destroy U.S. Rights, Says Truman," *Spokane Daily Chronicle*.

152. Ibid.

153. "Berlin Cold War Moves to Highly Explosive Stage," *Spokane Daily Chronicle* via the Associated Press, September 27, 1948, accessed May 2013.

154. William Batt Jr. to Clark Clifford, "President's Speech in Los Angeles," September 15, 1948, HSTL, accessed August 2012.

155. Ibid.

156. Ibid.

157. Ibid.

158. Philleo Nash, interview with Jerry N. Hess, HSTL, Washington, D.C., October 18, 1966, accessed September 2011, available online at http://www .trumanlibrary.org/oralhist/nash7.htm#370.

159. Ibid.

160. Richard Norton Smith, *Thomas E. Dewey and His Times* (New York: Simon & Schuster, 1982), 508.

161. Bray, "Recollections of the 1948 Campaign," HSTL.

162. "Communists Solid for Dewey," *New York Times*, September 28, 1948, accessed April 2013.

163. Ibid.

164. Ibid.

165. Margaret Truman, *Harry S. Truman*, 21.

166. Ibid; Bray, "Recollections of the 1948 Campaign"; "Cattleman's Triumph," *Time*, January 27, 1947, accessed November 2012; Truman campaign schedule with Research Division fact-finding assignment, undated, John E. Barriere Papers, HSTL, accessed November 4, 2012; Redding, *Inside the Democratic Party*, 273; Jay Mondy, *Time to Lay By* (Bloomington, Ind.: Trafford Publishing, 2010), 163.

167. Gene Curtis, "Only in Oklahoma: Welcome Mat Rolled Out for Truman Tour," *Tulsa World*, September 7, 2007, accessed April 2013.

168. Harry Truman, Address at Skelly Stadium, Tulsa, Oklahoma, September 29, 1948, Public Papers of the Presidents, HSTL via The American Presidency Project.

169. Ibid.

170. Ben Shapiro, *Project President: Bad Hair and Botox on the Road to the White House* (Nashville, Tenn.: Thomas Nelson, 2008), 16.

171. Curtis, "Only in Oklahoma," *Tulsa World*.

172. George F. Jenks, "Dewey Expects to Reveal Stand on Foreign Policy," *Toledo Blade*, September 29, 1948, accessed May 2013.

173. "Dewey Asks Stand Against Aggression," *Southeast Missourian* via the Associated Press, October 1, 1948, accessed May 2013.

174. Hoeber, interview with Jerry N. Hess, HSTL; Harry Truman, "Address in Louisville, Kentucky," September 30, 1948, Public Papers of the Presidents, HSTL, accessed October 2012.

175. Truman, "Address in Louisville, Kentucky," HSTL.

176. "Vishinsky in Violent Attack," *Southeast Missourian* via the Associated Press, October 1, 1948, accessed May 2013.

5. OCTOBER

1. Daniel F. Harrington, *Berlin on the Brink: The Blockade, the Airlift and the Early Cold War* (Lexington: University Press of Kentucky, 2012), 188.

2. Brian Burnes, *Harry S. Truman: His Life and Times* (Kansas City, Mo.: Kansas City Star Books, 2003), 164–165.

3. Clark Clifford to William L. Batt Jr., October 1, 1948, CCP, Box 21, Batt Correspondence 1948–1949, HSTL.

4. "Why They Came Out," *Time*, October 18, 1948, accessed April 2012.

5. "National Affairs: Dogi Cligin & the West," *Time*, October 4, 1948, accessed October 2012.

6. "Scripps-Howard Newspapers Support Dewey Campaign," *Lewiston Evening Journal*, October 14, 1948, accessed June 2012.

7. David M. Jordan, *FDR, Dewey, and the Election of 1944* (Bloomington: Indiana University Press, 2011), 235.

8. Ibid., 244.

9. Ibid., 251.

10. "Dewey Held to Net 14 States," *New York Times*, October 4, 1948, Elsey Papers Box 35, HSTL, October 6, 1948, accessed December 2012.

11. George Gallup, "Dewey Now Leads in 11 of 12 Populous Eastern States," *Philadelphia Evening Bulletin*, Elsey Papers Box 35, HSTL, October 6, 1948, accessed December 2012.

12. "Fireworks," undated, the Papers of Chester Heslep, the Speeches of Harry Truman 1948, box 2, HSTL, accessed December 2012.

13. "Large Crowd to See President, Changes Plans for Brief Stop," *The Daily News* [Batavia, N.Y.], October 9, 1948, accessed December 2012.

14. Mark Graczyk, "Hidden History: Harry & Ike Visit Batavia, 1948–1952," *The Daily News Online*, November 4, 2012, available online at http://thedaily newsonline.com/blogs/mark_my_words/article_ee98a1ae-1737-11e2-9a03-001 a4bcf887a.html, accessed December 2012.

15. Ibid.

16. "Dulles was Not Informed of Truman's Vinson Plan," *New York Times*, October 9, 1948, accessed May 2013.

17. "Mission Idea Denounced by Thurmond," *The Spartansburg Herald* via the Associated Press, October 11, 1948, accessed May 2013.

18. "Presidential Candidates to Speak Tonight on Labor Issues," Associated Press, October 11, 1948, accessed May 2013.

19. David Lawrence, "Truman's Plan to Send Vinson to Moscow Called One of His Worst Blunders," *Toledo Blade*, October 10, 1948, accessed May 2013; Harrington, *Berlin on the Brink*, 190–195.

20. Paul Gallico, untitled column, *Toledo Blade* via the Associated Press, October 11, 1948, accessed May 2013.

21. "London Paper Says Truman Blundered," *Lewiston Daily Sun* via the Associated Press, October 11, 1948, accessed May 2013.

22. Reader letter to the *Pittsburgh Post-Gazette*, October 19, 1948, accessed December 2013.

23. "President, GOP Nominee Both Start New Campaign Tours," United Press, October 11, 1948, accessed May 2013.

24. Harry Truman, "Rear Platform and Other Remarks in Ohio," HSTL, accessed May 2013.

25. Ibid.

26. Martin Halpern, *UAW Politics in the Cold War Era* (Albany: State University of New York Press, 1988), 204.

27. Ibid.

28. Ibid.

29. "Taft Tells South it Gains with GOP," *New York Times*, October 13, 1948, accessed May 2013.

30. Bette Richards (née Bunker), e-mails to the author, June 8 and June 13, 2013.

31. Clark Clifford, interview with Jerry N. Hess, Washington, D.C., May 10, 1971, accessed September 2011, available online at http://www.trumanlibrary.org.

32. Clark Clifford, *Counsel to the President: A Memoir* (New York: Random House, 1991), 235–236; William J. Bray, Recollections of the 1948 Campaign, accessed May 2012, available online at www.trumanlibrary.org.

33. "If I Hadn't Been There," *Time*, October 23, 1948, accessed June 2013.

34. "Dewey Lashes at Meddling by Truman," *The Milwaukee Sentinel*, October 13, 1948, accessed May 2013.

35. "U.S. Calls Russia 'Wrecker of the World,'" Associated Press, October 13, 1948, accessed May 2013.

36. Anne Applebaum, *Gulag: A History* (New York: Anchor, 2004), 44, 92; S. Usher, "Confessions to the Lie," *The Manitoba Ensign*, March 26, 1949, accessed May 2013.

37. "Russians Yearn to Cooperate," *The Milwaukee Sentinel*, October 13, 1948, accessed May 2013.

38. "Airlift Set for Winter," The Associated Press, October 13, 1948, accessed May 2013.

39. "Truman Assails Dewey's Stand on Atomic Energy," *St. Petersburg Times*, October 15, 1948, accessed May 2013.

40. Harry Truman, speech in Milwaukee, October 14, 1948, HSTL via the American Presidency Project, accessed May 2013.

41. Ibid.

42. George Gallup, "Thurmond Leading in 4 States; Truman, Dewey in Hot Race in 2," Associated Press, October 15, 1948, accessed May 2013.

43. Irwin Ross, *The Loneliest Campaign: The Truman Victory of 1948* (Portsmouth: Greenwood Publishing Group, 1977), 64.

44. Charles Ross, "How Truman Did It," *Collier's*, December 25, 1948, accessed December 2012.

45. Ibid.; George Elsey, *An Unplanned Life: A Memoir* (Columbia: University of Missouri Press, 2005), 165–166; India Edwards, interview with Jerry N. Hess, Washington, D.C., January 16, 1969, HSTL, accessed October 2012.

46. Ross, *The Loneliest Campaign*, 221.

47. Elsey, *An Unplanned Life*, 170.

48. Cynthia Harrison, *On Account of Sex: The Politics of Women's Issues, 1945–1948* (Berkeley: University of California Press, 1988), 54–55.

49. Ibid., 55.

50. Edwards, interview with Jerry N. Hess, HSTL.

51. Ibid.

52. George Elsey, oral interview with Charles T. Morrissey, February 17, 1964, HSTL, accessed December 2011.

53. Ross, "How Truman Did It"; Clifford, interview with Jerry N. Hess.

54. "Text of Executive Order," *New York Times*, October 15, 1948, accessed June 2013.

55. Robert K. Dean, "The Quiet Death of Universal Military Training: How America Lost an Opportunity to Close Civil-Military Gap," published online by the Virginia Military Institute, February 2008, accessed June 2013, available online at www.vmi.edu.

56. Russell Kirk, Jeffrey Nelson, and James McClellan, *The Political Principles of Robert A. Taft* (Edison, N.J.: Transaction Publishers, 2010), 79–80.

57. "U.S., British Combine Airlift Units as Guns Heard in Berlin," *Lewiston Morning Tribune*, October 15, 1948, accessed June 2013.

58. Wes Gallacher, "Clay Says Way to Halt Soviets is By Firmness," Associated Press, October 15, 1948, accessed June 2013.

59. "Reds Declare Move Forced by 'Smuggling,'" Associated Press, October 17, 1948, accessed June 2013.

60. Louis Nevin, "3 Powers Denounce Russ, Soviets Tighten Blockade," Associated Press, October 17, 1948, accessed June 2013.

61. Anthony Leviero, "Truman Defends Vinson Trip Idea, Bars Appeasement," *New York Times*, October 18, 1948, accessed May 2013.

62. Ibid.

63. Harry Truman, Address in Miami at the American Legion Convention, October 18, 1948, Public Papers of the Presidents, HSTL, accessed May 2013.

64. Ibid.

65. Ibid.

66. Ibid.

67. Ibid.

68. Ibid.

69. Ibid.

70. James David Barber, *The Pulse of Politics: Electing Presidents in the Media Age* (New Brunswick, N.J.: Transaction Publishers, 1980), 50.

71. Harry Truman to Mary Jane Truman, October 20, 1948, quoted in Monte M. Poen, ed., *Letters Home by Harry Truman* (New York: G. P. Putnam's Sons, 1984), 226–227.

72. Carl Anthony, "Harry Truman & Tallulah Bankhead Bond over Bourbon . . . and Civil Rights," CarlAnthony.com, August 22, 2011, accessed November 2012; Anthony Leviero, "Truman Declares Democrats Design Better Life in U.S.," *New York Times*, October 22, 1948, accessed June 2013; "I'm for Truman, He's Human, Tallulah Bankhead Says," United Press, October 22, 1948, accessed June 2013.

73. Harry Truman, "Address on Radio Program Sponsored by the International Ladies Garment Workers Union Campaign Committee," Public Papers of the Presidents, HSTL via the American Presidency Project.

74. Harry Truman, "Rear Platform Remarks in Pennsylvania," October 23, 1948, accessed June 2013, available online at www.trumanlibrary.org.

75. "Dewey Starts Final Tour Monday," *St. Petersburg Times*, October 23, 1948, accessed June 2013.

76. Harry Truman, "Address in Johnstown, Pennsylvania," October 23, 1948, HSTL via the American Presidency Project, accessed June 2013.

77. Ibid.

78. Edwin Bleachler, "100,000 Cheer Truman on 10-Mile Parade Route," *Pittsburgh Press*, October 24, 1948, accessed June 2013.

79. Harry Truman, "Rear Platform Remarks in Indiana," October 25, 1948, HSTL, accessed June 2013.

80. Ibid.

81. Harry Truman, "Address in the Memorial Auditorium, Gary, Indiana," October 25, 1946, HSTL, accessed May 2013.

82. Ibid.

83. Ibid.

84. Ibid.

85. Douglas B. Cornell, "Truman Fears Dictatorship Under the GOP," *Lewiston Daily Sun* via the Associated Press, October 26, 1948, accessed May 2013.

86. Harry S. Truman, "Address in Chicago Stadium," October 25, 1948, HSTL, accessed December 2011.

87. Ibid.

88. Ibid.

89. Ibid.

90. William J. Bray, "Recollections of the 1948 Campaign," August 1964, HSTL, accessed May 2012.

91. Paul Block Jr., "President Rips into Dewey as Pawn of Totalitarianism," *Pittsburgh Post-Gazette*, October 26, 1948, accessed June 2013.

92. Harry Truman to Mary Jane Truman, October 25, 1948, quoted in Poen, *Letters Home by Harry Truman*, 227.

93. "Campaigns Move Ahead in Final Week of Action," Associated Press, October 26, 1948, accessed May 2013.

94. James Hagerty, "Dewey Far in Lead; A Tie in the Senate Strong Possibility," *New York Times*, October 25, 1948, accessed June 2013.

95. J. Frank Tragle, "Truman May Be Out to Aid Running Mates," Associated Press, October 25, 1948, accessed June 2013.

96. Thomas L. Stokes, "Southern Splinter Party is Used to Dignify Motives of Interests," *Toledo Blade*, October 25, 1948, accessed June 2013.

97. *The Atlanta Journal-Constitution*, via "The Editors' Roundtable," *The Tuscaloosa News*, October 25, 1948, accessed June 2013.

98. Elsey, interview with Morrissey, HSTL.

99. Clifford, *Counsel to the President*, 194.

100. Harry Truman, "Rear Platform and Other Informal Remarks in Indiana and Ohio," October 26, 1948, HSTL, accessed April 2013.

101. Ibid.

102. Ibid.

103. "Truman, Dewey Hurl Verbal Blasts in Campaign," *Lewiston Morning Tribune* via the Associated Press, October 27, 1948, accessed April 2013.

104. "New Low in Mud-Slinging Says Dewey, Truman Accuses GOP of False Promises," *Southeast Missourian*, October 27, 1948, accessed December 2013.

105. "Frances Dewey Has Never Been in White House," *Boston Globe*, October 27, 1948, accessed June 2013.

106. Lyle C. Wilson, "Republicans Confident Dewey Will Win, But Worry About Senate," United Press, October 27, 1948, accessed April 2013.

107. James E. Roper, "Russia Invited to Accept, Outside U.N., Formula for Settlement of Berlin Crisis," United Press, October 27, 1948, accessed May 2013.

108. John B. McDermott, "Says Soviets Building Big Police Force," United Press, October 27, 1948, accessed June 2013.

109. Richard Norton Smith, *Thomas E. Dewey and His Times* (New York: Simon & Schuster, 1982), 516; John Hightower, "Fall of Mudken Reported in Chinese Civil War," Associated Press, October 29, 1948, accessed June 2013.

110. David McCullough, *Truman* (New York: Simon & Schuster, 1992), 701.

111. Kenneth Birkhead, oral interview with George A. Barnes, Washington, D.C., John F. Kennedy Library Oral History Project, July 1, 1964, John F. Kennedy Library, accessed June 2012.

112. Frank K. Kelly, interview with Niel M. Johnson, April 15, 1988, HSTL, accessed April 2012.

113. Frank K. Kelly, *Harry Truman and the Human Family* (Santa Barbara, Calif.: Capra Press, 1998), 74.

114. Ibid.

115. Kelly, interview with Niel M. Johnson, HSTL.

116. "The Road Shows," *Time*, October 25, 1948, accessed April 2012.

117. Ibid.

118. "Quincy, Massachusetts (First Parish Church, Quincy Square, 7:30 a.m.)," Rear Platform and Other Informal Remarks in Massachusetts, Rhode Island, Connecticut, and New York, October 28, 1948, HSTL, accessed October 2012.

119. Gallup Historical Presidential Job Approval Statistics, Gallup, undated, accessed March 2013, available online at http://www.gallup.com/poll/116677 /presidential-approval-ratings-gallup-historical-statistics-trends.aspx.

120. Rear Platform and Other Informal Remarks in Massachusetts, Rhode Island, Connecticut, and New York, October 28, 1948, HSTL.

121. "Bridgeport, Connecticut (Rear platform, 2:23 p.m.)," Rear Platform and Other Informal Remarks in Massachusetts, Rhode Island, Connecticut, and New York, October 28, 1948, HSTL, accessed October 2012.

122. Meyer Berger, "President in 9-Mile Tour Gets Spectacular Greeting," *New York Times*, October 28, 1948, accessed November 2012.

123. Oscar Chapman, interview with Jerry N. Hess, Washington, D.C., April 28, 1972, HSTL, accessed September 2011, available online at http://www.truman library.org/oralhist/chapman3.htm#91.

124. Ibid; Winston Churchill, "The Sinews of Peace," March 5, 1946, National Churchill Museum archives, accessed August 2010.

125. Berger, "President in 9-Mile Tour Gets Spectacular Greeting."

126. Ibid.

127. Harry Truman, "Rear Platform and Other Informal Remarks in Massachusetts, Rhode Island, Connecticut, and New York," October 28, 1948, HSTL, accessed October 2012.

128. Berger, "President in 9-Mile Tour Gets Spectacular Greeting," *New York Times*.

129. Franklin D. Mitchell, *Harry S. Truman and the News Media: Contentious Relations, Belated Respect* (Columbia: University of Missouri Press, 1998), 44.

130. Donald S. Dawson, interview with James Fuchs, Washington, D.C., August 8, 1977, HSTL, accessed May 2012, available online at http://www.truman library.org/oralhist/dawsond.htm.

131. Ibid.

132. Harry S. Truman: "Address in Harlem, New York, Upon Receiving the Franklin Roosevelt Award," October 11, 1952. Online by Gerhard Peters and

John T. Woolley, *The American Presidency Project*. http://www.presidency.ucsb.edu/ws/?pid=14295.

133. William Batt Jr. to Gael Sullivan and Clark Clifford, April 20, 1948, "The Negro Vote," CCP, Box 21, Batt Correspondence File, accessed August 2012.

134. Ibid.

135. *Congressional Record*, House, 79th Cong., 1st sess. (July 12, 1945): 7485.

136. Batt to Sullivan and Clifford, April 20, 1948.

137. Ibid.

138. Ibid.

139. Ibid.

140. Philleo Nash, oral interview with Jerry N. Hess, Washington, October 18, 1966, HSTL, accessed September 2011, available online at http://www.truman library.org/oralhist/nash7.htm#329.

141. Alice Allison Dunnigan, *A Black Woman's Experience: From Schoolhouse to White House* (Philadelphia: Dorrance Publishing, 1974), 228, 233.

142. Johannes Hoeber, interview with Jerry N. Hess, Washington, D.C., September 13, 1966, HSTL, accessed April 2012.

143. William Batt Jr., oral interview with Jerry N. Hess, July 26, 1966, HSTL, available online at http://www.trumanlibrary.org/oralhist/battw.htm, accessed May 2011.

144. Johannes Hoeber, oral interview with Jerry N. Hess, HSTL; Jim Grebe, "Leon Milton Birkhead," Dictionary of Unitarian & Universalist Biography, Unitarian Universalist Association, accessed September 2012, available online at http://www25.uua.org/uuhs/duub/articles/leonmiltonbirkhead.html.

145. Johannes Hoeber, oral interview with Jerry N. Hess, HSTL.

146. Philleo Nash, interview with Jerry N. Hess, October 24, 1966, HSTL, available online at http://www.trumanlibrary.org/oralhist/nash8.htm, accessed March 2013.

147. Ibid.

148. Ibid.

149. Harry Truman, Address in Harlem, New York, Upon Receiving the Franklin Roosevelt Award, October 29, 1948, HSTL, accessed September 2012.

150. Michael Gardner et al., *Harry Truman and Civil Rights: Moral Courage and Political Risks* (Carbondale: Southern Illinois University Press, 2003), 137.

151. Anthony Leviero, "President Reviews Civil Rights Plea; In Harlem, He Repeats Views That Caused Southerners to Revolt Last Winter," *New York Times*, October 30, 1948, accessed March 2013.

152. "Wallace Lashes Truman Tactics," *Lewiston Morning Tribune*, October 30, 1948, accessed March 2013.

153. "Thurmond Says Truman's Acts Yellow, Red," *Sarasota Herald-Tribune*, October 31, 1948, accessed March 2013.

154. "Truman, 'Shadow' Cross Trails," *The Dispatch* (Lexington, N.C.) via the Associated Press, October 29, 1948, accessed March 2013.

155. Clifford, *Counsel to the President*, 237.

156. "St. Louis Union Station's Architecture an Eclectic Mix of Romanesque Styles," St. Louis Union Station online, accessed March 2013.

157. Harry Truman speech in St. Louis, Missouri, Rear Platform Remarks in Ohio, Indiana, Illinois, and Missouri, Public Papers of the President, HSTL, accessed March 2013.

158. Ross, "How Truman Did It," *Collier's*; Anthony Leviero, "Dewey Pledges Aid to Unity at Home, Peace in World, As He Ends Campaign; Truman in St. Louis, Predicts Victory," *New York Times*, October 30, 1948, accessed June 2013.

159. Harry Truman, "Address at the Kiel Auditorium, St. Louis, Missouri," October 30, 1948, Public Papers of the Presidents, HSTL, accessed October 2012.

160. Ibid.

161. Ibid.

162. Ibid.

163. Leviero, "Dewey Pledges Aid to Unity at Home."

164. McCullough, *Truman*, 703.

6. NOVEMBER 2, 1948

1. Harry Truman, "Radio Remarks in Independence on Election Eve," November 1, 1948, HSTL via the American Presidency Project, accessed September 2011.

2. Paul F. Boller Jr., *Presidential Campaigns: From George Washington to George W. Bush* (Oxford: Oxford University Press, 2004), 272.

3. Harry Truman, News Conference, April 17, 1952, quoted by Raymond H. Geselbracht, "Harry Truman Speaks," HSTL, accessed May 2013.

4. "Home State Voters to Hear Final Dewey, Truman Talks," *Spokane Daily Chronicle*, October 30, 1948, accessed March 2013; Renee Critcher Lyons, "The Second Shall Be First: The 1948 Presidential Election," ourwhitehouse.org, 2012, accessed March 2013.

5. Charles Ross, "How Truman Did It," *Collier's*, December 25, 1948, accessed December 2012.

6. Harry S. Truman, "Address in Chicago Stadium," October 25, 1948, HSTL, accessed December 2011.

7. Clark Clifford interview with Jerry N. Hess, Washington, D.C., May 10, 1971, accessed September 2011, available online at http://www.trumanlibrary.org.

8. Donald, *Citizen Soldier*, 88.

9. Jonathan Daniels, *The Man of Independence* (Columbia: University of Missouri Press, 1998), 362.

10. David McCullough, *Truman* (New York: Simon & Schuster, 1992), 705.

11. Ibid.

12. Ibid., 707.

13. Ibid.

14. Ibid, 708–709.

15. Monte M. Poen, ed., *Letters Home by Harry Truman* (New York: G. P. Putnam's Sons, 1984), 228.

16. "Remarks at the Victory Celebration in Independence," November 3, 1948. The American Presidency Project, University of California, Santa Barbara. Available online at http://www.presidency.ucsb.edu/ws/index.php?pid=13084&st=&st1=, accessed October 2012.

17. Anthony Leviero, "President Tells Union Men it Is Their Fault if Labor Law Is Kept," *New York Times*, June 9, 1948, accessed December 2011.

18. "Truman Rejects Crow Dinner," *Southeast Missourian*, November 4, 1948, accessed December 2013.

7. THE WORLD ACCORDING TO HARRY TRUMAN

1. William Batt Jr., oral interview with Jerry N. Hess, July 26, 1966, HSTL, available online at http://www.trumanlibrary.org/oralhist/battw.htm, accessed May 2011.

2. "The Opening Speeches," *Pittsburgh Post-Gazette*, September 22, 1948, accessed April 2011.

3. Clark Clifford, interview with Jerry N. Hess, HSTL, Washington, D.C., May 10, 1971, accessed September 2011, available online at http://www.trumanlibrary.org/, HSTL.

4. Philleo Nash, interview with Jerry N. Hess, HSTL, Washington, D.C., October 18, 1966, accessed September 2011, available online at http://www.truman library.org/oralhist/nash7.htm#370.

5. Richard D. McKinzie, interview with Jerry N. Hess, New York, HSTL, August 23, 1973, accessed April 2012.

6. Omar H. Ali, *In the Balance of Power: Independent Black Politics and Third-Party Movements in the United States* (Chicago: University of Chicago Press, 2009), 127; "The Election of 1948," The Miller Center, University of Virginia, accessed August 2013, available online at www.millercenter.org.

7. James K. Libbey, *Dear Alben: Mr. Barkley of Kentucky* (Lexington: University Press of Kentucky, 1979), 97.

8. Clifford, interview with Jerry N. Hess, HSTL.

9. Clark Clifford to Matthew Connelly, November 29, 1948, Batt Correspondence file, Box 21, Clifford Papers, HSTL, accessed August 25, 2012.

10. Charles Ross, "How Truman Did It," *Colliers*, December 25, 1948, accessed December 2012.

11. George Elsey, oral interview with Charles T. Morrissey, February 17, 1964, HSTL, accessed December 2011.

12. David Paul Kuhn, "Vacation Politics," CBS News, December 5, 2007, available online at http://www.cbsnews.com/2100–250_162–607234.html, accessed January 2013.

13. Cabell Phillips, *The Truman Presidency* (London: Macmillan, 1966), 248–249.

14. Steven R. Goldzwig, *Truman's Whistle-Stop Campaign* (College Station: Texas A&M University Press, 2008), 59–60.

15. Harold I. Gullan, *The Upset that Wasn't: Harry S. Truman and the Crucial Election Victory of 1948* (Chicago: Ivan R. Dee, 1998), 214–215.

16. Batt to Clifford, April 22, 1948, Clifford Papers Box 22, Batt file, HSTL, accessed August 25, 2012.

17. Ross, "How Truman Did It."

18. Ronald T. Farrar, *Reluctant Servant: The Story of Charles G. Ross* (Columbia: University of Missouri Press, 1969), 191.

19. Ross, "How Truman Did It."

20. Goldzwig, *Truman's Whistle Stop Campaign*, 109.

AFTERWORD: THE LEGACY OF TRUMAN'S
TRIUMPH AND DEWEY'S DEFEAT

1. Michael Bowen, *The Roots of Modern Conservatism* (Chapel Hill: University of North Carolina Press, 2011), 3.

2. Mark Memmott, "How Did Strom Thurmond Last Through His 24-Hour Filibuster?" NPR.org, March 7, 2013, accessed December 2013.

3. Joseph Crespino, *Strom Thurmond's America* (New York: Hill and Wang, 2012), 158–159.

4. Adam Clymer, "Strom Thurmond, Foe of Integration, Dies at 100," *New York Times*, June 27, 2003, accessed December 2013.

5. John C. Culver and John Hyde, *American Dreamer: A Life of Henry A. Wallace* (New York: W. W. Norton, 2001), 339, 518, 521.

6. "William L. Batt, Jr.," Secretaries of L&I, PA Manual, 1957–1958, available online at http://www.psp.state.pa.us/portal/server.pt/gateway/PTARGS_6_2_73337_10453_552770_43/, accessed January 2013.

7. David D. Lloyd Files, biographical sketch, HSTL, accessed June 2012.

8. "Frank Kelly Lecture," Nuclear Age Peace Foundation, https://www.wagingpeace.org/menu/programs/public-events/frank-kelly-lecture/, accessed August 2013.

9. Francis W. Hoeber, e-mail to the author, August 15, 2013.

10. Kenneth Birkhead, interview with Jerry N. Hess, July 7, 1966, HSTL, accessed March 2011, available online at http://www.trumanlibrary.org/oralhist/birkhead.htm; David Birkhead, interview with the author, June 21, 2012; David Birkhead, e-mail to the author, June 22, 2012.

11. Herochik, "A Life of Activism: Initiative Backer Phil Dreyer, From Past to Present," *Portland Business Journal*, September 8, 2002.

12. John E. Barriere Personal Papers, John F. Kennedy Presidential Library and Museum, accessed August 2013; Rep. Barney Frank, "John E. Barriere," *capitolwords* 144, no. 49 (April 28, 1988), available online at http://capitolwords.org/date/1998/04/28/E689_john-e-barriere/, accessed August 2013

13. Emily Schultheis, "Exit Polls 2012: How President Obama Won," Politico, November 7, 2012, accessed November 2013; "2012 Election Campaign Results," *Washington Post*, November 2012, accessed November 2013; Michael Kranish, "The Story Behind Mitt Romney's Loss in the Presidential Campaign to President Obama," *The Boston Globe*, December 22, 2012, accessed November 2012.

14. Pete Kasperowicz, "Boehner Defends 'Do Nothing' House," *The Hill*, available online at http://thehill.com/blogs/regwatch/legislation/192039-boehner-defends-do-nothing-house.

Index